German Grammar

HARPERCOLLINS COLLEGE OUTLINE

German Grammar

Linda C. DeMeritt, Ph.D.
Allegheny College

HarperPerennial
A Division of HarperCollinsPublishers

HarperCollins books may be purchased for educational, business, or sales promotional use. For information, please write: Special Markets Department, Harper-Collins Publishers, Inc., 10 East 53rd Street, New York, NY 10022.

Editor: Wallace Sue
Project Manager: Jonathan Brodman
Developed by American Bookworks Corporation

Library of Congress Cataloging-in-Publication Data

DeMeritt, Linda C., 1953–
    German Grammar / Linda C. DeMeritt. — 1st ed.
        p.   cm. — (HarperCollins college outline)
    ISBN 0-06-467159-3
    1. German language—Grammar—1950– 2. German language—Textbooks
for foreign speakers—English. I. Title. II. Series
PF3112.D37 1993
438.2'421—dc20   93-36134

98 JE/RRD 10 9 8 7 6 5 4 3

Contents

Acknowledgments...vii

Preface...ix

Part One: The German Case System...1

1   Nouns and Articles 3

2   The Cases: Nominative, Accusative, Dative, Genitive 27

3   Pronouns...49

4   Prepositions 77

5   Adjectives and Adverbs 104

6   Numbers and Time Expressions..128

Part Two: German Verbs...145

7   Verb Tenses 147

8   The Passive Voice...192

9   The General Subjunctive 211

10 The Special Subjunctive: Indirect Discourse 232

11 Special Problems with Verbs..245

Part Three: German Word Order 269

12 Principles of German Word Order..271

13 Conjunctions..285

Vocabulary...301

Appendix A: Grammatical Tables...340

Appendix B: Principal Parts of Strong and Irregular Weak Verbs.....344

Index..347

Acknowledgments

I would like to thank many friends, colleagues, and students for their help and suggestions during the preparation of this book. Special thanks go to my colleagues Peter Ensberg (Allegheny College), Jochen Richter (Allegheny College), and Ilse Winter (Denison University) for their careful reading of specific chapters of the original manuscript. Kristin Springorum and Matthias Stausberg—our most recent German-language assistants at Allegheny—deserve special mention for their invaluable and creative input concerning the illustrative examples and exercises. I would like to thank my editor, Wallace Sue (Michigan State University), for his many helpful suggestions and thoughtful comments on the entire text. Finally, I wish to thank David Thorstad for his careful copyediting, Jonathan Brodman for his support throughout the project, and Fred Grayson for the opportunity to write this text.

Preface

German Grammar offers a systematic grammar review to students at the intermediate or advanced-intermediate level. It can be used as a supplemental text in conjunction with literary and/or cultural readers or as the core text in courses centered more exclusively on grammar review. Because the answers to all exercises are provided, it may also be used outside the classroom as a reference or self-study tool.

This textbook has been designed to make German grammar accessible to the student. Its explanations are thorough but concise and to the point; the language used is clear and easy to understand. Frequent tables, charts, and summaries are included. Grammar explanations are illustrated with numerous examples.

The text is based on the premise that mastery of the language comes from active application and practice. Thus each grammar explanation is followed immediately by extensive practice exercises of that particular point. In addition, numerous review exercises summarize the larger questions of grammar. The answers to all exercises are included at the conclusion of each chapter. In this manner, the student receives immediate feedback and is able to ascertain whether a particular grammatical feature has been mastered.

The vocabulary used in the examples and exercises is drawn from natural and everyday German. It is up-to-date and designed to keep the interest of student and teacher alike. All words are listed in the vocabulary at the end of the book.

German Grammar is divided into thirteen chapters. The first part of the book focuses on the German case system and presents nouns and articles, the cases, pronouns, prepositions, adjectives and adverbs, and the expression of numbers and time. The second section is devoted to German verbs and is divided into chapters on verb tenses, the passive voice, the general subjunctive, the special subjunctive, and special problem areas with verbs. The final section of the book deals with German word order in chapters covering the principles of word order and conjunctions. There are two appendixes, one presenting grammatical charts and tables and the other a list of the principal parts of strong and irregular verbs. The book may be covered sequentially or in a random order. Frequent cross-references and a complete index at the end of the book facilitate the latter approach.

PART ONE:
THE GERMAN
CASE SYSTEM

1

Nouns and Articles

In order to use a noun correctly in German, we must know its gender and number. The gender of a noun in German can be either masculine, neuter, or feminine. In contrast to English, the determination of gender in German is not natural but grammatical. This means that the gender of a noun must be learned when memorizing vocabulary. However, some patterns can aid in predicting gender.

Number refers to the singular and plural forms of a noun. In contrast to English, where most plural nouns are formed by adding -s, German plural formation includes a variety of different possibilities. Therefore, plural forms must be learned when memorizing vocabulary. However, as with the prediction of gender, there are some patterns that can be used to help guess the plural of a German noun.

The gender, number, and case (chapter 2) of a noun in German are marked by the definite or indefinite article. Other words, called **der**-*words and* **ein**-*words, take the same endings as the articles and also mark the gender, number, and case of German nouns.*

CAPITALIZATION

In German, all nouns are capitalized.

Die Frau hat eine Woche Ferien.
The woman has a week's vacation.

Mein **V**ater hat ein neues **A**uto gekauft.
My father bought a new car.

Das **E**ssen in der **M**ensa ist oft schlecht.
The food in the student cafeteria is frequently bad.

Many different parts of speech can act as nouns. In such a case, they also are capitalized. Thus a more encompassing rule for capitalization is that all words that *function* as nouns are capitalized.

VERB	Das **S**chnellfahren macht mir Spaß.
	Driving fast is fun for me.
ADJECTIVE	Die **S**chwarzhaarige ist am größten.
	The black-haired woman is the tallest.
PRONOUN	Der Schizophrene hat ein gespaltenes **I**ch.
	The schizophrenic has a split sense of self.
ADVERB	Das **H**eute interessiert mich mehr als das **G**estern.
	Today interests me more than yesterday.

Capitalization of Proper Names

In contrast to English usage, in German proper names are capitalized only when used as nouns. Compare the following groups of sentences. In the first sentence of the pairs below, the proper name is used as an adjective and is therefore not capitalized; in the second, it is used as a noun and is capitalized.

ADJECTIVE	Ich mag **f**ranzösischen Wein.
	I like French wine.
NOUN	Die **F**ranzosen unterstützen ein politisch vereinigtes Europa.
	The French support a politically united Europe.
ADJECTIVE	Die **a**merikanische Sprache ist nicht leicht.
	The American language is not easy.
NOUN	Ich bin **A**merikaner.
	I am an American.

For titles and geographical names, however, proper names are capitalized even when used as adjectives.

der Atlantische Ozean	*the Atlantic Ocean*
die Deutsche Bundesbank	*the German Federal Reserve*
die Deutsche Bundesbahn	*the German Federal Railway*
die Schweizer Alpen	*the Swiss Alps*
der Hamburger Hafen	*the harbor of Hamburg*

Exercise 1: *Capitalize where appropriate.*

1. Die deutschen häuser sind meistens aus stein.
2. Wir haben seit zwei wochen englisches wetter.
3. Die amerikanerinnen rasieren sich oft die beine.
4. Wo ist mein deutsches wörterbuch?
5. Der schnellste wird gewinnen.
6. Das lernen einer fremdsprache ist oft schwer.
7. Du sprichst ausgezeichnet deutsch. Du hast kaum einen amerikanischen akzent.
8. Das schönste an den deutschen schulen sind die ferien.
9. Der persische golf grenzt an viele arabische staaten.
10. Heute bin ich der bessere, mein lieber!

GENDER

All German nouns have a grammatical gender—either masculine, neuter, or feminine. Gender is indicated through the article of the noun: **der** for masculine nouns, **das** for neuter nouns, and **die** for feminine nouns in the singular.

Gender for Human Beings

The grammatical gender of human beings usually corresponds to biological gender. Thus, *the man* is masculine: **der Mann**; a *child* of unspecified sex is neuter: **das Kind**; and *the woman* is feminine: **die Frau**. There are some exceptions to this correspondence, the most notable being **das Mädchen** (*the young girl*) and **das Fräulein** (*the unmarried young woman*). The latter form (**das Fräulein**) is considered old-fashioned and is avoided generally. Here are some additional examples of masculine, neuter, and feminine nouns with biological, or natural, gender:

der Vater	*father*	der Freund	*male friend*
der Bruder	*brother*	der Student	*male student*
der Onkel	*uncle*	der Lehrer	*male teacher*
der Neffe	*nephew*	der Arzt	*male doctor*
der Sohn	*son*	der Sekretär	*male secretary*

das Baby	*baby*

die Mutter	*mother*	die Freundin	*female friend*
die Schwester	*sister*	die Studentin	*female student*
die Tante	*aunt*	die Lehrerin	*female teacher*
die Nichte	*niece*	die Ärztin	*female doctor*
die Tochter	*daughter*	die Sekretärin	*female secretary*

Gender for Other Nouns

The grammatical gender of other nouns does not correspond to biological gender. This is different from English, where nouns referring to inanimate objects and abstractions are neuter. In German, such nouns may be masculine, neuter, or feminine. For example, *the carpet* is masculine: **der Teppich**; *the window* is neuter: **das Fenster**; and *the door* is feminine: **die Tür**. Here are some additional examples of masculine, neuter, and feminine nouns where gender is strictly grammatical.

der Kaffee	*coffee*	der Fluß	*river*
der Bleistift	*pencil*	der Apfel	*apple*
der Hund	*dog*	der Tisch	*table*
der Text	*text*	der Teufel	*devil*
der Ausgang	*exit*	der Eingang	*entrance*
das Pferd	*horse*	das Projekt	*project*
das Problem	*problem*	das Dorf	*village*
das Buch	*book*	das Wasser	*water*
das Klavier	*piano*	das Boot	*boat*
das Radio	*radio*	das Kleid	*dress*
die Musik	*music*	die Schule	*school*
die Universität	*university*	die Stadt	*city*
die Prüfung	*test*	die Sprache	*language*
die Familie	*family*	die Fabrik	*factory*
die Milch	*milk*	die Straße	*street*

Because gender is often essential for determining the function of the noun within the sentence, and because there are no logical rules for its prediction, *the definite article must be learned along with the corresponding noun when memorizing vocabulary.*

Gender Prediction

Having said that gender must be memorized, here are some noun groups useful for its prediction in specific cases.

MASCULINE GENDER GROUPS

Nouns referring to male human beings, their professions, and their nationalities are masculine.

der Vater	*father*	der Lehrer	*male teacher*
der Student	*male student*	der Ingenieur	*male engineer*
der Deutsche	*male German*	der Amerikaner	*male American*

Names of the days of the week, the months, and the seasons are masculine.

der Montag	*Monday*	der Freitag	*Friday*
der Dienstag	*Tuesday*	der Samstag	*Saturday*
der Mittwoch	*Wednesday*	der Sonntag	*Sunday*
der Donnerstag	*Thursday*		

der Januar	*January*	der Juli	*July*
der Februar	*February*	der August	*August*
der März	*March*	der September	*September*
der April	*April*	der Oktober	*October*
der Mai	*May*	der November	*November*
der Juni	*June*	der Dezember	*December*

der Winter	*winter*	der Sommer	*summer*
der Frühling	*spring*	der Herbst	*fall*

The four points of the compass are masculine.

der Norden	*North*	der Osten	*East*
der Süden	*South*	der Westen	*West*

NEUTER GENDER GROUPS

Nouns referring to young persons or animals are generally neuter.

das Kind	*child*	das Baby	*baby*
das Kalb	*calf*	das Lamm	*lamb*

Nouns ending with the diminutive suffixes **-chen** or **-lein** are always neuter. Both suffixes impart the meaning of *small* or *dear* and both usually cause the base word to umlaut. The suffix **-chen** is more common than **-lein**.

das Mädchen	*girl*	das Büchlein	*little book*
das Heftchen	*little notebook*		

Infinitives used as nouns are always neuter.

das Rauchen	*smoking*	das Wandern	*hiking*
das Fahren	*driving*		

Names of towns and cities and most states, countries, and continents are neuter. However, the article is only used when the name is modified.

das unruhige Los Angeles   *turbulent Los Angeles*
das riesengroße Kanada   *huge Canada*

A few country names are not neuter. The most common of these exceptions include:

die Türkei (*feminine*)   *Turkey*
die Schweiz (*feminine*)   *Switzerland*
die Vereinigten Staaten (*plural*)   *the United States*
die USA (*plural*)   *the US*
die Niederlande (*plural*)   *the Netherlands*
der Iran (*masculine*)   *Iran*
der Irak (*masculine*)   *Iraq*

FEMININE GENDER GROUPS

Nouns referring to female human beings, their professions, and their nationalities, often formed by adding the suffix -**in** to the masculine noun, are feminine.

die Mutter	*mother*	die Lehrerin	*female teacher*
die Studentin	*female student*	die Ingenieurin	*female engineer*
die Deutsche	*female German*	die Amerikanerin	*female American*

Most nouns ending in an unstressed -**e** are feminine.

die Methode	*method*	die Maschine	*machine*
die Brücke	*bridge*	die Sonne	*sun*
die Minute	*minute*	die Fete	*party*

Common exceptions:

das Ende *end*   das Auge *eye*   der Name *name*

Nouns ending in the suffixes -**ei**, -**ie**, -**ik**, -**ion**, -**heit**, -**keit**, -**schaft**, -**tät**, -**ung**, -**ur** are always feminine.

die Bäckerei	*bakery*	die Freundlichkeit	*friendliness*
die Psychologie	*psychology*	die Gesellschaft	*society*
die Mathematik	*mathematics*	die Universität	*university*
die Religion	*religion*	die Zeitung	*newspaper*
die Krankheit	*illness*	die Kultur	*culture*

Exercise 2: *Fill in the correct definite article. All of the nouns are either included in the lists above or can be predicted by means of the gender categories.*

1. _____ Minute
2. _____ Prüfung
3. _____ Dörfchen
4. _____ Ende
5. _____ Lernen
6. _____ Student
7. _____ Schweizerin
8. _____ Herbst
9. _____ Bankkauffrau
10. _____ Montag
11. _____ Woche
12. _____ Sohn
13. _____ Mutter
14. _____ Tätigkeit
15. _____ Musik

Nouns with Two Genders

A few German nouns have two genders and, accordingly, two different meanings.

der See -n	*lake*	die See -n	*sea*
der Leiter -	*director*	die Leiter -n	*ladder*
der Tor -en	*fool*	das Tor -e	*gate, goal in a game*
der Band ⁝e	*(book) volume*	das Band ⁝er	*ribbon*
das Steuer -	*steering wheel*	die Steuer -n	*tax*

PLURAL FORMATION

The article for all plural nouns in German is **die**, regardless of whether that noun is masculine, neuter, or feminine in the singular.

In English, the plural form is created by adding **-s** to the noun. There are very few exceptions to this rule (*children, geese, foxes, syllabi*), making plural formation an easy matter for the most part. In German, however, several different endings are possible for the plural form. Therefore, *the plural form of a noun must be memorized when learning vocabulary.*

Plural Endings

The examples below indicate the four different plural endings that are common for German nouns.

PLURAL FORMATION WITH NO ENDING + UMLAUT SOMETIMES

Nouns in this group form their plural with no ending, but sometimes the stem vowel is umlauted. Masculine nouns frequently umlaut; neuter nouns never umlaut. There are only two feminine nouns in this group.

der Apfel	die Äpfel	*apple*
der Bruder	die Brüder	*brother*
der Vater	die Väter	*father*
der Teufel	die Teufel	*devil*

der Amerikaner	die Amerikaner	*American*
der Onkel	die Onkel	*uncle*
das Mädchen	die Mädchen	*young girl*
das Heftchen	die Heftchen	*little notebook*
das Büchlein	die Büchlein	*little book*
die Tochter	die Töchter	*daughter*
die Mutter	die Mütter	*mother*

PLURAL FORMATION WITH -*e* + UMLAUT SOMETIMES

Nouns in this group form their plural with -**e** plus an umlaut some-times. Masculine nouns frequently umlaut; neuter nouns never umlaut; feminine nouns always umlaut.

der Hund	die Hunde	*dog*
der Arm	die Arme	*arm*
der Tisch	die Tische	*table*
der Bleistift	die Bleistifte	*pencil*
der Text	die Texte	*text*
der Freund	die Freunde	*friend*
der Sekretär	die Sekretäre	*secretary*
der Ingenieur	die Ingenieure	*engineer*
der Tag	die Tage	*day*
der Sohn	die Söhne	*son*
der Eingang	die Eingänge	*entrance*
der Ausgang	die Ausgänge	*exit*
der Arzt	die Ärzte	*doctor*
der Fluß	die Flüsse	*river*
das Heft	die Hefte	*notebook*
das Boot	die Boote	*boat*
das Pferd	die Pferde	*horse*
das Problem	die Probleme	*problem*
das Klavier	die Klaviere	*piano*
das Projekt	die Projekte	*project*
die Stadt	die Städte	*city*
die Nacht	die Nächte	*night*
die Hand	die Hände	*hand*

PLURAL FORMATION WITH -*er* + UMLAUT WHERE POSSIBLE

Nouns in this group form their plural by adding -**er** plus an umlaut wherever possible. There are no feminine nouns in this group.

| der Wald | die Wälder | *woods* |
| der Mann | die Männer | *man* |

das Kind	die Kinder	*child*
das Kleid	die Kleider	*dress*
das Haus	die Häuser	*house*
das Wort	die Wörter	*word*
das Buch	die Bücher	*book*

PLURAL FORMATION WITH -(e)n

Nouns in this group form their plural by adding **-n** or **-en**. These nouns never add an umlaut. The majority of them are feminine.

die Schwester	die Schwestern	*sister*
die Tante	die Tanten	*aunt*
die Nichte	die Nichten	*niece*
die Familie	die Familien	*family*
die Methode	die Methoden	*method*
die Maschine	die Maschinen	*machine*
die Brücke	die Brücken	*bridge*
die Sonne	die Sonnen	*sun*
die Minute	die Minuten	*minute*
die Bäckerei	die Bäckereien	*bakery*
die Religion	die Religionen	*religion*
die Krankheit	die Krankheiten	*disease*
die Gesellschaft	die Gesellschaften	*society*
die Universität	die Universitäten	*university*
die Zeitung	die Zeitungen	*newspaper*
die Prüfung	die Prüfungen	*test*
die Schule	die Schulen	*school*
die Straße	die Straßen	*street*
die Sprache	die Sprachen	*language*
die Fabrik	die Fabriken	*factory*

| das Ende | die Enden | *end* |
| das Auge | die Augen | *eye* |

| der Student | die Studenten | *student* |
| der Name | die Namen | *name* |

A subgroup of this category is nouns that end in the suffix **-in**. These nouns always add **-nen** to form their plurals.

die Lehrerin   die Lehrerinnen   *female teacher*
die Studentin   die Studentinnen   *female student*

General Patterns in Plural Formation

If you have to guess a plural form, some general patterns may help you.

1. For monosyllabic nouns (nouns of one syllable): most masculine nouns add -**e**, sometimes with an umlaut; most feminine nouns add -**e**, with an umlaut where possible; most neuter nouns add -**er**, with an umlaut where possible; some neuter nouns add -**e**.
2. For polysyllabic nouns (nouns of more than one syllable): masculine and neuter nouns ending in -**el**, -**en**, -**er**, -**chen**, -**lein** add no ending, with an umlaut sometimes for the masculine nouns; most other masculine and neuter nouns add -**e**, with an umlaut sometimes for the masculine nouns; feminine nouns add -(**e**)**n**; feminine nouns ending in -**in** add -**nen**.

Because of the many exceptions to these patterns, however, it is best to memorize individual plural forms.

Exercise 3: *Supply the correct plural forms. All of the nouns are either included in the lists above or can be correctly guessed by means of the preceding guidelines for plural formation.*

1. der Tag
2. die Ingenieurin
3. das Klavier
4. das Zimmer
5. die Tochter
6. der Wagen
7. die Stadt
8. die Wohnung
9. das Kind
10. die Neuigkeit
11. die Brücke
12. die Blume
13. die Fabrik
14. das Mädchen
15. das Auge

Problem Areas in Plural Formation

NOUNS WITH TWO PLURAL FORMS

A few German nouns have two different plural forms and, accordingly, two different plural meanings. The most common of these are:

das Wort   die Worte   *words* in a connected sequence
das Wort   die Wörter   *unconnected words*, as in **das Wörterbuch**
die Bank   die Banken   *banks*
die Bank   die Bänke   *benches*

ENGLISH PLURAL/GERMAN SINGULAR NOUNS

Some nouns that are plural in English are singular in German. Some common examples are:

die Schere -n	*scissors*
die Brille -n	*eyeglasses*
die Hose -n	*pants*
der Inhalt -e	*contents*
die Statistik -en	*statistics*
die Polizei	*police*
die Treppe -n	*stairs*

Mein Mann hat **eine** neue **Hose** gekauft.
My husband bought new pants.

Die Schere ist ein unentbehrliches Haushaltsgerät.
Scissors are an indispensable household item.

Die Polizei war sehr schnell an der Unfallstelle.
The police were at the site of the accident very quickly.

Der Mathematiker fertigt **eine Statistik** an.
The mathematician is preparing the statistics.

When these nouns are used in the plural, they refer to two or more, or a set, of the objects.

Ich habe zwei **Brillen**, eine zum Lesen und eine zweite zum Fahren.
I have two pairs of glasses, one (pair) for reading and a second (pair) for driving.

Ich habe mir heute drei **Hosen** gekauft, eine Freizeithose und zwei Hosen für die Arbeit.
I bought three pairs of pants today, one for after work and two pairs for work.

In diesem Gebäude gibt es zwei **Treppen**. Eine führt in den Keller, die andere zum Dachgeschoß.
There are two stairways in this building. One goes to the basement; the other goes to the attic.

GERMAN NOUNS THAT ARE ALWAYS PLURAL

Other German nouns can only be used in the plural. Some of these are singular in English.

die Geschwister	*siblings*
die Eltern	*parents*
die Ferien	*vacation*
die Möbel	*furniture*

Exercise 4: *Translate the sentences into German. Be careful with the verb forms.*

1. The scissors aren't sharp enough.
2. Vacation starts tomorrow.
3. I'm always losing my glasses.
4. The contents are breakable.
5. Her words were incomprehensible.
6. These pairs of pants don't fit any longer.
7. The furniture is brand new.
8. The police arrest the burglar.
9. I fell down the stairs.
10. Statistics are an important part of mathematics.

COMPOUND NOUNS

Whereas in English nouns frequently stand next to each other, in German they are combined to form a single compound noun. This is a very common method of new word formation in German. By learning to take apart and analyze the component parts of compound nouns, you can increase your vocabulary greatly.

For a compound noun, the gender and plural are determined by the final noun in the compound.

der Lohn ¨e (*wages, salary*) + **die** Erhöhung **-en** (*rise, increase*) =
   die Lohnerhöhung **-en** (*wage increase*)
das Wasser (*water*) + **der** Fall ¨e   (*fall, descent*) =
   der Wasserfall ¨e (*waterfall*)

Sometimes, a connecting sound is inserted between the elements of a compound noun. The most frequent of these connecting sounds are **s** and **(e)n**.

die Respekt**s**person   *person held in respect*
die Prüfung**s**arbeit   *examination paper*
die Nase**n**spitze   *tip of the nose*

Compound nouns can also be formed with parts of speech other than two nouns, for example, with verbs or adjectives.

kaufen (*verb*) + das Haus = das **Kaufhaus**   *department store*
rollen (*verb*) + die Treppe = die **Rolltreppe**   *escalator*
klein (*adjective*) + die Stadt = die **Kleinstadt**   *small provincial town*

Exercise 5: *Form the compound noun from the words given, following the model. Indicate gender and plural forms, and translate the compound noun into English.*

Example: das Haus ⁼er + der Schlüssel - =
der Hausschlüssel *house key* **die Hausschlüssel**

1. der Sommer - + das Haus ⁼er =
2. die Hand ⁼e + der Schuh -e =
3. das Haus ⁼er + die Aufgabe -n =
4. das Land ⁼er + die Karte -n =
5. der Abend -e + das Kleid -er =
6. die Wache -n + n (connecting sound) + der Tag -e =
7. neu (adjective) + das Jahr =
8. schreiben (verb) + der Tisch -e =

ARTICLES

Articles are used to mark nouns. There are two types of articles: the definite article (*the*) and the indefinite article (*a, an*).

The Definite Article

The definite article (*the*) in German is **der** for masculine nouns, **das** for neuter nouns, and **die** for feminine and plural nouns.

The Indefinite Article

The indefinite article (*a, an*) in German is **ein** for masculine and neuter nouns, and **eine** for feminine nouns. Logically, there can be no indefinite article, which is singular, for the plural of a noun.

Article Usage in German

Although the article is used similarly in German and English for the most part, there are some important differences between the two languages that should be noted.

THE DEFINITE ARTICLE WITH ABSTRACT CONCEPTS

German uses the definite article to designate abstract or general concepts, whereas English usually does not.

Der Tod kommt immer zu schnell.
Death always comes too quickly.

Ist **der Mensch** angeboren gut oder schlecht?
Is humankind inherently good or evil?

So ist **das Leben**!
That's life!

THE DEFINITE ARTICLE WITH SEASONS AND MEALS

Unlike English, German uses the definite article to designate the seasons and meals.

Wenn **der Herbst** kommt, fällt das Laub von den Bäumen.
When autumn comes the leaves fall from the trees.

Der Winter ist die kälteste Jahreszeit.
Winter is the coldest time of the year.

Wir servieren **das Abendessen** um acht Uhr.
We are serving dinner at 8 o'clock.

THE DEFINITE ARTICLE WITH NAMES OF COUNTRIES

German uses the definite article with the names of countries that are masculine, feminine, or plural.

Der Irak grenzt an **den Iran.**
Iraq borders on Iran.

Die Schweiz hat vier offizielle Sprachen.
Switzerland has four official languages.

Die Niederlande sind ein kleines Land an der Nordsee.
The Netherlands is a small country on the North Sea.

Countries or cities that are neuter use the definite article only if they are modified in some way. Compare the following sets of sentences:

Berlin ist heute immer noch aufregend.
Berlin is still exciting today.

Italien liegt in Südeuropa.
Italy is located in southern Europe.

Das Berlin der zwanziger Jahre war eine aufregende Stadt.
Berlin of the twenties was an exciting city.

Das schöne Italien ist ein beliebter Ferienort.
Beautiful Italy is a favorite vacation spot.

THE DEFINITE ARTICLE IN IDIOMATIC PREPOSITIONAL PHRASES

German includes the definite article in certain idiomatic prepositional phrases, including prepositional phrases with the days of the week and months, where English does not.

Am Montag fängt die Schule wieder an.
School begins again on Monday.

Im Februar gibt es meistens Schnee.
There's usually snow in February.

Ich fühle mich nicht wohl, deshalb bleibe ich heute **im Bett**.
I don't feel well; therefore I'm going to stay in bed today.

Fährst du **mit dem Zug** oder **mit dem Auto**?
Are you going by train or by car?

THE DEFINITE ARTICLE WITH PARTS OF THE BODY

German uses the definite article with parts of the body and articles of clothing when ownership is clear. English usually uses the possessive adjective. Compare the German and English sentences.

Ich habe mir **den Arm** gebrochen.
I broke my arm.

Der Magen tut mir weh.
My stomach hurts.

Nimm **die Hände** aus den Taschen!
Take your hands out of your pockets.

Zieh **den Mantel** an, wenn du nach draußen gehst!
Put on your coat when you go outside.

Mach dir bitte **die Schuhe** sauber!
Please wipe off your shoes.

OMISSION OF THE INDEFINITE ARTICLE

German omits the indefinite article after the verbs **sein**, **werden**, and **bleiben** if the following noun designates a person's membership in a group or social status, for example, a profession, nationality, or religion.

Sie ist Oberärztin.
She's a head physician.

Er ist Witwer.
He's a widower.

Sie ist Lehrerin.
She's a teacher.

Der Student ist Fußballspieler.
The student is a football player.

However, if such a noun is modified by an attributive adjective, the indefinite article is used. Compare the following sentences with those above.

Sie ist **eine** sehr kompetente Oberärztin.
She's a very competent head physician.

Er ist **ein** trauriger Witwer.
He's a sad widower.

Sie ist **eine** ausgezeichnete Lehrerin.
She's an excellent teacher.

Der Student ist **ein** ausgezeichneter Fußballspieler.
The student is an excellent football player.

Exercise 6: *Fill in the article, if necessary.*

1. _____ Frühstück bekommt man hier zwischen sieben und neun Uhr morgens.
2. Im Norden ist _____ Winter sehr lang und kalt.
3. _____ Deutschland liegt in Mitteleuropa.
4. _____ USA grenzen an _____ Kanada.
5. _____ Leben ist kurz.
6. In Deutschland fährt man oft mit _____ Zug.
7. Man geht _____ Samstag auch in _____ Schule.
8. Dauert _____ Liebe wirklich ewig?
9. Ich möchte _____ Lehrer werden. Ich kann bestimmt _____ guter Lehrer werden.
10. Ich muß mir _____ Hände waschen.
11. An Feiertagen fällt _____ Schule aus.
12. Nach ihrem Studium wird sie _____ Rechtsanwältin.
13. _____ Sommer ist die wärmste Jahreszeit.
14. Der Bischof ist _____ Katholik.
15. Dr. Müller ist und bleibt _____ Geschäftsführerin.

DER-*WORDS*

There is a group of words that takes the same endings as the definite article. These words are called **der**-words. Here are the most common **der**-words.

all-	*all*
dies-	*this*
jed-	*each, every*
jen-	*that, that one*
manch-	singular: *many a*; plural: *several, some*
solch-	*such*
welch-	*which*

The Use of jen- and dies-

Jen- is rarely used except in contrast constructions with **dies**-.

Diese Lampe gefällt mir sehr; **jene** Lampe ist zu groß für die Wohnung.
I like this lamp a lot; that lamp is too large for the apartment.

Jen- together with **dies**- can sometimes mean *the former/the latter*.

Meine Eltern wohnen in Florida und Michigan. **Jener** Staat ist im Winter schön; **dieser** Staat ist im Sommer schön.
My parents live in Florida and Michigan. The former state is nice in the winter; the latter state is beautiful in the summer.

To express *that*, German would normally use **dieser** or a demonstrative pronoun (see chapter 3).

An **diesem Tag** (**dem Tag**) war ich einfach zu müde um mitzuspielen.
On that (particular) day I was simply too tired to participate.

The Use of all-

When followed by an additional **der**-word or **ein**-word, the ending on **all** is optional. The additional **der**-word or **ein**-word takes its normal ending as if **all** were not there.

All seine Geschwister wohnen in Europa.
All of his brothers and sisters live in Europe.

Sie mußten **all die** Telefonanrufe nach Europa bezahlen.
They had to pay for all of the telephone calls to Europe.

Exercise 7: *Replace the definite article with the cued* **der**-*word. Remember that the ending will remain the same.*

1. Der Wagen gehört mir.   (dies-)
2. Wollen wir die Stadt besuchen?   (jed-)
3. Die Frau ist meine Professorin.   (welch-)
4. Die Lösungen stehen am Ende des Kapitels.   (all-; jed-)
5. Der erste See ist kleiner als der zweite.   (dies-; jen-)
6. Willst du die Filme sehen?   (solch-)
7. In dem Zimmer wird nicht geraucht.   (dies-)
8. Das Märchen hat meinen Kindern nicht gefallen.   (welch-)
9. Die Burg ist über 500 Jahre alt.   (dies-)
10. Die Leute sprechen mehr als drei Fremdsprachen.   (manch-)

EIN-*WORDS*

There is a group of words that takes the same endings as the indefinite article. These words are called **ein**-words. The **ein**-words include all of the possessive adjectives and the negative **kein**.

Possessive Adjectives

A possessive adjective indicates a relationship of ownership between people or things. Here is a list of the possessive adjectives.

mein	*my*
dein	*your* (informal singular)
sein	*his*
sein	*its*
ihr	*her*
unser	*our*
euer	*your* (informal plural)
ihr	*their*
Ihr	*your* (formal)

When referring to inanimate objects, the possessive adjective *its* may be translated into German as either **sein** or **ihr**, depending on the gender of the noun that possesses.

Jeder Staat hat **seine** Sehenswürdigkeiten.
Every state has its tourist attractions.

Here **sein** is used because the possessor (**der Staat**) is masculine.

Jedes Land hat **seine** Sehenswürdigkeiten.
Every country has its tourist attractions.

Here **sein** is used because the possessor (**das Land**) is neuter.

Jede Stadt hat **ihre** Sehenswürdigkeiten.
Every city has its tourist attractions.

Here **ihr** is used because the possessor (**die Stadt**) is feminine.

Exercise 8: *Supply the appropriate possessive adjective meaning* its. *Watch the gender of the object that possesses and remember that the ending on the possessive adjective will be the same as the indefinite article ending.*

1. Das Fahrrad ist kaputt. Ein Reifen ist platt.
2. Ich nehme die Wohnung wegen eines großen Badezimmers.
3. Der Rock mit einer grellen Farbe gefällt mir nicht.
4. Die Vase mit einer Blume sieht schön aus.
5. Der Wagen ohne einen Motor ist sehr billig.

Because German has three forms equivalent to *you* (see chapter 3), it also has three different forms for *your.* For the second person familiar singular (**du**) the possessive adjective is **dein.** For the second person familiar plural (**ihr**) the possessive adjective is **euer.** (**Euer** is shortened to **eur-** when an ending is added.) For the formal form (**Sie**) the possessive adjective is **Ihr,** which is always capitalized. Study the following examples.

Hast du schon an **deine** Eltern geschrieben?

Habt ihr schon an **eure** Eltern geschrieben?

Haben Sie schon an **Ihre** Eltern geschrieben?

Have you already written to your parents?

Exercise 9: *Supply the appropriate possessive adjective meaning* your. *Remember that the ending on the possessive adjective will be the same as on the indefinite article.*

1. Kannst du mir bitte einen Kugelschreiber leihen?
2. Habt ihr schon wieder einen Schlüssel verloren?
3. Mit einer Erkältung mußt du im Bett bleiben.
4. Wann bekommen Sie ein neues Auto?
5. Ihr habt einen Termin vergessen.

Exercise 10: *Supply the appropriate possessive adjective. Remember that the ending will be the same as on the indefinite article.*

1. Ich lese ein Buch.   (*my*)
2. Können Sie mir bitte ein Buch geben?   (*your*)
3. Die Frau fährt mit einem neuen Auto nach Hause.   (*her*)

   4. Der Mann fand eine Katze im Keller.   (*his*)
   5. Was machen wir jetzt? Ein Koffer ist verlorengegangen.   (*our*)
   6. Diese Gegend mit einem See ist ideal für die Ferien.   (*its*)
   7. Wir sollten uns bald treffen, um eine Reise zu planen.   (*our*)
   8. Ich habe gestern einen Hund ins Tierheim gebracht.   (*my*)
   9. Wegen eines Beinbruchs kann der Sportler nicht trainieren.   (*his*)
   10. Mit einem Mikrowellengrill dauert das Kochen nicht lange.   (*my*)

The Negative kein

The negative form of **ein** is **kein**. It corresponds to *not a*, *not any*, or *no* in English.

Er hat **kein** Diplom.
He has no degree. (He doesn't have a degree.)

Ich will **keine** Hilfe von dir.
I want no help from you. (I don't want any help from you.)

Das Ehepaar hat **keine** Kinder.
*The married couple has no children. (The married couple doesn't have
   any children.)*

Exercise 11: *Translate into German.*

   1. I don't have any time.
   2. There are no tourists here.
   3. She has no car.
   4. I don't see any people here.
   5. Don't you have a ticket?

KEIN VS. NICHT

Kein is used only to negate a noun preceded by an indefinite article or by no article at all. Otherwise **nicht** is used.

NO ARTICLE	Ist er Student?
	Nein, er ist **kein** Student.
INDEFINITE ARTICLE	Ist er ein fleißiger Student?
	Nein, er ist **kein** fleißiger Student.

Exercise 12: Kein *or* **nicht**? *Answer the questions in the negative, using* **kein** *or* **nicht** *as appropriate.*

   1. Ist München eine kleine Stadt?
   2. Ist München die Hauptstadt von Deutschland?
   3. Ist das ein neuer Computer?
   4. Ist das sein neuer Computer?

5. Gibt es hier gute Restaurants?
6. Gibt es hier viele Restaurants?

NICHT EIN

Nicht ein is used only to emphasize the **ein** in the sense of *not one, not a single one.*

Der Makler gab mir **nicht einen** guten Tip.
The broker didn't give me a single good tip.

Nicht ein Fahrer wurde bei dem Unfall verletzt.
Not one driver was injured in the accident.

Exercise 13: *Translate into German.*

1. Not one student understands the sentence.
2. Not one answer was correct.
3. I don't want to make a single mistake.
4. She hasn't sold a single book.
5. Not one child is crying.

The Use of manch ein, solch ein, so ein, *and* welch ein

The **der**-words **manch-** and **solch-** are used primarily in the plural. In the singular, **manch ein** and **solch ein** or, even more commonly, **so ein** are used. **Manch ein** means *many a;* **solch ein** and **so ein** mean *such a.* Note that **manch** and **solch** are not declined; **ein** receives the normal **ein**-word ending.

Manch ein Geschäftsmann ist unehrlich.
Many a businessman is dishonest.

Ich lese **solch einen/so einen** Roman nicht gern.
I don't like to read such a/that kind of a novel.

Welch ein means *what a* and usually expresses surprise or disbelief. Similar to **manch ein** and **solch ein**, **welch** is not declined and **ein** takes normal **ein**-word endings.

Welch eine Überraschung! *What a surprise!*
Welch ein Durcheinander! *What a mess!*

The Use of was für (ein)

The expression **was für ein**, like **welch ein**, is sometimes used to express surprise or disbelief and corresponds to *what a.*

Was für eine Überraschung! *What a surprise!*
Was für ein Durcheinander! *What a mess!*

Was für ein is also a common idiom meaning *what kind of a.*

Was für ein Boot haben Sie gekauft?   *What kind of a boat did you buy?*

Was für ein Buch will sie lesen?   *What kind of a book does she want to read?*

For plural nouns, **was für** alone is used.

Was für Menschen sind sie?   *What kind of people are they?*

Was für Filme haben Sie gern?   *What kind of movies do you like?*

In the expression **was für (ein)**, **für** does not function as a preposition and therefore does not govern the case of the following noun. Instead, case is determined by the function of the noun in the sentence. Study the examples below.

In **was für einem** Haus wollen Sie wohnen?
In what kind of a house do you want to live?

Here case is determined by the either-or preposition *in*, which in this example is dative because there is no change of position.

Was für ein Mensch bist du?
What kind of a person are you?

Here the nominative is called for because **Mensch** is the subject of the sentence.

Exercise 14: *Translate into German, using* **manch ein**, **solch ein**, **so ein**, **welch ein**, *or* **was für (ein)**.

1. What a man!   (two possibilities)
2. Such (that kind of) food doesn't taste good to me.   (two possibilities)
3. Many a worker in America has no health insurance.
4. What a day!   (two possibilities)
5. What kind of a teacher is she?
6. I didn't understand many a question.
7. We find such a film boring.   (two possibilities)
8. What kind of pictures did she take?

Exercise 15: *Fill in the correct ending, as necessary.*

1. Was für ein__ Baum ist das?
2. Was für ein__ Temperatur haben wir heute?

3. In was für ein__ Welt leben wir?
4. Was für ein__ Programm gab es gestern abend im Fernsehen?
5. Was für ein__ Job hat die Frau?
6. Mit was für ein__ Frau ist er verheiratet?
7. Was für ein__ Farbe hat Ihr neues Auto?
8. Was für ein__ Wochentag haben wir heute?

ANSWERS TO EXERCISES

1.

1. Die deutschen Häuser sind meistens aus Stein.
2. Wir haben seit zwei Wochen englisches Wetter.
3. Die Amerikanerinnen rasieren sich oft die Beine.
4. Wo ist mein deutsches Wörterbuch?
5. Der Schnellste wird gewinnen.
6. Das Lernen einer Fremdsprache ist oft schwer.
7. Du sprichst ausgezeichnet Deutsch. Du hast kaum einen amerikanischen Akzent.
8. Das Schönste an den deutschen Schulen sind die Ferien.
9. Der Persische Golf grenzt an viele arabische Staaten.
10. Heute bin ich der Bessere, mein Lieber!

2.

1. die Minute
2. die Prüfung
3. das Dörfchen
4. das Ende
5. das Lernen
6. der Student
7. die Schweizerin
8. der Herbst
9. die Bankkauffrau
10. der Montag
11. die Woche
12. der Sohn
13. die Mutter
14. die Tätigkeit
15. die Musik

3.

1. die Tage
2. die Ingenieurinnen
3. die Klaviere
4. die Zimmer
5. die Töchter
6. die Wagen
7. die Städte
8. die Wohnungen
9. die Kinder
10. die Neuigkeiten
11. die Brücken
12. die Blumen
13. die Fabriken
14. die Mädchen
15. die Augen

4.

1. Die Schere ist nicht scharf genug.
2. Die Ferien beginnen morgen.
3. Ich verliere immer meine Brille.
4. Der Inhalt ist zerbrechlich.
5. Ihre Worte waren unverständlich.
6. Diese Hosen passen nicht mehr.
7. Die Möbel sind ganz neu.
8. Die Polizei verhaftet den Einbrecher.
9. Ich fiel die Treppe hinunter.
10. Statistik ist ein wichtiger Teil der Mathematik.

5.

1. das Sommerhaus *summer house* die Sommerhäuser
2. der Handschuh *glove* die Handschuhe
3. die Hausaufgabe *homework assignment* die Hausaufgaben
4. die Landkarte *map of a country* die Landkarten
5. das Abendkleid *evening gown* die Abendkleider
6. der Wochentag *day of the week* die Wochentage
7. das Neujahr *New Year's*
8. der Schreibtisch *desk* die Schreibtische

6.

1. Das Frühstück bekommt man hier zwischen sieben und neun Uhr morgens.
2. Im Norden ist der Winter sehr lang und kalt.
3. Deutschland liegt in Mitteleuropa.
4. Die USA grenzen an Kanada.
5. Das Leben ist kurz.
6. In Deutschland fährt man oft mit dem Zug.
7. Man geht am Samstag auch in die Schule.
8. Dauert die Liebe wirklich ewig?
9. Ich möchte Lehrer werden. Ich kann bestimmt ein guter Lehrer werden.
10. Ich muß mir die Hände waschen.
11. An Feiertagen fällt die Schule aus.
12. Nach ihrem Studium wird sie Rechtsanwältin.
13. Der Sommer ist die wärmste Jahreszeit.
14. Der Bischof ist Katholik.
15. Dr. Müller ist und bleibt Geschäftsführerin.

7.

1. Dieser Wagen
2. jede Stadt
3. Welche Frau
4. Alle Lösungen; jedes Kapitels
5. Dieser See ist kleiner als jener.
6. solche Filme
7. diesem Zimmer
8. Welches Märchen

9. Diese Burg
10. Manche Leute

8.

1. sein Reifen
2. ihres großen Badezimmers
3. seiner grellen Farbe
4. ihrer Blume
5. ohne seinen Motor

9.

1. deinen Kugelschreiber
2. euren Schlüssel
3. deiner Erkältung
4. Ihr neues Auto
5. euren Termin

10.

1. mein Buch
2. Ihr Buch
3. ihrem neuen Auto
4. seine Katze
5. Unser Koffer
6. ihrem See
7. unsere Reise
8. meinen Hund
9. seines Beinbruchs
10. meinem Mikrowellengrill

11.

1. Ich habe keine Zeit.
2. Es gibt keine Touristen hier.

3. Sie hat kein Auto.
4. Ich sehe keine Leute hier.
5. Hast du keine Karte?

12.

1. Nein, München ist keine kleine Stadt.
2. Nein, München ist nicht die Hauptstadt von Deutschland.
3. Nein, das ist kein neuer Computer.
4. Nein, das ist nicht sein neuer Computer.
5. Nein, es gibt hier keine guten Restaurants.
6. Nein, es gibt hier nicht viele Restaurants.

13.

1. Nicht ein Student versteht den Satz.
2. Nicht eine Antwort war richtig.
3. Ich will nicht einen Fehler machen.
4. Sie hat nicht ein Buch verkauft.
5. Nicht ein Kind weint.

14.

1. Welch ein Mann! Was für ein Mann!
2. So ein Essen schmeckt mir

nicht. Solch ein Essen schmeckt mir nicht.
3. Manch ein Arbeiter in Amerika hat keine Krankenversicherung.
4. Welch ein Tag!
   Was für ein Tag!
5. Was für eine Lehrerin ist sie?
6. Ich habe manch eine Frage nicht verstanden.
7. Wir finden so einen Film langweilig. Wir finden solch einen Film langweilig.
8. Was für Bilder hat sie gemacht?

15.

1. ein
2. eine
3. einer
4. ein
5. einen
6. einer
7. eine
8. einen

2

The Cases: Nominative, Accusative, Dative, Genitive

To use a noun correctly in German, you must know not only its gender and number (chapter 1), you must also know its case. Case means the function of a noun (or pronoun) within a sentence. In contrast to gender and number, case cannot be simply looked up in a dictionary and memorized. This chapter explains each of the cases in detail and provides exercises to help you identify them.

THE PRINCIPLE OF CASE

Case refers to the function of the noun (or pronoun) within a sentence. In other words, case marks the relationship of a noun (or pronoun) to the other words in the sentence.

Case in English

English has three cases: nominative, objective, and possessive.

The nominative case is used for the subject of the sentence.

*The **woman** walked across the room.*
*The **student** is tired of studying.*

The objective case is used for the direct object, the indirect object, or the object of a preposition.

DIRECT OBJECT   *The child threw the **ball** into the water.*
INDIRECT OBJECT   *On Mother's Day I gave my **mother** flowers.*
OBJECT OF THE PREPOSITION *to*   *We're taking the train to the **city**.*

The possessive case shows ownership.

***Germany's** weather is colder than ours.*
*My **neighbor's** cat was lost.*

Case in English is not marked except for the possessive *'s* and in pronoun usage (*I* vs. *me*; *he* vs. *him*; *she* vs. *her*; *we* vs. *us*; *they* vs. *them*). Instead, English usually uses word order to determine the relationship between words. Thus in the sentence *The woman sees the man*, the word order tells us who sees and who is seen. In other words, the word order tells us who/what the subject is as opposed to who/what the direct object is.

Case in German

German has four cases: the nominative case, the accusative case, the dative case, and the genitive case. Case in German is marked not by word order as in English, but by the form of the article and, less frequently, by endings on the noun. Below is a chart of the definite article in all of its possible forms, each determined by the gender, number, and case of the following noun.

	MASC.	NEUT.	FEM.	PLURAL
NOM.	der	das	die	die
ACC.	den	das	die	die
DAT.	dem	dem	der	den
GEN.	des	des	der	der

The sentence above (*The woman sees the man*) can be rendered in German in one of two possible ways:

Die Frau sieht **den** Mann.
Den Mann sieht **die** Frau.

Although the first version would be the more common, both versions are possible and mean essentially the same thing because the article, and not word order, marks grammatical case.

THE NOMINATIVE CASE

Nominative Forms

The **der**-words and **ein**-words (chapter 1) for the nominative case follow.

	MASC.	NEUT.	FEM.	PLURAL
Der-words	der	das	die	die
Ein-words	ein	ein	eine	keine

Usage of the Nominative Case

The nominative case is used in two common ways.

NOMINATIVE AS THE SUBJECT

Used as the subject, the nominative case answers the questions **Wer?** or **Was?** (*Who?* or *What?*).

Der Kaffee schmeckt gut. (Was schmeckt gut?)
The coffee tastes good. (What tastes good?)

Die Sonne scheint. (Was scheint?)
The sun is shining. (What's shining?)

Das Bild hängt an der Wand. (Was hängt an der Wand?)
The picture is hanging on the wall. (What's hanging on the wall?)

Die Touristen sind sehr müde. (Wer ist sehr müde?)
The tourists are very tired. (Who's very tired?)

Die Studentin kommt in die Vorlesung. (Wer kommt in die Vorlesung?)
The student comes to the lecture. (Who's coming to the lecture?)

NOMINATIVE AS A PREDICATE NOUN

A predicate noun may occur after the verbs **sein**, **werden**, and **bleiben**. It defines the subject of the sentence.

Dieses Museum ist **der Höhepunkt** der Reise.
This museum is the high point of the trip.

Der Junge wird **ein guter Fußballspieler**.
The boy is becoming a good football player.

Er ist und bleibt **mein bester Freund**.
He is and will remain my best friend.

It may be helpful to think of the verb as an equals sign in such expressions.

The museum = the high point of the trip.

The museum and *the high point* are equivalents, and therefore both are in the nominative case.

Exercise 1: *Fill in the correct nominative endings, where necessary.*

1. D__ Frau sitzt im Restaurant.
2. D__ Kind spielt mit dem Ball.
3. Wie heißt dies__ Politikerin?
4. Welch__ Zug hat Verspätung?
5. Wann beginnt dein__ Vorlesung?
6. Ein__ Mann im Zug sah aus dem Fenster.
7. Der BMW ist ein__ schnelles Auto.
8. Mein__ Schuhe sind schmutzig.
9. Sein__ Noten waren ein__ Katastrophe.
10. Mein__ Großmutter ist sehr krank.

THE ACCUSATIVE CASE

Accusative Forms

The **der**-words and **ein**-words for the nominative and accusative cases follow.

	MASC.	NEUT.	FEM.	PLURAL
NOM.	der	das	die	die
ACC.	den	das	die	die
NOM.	ein	ein	eine	keine
ACC.	einen	ein	eine	keine

Note that the only difference between the nominative and accusative endings occurs in the masculine.

Usage of the Accusative Case

The accusative case is used in five common ways.

ACCUSATIVE AS THE DIRECT OBJECT

Used as the direct object, the accusative noun receives the action of the verb. It answers the question **Wen?** or **Was?** (*Whom?* or *What?*).

Manfred mag **diese Gitarrenmusik**. (Was mag Manfred?)
Manfred likes this guitar music. (What does Manfred like?)

Gestern schrieb sie **einen Brief**. (Was schrieb sie gestern?)
Yesterday she wrote a letter. (What did she write yesterday?)

Ich sehe **eine Frau**. (Wen sehe ich?)
I see a woman. (Whom do I see?)

Tina ruft **ihre Familie** an. (Wen ruft Tina an?)
Tina is calling her family. (Whom is Tina calling?)

Exercise 2: *Fill in the correct accusative forms.*

1. Ich lese _____.   (die Zeitung)
2. Die Frau fragt _____.   (die Schüler)
3. Peter trägt nie _____.   (eine Krawatte)
4. Der Junge putzt _____.   (jedes Zimmer)
5. Die Katze frißt _____.   (die Maus)
6. Anna kennt hier _____.   (keine Person)
7. Die Studenten besuchen _____.   (das Museum)
8. Ich erwarte _____ am Bahnhof.   (mein Freund)
9. Morgen sehen wir _____.   (der Film)
10. _____ haben wir letztes Jahr gekauft.   (unser Haus)
11. Sie hält _____ in der Hand.   (ein Buch)
12. Sie liebt _____.   (dieser Mann)
13. Der Mechaniker repariert _____.   (der Wagen)
14. Die Schüler schreiben zweimal in der Woche _____.   (eine Klausur)
15. Die Schriftstellerin gibt _____ aus ihrem Buch.   (eine Lesung)

ACCUSATIVE WITH DURATIVE AND DEFINITE TIME EXPRESSIONS

The accusative case is used with durative and definite time expressions without a preposition. A durative time expression expresses duration and answers the question **Wie lange**? (*How long?*). A definite time expression pinpoints a specific time and answers the question **Wann**? (*When?*).

Wir haben **eine Woche** Ferien. (Wie lange?)
We have a one-week vacation. (How long?)

Ich hatte **den ganzen Tag** Orchesterprobe. (Wie lange?)
I had orchestra rehearsal the whole day (all day). (How long?)

Nächste Woche beginnen meine Ferien. (Wann?)
Next week my vacation begins. (When?)

Nächsten Freitag muß ich zur Orchesterprobe. (Wann?)
Next Friday I have to go to orchestra rehearsal. (When?)

ACCUSATIVE WITH EXPRESSIONS OF MEASUREMENT

The accusative case is used to express distance, space, and other kinds of measurements.

Diese Straße ist nur **einen Kilometer** lang.
This street is only one kilometer long.

Ich möchte bitte **ein Kilo** Kartoffeln.
I would like one kilogram of potatoes, please.

Das Mädchen ist schon **einen Meter** groß.
The girl is already a meter tall.

Das kostet nur **eine Mark**.
That only costs one mark.

ACCUSATIVE WITH THE EXPRESSION *ES GIBT*

The accusative case is always used with the idiomatic expression **es gibt**, which means *there is* or *there are*.

Es gibt **keine Wohnungen** mehr für die Studenten.
There are no longer any apartments for the students.

Es gibt **keinen Teppich** in diesem Zimmer.
There is no rug in this room.

Gibt es **ein Restaurant** in dieser Straße?
Is there a restaurant on this street?

ACCUSATIVE AFTER CERTAIN PREPOSITIONS

The accusative case is used after the accusative prepositions and, under certain conditions, the either-or prepositions. Prepositions are discussed in depth in chapter 4.

Exercise 3: *Fill in the blank with the correct nominative or accusative ending, if necessary.*

1. Familie Meier fährt jed__ Jahr nach Italien.
2. Mein__ Vater ist kein__ junger Mann.
3. Christine ißt ihr__ Salat ohne Dressing.
4. Wir bleiben ein__ Monat im Ausland.
5. Ich bringe mein__ Tennisschläger mit.
6. Es gibt kein__ Lösung für dieses Problem.
7. Wir sehen solch__ Filme nicht bis zu Ende.
8. D__ Leute demonstrieren gegen Atomkraftwerke.
9. Welch__ Geschenk ist für mich?
10. Ich verbringe jed__ Tag mit meiner Familie.
11. Unser__ Freunde schicken uns sicher ein__ Ansichtskarte aus Griechenland.
12. Ich habe ein__ Messer und ein__ Gabel, aber kein__ Löffel gefunden.
13. D__ Studentin sucht ein__ großen, alten Tisch.
14. Kannst du bitte d__ Fenster zumachen?

15. D__ Blumen auf der Wiese heißen Gänseblümchen.
16. Rock und Roll ist ihr__ Lieblingsmusik.
17. Gibt es ein__ Park in der Nähe?
18. Jed__ Morgen jogge ich ein__ Kilometer.

THE DATIVE CASE

Dative Forms

The **der**-words and **ein**-words for the nominative, accusative, and dative cases follow.

	MASC.	NEUT.	FEM.	PLURAL
NOM.	der	das	die	die
ACC.	den	das	die	die
DAT.	dem	dem	der	den (n)
NOM.	ein	ein	eine	keine
ACC.	einen	ein	eine	keine
DAT.	einem	einem	einer	keinen (n)

Plural nouns in the dative case add **-n** unless the noun ends in **-n** or **-s** in the nominative plural.

Usage of the Dative Case

The dative case is used in five common ways.

DATIVE AS THE INDIRECT OBJECT

The indirect object is usually the person to whom something is given or for whom something is done. The dative case thus answers the question **Wem**? (*To whom?* or *For whom?*).

Ich schreibe **meinem Freund** einen Liebesbrief. (Wem schreibe ich einen Liebesbrief?)
I'm writing a love letter to my boyfriend. (To whom am I writing a love letter?)

Die Chefin schickte **ihrer Sekretärin** Blumen zum Geburtstag. (Wem schickte die Chefin Blumen?)
The boss sent her secretary flowers for her birthday. (To whom did the boss send flowers?)

Die Babysitterin erzählt **dem Kind** eine Geschichte. (Wem erzählt die Babysitterin eine Geschichte?)
The babysitter tells the child a story. (To whom is the babysitter telling a story?)

Der Vater bestellt **seiner Tochter** das Essen. (Wem bestellt der Vater das Essen?)

The father orders the meal for his daughter. (For whom does the father order the meal?)

Ich bringe **meinen Gästen** Milch und Zucker für den Kaffee. (Wem bringe ich Milch und Zucker?)

I'm bringing my guests milk and sugar for their coffee. (To whom am I bringing milk and sugar?)

American students frequently find it difficult to distinguish between the direct object, which takes the accusative case, and the indirect object, which takes the dative case. The key to the difference lies in the questions we have set up for the two cases: *Whom?* or *What?* (accusative) versus *To whom?* or *For whom?* (dative).

Note the word order in the examples above, which each contain two noun objects: the indirect object (dative) precedes the direct object (accusative).

Ich erklärte **meinem Vater** (indirect object/dative case) **meine Sommerpläne** (direct object/accusative case).

Exercise 4: *Determine whether the nouns are accusative or dative and fill in the correct form of the article. Use the questions* Whom?/What? *and* To whom?/For whom? *to determine whether the nouns are direct or indirect objects.*

1. Der Fahrer zeigt d__ Polizistin d__ Führerschein.
2. Der Photograph schickt d__ Brautpaar d__ Photos.
3. Jeden Sonntag besuche ich mein__ Großmutter.
4. Jeden Samstag besuche ich ein__ Kunstmuseum.
5. Ich lese so ein__ Roman gern.
6. Ich lese mein__ Sohn so ein__ Roman gern vor.
7. Die Geschäftsfrau liefert ihr__ Kunden d__ Waren.
8. Das Mädchen erzählt ihr__ Freundin ein__ Geheimnis.
9. Die Austauschstudentin bringt ihr__ Gastfamilie ein__ Geschenk mit.
10. Nicole kauft ihr__ Freundinnen kein__ Zigaretten mehr.

DATIVE WITH DATIVE VERBS

Some verbs can take only a dative object. The most common of these are:

antworten	*to answer*
danken	*to thank*

folgen	*to follow*
gefallen	*to be pleasing to, to like*
gehören	*to belong to*
gelingen	*to succeed (at)*
glauben	*to believe*
helfen	*to help*
leid tun	*to be sorry*
passen	*to fit*
passieren	*to happen*
schmecken	*to taste*
weh tun	*to hurt*

The Use of *antworten*. Note that **antworten** is used to answer a person. The verb **beantworten** (plus accusative) is used to answer a question. Compare the following sentences:

Die Studentin antwortet **der** Professorin.
The student answers the professor.
BUT
Die Studentin beantwortet **die** Fragen korrekt.
The student answers the questions correctly.

The Use of *glauben*. Note that **glauben** can take an impersonal accusative object, usually **es** or **das**.

Das glaube ich.
I believe that.

Exercise 5: *Complete with the correct dative form of the nouns in parentheses.*

1. Das Heft gehört _____.   (die Schülerin; der Schüler)
2. Die Erbsen schmecken _____ nicht.   (das Baby; die Kinder)
3. Die Krankenschwester hilft _____.   (die Patientin; die Patienten)
4. Es tut _____ leid, daß wir nicht kommen.   (unsere Kollegen; unsere Freunde)
5. Ich danke _____ für alles.   (meine Eltern)
6. Die Touristen folgen _____.   (der Reiseleiter)
7. Was ist _____ passiert?   (deine Schwester; dein Bruder)
8. Das Knie tut _____ weh.   (der Sportler; die Sportlerin)
9. Das Kleid paßt _____ nicht mehr.   (meine Tochter)
10. Der Zeuge antwortet _____ auf seine Fragen.   (der Richter)

The Use of *gefallen*. The use of the dative verb **gefallen** is particularly problematic for American students. It may be helpful to translate it initially as *to be pleasing to*, rather than as the more idiomatic *to like*. Study the usage of the verb and its English equivalents carefully in the following examples:

Die neue Hose gefällt **meinem Vater**.
The new pair of pants is pleasing to my father.
My father likes the new pair of pants.

Das kalte Wetter gefällt **den Touristen** nicht.
The cold weather is not pleasing to the tourists.
The tourists don't like the cold weather.

Exercise 6: *Translate into English. If you find it helpful, translate first with* to be pleasing to *and then with* to like.

1. Es gefällt den Austauschstudenten in Deutschland.
2. Die Grammatik gefällt den Studenten nicht.
3. Was gefällt deiner Familie hier so gut?
4. Die Wälder gefallen dem Wanderer.
5. Das rote Motorrad gefällt mir besonders gut!
6. Dem kleinen Jungen gefallen seine neuen Schuhe nicht.
7. Gefällt deiner Schwester ihre neue Wohnung?

Exercise 7: *Translate into German. If you find it helpful, rephrase the English first with* to be pleasing to *and then translate into German.*

1. My father likes the new pair of pants.
2. The student likes her professor.
3. The American likes the beer in Germany.
4. The tourists like the museums in Europe.
5. I like this red dress.
6. Do you (**du**) like the music of Ludwig van Beethoven?
7. Which picture do you (**du**) like?

DATIVE WITH CERTAIN ADJECTIVES

The dative case is used with certain adjectives and their opposites. Here are some of the most common of these adjectives.

ähnlich	*similar*	gleich	*equal, indifferent*
angenehm	*pleasant*	leicht	*easy*
bekannt	*known*	lieb	*dear, agreeable*
böse	*angry*	möglich	*possible*
dankbar	*thankful*	nahe	*near, close*
egal	*all the same, indifferent*	nützlich	*useful*
fremd	*strange*	recht	*agreeable*
freundlich	*friendly*	teuer	*expensive*

treu	constant, faithful	wert	dear, valuable
unbegreiflich	incomprehensible	willkommen	welcome,
unmöglich	impossible		acceptable

It is impossible to memorize all adjectives that take the dative case, but you can develop a sense for them. Note in the examples below that these adjectives nearly always pose one of the questions that we identified as typical for the dative case: *To whom?* or *For whom?*.

Es ist **unserem Freund** unmöglich, morgen zu kommen.
It's impossible for our friend to come tomorrow.

Der Roman war **den Studenten** einfach unbegreiflich.
The novel was simply incomprehensible to the students.

Sie sieht **ihrem Vater** ähnlich.
She looks like her father. (She is similar to her father.)

Das große Auto ist **mir** zu teuer.
The large car is too expensive for me.

Exercise 8: *Complete with the dative forms of the nouns.*

1. Ein starker Wind ist _____ sehr willkommen.   (ein Segler)
2. _____ war die Diskussion ganz egal.   (unsere Schwester)
3. Ich bin _____ für alles dankbar.   (meine Eltern)
4. Der Skandal ist _____ höchst unangenehm.   (die Politikerin)
5. Die Pause ist _____ willkommen.   (die Studenten)
6. Deine Anwesenheit ist _____ viel wert.   (meine Familie)
7. Sie bleibt _____ treu.   (ihr Mann)
8. Er ist _____ böse.   (sein Gegenspieler)
9. Diese Tatsache war _____ sehr wohl bekannt.   (die Wissenschaftler)
10. _____ war die neue Umgebung vollkommen fremd.   (die Touristin)

DATIVE IN TIME EXPRESSIONS

The dative is used in time expressions after the prepositions **an** (*on, in*), **in** (*in*), and **vor** (*ago*).

am Montag   *on Monday*
am Abend   *in the evening*

in einer Woche   *in a week*
in einem Monat   *in a month*

vor einer Woche   *a week ago*
vor einem Jahr   *a year ago*

DATIVE AFTER CERTAIN PREPOSITIONS

The dative case is used after the dative prepositions and, under certain conditions, the either-or prepositions. Prepositions are discussed in depth in chapter 4.

Exercise 9: *Complete with the correct nominative, accusative, or dative ending, if necessary.*

1. Ich vermisse mein__ Freund sehr.
2. Dies__ Sommer müssen wir d__ Haus streichen.
3. D__ Professorin schreibt ein__ Empfehlungsbrief.
4. Möchtest du ein__ Tasse Kaffee?
5. D__ Professor liest sein__ Studenten ein__ Diktat vor.
6. Jed__ Tag bringt sie ihr__ Freundin ein__ Blume mit.
7. Unser__ Hund hat d__ Wasser gern.
8. Ich folge immer dein__ Rat.
9. Das ist mein__ Kugelschreiber.
10. Er ist sein__ Trainer dankbar für seinen Erfolg.
11. Gibt es hier kein__ Bäckereien?
12. Welch__ Buch gefällt d__ Kind am besten?
13. Ich werde mein__ Tochter ein__ Computer kaufen.
14. D__ Professor gefällt dein__ Thema sehr gut.
15. Mathematik ist d__ Studentin zu langweilig.

THE GENITIVE CASE

Genitive Forms   DER-WORD AND EIN-WORD CHARTS

The **der**-words and **ein**-words for all four cases in German (nominative, accusative, dative, and genitive) follow.

	MASC.	NEUT.	FEM.	PLURAL
NOM.	der	das	die	die
ACC.	den	das	die	die
DAT.	dem	dem	der	den (n)
GEN.	des (s, es)	des (s, es)	der	der
NOM.	ein	ein	eine	keine
ACC.	einen	ein	eine	keine
DAT.	einem	einem	einer	keinen (n)
GEN.	eines (s, es)	eines (s, es)	einer	keiner

Note the endings (**s**, **es**) after the masculine and neuter articles. This indicates that the masculine or neuter noun itself receives an ending in the genitive case.

GENITIVE NOUN ENDINGS

Most masculine and neuter nouns in the genitive case add **-s** or **-es** according to the following two rules.

General Rule. In general, **-es** is added to nouns of one syllable and **-s** is added to nouns of more than one syllable.

One syllable:	NOMINATIVE	GENITIVE	
	der Mann	des Mann**es**	*man*
	der Text	des Text**es**	*text*
	das Kind	des Kind**es**	*child*
	das Buch	des Buch**es**	*book*

More than one syllable:	NOMINATIVE	GENITIVE	
	der Vater	des Vater**s**	*father*
	der Teppich	des Teppich**s**	*carpet*
	das Telefon	des Telefon**s**	*telephone*
	das Fenster	des Fenster**s**	*window*

Rule for Nouns Ending in an *s* Sound. Nouns ending in an **s** sound (**-s**, **-ß**, **-x**, **-z**, **-sch**), regardless of the number of syllables, add **-es**.

NOMINATIVE	GENITIVE	
der Gruß	des Gruß**es**	*greeting*
der Komplex	des Komplex**es**	*complex*
das Glas	des Glas**es**	*glass*
das Gesetz	des Gesetz**es**	*law*

An exception to this rule is nouns ending in **-mus**; they do not add any ending.

NOMINATIVE	GENITIVE	
der Patriotismus	des Patriotismus	*patriotism*
der Optimismus	des Optimismus	*optimism*

Usage of the Genitive Case

The genitive case is used in three common ways.

GENITIVE FOR POSSESSION

The genitive case expresses a relationship of ownership between two nouns. Thus it answers the question **Wessen?** (*Whose?*).

In English, possession is shown either by means of an *'s* or with the preposition *of*.

my mother*'s* car   the car *of* my mother
our neighbor*'s* dog   the dog *of* our neighbor

In German, the genitive case is, with the exception of people's names (discussed below), expressed with a construction similar to the English prepositional phrase. *The key to correct usage of the genitive case in German is always to rephrase possession with the preposition "of."* Thus the genitive case answers the question *Of whom?* or *Of what?*.

Die Mechanikerin muß das Auto **meines Vaters** reparieren.
The mechanic must repair the car of my father.

Das ist das Werk **des Künstlers**.
That is the work of the artist.

Das Fahrrad **der Studentin** war kaputt.
The bicycle of the student was broken.

Exercise 10: *Rephrase the possessive construction using* of *and translate it into German.*

1. Here is the woman's address.
2. He is the children's father.
3. That is the dog's bone.
4. She is wearing her girlfriend's dress.
5. The house's window was broken.
6. Here is her sister's car.
7. The player's leg was broken.
8. May I use your friend's pencil?

Exercise 11: *Supply the correct genitive form of the noun in parentheses. Make sure you add endings to the nouns where necessary.*

1. Die Sirene _____ war laut. (der Krankenwagen)
2. Ich mag den Kuchen _____ am liebsten. (diese Bäckerei)
3. Die Erklärung _____ war unverständlich. (der Text)
4. Ich wohne noch in dem Haus _____. (meine Kindheit)
5. Die Lösungen _____ stehen am Ende _____. (die Übungen; jedes Kapitel)
6. Ich vergesse den Namen _____. (der Mann; das Kind)
7. Die Tochter _____ heißt Stephanie. (meine Schwester)
8. Dieses Buch analysiert die Grundsätze _____. (der Sozialismus)
9. Die Interpretation _____ ist zweideutig. (das Gesetz)
10. Die Farbe _____ gefällt ihm nicht. (ihr Kleid)

Genitive with Names of People. If the name of a person is the possessor, genitive is expressed with an **s**, without an apostrophe.

Wagners Musik	*Wagner's music*
Karins Wohnung	*Karin's apartment*
Mariannes Studenten	*Marianne's students*

An apostrophe, without the **s**, is used if the name ends in an **s** sound.

Fritz' Auto	*Fritz's car*
Hans' Buch	*Hans's book*

Dative as a Substitute for Genitive. In spoken German, the genitive case frequently is replaced by the preposition **von** plus the dative case.

das Heft der Studentin	das Heft von der Studentin
	the notebook of the student
die Tochter des Mannes	die Tochter von dem Mann
	the daughter of the man
der Name des Berges	der Name von dem Berg
	the name of the mountain
Helgas Freund	der Freund von Helga
	Helga's friend

GENITIVE TO DENOTE INDEFINITE TIME

The genitive case is used to indicate indefinite time.

eines Tages	*one day; someday*
eines Morgens	*one morning; some morning*
eines Abends	*one evening; some evening*

When used as an expression of indefinite time, the feminine noun **die Nacht** behaves like the masculine nouns above and takes masculine endings: **eines Nachts**.

Summary of Case in Time Expressions. It may be useful to recall and summarize the cases for time expressions here.

The accusative case is used for definite and durative time expressions.
The dative case is used for time expressions preceded by the prepositions **an**, **in**, and **vor**.
The genitive case is used for indefinite time expressions.

GENITIVE AFTER CERTAIN PREPOSITIONS

The genitive case is used after the genitive prepositions, discussed in chapter 4.

Exercise 12: *Complete with the correct nominative, accusative, dative, or genitive endings.*

1. Die Frau vermißt ihr__ Liebhaber.
2. Die Polizei glaubte d__ Einbrecher nicht.
3. D__ Regen hat ein__ Woche lang nicht aufgehört.
4. Ein__ Nacht__ hat jemand unser__ Wagen gestohlen.
5. D__ Lärm d__ Kinder war mein__ Nachbarin unangenehm.
6. D__ Stimme d__ Reporter__ war grell.
7. Jed__ Sommer verbringen d__ Freunde ein__ Monat zusammen am Bodensee.
8. D__ Eltern mein__ Freundin sind geschieden.
9. Ich habe d__ Zug verpaßt.
10. D__ Geschwindigkeit d__ Auto__ war d__ Passagiere__ sehr gefährlich.
11. Der Austauschstudent schreibt sein__ Eltern ein__ Brief.
12. D__ Kosten dies__ Projekt__ sind unbezahlbar.
13. D__ Mutter gab ihr__ Sohn ein wenig Geld.
14. D__ Fahrer d__ Wagen__ war bestimmt betrunken.
15. Der Hund mein__ Freund__ ist braun und weiß.

WEAK NOUNS

There is a group of nouns that adds the ending -(**e**)**n** in all cases except the nominative singular. These nouns usually refer to living creatures and are, with only one exception, masculine. They are called *weak nouns* or *masculine N-nouns*.

Weak Noun Forms

Most weak nouns add -**en** in all cases except the nominative singular. Nouns that already end in -**e** add -**n**. Here are some examples of weak noun declension.

ENGLISH		*human being*	*student*	*boy*
SINGULAR	NOM.	der Mensch	der Student	der Junge
	ACC.	den Mensch**en**	den Student**en**	den Jung**en**
	DAT.	dem Mensch**en**	dem Student**en**	dem Jung**en**
	GEN.	des Mensch**en**	des Student**en**	des Jung**en**
PLURAL		die Mensch**en**	die Student**en**	die Jung**en**

Der Herr (*gentleman*) and **der Nachbar** (*neighbor*) add **-n** only, not **-en** as expected.

SINGULAR	NOM.	der Herr	der Nachbar
	ACC.	den Herr**n**	den Nachbar**n**
	DAT.	dem Herr**n**	dem Nachbar**n**
	GEN.	des Herr**n**	des Nachbar**n**
PLURAL		die Herr**en**	die Nachbar**n**

A few weak nouns deviate slightly from this pattern in that they add **-(e)ns** in the genitive singular. These exceptions do not refer to living creatures. This group includes:

der Buchstabe	*letter*	der Glaube	*belief*
der Friede	*peace*	der Name	*name*
der Gedanke	*thought*	der Wille	*will*

SINGULAR	NOM.	der Name	der Gedanke
	ACC.	den Name**n**	den Gedanke**n**
	DAT.	dem Name**n**	dem Gedanke**n**
	GEN.	des Name**ns**	des Gedanke**ns**
PLURAL		die Name**n**	die Gedanke**n**

One neuter noun, **das Herz** (*heart*), adds the same endings except in the accusative singular.

SINGULAR	NOM.	das Herz
	ACC.	das Herz
	DAT.	dem Herz**en**
	GEN.	des Herz**ens**
PLURAL		die Herz**en**

Identification of Weak Nouns

Because it is difficult to predict which nouns are weak, it is best to keep a list of those weak nouns you encounter most frequently and memorize them. However, the following rule may help you recognize the majority of such nouns:

All masculine nouns referring to living beings are weak if

1. they have two or more syllables and end in an unstressed **-e**.

der Junge	*boy*	der Löwe	*lion*	der Kollege	*colleague*
der Neffe	*nephew*	der Affe	*ape*	der Franzose	*Frenchman*

OR

2. they have two or more syllables with the stress on the final syllable.

der Advokát	*lawyer*	der Kandidát	*candidate*
der Dirigént	*conductor*	der Philosóph	*philosopher*
der Elefánt	*elephant*	der Studént	*student*
der Kamerád	*comrade*	der Touríst	*tourist*

Exercise 13: *Supply the correct form of the weak noun.*

1. der Student
   _____ wohnt in Berlin.
   Ich kenne _____.
   Der Staat gibt _____ Bafög.
   Die Wohnung _____ ist sehr klein.
2. der Nachbar
   _____ ist ein alter Mann.
   Ich sehe _____ jeden Morgen.
   Unsere Parties gefallen _____ nicht.
   Der Garten _____ ist sehr gepflegt.
3. (Sein Name) _____ ist Patrick.
4. (Die Menschen) _____ sehen (die Affen) _____ und (ein Löwe) _____ im Zoo.
5. Die Pläne (der Tourist) _____ waren unrealistisch.
6. Man gab (der Held) _____ ein Ehrenzeichen.
7. Du bleibst ewig in (mein Herz) _____.
8. Ich kann (dieser Buchstabe) _____ nicht lesen.
9. Die kurze Dauer (der Friede) _____ war keine Überraschung.
10. Ich kenne die Eltern (der Junge) _____ nicht.

CASE IN SENTENCE FRAGMENTS AND APPOSITIVES

Sentence Fragments

To determine the case for nouns in sentence fragments, complete the fragment in your thoughts. For example:

Hast du deine Mutter gestern gesehen? Nein, mein**en** Vater.
Did you see your mother yesterday? No, my father.

To determine the case of *my father*, complete the thought in your head: *No, I saw my father.* Now it is clear that *father* is a direct object and is therefore accusative in the German equivalent.

Similarly:

Kannst du Brigitte einen Kugelschreiber leihen? Nein, nur ein**en** Bleistift.
Can you lend Brigitte a pen? No, (I can lend her) only a pencil.

Welchem Schüler gibst du Nachhilfestunden? **Dem** Junge**n** da.
Which pupil do you give tutoring to? (I give tutoring) to that boy there.

Appositives

Sometimes a fragment occurs within a sentence. These fragments are called *appositives* and they take the same case as the noun to which they refer.

Hast du meinen Vater, **einen alten Mann mit grauem Haar**, gesehen?
Have you seen my father, an old man with gray hair?

Ich gebe dem Mädchen da, **einer Schülerin aus der zehnten Klasse**, Nachhilfestunden.
I'm giving tutoring to that girl there, a pupil from the tenth grade.

Exercise 14: *Complete with the correct case ending.*

1. Wen hast du zur Party eingeladen? Nur mein___ Freund und mein___ beste Freundin.
2. Wer repariert das Auto? D___ Mechaniker.
3. Ich heirate Georg, ein___ Freund aus der Schulzeit.
4. Ich habe keine Katze, nur ein___ Hund.
5. Welchen Deutschkurs belegst du? D___ Kurs für Anfänger.
6. Welcher Wochentag ist dein Lieblingstag? D___ Freitag.
7. Helmut Kohl, d___ Bundeskanzler, ist Mitglied der CDU.
8. Wen besuchst du morgen? Mein___ Bruder und mein___ Schwester.
9. Das ist Frau Schmidt, ein___ pensionierte Beamte.
10. Ich liebe beides, d___ Leben und d___ Friede___.

REVIEW EXERCISES

Exercise 15: *Complete with the correct form of the nouns in parentheses. (This is a comprehensive exercise, testing everything you have learned in this chapter.)*

1. Die Antwort (der Schüler) _____ gefällt (die Lehrerin) _____ nicht.
2. Ich mag (der Rhythmus) _____ der Musik.
3. Die Verkäuferin sieht (der Ladendieb) _____ nicht.

4. Es ist (meine Eltern) _____ gleich, ob wir sie heute oder morgen besuchen.
5. Der Preis (der Wagen) _____ ist viel zu hoch.
6. (Diese Farbe) _____ gefällt mir ausgesprochen gut!
7. Die Studenten folgen (die Anweisungen) _____ (der Professor) _____ haargenau.
8. Es gibt (kein Grund) _____ dafür.
9. Das kann wirklich nur (deine Tante) _____ passieren!
10. Der Bericht (der Journalist) _____ war hervorragend.
11. Die Gastgeberin war (ihre Gäste) _____ sehr freundlich.
12. Wem glaubst du? (Der Mann) _____ oder (die Frau) _____?
13. Ich schenke (meine Tochter) _____ (ein Sportwagen) _____.
14. (Kein Mensch) _____ kann mir erklären, wo (der Bahnhof) _____ ist.
15. Die Sekretärin hat (eine Kopie) _____ (das Protokoll) _____.

Exercise 16: *Complete with the correct nominative, accusative, dative, or genitive case ending, if necessary.*

1. Dein__ Ideen sind d__ anderen Schüler__ gleich.
2. Die Großmutter erzählt ihr__ Enkelkinder__ ein__ Geschichte.
3. Wir verbringen jed__ Sommer ein__ Woche an der Nordsee.
4. Fußball ist ein__ sehr populäre Sportart in Europa.
5. Die Professorin erläutert d__ Studenten ihr__ Theorie.
6. Ich kaufe heute ein__ Anzug.
7. D__ Kriminalkommissar untersucht d__ Tatort.
8. Ich habe kein__ Briefmarken mehr übrig.
9. Die Kellnerin bringt d__ Gast ein__ Glas Wasser.
10. Dies__ Ort ist mein__ Lieblingsort.
11. Die neue Maschine war d__ Techniker sehr nützlich.
12. Die Ärztin sieht ihr__ Patienten täglich.
13. Es gibt kein__ Erklärung für diesen Vorfall.
14. Ich verkaufe dies__ Plattenspieler.
15. Am Sonntag geht d__ ganze Familie im Park spazieren.
16. Ilse hat ein__ Schwester, aber sie hat kein__ Bruder.
17. D__ Lehrerin betritt d__ Klassenzimmer.
18. Sie liest jed__ Buch von Hemingway dreimal.
19. Ich möchte ein___ Kaffee und ein___ Stück Kirschtorte.
20. Ich bin die Tochter des Professors, ein___ stadtbekannten Mann___.

ANSWERS TO EXERCISES

1.

1. Die
2. Das
3. diese
4. welcher
5. deine
6. Ein
7. ein
8. Meine
9. Seine; eine
10. Meine

2.

1. die Zeitung
2. die Schüler
3. eine Krawatte
4. jedes Zimmer
5. die Maus
6. keine Person
7. das Museum
8. meinen Freund
9. den Film
10. Unser Haus
11. ein Buch
12. diesen Mann
13. den Wagen
14. eine Klausur
15. eine Lesung

3.

1. jedes
2. Mein; kein
3. ihren
4. einen
5. meinen
6. keine
7. solche
8. Die
9. Welches
10. jeden
11. Unsere; eine
12. ein; eine; keinen
13. Die; einen
14. das
15. Die
16. ihre
17. einen
18. Jeden; einen

4.

1. der; den
2. dem; die
3. meine
4. ein
5. einen
6. meinem; einen
7. ihren; die
8. ihrer; ein
9. ihrer; ein
10. ihren; keine

5.

1. der Schülerin; dem Schüler
2. dem Baby; den Kindern
3. der Patientin; den Patienten
4. unseren Kollegen; unseren Freunden
5. meinen Eltern
6. dem Reiseleiter
7. deiner Schwester; deinem Bruder
8. dem Sportler; der Sportlerin
9. meiner Tochter
10. dem Richter

6.

1. (In Germany it is pleasing to the exchange students.)
   The exchange students like it in Germany.
2. (Grammar is not pleasing to the students.)
   The students don't like grammar.
3. (What is so pleasing to your family here?)
   What does your family like here so much?
4. (The forests are pleasing to the hiker.)
   The hiker likes the forests.
5. (The red motorcycle is especially pleasing to me!)
   I especially like the red motorcycle!
6. (His new shoes are not pleasing to the little boy.)
   The little boy doesn't like his new shoes.
7. (Is her new apartment pleasing to your sister?)
   Does your sister like her new apartment?

7.

1. (The new pair of pants is pleasing to my father.)
   Die neue Hose gefällt meinem Vater.
2. (Her professor is pleasing to the student.)
   Ihr Professor/Ihre Professorin gefällt der Studentin.
3. (The beer in Germany is pleasing to the American.)
   Das Bier in Deutschland gefällt dem Amerikaner/der Amerikanerin.
4. (The museums in Europe are pleasing to the tourists.)
   Die Museen in Europa gefallen den Touristen.
5. (This red dress is pleasing to me!)
   Mir gefällt dieses rote Kleid!
6. (Is the music of Ludwig van Beethoven pleasing to them?)
   Gefällt ihnen die Musik von Ludwig van Beethoven?
7. (Which picture is pleasing to you?)
   Welches Bild gefällt dir?

8.

1. einem Segler
2. Unserer Schwester
3. meinen Eltern
4. der Politikerin
5. den Studenten
6. meiner Familie
7. ihrem Mann
8. seinem
9. den Wissenschaftlern
10. Der Touristin

9.

1. meinen
2. Diesen; das
3. Die; einen
4. eine
5. Der; seinen; ein
6. Jeden; ihrer; eine
7. Unser; das
8. deinem
9. mein
10. seinem
11. keine
12. Welches; dem
13. meiner; einen
14. Dem; dein
15. der

10.

1. Here is the address of the woman.
   Hier ist die Adresse der Frau.
2. He is the father of the children.
   Er ist der Vater der Kinder.
3. That is the bone of the dog.
   Das ist der Knochen des Hundes.
4. She is wearing the dress of her girlfriend.
   Sie trägt das Kleid ihrer Freundin.
5. The window of the house was broken.
   Das Fenster des Hauses war kaputt.
6. Here is the car of her sister.
   Hier ist das Auto ihrer Schwester.
7. The leg of the player was broken.
   Das Bein des Spielers war gebrochen.
8. May I use the pencil of your friend?
   Darf ich den Bleistift deines Freundes/deiner Freundin benutzen?

11.

1. des Krankenwagens
2. dieser Bäckerei
3. des Textes
4. meiner Kindheit
5. der Übungen; jedes Kapitels
6. des Mannes; des Kindes
7. meiner Schwester
8. des Sozialismus
9. des Gesetzes
10. ihres Kleides

12.

1. ihren
2. dem
3. Der; eine
4. Eines Nachts; unseren
5. Der; der; meiner
6. Die; des Reporters
7. Jeden; die; einen
8. Die; meiner
9. den
10. Die; des Autos; den Passagieren
11. seinen; einen
12. Die; dieses Projekts
13. Die; ihrem
14. Der; des Wagens
15. meines Freundes

13.

1. Der Student
   den Studenten
   dem Studenten
   des Studenten
2. Der Nachbar
   den Nachbarn
   dem Nachbarn
   des Nachbarn
3. Sein Name
4. Die Menschen; die Affen; einen Löwen
5. des Touristen
6. dem Helden
7. meinem Herzen
8. diesen Buchstaben
9. des Friedens
10. des Jungen

14.

1. meinen; meine
2. Der
3. einen
4. einen
5. Den
6. Der
7. der
8. Meinen; meine
9. eine
10. das; den Frieden

15.

1. des Schülers; der Lehrerin
2. den Rhythmus
3. den Ladendieb
4. meinen Eltern
5. des Wagens
6. Diese Farbe
7. den Anweisungen; des Professors
8. keinen Grund
9. deiner Tante
10. des Journalisten
11. ihren Gästen
12. Dem Mann; der Frau
13. meiner Tochter; einen Sportwagen
14. Kein Mensch; der Bahnhof
15. eine Kopie; des Protokolls

16.

1. Deine; den anderen Schülern
2. ihren Enkelkindern; eine
3. jeden; eine
4. eine
5. den; ihre
6. einen
7. Der; den
8. keine
9. dem; ein
10. Dieser; mein
11. dem
12. ihre
13. keine
14. diesen
15. die
16. eine; keinen
17. Die; das
18. jedes
19. einen; ein
20. eines Mannes

3

Pronouns

*P*ronouns replace nouns. There are many different kinds of pronouns—for example, personal, demonstrative, interrogative, indefinite, reflexive, and relative. The most common are the personal pronouns, corresponding to English **I**, **you**, **he**, **she**, **it**, **we**, **they**.

Pronouns are declined according to number, gender, and case. They must agree with their antecedent. In other words, they must indicate the same number, gender, and case as the noun that they replace. In this chapter we will introduce the meanings and forms of the various pronouns and practice replacing nouns with them.

PERSONAL PRONOUNS

Listed below are the forms of the personal pronouns in the nominative, accusative, and dative cases.

Forms

SINGULAR	1st person	2nd person familiar	2nd person formal	3rd person		
	I	*you*	*you*	*he*	*it*	*she*
NOM.	ich	du	Sie	er	es	sie
ACC.	mich	dich	Sie	ihn	es	sie
DAT.	mir	dir	Ihnen	ihm	ihm	ihr

PLURAL	*we*	*you*	*you*	*they*
NOM.	wir	ihr	Sie	sie
ACC.	uns	euch	Sie	sie
DAT.	uns	euch	Ihnen	ihnen

Note that the first person singular (*I*) is not capitalized in German: **ich**. The second person formal, singular and plural (*you*), is capitalized in all cases in German: **Sie, Sie, Ihnen**.

Note that the third person personal pronouns in both singular and plural correspond very closely to the endings of the definite article. This may help you to remember the forms. Compare:

	DEFINITE ARTICLE				PERSONAL PRONOUNS			
NOM.	der	das	die	die	er	es	sie	sie
ACC.	den	das	die	die	ihn	es	sie	sie
DAT.	dem	dem	der	den	ihm	ihm	ihr	ihnen

The Difference between du, ihr, and Sie

As you can see from the chart above, German distinguishes between formal (**Sie**) and informal (**du**, **ihr**) personal pronouns in the second person. In informal usage there is a further distinction between singular (**du**) and plural (**ihr**).

Because English makes no such distinctions, it is frequently difficult for English speakers to know when to use the informal as opposed to the formal form of address. In general, the informal form of address should be used with family members, friends, and children or young adolescents. In addition, members of a close group, such as students or athletes on a team, tend to use the familiar form of address to convey solidarity. The formal form of address implies distance and respect. When in doubt, it is probably wise to err on the side of caution and use the formal form of address.

The formal **Sie** in all of its forms is always capitalized. The informal **du** and **ihr** are not capitalized except in letters, as demonstrated below.

Lieber Peter! Vielen Dank für **D**einen langen Brief. Ich hoffe, es geht **D**ir mittlerweile besser. Wann kommt **I**hr wieder nach Hause? . . . Mit freundlichen Grüßen von **D**einer Monika.

Dear Peter, Thanks a lot for your letter. I hope that you're doing better in the meantime. When are you (guys) coming back home? . . . All the best from your friend, Monika.

Exercise 1: *Replace the boldface pronoun with the cue pronoun.*

1. Sprich nicht so schlecht von **mir**!   (er; sie [*she*]; wir; sie [*they*])
2. Er trifft **dich** in der Stadt.   (ich; er; sie [*she*]; wir; ihr; sie [*they*]; Sie)

3. Das Reisebüro bucht eine Reise für **mich** nach Italien.   (du; er; sie [*she*]; wir; ihr; sie [*they*]; Sie)

4. Sie hilft **mir** sehr.   (du; er; sie [*she*]; wir; ihr; sie [*they*]; Sie)

Exercise 2: *Supply the correct form of the personal pronoun.*

1. (ich)   _____ zahle die Rechnung.
2. (du)   Kommst _____ zur Klasse? Dann sehe ich _____ da.
3. (Sie)   Können _____ Schach spielen? Sind _____ die Spielregeln bekannt?
4. (wir)   _____ gefällt die Dreizimmerwohnung besser.
5. (ich; du)   _____ gehe morgen abend nur dann ins Kino, wenn _____ mitkommst.
6. (ich)   Herr Ober, können Sie _____ bitte noch eine Suppe bringen?
7. (wir; ihr)   Diese Katze gehört _____, nicht _____!
8. (sie [*they*])   Als ich _____ meine Geschichte erzählte, waren _____ sehr schockiert.
9. (wir; ihr)   Können _____ zu _____ kommen?
10. (sie; du)   _____ liebt _____ sehr.

Exercise 3: *Replace the boldface words with the appropriate personal pronoun.*

1. Kennst du **meinen Bruder**?
2. Ich sah **deine Eltern** gestern abend in der Diskothek!
3. **Die Arbeiter** haben jetzt Mittagspause.
4. Sie telefoniert mit **ihren Eltern**.
5. **Meine Schwester und ich** gehen zusammen einkaufen.
6. Ich habe ein Geschenk für **dich und deine Freundin**.
7. **Die Studentin** lernt bis spät in die Nacht.
8. Er machte **seiner Frau** etwas zu essen.
9. Der Pfadfinder hilft **dem alten Mann**.
10. **Die Professorin** hat **der Studentin** eine schlechte Note gegeben.
11. **Meine Geschwister** sind alle älter als ich.
12. **Der Autofahrer** hat **den Polizisten** nach dem Weg gefragt.
13. **Der gefährliche Hund** hat **die Briefträgerin** gebissen.
14. **Meine Freunde und ich** fahren morgen zusammen in Urlaub.
15. **Peter und Christine** heiraten bald.

Gender Agreement of Personal Pronouns

Personal pronouns agree with their antecedent in number, case, and gender. As you know, inanimate objects in German have grammatical, not natural, gender (see chapter 1). In the singular, the gender of a pronoun must agree with the gender of the noun it replaces.

Der Tisch ist rot.   **Er** ist rot.
The table is red.   *It is red.*

Das Fenster ist zu.   **Es** ist zu.
The window is closed.   *It is closed.*

Die Tür ist auf.   **Sie** ist auf.
The door is open.   *It is open.*

There is one frequent exception to personal pronoun gender agreement. With the neuter noun **das Mädchen** it has become common to use the feminine personal pronoun, **sie**, especially in the spoken language.

Das Mädchen geht zur Schule.   **Sie** geht zur Schule.
The girl goes to school.   *She goes to school.*

The personal pronoun for all nouns in the plural is **sie**.

Die Tische sind rot.   **Sie** sind rot.
The tables are red.   *They are red.*

Die Fenster sind zu.   **Sie** sind zu.
The windows are closed.   *They are closed.*

Die Türen sind offen.   **Sie** sind offen.
The doors are open.   *They are open.*

Exercise 4: *Replace the boldface words with the appropriate personal pronoun.*

1. Der Musiker spielt **die Flöte** wunderbar.
2. **Der Kühlschrank** ist kaputt.
3. Ich habe **das Geschirr** gestern gespült.
4. Gisela kauft **den Schal**.
5. Schreib **den Lebenslauf** bitte zu Ende!
6. Ich trinke **die Tasse Tee** schnell aus.
7. Sie besuchen **zwei Kirchen** in Köln.
8. Der Student bekommt **den Ferienjob** nicht.
9. Ich habe **die Uhr** verloren.
10. Sie löst **die Kreuzworträtsel** gern.
11. **Die Schiffe** werden in zwei Wochen den Hafen erreichen.
12. Er hat **das letzte Brötchen** zum Frühstück gegessen.
13. Meine Mutter verkauft **das Auto**.
14. Ich finde **dieses Buch** ungeheuer interessant.
15. Ich habe **meine Kontaktlinsen** verloren.

Word Order of Accusative and Dative Pronouns

When a sentence has two noun objects, the indirect object (IO) precedes the direct object (DO) (see chapter 2).

       IO   DO

Ich schenke **meiner Mutter eine Bluse**.

I'm giving my mother a blouse.

       IO   DO

Sie erzählt **den Kindern eine Geschichte**.

She tells the children a story.

When a sentence has two pronoun objects, the order is reversed and the direct object (DO) precedes the indirect object (IO).

      DO   IO

Ich schenke **sie** (die Bluse) **ihr** (meiner Mutter).

I'm giving it (the blouse) to her (my mother).

      DO   IO

Sie erzählt **sie** (eine Geschichte) **ihnen** (den Kindern).

She tells it (the story) to them (the children).

When a sentence has one noun and one pronoun object, the pronoun precedes the noun regardless of case.

Ich schenke **ihr** eine Bluse.
I'm giving her a blouse.

Ich schenke **sie** meiner Mutter.
I'm giving it to my mother.

Sie erzählt **ihnen** eine Geschichte.
She tells them a story.

Sie erzählt **sie** den Kindern.
She tells it to the children.

The use of the personal pronouns with prepositions is discussed in chapter 4.

Exercise 5: *Replace the boldface noun objects with pronoun objects. Change the word order if necessary.*

1. Wir mußten **dem Dieb** unser ganzes Geld geben.
2. Ich backe der kranken Frau **einen leckeren Kuchen** heute abend.
3. Sie öffnete **dem alten Mann** die Tür.
4. Die Kauffrau beschreibt **dem Kunden** die Vorteile dieses Autos.

5. Die Verwandten zeigen meiner Familie **die Umgebung**.
6. Der Kellner empfiehlt **dem Ehepaar** den Rotwein.
7. Ich wünsche **meiner Kollegin** alles Gute zum Geburtstag.
8. Der Juwelier hat seiner Frau **einen Diamantring** gekauft.
9. Gib dem Kind **das Messer** bitte nicht!
10. Sie hat ihrem Nachbarn **den Rasenmäher** geliehen.

Exercise 6: *Replace both noun objects with pronoun objects and change the word order as necessary.*

1. Die Mutter kauft ihrer Tochter einen Gebrauchtwagen.
2. Der Sprecher berichtet der Presse die Neuigkeiten.
3. Ich bringe meinen Eltern die Zeitung.
4. Das Spiel bietet dem Gewinner eine Weltreise.
5. Die Autorin widmet ihrer Großmutter ihr Buch.
6. Sie schenkt ihren Gästen das Photo.
7. Ich gebe der Professorin meine Hausarbeit.
8. Der Sportler reicht seinem Gegner die Hand.
9. Die Händlerin verkauft dem Kunden einen Teppich.
10. Der Vater bastelt seinem Sohn einen Papierdrachen.

REFLEXIVE PRONOUNS

Definition

A *reflexive pronoun* is a pronoun that refers back to the subject of the sentence. Compare the following sentence pairs:

NONREFLEXIVE	REFLEXIVE
Sie wäscht **es** (das Auto).	Sie wäscht **sich**.
She washes it (the car).	*She washes herself.*
Der Friseur rasiert **ihn** (den Mann).	Der Friseur rasiert **sich**.
The barber shaves him (the man).	*The barber shaves himself.*
Sie kauft **ihr** (der Frau) Blumen.	Sie kauft **sich** Blumen.
She buys her (the woman) flowers.	*She buys herself flowers.*

Forms

A reflexive pronoun may be either accusative or dative.

PERSONAL PRONOUN SUBJECT	ACCUSATIVE REFLEXIVE	DATIVE REFLEXIVE
ich	mich	mir
du	dich	dir
er/es/sie	sich	sich
wir	uns	uns
ihr	euch	euch
sie	sich	sich
Sie	sich	sich

Note that the only difference between the accusative and dative reflexive pronoun forms occurs in the **ich** and **du** forms.

Note that the reflexive pronoun for all third person forms, singular or plural (**er**, **es**, **sie** [*she*], and **sie** [*they*]), is identical: **sich**.

Note that the reflexive pronoun for **Sie** in both cases is not capitalized: **sich**.

Accusative or Dative?

The case of the reflexive pronoun is determined by the function of that pronoun within the sentence. A reflexive pronoun is accusative when it is the direct object of the sentence or when it follows an accusative preposition. A reflexive pronoun is dative when it is the indirect object of the sentence or when it follows a dative preposition, verb, or adjective. Study the following sentences:

ACCUSATIVE REFLEXIVE PRONOUNS

DIRECT OBJECT	Ich rasiere **mich**.
	I shave myself.
OBJECT OF AN ACCUSATIVE PREPOSITION	Du kämpfst nur gegen **dich**.
	You're only fighting yourself.

DATIVE REFLEXIVE PRONOUNS

INDIRECT OBJECT	Ich kaufte **mir** Blumen.
	I bought myself flowers.
OBJECT OF A DATIVE PREPOSITION	Ich habe viel Geld bei **mir**.
	I have a lot of money on me.
OBJECT OF A DATIVE VERB	Hast du **dir** weh getan?
	Did you hurt yourself?
OBJECT OF A DATIVE ADJECTIVE	Manchmal bin ich **mir** selber fremd.
	I don't know myself sometimes.

Reflexive Pronouns with Parts of the Body and Clothing

German uses a dative reflexive pronoun together with a definite article to show possession with parts of the body and clothing. English uses the possessive adjective in such constructions.

Ich wasche **mir** die Hände.	*I wash my hands.*
Ich habe **mir** den Arm gebrochen.	*I broke my arm.*
Ich ziehe **mir** das Hemd aus.	*I'm taking my shirt off.*

Reflexive Constructions to Express Reciprocity

The plural reflexive pronouns (**uns**, **euch**, **sich**) may be used to express reciprocity in the sense of *each other*. **Einander**, which never changes its form, may be substituted for the reflexive pronoun in such expressions.

Wann sehen wir **uns** wieder? Wann sehen wir **einander** wieder?
When will we see each other again?

Habt ihr **euch** sehr vermiβt? Habt ihr **einander** sehr vermiβt?
Did you (guys) miss each other a lot?

Selbst and selber

Selbst and **selber** are adverbs meaning *-self* that may be used to intensify the reflexive pronoun. They may not, however, replace the reflexive pronoun. **Selbst** and **selber** never change their form.

Ich will dir helfen, aber zuerst muβ ich mir **selbst/selber** helfen.
I want to help you, but first I have to help myself. (emphasis on *myself*)

Durch solche Handlungen verletzt du nur dich **selbst/selber.**
You only hurt yourself by such actions. (emphasis on *yourself*)

Selbst and **selber** may intensify parts of speech other than reflexive pronouns.

Morgen spricht der Chef **selbst/selber** mit uns.
Tomorrow the boss himself is going to speak with us.

Nur ich **selbst/selber** bin für den Fehler verantwortlich.
I alone am responsible for the mistake.

If **selbst** (but never **selber**) precedes a noun, it corresponds to English *even.*

Selbst sie konnte das Rätsel nicht lösen.
Even she couldn't solve the puzzle.

Reflexive Verbs

Some verbs are always used with reflexive pronouns to express certain meanings. These verbs are called *reflexive verbs*. They will be treated in detail in chapter 11.

Exercise 7: *Supply the correct reflexive or personal pronoun.*

1. Sie sieht _____ im Spiegel.   (*herself*)
2. Sie sieht _____ im Spiegel.   (*him*)
3. Ich putze _____ die Zähne.
4. Ich schenke _____ ein neues Auto.   (*myself*)
5. Dann schenke ich _____ mein altes Auto.   (*her*)
6. Die Schauspielerin schminkt _____.   (*herself*)
7. Die Assistentin schminkt _____.   (*her*)
8. Niemand war da. Ich muβte _____ selber zum Geburtstag gratulieren.   (*myself*)
9. Er ist auβer _____ vor Freude.   (*himself*)
10. Kind, zieh _____ den Mantel an!

11. Kind, zieh _____ sofort an!
12. Sie hat _____ beide Arme gebrochen.
13. Sie hat _____ eine Geschichte vorgelesen.   (*him*)
14. Wir haben _____ heute verlobt.
15. Der Bauarbeiter gönnt _____ eine kurze Pause.   (*himself*)
16. Ich gebe _____ 15 Minuten Zeit!   (*them*)
17. Laβ _____ nicht beim Abschreiben erwischen!   (*yourself*)
18. Claudia hat _____ ein neues Kleid gekauft.   (*herself*)
19. Ihre Mutter hat _____ das Kleid bezahlt.   (*her*)
20. Ich habe _____ heute nicht rasiert.   (*myself*)

INTERROGATIVE PRONOUNS

There are two interrogative pronouns: **wer** (*who*) and **was** (*what*). The interrogative pronoun **wer** is declined as follows:

NOMINATIVE	**wer**
ACCUSATIVE	**wen**
DATIVE	**wem**
GENITIVE	**wessen**

NOMINATIVE	**Wer** klopft an die Tür?
	Who's knocking at the door?
ACCUSATIVE	**Wen** treffen Sie im Biergarten?
	Whom are you meeting in the beer garden?
DATIVE	**Wem** geben Sie die Rosen?
	To whom are you giving the roses?
GENITIVE	**Wessen** Schallplatte liegt hier?
	Whose record is lying here?

The interrogative **was** is not declined.

The use of interrogative pronouns with prepositions is discussed in chapter 4.

Exercise 8: *Complete with the correct form of the interrogative pronoun indicated.*

1. (*Whose*) _____ Brille ist das?
2. (*What*) _____ hast du zu Weihnachten bekommen?
3. (*Who*) _____ hat die Arbeit gemacht?
4. (*Who*) _____ hat das Geld gestohlen?
5. (*Who*) _____ kommt heute abend zum Essen?
6. (*What*) _____ gibt es zu essen?

7. (*To whom*) _____ schreibst du den langen Brief?
8. (*Whom*) _____ liebt sie?
9. (*Whom*) _____ haben Sie angerufen?
10. (*Whose*) _____ Telefonnummer wählst du?
11. (*Whom*) _____ möchtest du für morgen abend einladen?
12. (*To whom*) _____ hast du noch keine Einladung gegeben?
13. (*Whom*) _____ habt ihr gestern beim Einkaufen getroffen?
14. (*Whose*) _____ Musik gefällt dir am besten?
15. (*What*) _____ spielt heute abend im Theater?

THE INDEFINITE PRONOUN MAN

The indefinite pronoun **man** refers to no one in particular and corresponds to *one*, *you*, *they*, or *people* in English. Study the following examples:

Hier darf man nicht rauchen.
One is not allowed to smoke here. No smoking here.

So etwas tut man nicht.
One doesn't do that. That's just not done.

Man muβ nicht jeden Tag Fleisch essen.
You don't have to eat meat every day.

In der Kirche soll man ruhig sein.
You should be quiet in church.

Man, as a pronoun, cannot be replaced by another pronoun. Instead it is repeated. Compare this with the usage of *one* in English which is often replaced by *he/she*.

Wenn **man** fünf Kilometer joggt, wird **man** müde.
When one jogs five kilometers, one (he/she) becomes tired.

Wenn **man** müde ist, soll **man** ins Bett gehen.
If one is tired, one (he/she) should go to bed.

Man is the nominative form. It is declined for the accusative and dative cases as follows:

NOMINATIVE	**man**
ACCUSATIVE	**einen**
DATIVE	**einem**

ACCUSATIVE   Es freut **einen** nicht, wenn man krank ist.
                It doesn't make you happy when you're sick.

DATIVE   Wenn man jung ist, gehört **einem** noch die Zukunft.
                When you're young, the future still belongs to you.

The reflexive pronoun for **man** is **sich**.

Man duscht **sich** normalerweise mit warmem Wasser.
Normally one takes a shower with warm water.

Exercise 9: *Supply the correct form of* **man**. *Then translate the sentences into idiomatic English.*

    1. Es tut _____ weh, wenn man hinfällt.
    2. Man soll _____ die Zähne jeden Abend putzen. (*reflexive pronoun*)
    3. _____ fährt schnell auf der Autobahn.
    4. Hier darf _____ nicht schwimmen gehen.
    5. Wenn _____ eine Erkältung hat, hat _____ oft Fieber.
    6. Man trifft _____ oft in einem Biergarten. (*reflexive pronoun*)
    7. Von hier aus sieht der Polizist _____ nicht.
    8. Die Politiker sagen _____ nicht immer die Wahrheit.
    9. Normalerweise trinkt _____ Kaffee morgens.
  10. Das Buch erklärt _____, wie _____ den Computer bedient.

Exercise 10: *Translate into correct German.*

    1. In America they shower/one showers every morning.
    2. You/one may drive fast on this road.
    3. If you are/one is sick, you go/one goes to the doctor.
    4. Love makes you/one crazy.
    5. Does a black cat really bring you/one bad luck?

DEMONSTRATIVE PRONOUNS

Demonstrative pronouns are used instead of personal pronouns for emphasis. They are usually placed at or near the beginning of the sentence. In most cases, the English equivalent is a personal pronoun (*he, she, it,* etc.) or, to convey emphasis, *this one* or *that one.*

The forms of the demonstrative pronouns correspond to those of the definite article, except in the dative case plural, where **den** is extended to become **denen**. Genitive forms occur only rarely and will not be treated here.

	MASC.	NEUT.	FEM.	PLURAL
NOM.	der	das	die	die
ACC.	den	das	die	die
DAT.	dem	dem	der	denen

The number and gender of the demonstrative pronoun are determined by its antecedent. The case is determined by the function of the demonstrative pronoun within the sentence.

Kennst du Gabriele? Ja, **die** kenne ich gut.
Do you know Gabriele? Yes, I know her well.

Willst du mit meinen Eltern fahren? Ja, mit **denen** fahre ich gern.
Do you want to drive with my parents? Yes, I like driving with them.

For additional emphasis, the demonstrative pronoun is sometimes combined with **dort**, **da**, or **hier**. The English equivalent is **this one (here)** or **that one (there)**.

Kaufst du diese Bluse? Nein, **die dort** gefällt mir besser.
Are you going to buy this blouse? No, I like that one there better.

Wohnst du in dieser Wohnung? Nein, in **der da**.
Do you live in this apartment? No, in that one there.

Dies- can also be used as a demonstrative pronoun. As such, it takes the same endings as the demonstrative pronoun listed above. The English equivalent is *this one* or *that one*.

Kaufst du diese Bluse? Nein, **diese** gefällt mir besser.
Are you going to buy this blouse? No, I like this one better.

Wohnst du in dieser Wohnung? Nein, in **dieser**.
Do you live in this apartment? No, in this one.

Exercise 11: *Supply the appropriate demonstrative pronoun.*

1. Magst du den Anzug? Ja, _____ kaufe ich.
2. Möchten Sie einen Roman von Günter Grass kaufen? Ja, _____ hier habe ich noch nicht gelesen.
3. Wohnt er noch bei seiner Mutter? Ja, bei _____ wohnt er wahrscheinlich ewig.
4. Welche Hose gefällt dir am besten? _____ da.
5. Besucht sie die Vorlesung von Professor Hartmann? Nein, _____ von Professor Richter interessiert sie mehr.
6. Kennst du die Frau da? Nein, _____ habe ich nie vorher gesehen.

7. Sollen wir mit Claudia und Klaus zusammen arbeiten? Ja, mit _____ kann man gut zusammen arbeiten.
8. Hast du dieses Buch gelesen? _____ hat mir überhaupt nicht gefallen!
9. Möchtest du noch ein Stück von der Kirschtorte? Nein danke, _____ schmeckt mir nicht besonders gut.
10. Mit welchem Zug kann ich nach Düsseldorf fahren? Mit _____ da.

DER-*WORDS AS PRONOUNS*

The **der**-words may be used as pronouns to replace previously mentioned nouns. They take the number and gender of the noun to which they refer. Their case is determined by their function in the sentence. When used as a pronoun, the **der**-words correspond to the following in English:

all-   *all (of them)* (plural)
dies-   *this one, these*
jed-   *each one, every one*
jen-   *that one, those*
manch-   *some, some of them* (plural)
solch-   *such things, ones like that* (plural)
welch-   *which one(s)*

Willst du dieses Buch? **Welches** meinst du?
Do you want this book? Which one do you mean?

Sollen wir diese alten Gläser durchsuchen? **Manche** sind noch schön.
Should we look through these old glasses? Some of them are still pretty.

Welche Filme von Wim Wenders habt ihr gesehen? **Jeden.**
Which movies by Wim Wenders have you (guys) seen? Every one of them.

Jen-, when used as a **der**-word (see chapter 1) or a pronoun, is contrasted frequently with **dies-**.

Welches Buch willst du? **Dieses** oder **jenes**?
Which book do you want? This one or that one?

In this type of contrastive construction, **jen-** can correspond to *the former* and **dies-** to *the latter*.

Johann bekam eine Note in Deutsch und in Chemie. Er war froh über **jene**, aber enttäuscht über **diese**.

Johann received a grade in German and in chemistry. He was happy about the former but disappointed with the latter.

Exercise 12: *Supply the appropriate German equivalent.*

1. Welcher Satz ist grammatikalisch richtig? _____ oder _____?
   (*This one; that one*)
2. Kaufst du die Blumen? Nein, _____ gefallen mir nicht.   (*ones like that*)
3. Kennen Sie Ihre Nachbarn? Noch nicht _____. (*all of them*)
4. Ich habe alle Bücher von der Autorin gelesen. _____ ist ein bißchen anders.   (*Each one*)
5. Manche Probleme sind leicht; _____ sind schwer.   (*some*)
6. Ich möchte bitte mit meiner Schwester sprechen. Mit _____?
   (*which one*)
7. Sammelst du deutsche Briefmarken? Ja, ich habe _____ von 1949 bis 1993.   (*all of them*)
8. Hast du ein paar neue CDs? Ja, _____ habe ich mir gestern gekauft, aber _____ habe ich schon etwas länger.   (*these; those*)
9. _____ weiß heutzutage, daß man nicht rauchen soll.   (*Everyone*)
10. Es gibt hier zwei Stadtautobahnen, aber _____ führt in die Innenstadt?   (*which one*)

EIN-*WORDS AS PRONOUNS*

The **ein**-words may be used as pronouns to replace nouns previously mentioned. Their gender and number are determined by the noun to which they refer. Their case is determined by their function within the sentence.

When used as a pronoun, the **ein**-word takes a **der**-word ending. This means that the masculine nominative pronoun has the ending -**er** and the neuter nominative and accusative pronouns have the ending -**es**. Compare the endings in the following sentences:

ein-WORD AS POSSESSIVE ADJECTIVE	**ein**-WORD AS PRONOUN
Hier ist mein Mantel.	Wo ist dein**er**?
Here's my coat.	*Where's yours?*
Darf ich Ihr Auto borgen?	Mein**es** ist kaputt.
May I borrow your car?	*Mine is broken.*

Here are some additional examples of **ein**-words used as pronouns.

Wessen Auto ist das? Es ist **ihres**.
Whose car is that? It's hers.

Hast du noch einen Kugelschreiber für mich? Nein, aber du kannst **meinen** haben.
Do you have another pen for me? No, but you can have mine.

In conversation, the **e** in the ending is usually omitted from the neuter nominative and accusative forms.

Du hast dein Zimmer und ich habe **meins**.

Exercise 13: *Supply the correct German equivalent.*

1. Ist das ihr Videorecorder oder _____? *(his)*
2. Das Kind hat sein Spielzeug verloren. Gib ihm _____! *(mine)*
3. Wessen Seminar finden Sie interessanter? _____ oder _____?
   (Hers; his) _____ interessiert mich. *(None/Not a one)*
4. Sabine, in welchem Zimmer soll ich schlafen? In _____ oder in _____? *(yours; hers)*
5. Hast du einen Bleistift für mich? Ja, hier ist _____. *(one)*
6. Darf ich bitte Ihr Fahrrad benutzen? _____ fährt schneller als _____. *(Yours; mine)*
7. Klaus, fahren wir mit meinem Auto oder mit _____? *(yours)*
8. Gib ihm bitte seinen Schlüssel! Nein, das ist nicht _____, das ist _____. *(his; hers)*
9. Können Sie mir einen Zahnarzt empfehlen? Ich kenne hier nämlich _____. *(none)*
10. Das ist nicht deine Brieftasche, das ist _____. *(mine)*

RELATIVE PRONOUNS

Definition

A *relative pronoun* introduces a *relative clause*. A relative clause provides additional information about a previously mentioned noun, the *antecedent*. In German, relative clauses are always set off by commas. Here are some examples of relative clauses in German and English.

Der Mann, **der da steht**, heißt Werner.
The man who is standing there is called Werner.

Ich kenne die Leute, **die in dem Haus wohnen**.
I know the people who live in that house.

Wie heißt das Buch, **das du liest**?
What is the name of the book that you are reading?

Die Frau, **der ich das Paket schicke**, ist die Herausgeberin meines
  Buches.
The woman to whom I'm sending the package is the editor of my book.

Das Wörterbuch, **mit dem ich arbeite**, ist veraltet.
The dictionary with which I am working is out-of-date.

Forms

The German relative pronouns are listed in the chart below.

	MASC.	NEUT.	FEM.	PLURAL
NOM.	der	das	die	die
ACC.	den	das	die	die
DAT.	dem	dem	der	den**en**
GEN.	des**sen**	des**sen**	der**en**	der**en**

Note that these forms are identical to the declension of the definite article except that the dative plural and all of the genitive forms have been
extended by **-(s)en**.

*The gender and number of the relative pronoun are determined by its
antecedent, that is, by the noun to which the relative pronoun refers. The
case of the relative pronoun is determined by its function within the relative
clause.*

The following examples illustrate relative pronouns in each of the four
cases, for all genders and number.

NOMINATIVE RELATIVE PRONOUNS

In these examples the relative pronoun functions as the subject of the
sentence and is therefore in the nominative case. The gender of the relative
pronoun is determined by the noun to which it refers. These examples
demonstrate each of the different genders and number: masculine, neuter,
feminine, and plural.

Der Mann, **der** uns morgen besucht, ist ein Freund der Familie.
The man who is visiting us tomorrow is a friend of the family.

Das Kind, **das** draußen spielt, ist sieben Jahre alt.
The child who's playing outside is seven years old.

Die Studentin, **die** Susi heißt, kommt heute nicht.
The student who is called Susi isn't coming today.

Die Leute, **die** das Haus kaufen, sind reich.
The people who are buying the house are rich.

ACCUSATIVE RELATIVE PRONOUNS

In the examples below the relative pronoun functions as object and is therefore in the accusative case.

Der Mann, **den** mein Vater gut kannte, ist gestorben.
The man, whom my father knew well, died.

Das Kind, **das** niemand leiden kann, benimmt sich immer schlecht.
The child whom nobody can stand always behaves badly.

Die Studentin, **die** ich morgen besuche, hilft mir beim Lernen.
The student whom I'm visiting tomorrow is helping me study.

Die Leute, **die** ich in Bonn kennengelernt habe, ziehen nach Berlin um.
The people whom I met in Bonn are moving to Berlin.

DATIVE RELATIVE PRONOUNS

In the next examples the relative pronoun functions as the indirect object or as the object of a dative verb or adjective and is therefore in the dative case.

Der Mann, **dem** der Arzt half, ist wieder gesund.
The man whom the doctor helped is healthy again.

Das Kind, **dem** die Großeltern das Geschenk schicken, ist brav.
The child to whom the grandparents are sending the present is well behaved.

Die Studentin, **der** er nicht glauben kann, lügt oft.
The student whom he cannot believe frequently lies.

Die Leute, **denen** die Situation unangenehm war, sind weggegangen.
The people for whom the situation was unpleasant went away.

GENITIVE RELATIVE PRONOUNS

In the following examples the relative pronoun indicates a relationship of ownership and is therefore in the genitive case.

Der Mann, **dessen** Brille verloren gegangen war, konnte nicht sehen.
The man whose glasses had been lost couldn't see.

Das Kind, **dessen** Zimmer ruhig liegt, schläft durch die Nacht.
The child whose bedroom is quiet sleeps through the night.

Die Studentin, **deren** Buch da liegt, kommt zurück.
The student whose book is lying there is coming back.

Die Leute, **deren** Geld gestohlen wurde, hatten keine Reiseschecks.
The people whose money was stolen didn't have any traveler's checks.

For the genitive, it is particularly important to remember that the gender and number of the relative pronoun are determined by the noun to which it refers. For example, in the first sentence **Mann**, and not **Brille**, determines that the relative pronoun is masculine singular: **dessen**. Similarly, in the second sentence, **Kind**, not **Zimmer**, determines the gender and number (neuter singular): **dessen**.

Word Order

The conjugated verb always stands at the end of the relative clause.

Der Mann, der uns morgen **besucht**, ist ein Freund der Familie.
Das Kind, dem die Großeltern das Geschenk **schicken**, ist brav.

The relative clause, always set off by commas, is usually placed immediately after its antecedent. However, if there is only one word remaining to finish the sentence, the relative clause may be placed after that word.

Du mußt die Rechnung, die du vom Arzt bekommen hast, bezahlen.
OR
Du mußt die Rechnung bezahlen, die du vom Arzt bekommen hast.
You have to pay the bill that you got from the doctor.

Exercise 14: *Supply the correct relative pronoun.*

1. Das ist die Frau, _____ im Lotto gewonnen hat.
2. Kennst du den Mann, _____ im Krankenhaus liegt?
3. Das ist der Professor, _____ keiner leiden kann.
4. Die Erdbeeren, _____ du gepflückt hast, sind noch grün.
5. Treffen wir uns bei der Brücke, _____ man von deinem Fenster aus sehen kann.
6. Das letzte Buch, _____ ich gelesen habe, war sehr traurig.
7. Die Fremdsprache, _____ sie lernt, ist eine offizielle Sprache der Vereinten Nationen.
8. Der Aufsatz, _____ ich schreibe, ist morgen fällig.
9. Eine Person, _____ sich so wichtig nimmt, ist mir unangenehm.
10. Wir kennen eine junge Regisseurin, _____ Filme bisher sehr gut waren.
11. Die Chefin lobte den Arbeiter, _____ Idee das war.
12. Ich trage das Kleid, _____ Farbe mir nicht gefällt, nicht.
13. Hier wohnt die Musikerin, _____ Musik so populär ist.
14. Die Eltern, _____ Kind so gut Klavier spielt, waren stolz.

15. Der Mann, _____ der Anzug nicht paßt, probiert einen anderen.
16. Ich wohne neben dem Haus, _____ lila Fenster hat.
17. Ich vertraue der Chirurgin, _____ mich morgen früh operieren wird.
18. Der Autohändler, _____ ich mein Auto verkauft habe, hat ein gutes Geschäft gemacht.
19. Die Bücher, _____ sie schreibt, gefallen mir gut.
20. Das ist die einzige Fußballmannschaft, _____ in dieser Saison noch nicht gewonnen hat.

Exercise 15: *Combine the sentences by making the second one into a relative clause. Watch your word order.*

1. Gib mir bitte das Buch! Du hast das Buch für mich gekauft.
2. Meinst du die Frau? Die Frau spricht mit Herrn Über.
3. Meine Zimmerkollegin räumt die Küche auf. Meine Zimmerkollegin hat den ganzen Tag gebacken.
4. Martina will nicht weiter studieren. Martina ist sehr intelligent.
5. Der Mann heißt Georg. Ich liebe den Mann.
6. Ich bringe das Auto zum Mechaniker. Seine Bremse ist kaputt.
7. Wir haben die Brote schnell gegessen. Du hast die Brote eingepackt.
8. Meine Gastfamilie in Deutschland heißt Martin. Ich bringe meiner Gastfamilie ein Bilderbuch aus Amerika mit.
9. Man verhaftet den Spion. Die Polizei folgte dem Spion wochenlang.
10. Die Touristin fährt nach Spanien. Ihre Ferien dauern sechs Wochen.
11. Ich kenne eine Studentin. Die Studentin hat sich beim Basketballspielen den Fuß gebrochen.
12. Der Schauspieler hat endlich seine Traumrolle bekommen. Dieser Schauspieler ist jetzt 65 Jahre alt.

Relative Pronouns with Prepositions

A relative pronoun may be the object of an accusative, dative, or either-or preposition. As always, the case of the relative pronoun is determined by its function in the relative clause, which in these examples is determined by the preposition. Gender and number are determined by the antecedent. Consult chapter 4 if you need to review the prepositions and their cases.

RELATIVE PRONOUNS WITH ACCUSATIVE PREPOSITIONS

Das Zimmer, **durch das** er ging, war leer.
The room through which he walked was empty.

Der Mann, **gegen den** er so lange kämpfte, hat endlich aufgegeben.
The man against whom he fought for such a long time finally gave up.

RELATIVE PRONOUNS WITH DATIVE PREPOSITIONS

Der Student, **mit dem** sie tanzt, sieht elegant aus.`
The student with whom she's dancing looks elegant.

Die Firma, **bei der** sie arbeitet, produziert Autos.
The company for which she works produces cars.

RELATIVE PRONOUNS WITH EITHER-OR PREPOSITIONS

Relative pronouns with either-or prepositions will take either the accusative or dative case according to the rules discussed in chapter 4. In the following examples the either-or preposition takes the accusative.

Der Tisch, **auf den** man den Computer stellte, brach zusammen.
The table upon which the computer was put broke.

Die Leute, **an die** wir schreiben, sind Verwandte.
The people to whom we are writing are relatives.

In these examples the either-or preposition takes the dative.

Das Haus, **in dem** die Familie wohnt, hat zwei Badezimmer.
The house in which the family lives has two bathrooms.

Das Fach, **an dem** sie interessiert ist, ist sehr schwer.
The subject in which she is interested is very difficult.

Exercise 16: *Supply the correct relative pronoun.*

1. Der Kandidat, für _____ ich stimme, ist kompetent.
2. Der Wald, durch _____ wir gehen, ist dunkel.
3. Heidi, auf _____ ich zwei Stunden wartete, kam gar nicht.
4. Ich habe die Tasse, aus _____ du trinkst, gerade gewaschen.
5. Die Liebesgeschichte, von _____ das Theaterstück handelt, ist sentimental.
6. Die Studentenorganisation, für _____ ich arbeite, demonstriert gegen Atomkraftwerke.
7. Medizin ist der Beruf, an _____ sie Interesse hat.
8. Die Universität, an _____ ich studiere, ist die älteste in Deutschland.
9. Die Probleme, von _____ man soviel hört, werden immer schlimmer.
10. Wie heißt der Mann, mit _____ ich tanze?
11. Die Situation, von _____ man spricht, wird immer kritischer.
12. In der Schweiz gibt es viele Berge, in _____ wir schön herumwandern können.

13. Das Fliegen, vor _____ so viele Angst haben, ist eigentlich sehr sicher.
14. Heidelberg ist eine Stadt, in _____ man viel Interessantes sehen kann.
15. Ich habe einige Freunde, für _____ ich alles tun würde.
16. Die Instrumente, mit _____ der Zahnarzt arbeitet, müssen absolut steril sein.
17. In diesem Kurort gibt es eine Heilquelle, aus _____ heißes Wasser entspringt.
18. Der Maler, über _____ wir uns unterhalten, malt Aquarelle.
19. Sie sind die Leute, vor _____ uns unsere Eltern immer gewarnt haben.
20. Die Agentin, mit _____ die Polizei zusammenarbeitet, heißt Meyer.

POSITION OF THE PREPOSITION

Note that in German, *the preposition always introduces the relative clause*. In English, the preposition may introduce the relative clause and frequently does so in formal speech. However, in less formal speech the preposition usually stands at the end of the relative clause. Thus the English sentences near the beginning of this section could also be stated as follows:

The room *that* he walked *through* was empty.
The student *whom* she's dancing *with* looks elegant.
The company *that* she works *for* produces cars.
The table *that* the computer was put *on* broke.

Do not let the informal English word order confuse you when making relative clauses in German.

Exercise 17: *Combine the sentences by making the second one into a relative clause. Remember that the preposition introduces the relative clause.*

1. Die Landschaft ist wunderschön. Wir fahren durch die Landschaft.
2. Die Gegend liegt in der Nähe von Mainz. Ich habe in dieser Gegend meine Jugend verbracht.
3. Der Kiosk war zu. Die zwei Männer trafen sich vor dem Kiosk.
4. Die Abendkasse macht in ein paar Minuten auf. Man holt die Karten an der Abendkasse ab.
5. Hast du den Film gesehen? Der Kritiker spricht so positiv über den Film.
6. Die Nachbarschaft hat zuviel Verkehr. Ich wohne in dieser Nachbarschaft.

7. Ich habe meinen Freund lange nicht gesehen. Ich bekam gerade diesen Brief von meinem Freund.
8. Ich habe viele Photos gemacht. Man kann die Hochzeitsparty auf den Photos sehen.
9. Die Frau ist schon verheiratet. Er ist in die Frau verliebt.
10. Die Theatersaison beginnt nächste Woche. Ich freue mich auf die Theatersaison.

Omission of the Relative Pronoun in English

In English, the relative pronoun is frequently omitted.

The house I own is situated on Lynn Drive.
(The house *that* I own is situated on Lynn Drive.)
The day we were married on was hot.
(The day *that* we were married on was hot.)
The plan he thought of is too complicated.
(The plan *that* he thought of is too complicated.)
The book she was reading was boring.
(The book *that* she was reading was boring.)
The person she's working with is competent.
(The person *whom* she's working with is competent.)

The relative pronoun cannot be omitted in German.

Exercise 18: *Reinsert the relative pronoun in the English sentence. Then translate into German.*

1. The woman he sees is my mother.
2. The shirt he's wearing is dirty.
3. The apartment she lives in is big.
4. The person she works for is intelligent.
5. The desk she's sitting at is large.
6. The letter she's writing is long.
7. The man standing there is called Mr. Tietz.

The Interrogatives as Relative Pronouns

The interrogatives **was** (*what*), **wer** (*who*), and **wo** (*where*) are frequently used as relative pronouns.

WAS AS A RELATIVE PRONOUN

Was is used as a relative pronoun to refer to the following sentence elements:

Indefinite Pronouns. Was is used as a relative pronoun to refer back to an indefinite pronoun. Here are some common indefinite pronouns.

alles	*everything*	nichts	*nothing*
einiges	*several things*	vieles	*much, a lot*
etwas	*something*	wenig	*little*
manches	*much*		

Ich sagte ihm alles, **was** ich weiβ.
I told him everything that I know.

Es gibt nichts, **was** sie noch nicht getan hat.
There's nothing that she hasn't already done.

Superlative Adjectival Nouns and *das*. Was is used as a relative pronoun to refer back to a superlative adjective used as a noun (see chapter 5) or to refer to **das**.

Das ist das Beste, **was** ich je gegessen habe.
That's the best thing that I have ever eaten.

Das, **was** ich wissen wollte, hat sie nicht erwähnt.
She didn't mention what (that which) I wanted to know.

Entire Clauses. When the relative clause refers back to an entire clause **was** must be used.

Sie hat mich nicht angerufen, **was** höchst ungewöhnlich war.
She didn't call me, which was highly unusual.

Neuter Ordinals. Was is used as a relative pronoun to refer back to **das letzte**, **das einzige**, or a neuter ordinal (**das erste**, **das zweite**, etc.).

Das ist das erste, **was** ich machen will, nachdem wir ankommen.
That's the first thing that I want to do after we arrive.

WER AS A RELATIVE PRONOUN

Wer is used as a relative pronoun when the antecedent is an unnamed person. It corresponds to English *whoever, anyone who,* or *a person who.*

Wer zu spät kommt, bekommt nichts zu essen.
Whoever comes late won't get anything to eat.

Wer in Deutschland jodeln kann, zählt als Bayer.
Anyone in Germany who can yodel is considered a Bavarian.

WO AS A RELATIVE PRONOUN

Wo is used as a relative pronoun when the antecedent is a place name.

München, **wo** meine Verwandten wohnen, ist sehr teuer.
Munich, where my relatives live, is very expensive.

Ich arbeite bei Bayer, **wo** man Chemikalien herstellt.
I work at Bayer where chemicals are produced.

In spoken German, **wo** is frequently substituted for a preposition indicating location with a relative pronoun.

Das Haus, **in dem** meine Familie wohnt, hat keine Garage.
The house in which my family lives doesn't have a garage.
OR
Das Haus, **wo** meine Familie wohnt, hat keine Garage.
The house where my family lives doesn't have a garage.

Wo is also used as a relative pronoun when the antecedent is an unknown or unnamed location. It corresponds to *wherever* in English.

Wo du bist, hat man Spaβ.
Wherever you are people have fun.

Exercise 19: *Supply* **was, wer,** *or* **wo.**

1. Er war schon überall, _____ es schön ist.
2. Meine Mutter besucht uns diese Woche, _____ mich sehr freut.
3. Du willst immer das, -_____ ich schon habe.
4. In ihrem Vortrag erwähnte sie manches, _____ mich sehr interessiert.
5. Essen wir im Restaurant, _____ wir uns kennengelernt haben!
6. Das ist etwas, _____ ich gar nicht verstehe.
7. Was ist das Nächste, _____ wir tun sollen?
8. _____ nicht arbeitet, bekommt kein Geld.
9. Das Einkaufszentrum, _____ man schön einkaufen kann, ist eine Fuβgängerzone.
10. Das Kind will kein Eis, _____ mich überrascht.
11. Das einzige, _____ mich an dieser Wohnung stört, ist der Straβenlärm.
12. Sie sagte mir nichts, _____ ich nicht schon wuβte.

A *WO*-COMPOUND AS A RELATIVE PRONOUN

Prepositions are not normally used with the relative pronoun **was**. Instead a **wo**-compound is used.

Sport ist das einzige, ~~für was~~ er sich interessiert.
Sport ist das einzige, **wofür** er sich interessiert.
Sports are the only thing in which he is interested.

Es gibt nichts, ~~über was~~ wir uns unterhalten können.
Es gibt nichts, **worüber** wir uns unterhalten können.
There is nothing about which we can talk.

In spoken German, a **wo**-compound is sometimes used instead of a preposition plus any relative pronoun.

Das Holz, **mit dem** das Haus gebaut wird, ist Zedernholz.
OR
Das Holz, **womit** das Haus gebaut wird, ist Zedernholz.
The wood with which the house is being built is cedar.

Das Museum, **vor dem** ich das Auto geparkt habe, befindet sich in der Hauptstraße.
OR
Das Museum, **wovor** ich das Auto geparkt habe, befindet sich in der Hauptstraße.
The museum in front of which I parked the car is located on Main Street.

Exercise 20: *Translate the English phrases into German using a* **wo**-*compound for the relative clause.*

1. Muβ ich mich darüber schämen? Nein, du hast nichts gemacht, _____. (*of which you have to be ashamed*)
2. Für welches Fach interessierst du dich? Es gibt vieles, _____. (*in which I am interested*)
3. In diesem Seminar haben wir über viele problematische Themen geredet. Das Problematischste, _____, war das Recht einer Frau auf Abtreibung. (*about which we talked*)
4. War sie stolz auf ihre Note? Ja, sie hat die beste Note in der Klasse bekommen, _____. (*of which she was very proud*)
5. Freut sich der Kranke auf den Besuch seiner Familie? Nein, es gibt nur noch wenig, _____. (*to which he looks forward*)
6. Habt ihr von den finanziellen Schwierigkeiten der Firma gehört? Nein, das ist etwas, _____. (*about which you/one doesn't hear much*)

ANSWERS TO EXERCISES

1.

1. ihm; ihr; uns; ihnen
2. mich; ihn; sie; uns; euch; sie; Sie
3. dich; ihn; sie; uns; euch; sie; Sie
4. dir; ihm; ihr; uns; euch; ihnen; Ihnen

2.

1. Ich
2. du; dich
3. Sie; Ihnen
4. Uns
5. Ich; du
6. mir
7. uns; euch
8. ihnen; sie
9. wir; euch
10. Sie; dich

3.

1. ihn
2. sie
3. Sie
4. ihnen
5. Wir
6. euch
7. Sie
8. ihr
9. ihm
10. Sie; ihr
11. Sie
12. Er; ihn
13. Er; sie
14. Wir
15. Sie

4.

1. sie
2. Er
3. es
4. ihn
5. ihn
6. sie
7. sie
8. ihn
9. sie
10. sie
11. Sie
12. es
13. es
14. es
15. sie

5.

1. Wir mußten ihm unser ganzes Geld geben.
2. Ich backe ihn der kranken Frau heute abend.
3. Sie öffnete ihm die Tür.
4. Die Kauffrau beschreibt ihm die Vorteile dieses Autos.
5. Die Verwandten zeigen sie meiner Familie.
6. Der Kellner empfiehlt ihm den Rotwein.
7. Ich wünsche ihr alles Gute zum Geburtstag.
8. Der Juwelier hat ihn seiner Frau gekauft.
9. Gib es dem Kind bitte nicht!
10. Sie hat ihn ihrem Nachbarn geliehen.

6.

1. Die Mutter kauft ihn ihr.
2. Der Sprecher berichtet sie ihr.
3. Ich bringe sie ihnen.
4. Das Spiel bietet sie ihm.
5. Die Autorin widmet es ihr.
6. Sie schenkt es ihnen.
7. Ich gebe sie ihr.
8. Der Sportler reicht sie ihm.
9. Die Händlerin verkauft ihn ihm.
10. Der Vater bastelt ihn ihm.

7.

1. sich
2. ihn
3. mir
4. mir
5. ihr
6. sich
7. sie
8. mir
9. sich
10. dir
11. dich
12. sich
13. ihm
14. uns
15. sich
16. ihnen
17. dich
18. sich
19. ihr
20. mich

8.

1. Wessen
2. Was
3. Wer
4. Wer
5. Wer
6. Was
7. Wem
8. Wen
9. Wen
10. Wessen
11. Wen
12. Wem
13. Wen
14. Wessen
15. Was

9.

1. einem
   It hurts (you) when you fall down.
2. sich
   You should brush your teeth every evening.
3. Man
   One drives/people drive fast on the Autobahn.
4. man
   You cannot go swimming here. No swimming allowed.
5. man; man
   If you have/one has a cold, you have/one has a fever often.
6. sich
   People often meet each other in a beer garden.
7. einen
   The policeman doesn't see one/you from here.
8. einem
   Politicians don't always tell people/one the truth.
9. man
   Normally one drinks/you drink coffee in the morning.

10. einem; man
   The book explains to you how
   you use the computer/how to
   use the computer.

10.

1. In Amerika duscht man sich
   jeden Morgen.
2. Man darf auf dieser Straße
   schnell fahren.
3. Wenn man krank ist, geht man
   zum Arzt.
4. Die Liebe macht einen verrückt.
5. Bringt einem eine schwarze
   Katze wirklich Pech?

11.

1. den
2. den
3. der
4. Die
5. die
6 die
7. denen
8. Das
9. die
10. dem

12.

1. Dieser; jener
2. solche
3. alle
4. Jedes
5. manche
6. welcher
7. alle
8. diese; jene
9. Jeder
10. welche

13.

1. seiner
2. meines
3. Ihres; seines; Keines
4. deinem; ihrem
5. einer
6. Ihres; meines
7. deinem
8. seiner; ihrer
9. keinen
10. meine

14.

1. die
2. der
3. den
4. die

5. die
6. das
7. die
8. den
9. die
10. deren
11. dessen
12. dessen
13. deren
14. deren
15. dem
16. das
17. die
18. dem
19. die
20. die

15.

1. Gib mir bitte das Buch, das du
   für mich gekauft hast!
2. Meinst du die Frau, die mit
   Herrn Über spricht?
3. Meine Zimmerkollegin, die den
   ganzen Tag gebacken hat, räumt
   die Küche auf.
4. Martina, die sehr intelligent ist,
   will nicht weiter studieren.
5. Der Mann, den ich liebe, heißt
   Georg.
6. Ich bringe das Auto, dessen
   Bremse kaputt ist, zum
   Mechaniker.
7. Wir haben die Brote, die du
   eingepackt hast, schnell
   gegessen.
8. Meine Gastfamilie in
   Deutschland, der ich ein
   Bilderbuch aus Amerika mit-
   bringe, heißt Martin.
9. Man verhaftet den Spion, dem
   die Polizei wochenlang folgte.
10. Die Touristin, deren Ferien
    sechs Wochen dauern, fährt
    nach Spanien.
11. Ich kenne eine Studentin, die
    sich beim Basketballspielen den
    Fuß gebrochen hat.
12. Der Schauspieler, der jetzt 65
    Jahre alt ist, hat endlich seine
    Traumrolle bekommen.

16.

1. den
2. den
3. die
4. der

5. der
6. die
7. dem
8. der
9. denen
10. dem
11. der
12. denen
13. dem
14. der
15. die
16. denen
17. der
18. den
19. denen
20. der

17.

1. Die Landschaft, durch die wir
   fahren, ist wunderschön.
2. Die Gegend, in der ich meine
   Jugend verbracht habe, liegt in
   der Nähe von Mainz.
3. Der Kiosk, vor dem die zwei
   Männer sich trafen, war zu.
4. Die Abendkasse, an der man die
   Karten abholt, macht in ein paar
   Minuten auf.
5. Hast du den Film, über den der
   Kritiker so positiv spricht,
   gesehen?
6. Die Nachbarschaft, in der ich
   wohne, hat zuviel Verkehr.
7. Ich habe meinen Freund, von
   dem ich gerade diesen Brief
   bekam, lange nicht gesehen.
8. Ich habe viele Photos, auf denen
   man die Hochzeitsparty sehen
   kann, gemacht.
9. Die Frau, in die er verliebt ist,
   ist schon verheiratet.
10. Die Theatersaison, auf die ich
    mich freue, beginnt nächste
    Woche.

18.

1. The woman whom he sees is my
   mother.
   Die Frau, die er sieht, ist meine
   Mutter.
2. The shirt that he's wearing is
   dirty.
   Das Hemd, das er trägt, ist
   schmutzig.
3. The apartment that she lives in
   is big.

Die Wohnung, in der sie wohnt,
ist groβ.

4. The person for whom she works
is intelligent.
Die Person, für die sie arbeitet,
ist intelligent.

5. The desk that she's sitting at is
big.
Der Schreibtisch, an dem sie
sitzt, ist groβ.

6. The letter that she's writing is
long.
Der Brief, den sie schreibt, ist
lang.

7. The man who's standing there is
called Mr. Tietz.
Der Mann, der dort steht, heiβt
Herr Tietz.

19

1. wo
2. was
3. was
4. was
5. wo
6. was
7. was
8. Wer
9. wo
10. was
11. was
12. was

20

1. Nein, du hast nichts gemacht,
worüber du dich schämen muβt.

2. Es gibt vieles, wofür ich mich
interessiere.

3. Das Problematischste, worüber
wir geredet haben, war das
Recht einer Frau auf
Abtreibung.

4. Ja, sie hat die beste Note in der
Klasse bekommen, worauf sie
sehr stolz war.

5. Nein, es gibt nur noch wenig,
worauf er sich freut.

6. Nein, das ist etwas, wovon man
nicht viel hört.

4

Prepositions

A *preposition usually precedes a noun or pronoun object, called the prepositional object, and indicates the function and meaning of that noun or pronoun within the rest of the sentence.*

*She always traveled **by** train.*
*The firefighter rescued the child **from** the burning house.*
*I enjoyed the day **in spite of** his foul mood.*
*He never went anywhere **without** her.*

In German, the prepositions govern one of the three objective cases. Accordingly, they are divided into four different groups, depending on the case they take: the accusative prepositions, the dative prepositions, the either-or prepositions, and the genitive prepositions. In the absence of general rules or guidelines determining these groupings, each preposition must be memorized with the case it governs.

The meanings of prepositions, in German and English, are highly idiomatic and cause numerous problems even for advanced speakers of the language. This chapter attempts to familiarize you with the basic meanings of each of the prepositions and to introduce the most common of their idiomatic meanings.

ACCUSATIVE PREPOSITIONS

Seven common prepositions govern the accusative case. Their most frequent meanings and common idioms are presented below.

bis

MEANING *UNTIL, BY*

Used to express time, **bis** means *until* or *by.*

Ich warte **bis nächste Woche**.
I'll wait until next week.

Die Hausaufgaben müssen **bis morgen** fertig sein.
The homework has to be done by tomorrow.

MEANING *AS FAR AS*

Used with locations, **bis** means *as far as.*

Wir fahren **bis München**.
We're going as far as Munich.

If the prepositional object is preceded by an article, **bis** must be followed by another preposition. This second preposition then governs the case of the object.

Sie ging **bis an** die Tür mit mir.
She went up to/as far as the door with me.

Maria joggt jeden Tag **bis zur** Hauptstraße.
Maria jogs up to/as far as the main street every day.

COMMON IDIOMS

von Kopf bis Fuß   *from head to toe*
von oben bis unten   *from top to bottom*

durch

MEANING *THROUGH*

Die Exkursion führt **durch die Wüste**.
The excursion leads through the desert.

Man kann **durch das schmutzige Fenster** gar nichts sehen.
You can't see a thing through the dirty window.

MEANING *THROUGH, BY MEANS OF*

Durch is used to express the impersonal agent of passive sentences (see chapter 8).

Das Haus wurde **durch den Wind** zerstört.
The house was destroyed by (means of) the wind.

COMMON IDIOMS

durch Zufall   *by accident, by chance*

entlang   **MEANING** *ALONG*

Entlang usually follows its object.

Wir fahren **die Küste entlang**.
We're driving along the coast.

Wir spazieren **den Weg entlang**.
We're walking along the path.

für   **MEANING** *FOR*

Ihr Herz schlägt nur **für ihren Freund**.
Her heart beats only for her boyfriend.

Nichts ist zu gut **für meine Tochter**.
Nothing is too good for my daughter.

gegen   **MEANING** *AGAINST*

Der Taxifahrer hat nichts **gegen ein Trinkgeld**.
The taxi driver has nothing against a tip.

Diese Zeitung ist **gegen den konservativen Bürgermeister**.
This newspaper is against the conservative mayor.

MEANING *APPROXIMATELY*

When used in time expressions, **gegen** means *around*, *about*, or *toward* (up to but not exceeding a time or number).

Ich komme **gegen Abend**.
I'll come toward evening.

ohne   **MEANING** *WITHOUT*

Sie schafft es auch **ohne ihren Mann**.
She'll also get along without her husband.

Ohne einen Computer dauert die Arbeit viel länger.
The work takes a lot longer without a computer.

um   **MEANING** *AROUND*

Du mußt mit dem Fahrrad **um das Hindernis** herumfahren.
You have to bicycle around the obstacle.

Sie wohnt gleich **um die Ecke**.
She lives right around the corner.

MEANING *AT*

When used in time expressions, **um** means *at*.

Das Schauspiel beginnt **um acht Uhr**.
The play begins at eight o'clock.

Exercise 1: *Supply the missing accusative prepositions or idioms.*

1. (*at*)   Diese Klasse beginnt _____ acht Uhr morgens.
2. (*Without*)   _____ eine Arbeitserlaubnis darf man nicht arbeiten.
3. (*against*)   Sie trägt die Jeans _____ den Willen ihrer Mutter.
4. (*until*)   Ich warte _____ drei.
5. (*by chance*)   Ich habe meinen Mann _____ kennengelernt.
6. (*from head to toe*)   Das Kind war _____ schmutzig.
7. (*until*)   Wir müssen heute nur _____ zur Mittagspause arbeiten.
8. (*for*)   Dieses Geschenk ist _____ die gesamte Familie.
9. (*along*)   Wir sind von Koblenz bis nach Köln den Rhein _____ gefahren.
10. (*through*)   Wir laufen langsam _____ die Innenstadt.

Exercise 2: *Fill in the correct accusative ending, where necessary.*

1. Man muß die Prüfung ohne ein__ Wörterbuch schreiben.
2. Wir wandern gern durch d__ Berge.
3. Die Mutter arbeitet für ihr__ Familie.
4. Die Gruppe macht eine Reise um d__ Welt.
5. Man kann nicht gegen d__ Wind segeln.
6. Wir haben den Weg auch ohne d__ Landkarte gefunden.
7. Mein Vater stellt einen Zaun um unser__ Grundstück herum auf.
8. Ich will etwas für mein__ Bruder kaufen.
9. Der Vogel fliegt durch d__ Luft.
10. Der Mann kämpft gegen sein__ Nachbar__.

DATIVE PREPOSITIONS

There are nine common dative prepositions. Their most frequent meanings and idioms are presented below.

aus

MEANING *FROM, TO ORIGINATE FROM*

With place names, **aus** means *from* in the sense of one's origin.

Sie kommt **aus Indien**.
She's from India.

Ich komme **aus den Vereinigten Staaten**.
I'm from the United States.

MEANING *OUT OF*

Heißes Wasser kam **aus dem Wasserhahn**.
Hot water came out of the water faucet.

Er lief **aus dem Klassenzimmer**.
He ran out of the classroom.

MEANING *MADE OUT OF*

Der Tisch ist **aus Holz**.
The table is made out of wood.

COMMON IDIOMS

aus Mitleid	*out of pity*
aus Angst	*out of fear, from fear*
aus diesem Grund	*for this reason*

außer

MEANING *EXCEPT FOR, BESIDES, OTHER THAN*

Außer meinem Bruder habe ich keine Geschwister.
Except for my brother I have no siblings.

MEANING *IN ADDITION TO, BESIDES*

Außer meinem Bruder habe ich auch zwei Schwestern.
In addition to my brother I also have two sisters.

COMMON IDIOMS

außer Atem	*out of breath*
außer Betrieb	*out of order*
außer Gefahr	*out of danger*

bei

MEANING *AT, WITH*

The preposition **bei** is used to indicate a place of business or someone's home.

Susie wohnt noch **bei ihren Eltern**.
Susie still lives with her parents/at her parents' house.

Man kauft Brot **bei einer Bäckerei**.
You buy bread at a bakery.

Sie arbeitet **bei Daimler-Benz**.
She works at Daimler-Benz.

Ich habe um zwei einen Termin **bei dem Arzt**.
I have a doctor's appointment at two.

MEANING *NEAR*

With locations, **bei** may also express proximity.

Studenten wollen **bei der Universität** wohnen.
Students want to live near the university.

Bad-Godesberg liegt **bei** Bonn.
Bad-Godesberg is near Bonn.

COMMON IDIOMS

Ich habe kein Geld **bei mir**.
I have no money with/on me.

Bei solchem Wetter gibt es nichts zu tun.
In this kind of weather there's nothing to do.

Beim Lesen muβ ich Ruhe haben.
While reading I have to have peace and quiet.

gegenüber

MEANING *ACROSS FROM, OPPOSITE*

Gegenüber can precede or follow its noun object.

Man baut das neue Rathaus **dem Marktplatz gegenüber**.
OR
Man baut das neue Rathaus **gegenüber dem Marktplatz**.
The new city hall is being built across from/opposite the marketplace.

Gegenüber must follow a pronoun object.

Uns gegenüber steht ein häβliches Hochhaus.
An ugly skyscraper is located across from us/opposite our house.

mit

MEANING *WITH, TOGETHER WITH*

Er feiert Weihnachten **mit seiner Familie**.
He is celebrating Christmas with his family.

Ich reise **mit meinem Mann** nach Deutschland.
I'm traveling to Germany with my husband.

MEANING *WITH, BY MEANS OF*

Die Professorin korrigiert die Aufsätze **mit einem roten Kugel-schreiber**.
The professor corrects the essays with a red pen.

MEANING *BY*

The preposition **mit** is used with means of transportation.

Ich fahre **mit dem Rad** zum Einkaufen.
I go shopping by bicycle/on my bicycle.

In Deutschland kommt man **mit dem Zug** überall hin.
In Germany you can go anywhere by train.

Note that the definite article is omitted in English, but maintained in German.

mit **dem** Zug   *by train*
mit **dem** Auto   *by car*

COMMON IDIOM

mit Gewalt   *by force*

nach

MEANING *AFTER*

In time expressions, **nach** means *after*.

Sie ist **nach einer Stunde** endlich zurückgekommen.
She finally came back after an hour.

Nach der Arbeit gehen wir ein Bier trinken.
We're going to go have a beer after work.

MEANING *TO*

Nach corresponds to English *to* when used with the names of cities and countries. Compare this meaning of **nach** with **zu**.

Viele Leute fliegen **nach Amerika**.
Many people fly to America.

Sie wollte **nach Toronto** fahren.
She wanted to travel to Toronto.

MEANING *ACCORDING TO*

When **nach** is equivalent to *according to*, it usually follows its object.

Den Politikern nach gibt es gar keine Rezession.
According to the politicians there isn't a recession at all.

Meiner Meinung nach ist das keine gute Idee.
That's not a good idea according to my opinion/in my opinion.

COMMON IDIOM

Ich gehe nach Hause.   *I'm going home.*

seit

MEANING *SINCE, FOR*

Sie wohnt **seit einem Monat** hier.
She's been living here for a month.

Seit requires the present tense in German if the action of the verb started in the past but is continued into the present. In English, the present perfect tense is used in such constructions. Compare the following German and English sentences:

Seit wann **bist** du in den Staaten?
*How long **have** you **been** in the States?*

Ich **studiere** seit September hier.
*I **have been studying** here since September.*

These constructions will be treated in more depth in chapter 7.

von

MEANING *FROM*

Sie kommt um halb zwei **von der Schule** nach Hause.
She comes home from school at 1:30.

Er bekam eine Warnung **von dem Polizisten**.
He received a warning from the police officer.

Do not confuse **aus** and **von**. Both correspond to English *from*, but **aus** is more specifically *to originate from*. Compare the following two sentences:

Er kommt **aus** Japan.
He comes from Japan (i.e., he lives there).

Er fliegt **von** Japan nach Deutschland.
He's flying from Japan to Germany.

MEANING *BY*

Musik **von Mozart** ist weltbekannt.
Music by Mozart is world famous.

MEANING *OF*

In colloquial German, you will frequently hear **von**, meaning *of*, as a substitute for the genitive case.

die Freundin **von Peter**	*Peter's girlfriend/the girlfriend of Peter*
das Auto **von meiner Mutter**	*my mother's car/the car of my mother*

zu

MEANING *TO*

Zu corresponds to English *to* when used with buildings and people. Do not confuse **zu** with **nach**, which also means *to* but is used with names of cities and countries.

Wir gehen **zu der Bibliothek**.
We're going to the library.

With people, the home or house is understood in German, but frequently explicitly stated in English.

Wir fahren **zu unseren Großeltern**.
We're driving to our grandparents' house.

Wir gehen **zu Paul**.
We're going to Paul's house.

COMMON IDIOMS

zu Weihnachten	*at Christmas*
zu Ostern	*at Easter*
zu dieser Zeit	*at this time*
Ich bin zu Hause.	*I am (at) home.*
Wir gehen zu Fuß.	*We're walking.*
zum Beispiel	*for example*
zum Schluß	*in conclusion*

Exercise 3: *Supply the missing dative prepositions or idioms.*

1. (to)   Wir fahren _____ unserer Oma.
2. (made out of)   Diese Vase ist _____ Glas.
3. (At; [to])   _____ Weihnachten fahre ich _____ Hause.
4. (at)   Du kannst _____ meinen Eltern übernachten.

5. (to)   Nächsten Sommer fährt Jutta _____ Europa.
6. (In; at)   _____ schlechtem Wetter bleibt man _____ Hause.
7. (out of order)   Die Maschine ist _____.
8. (by foot; by car)   Wir kommen nicht _____, sondern _____.
9. (from)   Meine Vorfahren sind vor 150 Jahren _____ Deutschland ausgewandert.
10. (at)   Wir haben uns Auskunft _____ der Touristen-Information geholt.

Exercise 4: *Fill in the correct dative ending.*

1. Unser__ Haus gegenüber gibt es einen Park.
2. Ich will mit mein__ Mutter sprechen.
3. D__ Zeitung nach gewinnt unser Kandidat die Wahl.
4. Ich höre gar nichts mehr von mein__ Freunde__.
5. Ich ging mit mein__ Freundin einkaufen.
6. Der Bettler hatte nichts außer sein__ Kleider__.
7. Mein__ Onkel gegenüber saß meine Tante.
8. Sie lieben einander seit d__ Schulzeit.
9. Ich habe einen Telefonanruf von ein__ alten Schulfreund bekommen.
10. Außer mein__ Gymnasium gibt es in unserer Stadt noch drei weitere Schulen.

EITHER-OR PREPOSITIONS

Either-or prepositions, sometimes called two-way prepositions or accusative-dative prepositions, govern either the accusative or the dative case.

Dative or Accusative?

Either-or prepositions take the accusative case when there is a change of position in relation to the object. The dative case is used when there is no change of position.

In the accusative case, the prepositional phrase answers the question **Wohin**? (*To where?*). In the dative case, the prepositional phrase answers the question **Wo**? (*Where?*). Compare the following sets of sentences:

ACCUSATIVE: CHANGE OF POSITION
Sie fährt **in die Stadt**. **Wohin** fährt sie?
She drives into the city.

Sie legt das Buch **auf den Tisch**. **Wohin** legt sie das Buch?
She puts the book on the table.

She geht **an das Telefon**. **Wohin** geht sie?
She goes to the telephone.

DATIVE: NO CHANGE OF POSITION
Sie kauft **in der Stadt** ein. **Wo** kauft sie ein?
She shops in the city.

Das Buch liegt **auf dem Tisch**. **Wo** liegt das Buch?
The book is lying on the table.

Sie ist seit 30 Minuten **an dem Telefon**. **Wo** ist sie?
She's been on the telephone for 30 minutes.

It is important to understand that the difference between accusative and dative is not simply one of motion versus no motion. In the sentences below there is motion, but no change of position in relation to the object. Therefore, the preposition takes the dative.

Er läuft **hinter dem Haus** herum.
He's running around behind the house.

(Although he is moving, he is not changing his position relative to the house.)

Der BMW fährt schnell **auf der Autobahn**.
The BMW drives fast on the expressway.

(Although the car is moving, it is not changing its position in relation to the expressway, i.e., it stays on the expressway.)

Now compare the sentences above to the following accusative examples where there is a change of position:

Er läuft **hinter das Haus**.
He runs behind the house.

(Initially he is not behind the house, but then he changes position.)

Der BMW fährt schnell **auf die Autobahn**.
The BMW drives onto the expressway fast.

(The car is presumably still on the entrance ramp to the expressway.)

There are nine common either-or prepositions.

an	**MEANING** *ON*

The preposition **an** is used with vertical surfaces such as walls or windows. Compare this meaning of **an** with **auf**, which is used with horizontal surfaces.

ACC.   Ich hänge das Bild **an die Wand**.
I'm hanging the picture on the wall.

DAT.   Das Bild hängt **an der Wand**.
The picture is hanging on the wall.

MEANING *TO, AT*

The preposition **an** can mean *to* or *up to* (*but no farther than*) with the accusative case. It can mean *at* with the dative case.

ACC.   Christa geht **an den Brunnen**.
Christa goes up to the fountain.

DAT.   Christa steht **an dem Brunnen**.
Christa is standing at the fountain.

ACC.   Michael fährt **an die Grenze**.
Michael drives up to the border.

DAT.   Michael steht **an der Grenze**.
Michael is standing at the border.

auf	**MEANING** *ON*

The preposition **auf** is used with horizontal surfaces such as tables or floors. Compare this meaning of **auf** with **an**, which is used with vertical surfaces.

ACC.   Sie stellt den Wecker **auf den Nachttisch**.
She puts the alarm clock on the night table.

DAT.   Der Wecker steht **auf dem Nachttisch**.
The alarm clock is standing on the night table.

COMMON IDIOMS

auf deutsch   *in German*
auf englisch   *in English*

hinter	**MEANING** *BEHIND, IN BACK OF*

ACC.   Sie versteckt das Geschenk **hinter den Sessel**.
She's hiding the present behind the armchair.

DAT. Das Geschenk ist **hinter dem Sessel**.
The present is behind the armchair.

in

MEANING *IN, INTO*

ACC. Er geht **in die Drogerie**.
He's going into the drugstore.

DAT. Er arbeitet **in der Drogerie**.
He works in the drugstore.

MEANING *TO*

When the preposition **in** is equivalent to English *to*, it always takes the accusative case.

ACC. Ich gehe **ins Theater**.
I'm going to the theater.

ACC. Das Kind geht **in die Schule**.
The child goes to school.

With names of feminine and plural countries, **in** is used with the definite article and corresponds to English *to*. Compare this to the usage of **nach** with neuter countries.

ACC. Wir fahren **in die Schweiz**.
We're traveling to Switzerland.

ACC. Wir fliegen **in die Vereinigten Staaten**.
We're flying to the United States.

neben

MEANING *NEXT TO, BESIDE*

ACC. Sie stellt den Videorecorder **neben den Fernseher**.
She puts the VCR next to the TV.

DAT. Der Videorecorder steht **neben dem Fernseher**.
The VCR is next to the TV.

über

MEANING *OVER, ABOVE*

ACC. Die Mutter hängt das Mobile **über das Kinderbett**.
The mother hangs the mobile above the crib.

DAT. Das Mobile hängt **über dem Kinderbett**.
The mobile is hanging above the crib.

MEANING *OVER, ACROSS*

When used to mean *over* or *across*, the preposition **über** always takes the accusative case.

ACC.   Das Boot fährt **über den See**.
    The boat travels across the lake. (The boat crosses the lake.)

ACC.   Ich gehe **über die Straβe**.
    I go across the street. (I cross the street.)

unter

MEANING *UNDER*

ACC.   Sie stellt das Auto **unter das Dach**.
    She's parking the car under the roof.

DAT.   Das Auto steht **unter dem Dach**.
    The car is (parked) under the roof.

COMMON IDIOMS

unter uns gesagt   *just between us*
unter vier Augen   *in private, in confidentiality*

vor

MEANING *IN FRONT OF, BEFORE*

ACC.   Er geht **vor das Haus**.
    He's walking to the front of the house.

DAT.   Er wartet **vor dem Haus** auf sie.
    He's waiting for her in front of the house.

MEANING *AGO*

In time expressions, **vor** corresponds to *ago* and always takes the dative case.

DAT.   **Vor einer Woche** fuhr sie ab.
    She left a week ago.

COMMON IDIOMS

vor allem   *above all*
vor Angst   *out of fear*
vor Freude   *for joy*

zwischen

MEANING *BETWEEN*

ACC.   Hilde setzte sich **zwischen ihre Mutter und ihren Vater**.
    Hilde sat down between her mother and her father.

DAT.   Hilde saβ **zwischen ihrer Mutter und ihrem Vater**.
Hilde was sitting between her mother and her father.

Exercise 5: *Describe the classroom using the correct either-or prepositions.*

Die Professorin sitzt (*in front of*) _____ der Klasse (*at*) _____ ihrem Schreibtisch. Sie schreibt oft (*on*) _____ die Tafel. Die Studenten sitzen (*next to*) _____ einander (*in*) _____ einem groβen Halbkreis. Ihre Bücher liegen (*on*) _____ dem Boden (*underneath*) _____ ihren Stühlen. (*In*) _____ dem Zimmer gibt es zwei Fenster. (*Between*) _____ den Fenstern steht eine groβe Blumenvase. Lampen hängen (*above*) _____ den Studenten. (*Behind*) _____ einem Vorhang in der Ecke gibt es ein Waschbecken. Bilder hängen überall (*on*) _____ den Wänden. Die Studenten nehmen einen Bleistift (*in*) _____ die Hand und beginnen, Aufgaben zu lösen.

Exercise 6: *Determine if the either-or preposition governs the accusative or dative case and supply the correct endings.*

1. Das Auto steht zwischen ein__ Lastwagen und ein__ Kleinbus.
2. Das Kind spielt hinter d__ Garage.
3. Das Brautpaar geht in d__ Kirche.
4. Die Schuhe stehen unter d__ Schrank.
5. Die Wiese liegt zwischen zwei Häuser__.
6. Der Hund sitzt vor d__ Tür.
7. Sie hängt die Lampe über d__ Tisch.
8. Der Hausmeister steigt auf d__ Leiter.
9. Die Antenne ist auf d__ Haus.
10. Martin liegt noch in d__ Bett.
11. Die Garderobe ist hinter d__ Tür.
12. Die Bergsteiger wanderten tagelang in d__ Berge__ herum.
13. Das Flugzeug kann nicht landen. Es fliegt seit einer Stunde über d__ Stadt.
14. Matthias hängt sein neuestes Bild an d__ Wand.
15. Wir müssen unseren Schäferhund an d__ Leine spazierenführen.
16. Es gibt einen Park hinter d__ Opernhaus.
17. Kannst du bitte in d__ Stadt gehen?
18. Neben d__ Haus haben wir noch eine sehr groβe Garage.
19. Der Unfall passierte genau vor mein__ Augen.
20. Steck deine Sachen schnell unter d__ Tisch!

SPECIAL MEANINGS FOR THE ACCUSATIVE, DATIVE, AND EITHER-OR PREPOSITIONS

In addition to their basic meanings, prepositions have special meanings when used together with specific verbs or adjectives. Because there is no way to know the meaning—or, with the either-or prepositions, case—of the preposition, these expressions must be learned as vocabulary items. Here is a list of some common special meanings for the prepositions.

ACCUSATIVE PREPOSITIONS

bitten um	*to ask for; to request*

DATIVE PREPOSITIONS

abhängig sein von	*to be dependent on*
begeistert sein von	*to be enthusiastic about*
fragen nach	*to ask about*
gratulieren zu	*to congratulate on*
handeln von	*to deal with; to treat*
Sehnsucht haben nach	*to long for*
sprechen von	*to speak about, of*
verheiratet sein mit	*to be married to*
verwandt sein mit	*to be related to*
zufrieden sein mit	*to be satisfied with*

EITHER-OR PREPOSITIONS

an

arbeiten an + *dat.*	*to work on*
denken an + *acc.*	*to think of*
glauben an + *acc.*	*to believe in*
Interesse haben an + *dat.*	*to have an interest in*
interessiert sein an + *dat.*	*to be interested in*
schreiben an + *acc.*	*to write to*
studieren an + *dat.*	*to study at*

auf

antworten auf + *acc.*	*to answer (something)*
beruhen auf + *dat.*	*to be based on*
böse sein auf + *acc.*	*to be angry at*
hoffen auf + *acc.*	*to hope for*
reagieren auf + *acc.*	*to react to*
trinken auf + *acc.*	*to drink to*
verrückt sein auf + *acc.*	*to be crazy about*
warten auf + *acc.*	*to wait for*

in

verliebt sein in + *acc.*	*to be in love with*

über

entsetzt sein über + *acc.*	*to be horrified at*
froh sein über + *acc.*	*to be happy about*
glücklich sein über + *acc.*	*to be happy about*
lachen über + *acc.*	*to laugh about; to laugh at*
sprechen über + *acc.*	*to talk about*

When used in a special construction as in those above, **über** always takes the accusative case.

vor

Angst haben vor + *dat.*	*to be afraid of*

There are many more special meanings for the prepositions. They can be found in any good dictionary and are listed under the appropriate verb or adjective, not the preposition.

Exercise 7: *Complete with the appropriate preposition.*

1. Er ist _____ die schlanke Frau verliebt.
2. Wie hat dein Chef _____ deinen Vorschlag reagiert?
3. Peter denkt oft _____ Fuβball.
4. Der Kunde war entsetzt _____ den Preis.
5. Die Soldaten tranken _____ das Ende des Krieges.
6. Wir hoffen _____ gutes Wetter.
7. Die Studentinnen sind verrückt _____ den neuen Professor.
8. Sie ist _____ der Königin verwandt.
9. Der Film handelt _____ einer berühmten Pianistin.
10. Sie arbeitet fleiβig _____ ihrem Aufsatz.
11. Ist der neue Lehrer _____ seinem Büro zufrieden?
12. Glaubst du _____ Gott?
13. Wir haben gestern abend sehr lange _____ euch gewartet.
14. Ich bin sehr interessiert _____ ihrer Briefmarkensammlung.
15. Meine Freunde waren _____ dem neuen Film begeistert.
16. Entschuldigung, das muβ _____ einem Irrtum beruhen.
17. Wir sprechen heute _____ die neue deutsche Literatur.
18. Anja, kannst du mir bitte _____ meine Frage antworten?
19. Monika schreibt einen Bewerbungsbrief _____ die Universität.
20. Die Geschäftsführerin gratuliert ihrem Mitarbeiter ganz herzlich _____ seiner Beförderung.

Exercise 8: *Supply the correct accusative or dative endings, where necessary.*

1. Der Briefträger hat Angst vor d__ Hund.
2. Der Demonstrant ist böse auf d__ Regierung.
3. Ich gratuliere dir zu dein__ Erfolg.
4. Unsere Nachbarin bittet um ein__ Ei.
5. Der Zorn der zwei Brüder beruht auf ein__ Mißverständnis.
6. Ich bin mit mein__ Note nicht zufrieden.
7. Die Studentin antwortet richtig auf d__ Frage.
8. Lach bitte nicht über mein__ Fehler!
9. Man wartet immer ungeduldig auf d__ Zahltag.
10. Ich habe große Sehnsucht nach d__ Süden.
11. Der Autosammler hatte Interesse an d__ Oldtimer.
12. Meine Schwester reagierte wütend auf d__ Brief ihres Freundes.
13. Jürgen hat sich in d__ Freundin seines Bruders verliebt.
14. Die Professorin war entsetzt über d__ Ergebnis der Klausur.
15. Wir hoffen sehr auf d__ Hilfe ihrer Organisation.
16. Meine Schwester studiert an d__ Universität Köln.
17. Meine Familie war sehr froh über eur__ Besuch.
18. Als Student ist man meistens abhängig von sein__ Eltern.
19. Dieser Roman handelt von d__ unglücklichen Liebe eines jungen Paares.
20. Trinken wir auf unser__ Zukunft zusammen!

CONTRACTIONS WITH THE PREPOSITIONS

In German, particularly in the spoken language, accusative, dative, and either-or prepositions are frequently contracted with the definite article. The following contractions are common:

CONTRACTIONS WITH ACCUSATIVE PREPOSITIONS

durch das = **durchs**
für das = **fürs**
um das = **ums**

CONTRACTIONS WITH DATIVE PREPOSITIONS

bei dem = **beim**
von dem = **vom**
zu dem = **zum**
zu der = **zur**

CONTRACTIONS WITH EITHER-OR PREPOSITIONS

ACCUSATIVE
an das = **ans**
in das = **ins**
auf das = **aufs**

DATIVE
an dem = **am**
in dem = **im**

Other contractions with the either-or prepositions are possible—for example **vorm**, **hinters**, or **übers**—but they are colloquial.

GENITIVE PREPOSITIONS

There are four common genitive prepositions.

anstatt, statt

MEANING *INSTEAD OF*

Anstatt is used in slightly more formal speech than **statt**.

Ich bekam von ihm **anstatt eines Briefes** nur eine Ansichtskarte.
Instead of a letter I only received a postcard from him.

Statt eines Anzugs trug er nur Jeans und ein Hemd.
Instead of a suit he wore just jeans and a shirt.

If the preposition is followed immediately by a noun, that noun does not take the normal genitive ending.

Anstatt Bier trank sie Wein.
She drank wine instead of beer.

trotz

MEANING *IN SPITE OF*

Marina lernte **trotz der lauten Musik**.
Marina was studying in spite of the loud music.

Das Fußballspiel findet **trotz des Regens** statt.
The soccer game is taking place in spite of the rain.

während

MEANING *DURING*

Während des Konzerts wurden 15 Leute ohnmächtig.
Fifteen people passed out during the concert.

Während des Vortrags bin ich eingeschlafen.
I fell asleep during the lecture.

wegen   MEANING *BECAUSE OF, DUE TO*

> **Wegen des schlechten Wetters** sind wir zu Hause geblieben.
> *We stayed at home because of the bad weather.*
>
> Er sah **wegen seiner grauen Haare** alt aus.
> *He looked old because of his gray hair.*

In spoken German, the genitive prepositions sometimes take the dative case.

> während **dem** Monat   wegen **seinem** Vater   trotz **dem** Auto

Exercise 9: *Supply the appropriate genitive prepositions and the correct endings, where necessary.*

1. (In spite of) _____ sein__ Pech__ gewann er das Spiel.
2. (during)   Der Strom ist _____ d__ Sturm__ ausgefallen.
3. (because of)   Er trinkt keinen Alkohol mehr _____ sein__ Gesundheit.
4. (in spite of)   Sie ist sehr aktiv _____ ihr__ Alter__.
5. (instead of)   Ich brauche Salz _____ Pfeffer__.
6. (because of)   Sie wählte Deutsch als Hauptfach _____ ihr__ Lehrerin im Gymnasium.
7. (because of)   Die Schule war _____ d__Tod__ des Rektors geschlossen.
8. (Because of)   _____ d__ Wetter__ konnten wir nicht weiter spielen.
9. (During)   _____ d__ Konzert__ wurde meine Schwester krank.
10. (Instead of)   _____ ein__ Regenschirm__ trägt sie einen Regenmantel.
11. (In spite of)   _____ sein__ Erkältung ging Klaus hinaus in den Regen.
12. (during)   Ich war _____ mein__ Studienzeit sehr faul.

COMPREHENSIVE EXERCISES

Exercise 10: *Complete with the appropriate preposition from the list.*

an   nach   ohne   um   zu

1. Ich kann _____ meine Brille nicht fahren.
2. Am Wochenende fahre ich _____ Hause.
3. Sie hat ein großes Interesse _____ Fremdsprachen.

4. Darf ich Sie _____ Ihren Namen bitten?

5. Ich besuche alle Verwandten _____ Hause.

an in nach während zu

6. Die Frau sah ihren Mann nur selten _____ der Fußballsaison.

7. Sie studiert _____ einer Uni in Österreich.

8. Viele Ausländer kommen _____ Amerika fürs Studium.

9. Bring diesen Brief bitte _____ der Post!

10. Ein großer Teil der Alpen liegt _____ der Schweiz.

an aus auf mit von

11. Im Sommer essen wir _____ der Terrasse.

12. Mein Mann kommt _____ Boston.

13. In dem Literaturkurs lesen wir *Tod in Venedig* _____ Thomas Mann.

14. Man ißt oft Pommes frites _____ Ketchup und Mayonnaise.

15. Das Thermometer hängt draußen _____ der Hauswand.

bei mit

16. Sie begießt die Blumen _____ Wasser.

17. _____ gutem Wetter haben wir ein Picknick.

18. Sie ist eine Frau _____ sehr viel Gefühl.

19. Wir haben _____ unseren Freunden übernachtet.

20. Michael wird _____ seinem neuen Spielzeug viel Spaß haben.

in hinter zwischen trotz um

21. Der Detektiv hatte sich _____ der Tür versteckt.

22. Räum deine Wäsche _____ den Kleiderschrank!

23. _____ Schule und Universität gehe ich für einige Zeit arbeiten.

24. Frau Krause konnte _____ ihrer Schlaftabletten nicht richtig einschlafen.

25. _____ den See herum stehen viele elegante Villen.

Exercise 11: *Supply the correct accusative, dative, or genitive ending, as necessary.*

1. Sie reagierte positiv auf d__ Vorschlag.

2. Die Tür wurde durch d__ Wind zugeschlagen.

3. Ich habe nie von dies__ Komponist__ gehört.

4. Für dies__ Jahreszeit ist es viel zu kalt.

5. Ohne ein__ Birne brennt eine Lampe nicht.

6. Sie fährt mit ihr__ Rad durch d__ Park.

7. Der Wald steht zwischen d__ zwei Dörfer__.

8. Die Katze schläft während d__ Tag__.

9. Wegen ein__ Termin__ bei d__ Zahnarzt komme ich nicht.
10. Trotz d__ Panne kam er rechtzeitig an.
11. Nach d__ Essen machen wir einen langen Spaziergang.
12. Herr Ober, setzen Sie den Champagner bitte auf d__ Rechnung!
13. Während d__ Fußballspiel__ saß Thorsten neben sein__ Freundin.
14. Die Opposition war gegen d__ Vorschlag der Regierung.
15. Die Forscher mußten sich durch d__ Regenwald kämpfen.
16. Ich werde dieses Haus nicht ohne mein__ Geld verlassen.
17. Außer d__ Großeltern war die gesamte Familie da.
18. Gegenüber mein__ Schule steht ein großes Sportzentrum.
19. Wir sind jetzt schon seit d__ frühen Morgen hier.
20. Meine Mutter stellte eine neue Blumenvase auf d__ Tisch.

Exercise 12: *Translate into idiomatic German.*

1. Can one say that in German?
2. In my opinion, she drives too fast.
3. She's picking up her friends at around 7.
4. The boy is dependent on his parents.
5. It rained every day except Tuesday. (present perfect tense)
6. I am waiting for the mail.
7. He wrote to the wrong address. (present perfect tense)
8. They're going home on Sunday.
9. She's putting her books on the desk.
10. The girl is playing behind the house.

DA-*COMPOUNDS*

A **da**-compound consists of **da** plus a preposition: **davon**, **damit**, **daneben**, **dahinter**, **dagegen**, etc. If the preposition begins with a vowel, an **r** must be inserted: **darüber**, **daran**, **darauf**, **darunter**, etc.

When the object of an accusative, dative, or either-or preposition is a pronoun and refers to an *inanimate object or concept*, a **da**-compound must be used. In other words, the **da**-compound substitutes for a preposition plus personal pronoun if that pronoun refers to something inanimate.

Ich lache **über den Film.**
I'm laughing about the movie.

Ich lache **darubër.**
I'm laughing about it.

Er spricht **von der Party**.
He speaks about the party.

Er spricht **davon**.
He speaks about it.

Das erinnert mich **an einen Witz**.
That reminds me of a joke.

Das erinnert mich **daran**.
That reminds me of it.

For *human beings* the preposition plus a personal pronoun is maintained. Compare the following sentences with those above:

Ich lache **über meinen Freund.**
I'm laughing about my friend.

Ich lache **über ihn.**
I'm laughing about him.

Er spricht **von den Leuten.**
He talks about the people.

Er spricht **von ihnen.**
He talks about them.

Er erinnert mich **an meinen Vater.**
He reminds me of my father.

Er erinnert mich **an ihn.**
He reminds me of him.

Exercise 13: *Substitute* **da**-*compounds for the boldface prepositional phrases.*

1. Die alte Frau liest immer **mit einer Brille.**
2. Er fährt **mit dem Wagen** in die Stadt.
3. Sie arbeitet den ganzen Tag **an dem Projekt.**
4. Seine Kollegen gratulieren ihm **zum Geburtstag.**
5. Die Wissenschaftlerin ist **an der Frage** interessiert.
6. Der Mantel hängt **hinter der Tür.**
7. Die Eltern sind glücklich **über den Erfolg ihrer Tochter.**
8. Die Spielzeuge liegen **auf dem Boden.**
9. Die Bluse paßt **zu diesem Rock.**
10. Wir haben noch lange **von der Torte** gegessen.
11. Wir sollten uns einmal **über unsere Zukunft** unterhalten.
12. Ich habe diesen Brief **mit meinem neuen Füller** geschrieben.

Exercise 14: *Substitute a* **da**-*compound or a preposition plus a pronoun for the boldface phrases, as appropriate.*

1. Er übernachtet **bei seinem Freund.**
2. Sie trank das Bier **aus der Flasche.**
3. Ich arbeite den ganzen Tag **mit dem Computer.**
4. Die Kinder tun alles **für ihre Eltern.**
5. Seine Sehnsucht **nach dem Tod** wurde immer stärker.
6. Die 70er Jahre waren besonders hart **für die Arbeiter der Stahlindustrie.**
7. Trinken wir **auf ein langes und gesundes Leben**!
8. Ich bin **mit der Arbeit** endlich fertig.
9. Die Kolonisten kämpften **gegen die Natur.**
10. Das Ehepaar hat nicht **an seinen Jahrestag** gedacht.
11. Ich schreibe einen Brief **an meinen Kollegen.**
12. Die Eltern waren sehr stolz **auf ihren Sohn.**
13. Die Schüler sind **mit ihrer Lehrerin** in den Zirkus gegangen.
14. Ich kann Ihnen **auf diese Frage** leider nicht antworten.

15. Die Studenten diskutierten lange **über die Politik.**
16. Das junge Ehepaar wohnte zunächst **bei den Eltern der Braut.**
17. Oh, entschuldigen Sie, ich habe Sie **für meinen Bruder** gehalten.
18. Die Einbrecher hielten sich **hinter dem Vorhang** versteckt.
19. Die junge Dame zog plötzlich eine Pistole **aus ihrer Handtasche.**
20. Für das Foto haben wir uns alle **neben das Denkmal** gestellt.

WO-COMPOUNDS

A **wo**-compound consists of **wo** plus a preposition: **womit**, **wovon**, **wogegen**, etc. If the preposition begins with a vowel, an **r** must be inserted: **worüber**, **woran**, **worauf**, **worin**, etc.

When the object of an accusative, dative, or either-or preposition is an interrogative pronoun and refers to an *inanimate object or concept*, a **wo**-compound must be used. A **wo**-compound is essentially the same as a **da**-compound, but is used for questions rather than statements. In other words, a **wo**-compound corresponds to the interrogative **was** plus a preposition.

Ich lache **über den Film.**　**Worüber** lachst du?
I'm laughing about the movie.　*What are you laughing about?*

Er spricht **von der Party**.　**Wovon** spricht er?
He's talking about the party　*What's he talking about?*

Das erinnert mich **an einen Witz**.　**Woran** erinnert dich das?
That reminds me of a joke.　*What does that remind you of?*

Informal German sometimes avoids the **wo**-compound with the preposition followed by **was**.

Über was lachst du?
Von was spricht er?
An was erinnert dich das?

For *human beings* the interrogative pronoun (**wen** or **wem**) is maintained. The preposition always precedes the interrogative pronoun and determines its case. Compare the following examples with those above:

Ich lache **über meinen Freund**.　**Über wen** lachst du?
I'm laughing about my friend.　*About whom are you laughing?*

Er spricht **von den Leuten.**　**Von wem** spricht er?
He's talking about the people.　*About whom is he talking?*

Er erinnert mich **an meinen Vater.**　**An wen** erinnert er dich?
He reminds me of my father.　*Of whom does he remind you?*

Exercise 15: *Ask questions, using* **wo**-*compounds for the boldface prepositional phrases.*

1. Der Kritiker ist begeistert **von diesem Film**.
2. Wir backen einen Kuchen **für die Party**.
3. Der Regen fällt **auf das Dach** herab.
4. Sie ist stolz **auf ihre Leistungen**.
5. Die Angestellte ist **mit ihrem Gehalt** nicht zufrieden.
6. Kleine Kinder haben oft Angst **vor der Dunkelheit**.
7. Das Mädchen spielte **mit dem Ball**.
8. Der Spezialist fragte **nach den Problemen**.
9. Der Sinn des Essens liegt **im Sattwerden**.
10. Wir sprechen heute **über die Außenpolitik Amerikas.**

Exercise 16: *Ask questions, using* **wo**-*compounds or the preposition plus the interrogative pronoun for the boldface phrases, as appropriate.*

1. Die Tochter fuhr zum Supermarkt **für ihre kranke Mutter**.
2. Ihre kleine Schwester glaubt noch **an den Osterhasen**.
3. Der Roman handelt **von einer Liebesgeschichte**.
4. Er ist nicht mehr **auf seinen Chef** böse.
5. Der Reporter sprach **mit den Augenzeugen**.
6. Der Alkoholiker hatte einen Termin **beim Arzt**.
7. Das Publikum ist **von dem Filmstar** begeistert.
8. Sie waren sehr froh **über die Geburt ihres zweiten Kindes**.
9. Die Sängerin sang zusammen **mit einem Fan**.
10. Die Mutter war entsetzt **über den neuen Ohrring ihres Sohnes**.
11. Die Lehrerin war sehr zufrieden **mit dem Ergebnis der Klassenarbeit**.
12. Eine Bohrmaschine benutzt man **zum Bohren**.
13. Sie hat einen Brief **von ihrem Bruder** erhalten.
14. Der Bräutigam tanzte **mit seiner Schwiegermutter**.
15. Er hat diese Grafik **mit dem Computer** erstellt.

ANSWERS TO EXERCISES

1.

1. um
2. Ohne
3. gegen
4. bis
5. durch Zufall
6. von Kopf bis Fuß
7. bis
8. für
9. entlang
10. durch

2.

1. ein
2. die
3. ihre
4. die
5. den
6. die
7. unser
8. meinen
9. die
10. seinen Nachbarn (singular)
    seine Nachbarn (plural)

3.

1. zu
2. aus
3. Zu; nach
4. bei
5. nach
6. Bei; zu
7. außer Betrieb
8. zu Fuß; mit dem Auto
9. aus
10. bei

4.

1. Unserem
2. meiner
3. Der
4. meinen Freunden
5. meiner
6. seinen Kleidern
7. Meinem
8. der
9. einem
10. meinem

5.

Die Professorin sitzt vor der Klasse an ihrem Schreibtisch. Sie schreibt oft an die Tafel. Die Studenten sitzen neben einander in einem großen Halbkreis. Ihre Bücher liegen auf dem Boden unter ihren Stühlen. In dem Zimmer gibt es zwei Fenster. Zwischen den Fenstern steht eine große Blumenvase. Lampen hängen über den Studenten. Hinter einem Vorhang in der Ecke gibt es ein Waschbecken. Bilder hängen überall an den Wänden. Die Studenten nehmen einen Bleistift in die Hand und beginnen, Aufgaben zu lösen.

6.

1. Dative: einem; einem
2. Dative: der
3. Accusative: die
4. Dative: dem
5. Dative: Häusern
6. Dative: der
7. Accusative: den
8. Accusative: die
9. Dative: dem
10. Dative: dem
11. Dative: der
12. Dative: den Bergen
13. Dative: der
14. Accusative: die
15. Dative: der
16. Dative: dem
17. Accusative: die
18. Dative: dem
19. Dative: meinen
20. Accusative: den

7.

1. in
2. auf
3. an
4. über
5. auf
6. auf
7. auf
8. mit
9. von
10. an
11. mit
12. an
13. auf
14. an
15. von
16. auf
17. über
18. auf
19. an
20. zu

8.

1. dem
2. die
3. deinem
4. ein
5. einem
6. meiner
7. die
8. meinen (singular)/meine (plural)
9. den
10. dem
11. dem
12. den
13. die
14. das
15. die
16. der
17. euren
18. seinen
19. der
20. unsere

9.

1. Trotz seines Peches
2. während des Sturmes
3. wegen seiner Gesundheit
4. trotz ihres Alters
5. (an)statt Pfeffer
6. wegen ihrer Lehrerin
7. wegen des Todes
8. Wegen des Wetters
9. Während des Konzerts
10. (An)statt eines Regenschirms
11. Trotz seiner Erkältung
12. während meiner Studienzeit

10.

1. ohne
2. nach
3. an
4. um
5. zu
6. während
7. an
8. nach
9. zu (zur)
10. in
11. auf

12. aus
13. von
14. mit
15. an
16. mit
17. Bei
18. mit
19. bei
20. mit
21. hinter
22. in
23. Zwischen
24. trotz
25. Um

11.

1. den
2. den
3. diesem Komponisten
4. diese
5. eine
6. ihrem; den
7. den zwei Dörfern
8. des Tages
9. eines Termins; bei dem (beim)
10. der
11. dem
12. die
13. des Fußballspiels; seiner
14. den
15. den
16. mein
17. den
18. meiner
19. dem
20. den

12.

1. Kann man das auf deutsch sagen?
2. Meiner Meinung nach fährt sie zu schnell.
3. Sie holt ihre Freunde gegen 7 Uhr ab.
4. Der Junge ist von seinen Eltern abhängig.
5. Es hat jeden Tag außer Dienstag geregnet.

6. Ich warte auf die Post.
7. Er hat an die falsche Adresse geschrieben.
8. Sie gehen am Sonntag nach Hause.
9. Sie legt ihre Bücher auf den Schreibtisch.
10. Das Mädchen spielt hinter dem Haus.

13.

1. damit
2. damit
3. daran
4. dazu
5. daran
6. dahinter
7. darüber
8. darauf
9. dazu
10. davon
11. darüber
12. damit

14.

1. bei ihm
2. daraus
3. damit
4. für sie
5. danach
6. für sie
7. darauf
8. damit
9. dagegen
10. daran
11. an ihn
12. auf ihn
13. mit ihr
14. darauf
15. darüber
16. bei ihnen
17. für ihn
18. dahinter
19. daraus
20. daneben

15.

1. Wovon ist der Kritiker begeistert?
2. Wofür backen wir einen Kuchen?
3. Worauf fällt der Regen herab?
4. Worauf ist sie stolz?
5. Womit ist die Angestellte nicht zufrieden?
6. Wovor haben kleine Kinder oft Angst?
7. Womit spielte das Mädchen?
8. Wonach fragte der Spezialist?
9. Worin liegt der Sinn des Essens?
10. Worüber sprechen wir heute?

16.

1. Für wen fuhr die Tochter zum Supermarkt?
2. Woran glaubt ihre kleine Schwester noch?
3. Wovon handelt der Roman?
4. Auf wen ist er nicht mehr böse?
5. Mit wem sprach der Reporter?
6. Bei wem hatte der Alkoholiker einen Termin?
7. Von wem ist das Publikum begeistert?
8. Worüber waren sie sehr froh?
9. Mit wem sang die Sängerin zusammen?
10. Worüber war die Mutter entsetzt?
11. Womit war die Lehrerin sehr zufrieden?
12. Wozu benutzt man eine Bohrmaschine?
13. Von wem hat sie einen Brief erhalten?
14. Mit wem tanzte der Bräutigam?
15. Womit hat er diese Grafik erstellt?

5

Adjectives and Adverbs

*O*ne *of the most difficult and frustrating areas of German grammar for English speakers is adjective endings. This chapter provides a review of adjective endings with emphasis placed on extensive practice. You will benefit from these exercises only if you approach the adjective endings systematically. Three questions must always be answered to ensure accuracy:*

1. What is the gender/number of the noun being modified?
2. What is the case of the noun being modified?
3. Which chart is appropriate?

Once these three questions are answered, the correct ending can be looked up in the appropriate chart in the appendix. At first, you may use the charts for reference. Eventually, however, these charts must be memorized.

The second part of this chapter deals with the comparative and superlative forms of adjectives and adverbs. German forms are similar to English forms: both add an **-er** *for the comparative and an* **-st** *for the superlative. However, whereas English uses* **more** *and* **most** *in certain cases, German has no corresponding alternate form.*

ATTRIBUTIVE ADJECTIVES, PREDICATE ADJECTIVES, AND ADVERBS

For this chapter, it is essential to know the difference between an *attributive adjective*, a *predicate adjective*, and an *adverb*. Study the three sentences below.

ATTRIBUTIVE ADJECTIVE	Er hört einen **interessanten** Vortrag.
	He's listening to an interesting lecture.
PREDICATE ADJECTIVE	Der Vortrag ist **interessant**.
	The lecture is interesting.
ADVERB	Der Vortrag beginnt **spät**.
	The lecture begins late.

An *attributive adjective*—called simply an adjective from now on—immediately precedes the noun that it modifies. These adjectives are part of the declensional system in German. In other words, they take certain endings, called adjective endings, according to the gender, number, and case of the noun they modify.

A *predicate adjective* does not precede the noun it modifies but rather is located in the predicate, that is, after the verb, which is usually **sein** or **werden**. A predicate adjective has no ending.

An *adverb*, like the predicate adjective, takes no ending. However, whereas the predicate adjective describes a noun (*How is the lecture? The lecture is interesting.*), the adverb describes a verb (*When does the lecture begin? The lecture begins late.*).

Exercise 1: *Identify the boldface word as an attributive adjective, a predicate adjective, or an adverb.*

1. Die Studentin ist sehr **fleißig**.
2. Ich esse nur **frisches** Gemüse.
3. Sie haben zu **jung** geheiratet.
4. Die Blumen sind **tot**.
5. Das Fleisch ist mir zu **salzig**.
6. Das **salzige** Fleisch schmeckt mir nicht.
7. Mein Mann trägt **enge** Jeans.
8. Die Sekretärin tippt **schnell**.
9. Sie sieht ihre Eltern nur **selten**.
10. Diese Arbeit wird **langweilig**.

ADJECTIVE ENDINGS

German has three different sets of adjective endings depending on what precedes the adjective: adjective endings after **der**-words, adjective endings after **ein**-words, and unpreceded adjective endings. Some textbooks call the unpreceded adjective endings *strong* and the adjective endings after **der**-words *weak*. The adjective endings after **ein**-words are mixed, that is, some are strong and some weak.

Adjective Endings after der-words

The following chart shows the declension of the **der**-words and the corresponding adjective ending. You should memorize this chart thoroughly.

	MASCULINE	NEUTER	FEMININE	PLURAL
NOM.	der groβe Mann	das groβe Kind	die groβe Frau	die groβen Häuser
ACC.	den groβen Mann	das groβe Kind	die groβe Frau	die groβen Häuser
DAT.	dem groβen Mann	dem groβen Kind	der groβen Frau	den groβen Häusern
GEN.	des groβen Mannes	des groβen Kindes	der groβen Frau	der groβen Häuser

Note that there are only two possible adjective endings in this chart: **-e** (within the box) and **-en** (outside of the box).

As you remember from chapter 1, the **der**-words are the definite article **der**, and **all-**, **dies-**, **jed-**, **jen-**, **manch-**, **solch-**, and **welch-**. Study the following examples:

NOMINATIVE Dieses schön**e** Haus steht leer.
This beautiful house is standing empty.

Manche bunt**en** Vögel bleiben im Winter da.
Some colorful birds don't migrate in the winter.

ACCUSATIVE Welches fern**e** Land wirst du besuchen?
Which distant country are you going to visit?

Wir haben auch solche grün**en** Fenster.
We also have such (this kind of) green windows.

DATIVE Wir haben Angst vor dem schrecklich**en** Gewitter.
We are afraid of the terrible thunderstorm.

Im nächst**en** Herbst kaufen sie ein Sommerhaus.
They're going to buy a summer house next fall.

GENITIVE Wegen des schlecht**en** Wetters bleiben wir zu Hause.
Because of the bad weather we're staying at home.

Haben Sie die Adresse der bankrott**en** Firma?
Do you have the address of the bankrupt company?

Exercise 2: *Supply the correct adjective endings.*

1. Alle jung__ Spieler betreten das Spielfeld.
2. Ich kenne diese alt__ Frau schon lange.
3. Welche schön__ Bluse paβt zu diesem Rock?
4. Ein Spaziergang durch den groβ__ Wald dauert eine Stunde.
5. Am Ende dieses interessant__ Romans gibt es eine Überraschung.

6. Ist Amerika wirklich ein Land der unbegrenzt__ Möglichkeiten?
7. Wegen der hoh__ Temperatur bleibe ich zu Hause.
8. Sie ist gern an der frisch__ Luft.
9. Gleich am Anfang des traurig__ Filmes weinte ich.
10. Jede modern__ Großstadt hat heute ihre Probleme.
11. Er reinigt den schmutzig__ Teppich.
12. Ich kann dieses kompliziert__ Formular nicht ausfüllen.
13. In welchem fern__ Land verbringst du deinen Urlaub?
14. Alle bewundern das faszinierend__ Panorama der Alpen.
15. Der Bürgermeister wohnt in jenem riesig__ Haus.

Adjective Endings after ein-words

The following chart shows the declension of the **ein**-words and the corresponding adjective ending.

	MASCULINE	NEUTER	FEMININE	PLURAL
NOM.	ein gro**ßer** Mann	ein gro**ßes** Kind	eine gro**ße** Frau	keine gro**ßen** Häuser
ACC.	einen gro**ßen** Mann	ein gro**ßes** Kind	eine gro**ße** Frau	keine gro**ßen** Häuser
DAT.	einem gro**ßen** Mann	einem gro**ßen** Kind	einer gro**ßen** Frau	keinen gro**ßen** Häusern
GEN.	eines gro**ßen** Mannes	eines gro**ßen** Kindes	einer gro**ßen** Frau	keiner gro**ßen** Häuser

This chart is identical to the **der**-word chart with three exceptions, enclosed in the box:

1. the masculine nominative (**ein großer Mann** vs. **der große Mann**)
2. the neuter nominative (**ein großes Haus** vs. **das große Haus**)
3. the neuter accusative (**ein großes Haus** vs. **das große Haus**)

Note that there is a certain logic to these exceptions. Since the **ein**-word shows no ending (**ein**), the attributive adjective must (**-er** and **-es**). Memorize these three exceptions to the **der**-word chart and you will have memorized the **ein**-word chart.

As you remember from chapter 1, the **ein**-words are the indefinite article **ein**, the possessive adjectives, and the negative **kein**. Study the following examples:

NOMINATIVE   Ihr Liebhaber ist ein verheiratet**er** Mann.
Her lover is a married man.

Sein blau**es** Hemd liegt auf dem Bett.
His blue shirt is lying on the bed.

ACCUSATIVE   Kennst du ihre nett**e** Schwester?
Do you know her nice sister?

Heute gibt es keine langweilig**en** Vorlesungen.
Today there are no boring lectures.

DATIVE   Sie wohnt in einem renoviert**en** Haus.
She lives in a renovated house.

Das Haus liegt einem elegant**en** Gebäude gegenüber.
The house is located across from an elegant building.

GENITIVE   Der Dieb stahl die Tasche einer unvorsichtig**en** Touristin.
The thief stole the purse of a careless tourist.

Während des lang**en** Fluges nach Europa lesen wir viel.
During the long flight to Europe we read a lot.

Exercise 3: *Supply the correct adjective endings.*

1. In Köln gibt es einen berühmt__ Dom.
2. Die Fluggesellschaft hat mein ganz__ Gepäck verloren.
3. Das ist eine toll__ Aussicht!
4. Sie erzählt von ihrer abenteuerlich__ Reise.
5. Wir suchen ein exklusiv__ Hotel.
6. Sie ist mit dem Plan ihres verrückt__ Mannes nicht einverstanden.
7. Für so ein elegant__ Kleid muß man viel bezahlen.
8. Wegen ihrer heiser__ Stimme kann man sie nicht hören.
9. Die Pension liegt in der Nähe eines berühmt__ Restaurants.
10. In einem unordentlich__ Zimmer kann man nichts finden.
11. Unser klein__ Kind kann schon zwei Wörter sagen.
12. Meine talentiert__ Mutter kann sehr schön singen.
13. Meine Schwester hat ein klein__ Kätzchen gefunden.
14. Die Wissenschaftlerin hatte plötzlich eine genial__ Idee.
15. Klaus ist ein sehr intelligent__ Student.

Unpreceded Adjective Endings

Unpreceded adjectives are preceded by neither a **der**-word nor an **ein**-word. The following chart shows the declension of the unpreceded adjectives.

	MASCULINE	NEUTER	FEMININE	PLURAL
NOM.	gut**er** Kaffee	gut**es** Bier	gut**e** Limonade	gut**e** Freunde
ACC.	gut**en** Kaffee	gut**es** Bier	gut**e** Limonade	gut**e** Freunde
DAT.	gut**em** Kaffee	gut**em** Bier	gut**er** Limonade	gut**en** Freunden
GEN.	gut**en** Kaffees	gut**en** Bieres	gut**er** Limonade	gut**er** Freunde

For the most part, this chart can be derived from the **der**-word chart. The adjective endings here correspond to the endings of the **der**-word itself: **der** becomes **-er**; **die** becomes **-e**; **das** becomes **-es**; etc. There are two exceptions, indicated by the box, where the **der**-word ending is not the same as the unpreceded adjective ending:

1. the masculine genitive (**guten**, not **gutes Kaffees**)
2. the neuter genitive (**guten**, not **gutes Bieres**)

Study the following sentences:

NOMINATIVE   Schwarz**er** Kaffee schmeckt mir nicht.
I don't like black coffee.

ACCUSATIVE   In Deutschland gibt es gut**es** Bier.
In Germany there's good beer.

DATIVE   Bei schlecht**em** Wetter fahren wir nicht.
We won't go in bad weather.

GENITIVE   Wegen schlecht**en** Wetters fahren wir nicht.
We aren't going because of bad weather.

Exercise 4: *Supply the correct adjective endings.*

1. Hier gibt es frisch__ Brot.
2. Am Rhein findet man groβ__ Weingebiete.
3. Sie singt mit laut__ Stimme.
4. Ich habe rot__ Wein gern.
5. Schmutzig__ Wasser ist nicht gesund.
6. Ich wünsche dir schön__ Ferien.
7. Wir verbringen ruhig__ Tage auf dem Land.
8. Dieses Resultat ist aus folgend__ Gründen ungültig.
9. Die Deutschen schlafen gern bei geöffnet__ Fenster.
10. Beim Frühstück trinke ich schwarz__ Kaffee.
11. Ende vorig__ Monats war ich noch in Deutschland.
12. Zum Mittagessen gab es ausgezeichnet__ Steaks.
13. Zufrieden__ Menschen leben länger!
14. Wir standen vor verschlossen__ Türen.
15. Trotz unglaublich__ Regens hat er im Garten gearbeitet.

Indefinite Numerals

The indefinite numerals **andere** (*other*), **einige** (*some*), **mehrere** (*several*), **viele** (*many*), and **wenige** (*few*) are considered to be adjectives. This means that they normally take the endings of the unpreceded adjectives and that any adjective following them will take the same ending. Study the following examples:

Augsburg hat viel**e** klein**e** Brunnen.
Augsburg has many small fountains.

Bei dieser Diät kannst du einige süße Sachen essen.
On this diet you can eat some sweet things.

Ich war mit mehreren guten Freunden in Urlaub.
I was on vacation with several good friends.

Exercise 5: *Complete with the correct form of the cue adjective.*

1. (nett) Wir haben auch noch andere _____ Leute kennengelernt.
2. (groβ) Claudia besitzt einige _____ Aquarien.
3. (schwierig) Man muβ mehrere _____ Hindernisse überwinden.
4. (lang) Bei der anstrengenden Arbeit muβten die Arbeiter viele _____ Pausen machen.
5. (gut) Es gibt nur wenige _____ Restaurants in dieser Stadt.
6. (schön) In anderen _____ Hotels hat man ein Schwimmbad.
7. (neu) Herr Kaiser hat sich einige _____ Anzüge gekauft.
8. (unzerstört) Nach dem Krieg gab es nur wenige _____ Städte.

Adjectival Nouns

Adjectival nouns are adjectives used as nouns. As nouns, they are capitalized. As adjectives, they take an adjective ending according to the rules already discussed in this chapter. This means that their ending will change according to gender, number, and case, and according to whether they are preceded by a **der**-word, **ein**-word, or nothing at all (unpreceded).

Masculine, feminine, and plural adjectives used as nouns usually designate people. Neuter adjectives used as nouns usually designate a thing or concept.

der Alte = *the old man*	ein Alter = *an old man*
die Alte = *the old woman*	eine Alte = *an old woman*
die Alten = *the old people*	keine Alten = *no old people*
das Alte = *the old thing*	ein Altes = *an old thing*

Neuter adjectives may also be used to designate a young child: **das Kleine** = *the small child.*

Similarly, the adjective **deutsch** is used as a noun to designate a German man or woman, the German people, or things German.

der Deutsche = *the German man*	ein Deutscher = *a German man*
die Deutsche = *the German woman*	eine Deutsche = *a German woman*
die Deutschen = *the German people*	keine Deutschen = *no Germans*
das Deutsche = *that which is German; the German thing*	

Note that whereas in English the noun (*man, woman, people, thing*) is usually stated, in German it is understood.

Study the changing endings in the following examples:

NOMINATIVE **Der** Alt**e** trat erst letztes Jahr in Pension.
The old man was pensioned just last year.

ACCUSATIVE Ich sehe ein**en** Alt**en** im Garten.
I see an old man in the garden.

DATIVE Kannst du d**em** Alt**en** helfen? Ich helfe d**er** Alt**en**.
Can you help the old man? I'm helping the old woman.

GENITIVE Ich habe die Telefonnummer d**er** Alt**en** vergessen.
I forgot the telephone number of the old people/the old woman.

Note the idiomatic usage of the preposition **an** in the following examples:

Das Unangenehme **an der Reise** ist die Weite.
The unpleasant thing about the trip is the distance.

Das Schöne **daran** ist der Preis.
The nice thing about it is the price.

Exercise 6: *Use the cue adjective as an adjectival noun. Check your endings and make sure each adjectival noun is capitalized.*

1. _____ ist unbeliebt bei den Kindern. (*the male relative:* verwandt)
2. _____ bekommen leicht einen Sonnenbrand. (*red-haired people:* rothaarig)
3. _____ am Gedicht ist seine Form. (*the interesting thing:* interessant)
4. Man kann mit _____ nicht sprechen. (*the impatient woman:* ungeduldig)
5. Seit dem 3. Oktober 1990 sind _____ vereint. (*the Germans:* deutsch)
6. Wirf bitte _____ weg, bevor du etwas Neues kaufst! (*the old thing, that which is old:* alt)
7. Man kann von _____ viel lernen. (*the intelligent woman:* intelligent)
8. _____ haben eine Verantwortung _____ gegenüber. (*the rich:* reich; *the poor:* arm)
9. _____ konnte noch nicht sprechen. (*the small child:* klein)
10. _____ hat die Goldmedaille gewonnen. (*a German woman:* deutsch)

11. _____ wird wieder gesund werden.   (*the ill man:* krank)
12. Ich glaube an _____ im Menschen.   (*the good:* gut)
13. _____ konnte nach einer Operation wieder sehen.   (*the blind woman:* blind)
14. _____ an ihr sind ihre Augen.   (*the intriguing thing:* faszinierend)
15. Die Ärztin half _____.   (*a ten-year-old boy*: zehnjährig)

Adjective Endings after Indefinite Pronouns

Adjectives following the indefinite pronouns **etwas**, **nichts**, **viel**, and **wenig** are considered to be nouns and accordingly are capitalized. They take strong adjective endings: **-es** in the nominative and accusative cases and **-em** in the dative case.

Es gibt wenig **Neues** zu berichten.
There is little new to report.

Sie hat mir von nichts **Neuem** erzählt.
She told me (about) nothing new.

Adjectives following the indefinite pronoun **alles** take a weak adjective ending: **-e** in the nominative and accusative cases and **-en** in the dative case.

Ich wünsche dir alles **Gute**.
I wish you well.

The adjective **ander-** is not capitalized in such constructions.

Hast du nichts **anderes** zu tun?
Don't you have anything else to do?

Exercise 7: *Supply the correct adjective endings.*

1. Alles Gut__ kommt von oben.
2. Hast du nichts Besser__ zu tun?
3. Er hat viel Gut__ für mich getan.
4. Sie hat mir von etwas Unverständlich__ erzählt.
5. Der Austauschstudent gibt seiner Gastfamilie etwas typisch Amerikanisch__.
6. Es gibt nichts Besonder__ über sie zu sagen.
7. Ich muß dir etwas Überraschend__ mitteilen.
8. Die Nachrichtensprecherin berichtete von wenig Erfreulich__.
9. Die Wissenschaftler fanden viel Interessant__ heraus.
10. Sie schenkt mir immer etwas Schön__.

Adjective Endings with Names of Cities

If the name of a city is used as an adjective, it always takes the ending -**er**.

Der Köln**er** Dom ist eine berühmte Kirche.
The Cologne Cathedral is a famous church.

In den München**er** Museen gibt es viel zu sehen.
There is a lot to see in the museums of Munich.

Adjectives in a Sequence

Adjectives in a sequence all take the same ending.

In Indien gibt es gut**es**, heiß**es**, würzig**es**, billig**es** Essen.
In India there is good, hot, spicy, inexpensive food.

Past Participles and Present Participles used as Adjectives

In German and in English, past or present participles may be used as adjectives. German past or present participles used as adjectives follow the same rules for adjective endings outlined above.

PAST PARTICIPLES

To review the formation of past participles, see chapter 7. The following examples show past participles used as adjectives:

Ein getippt**er** Brief ist leicht zu lesen.
A typed letter is easy to read.

Die gewaschen**en** Kleider riechen nach Seife.
The washed clothes smell like soap.

PRESENT PARTICIPLES

In German, the present participle is formed by adding **d** to the infinitive form of the verb. It corresponds to the infinitive plus *ing* in English. The following examples show present participles used as adjectives:

Er spricht mit zittern**der** Stimme.
He's speaking with a trembling voice.

Der bellen**de** Hund störte die Nachbarn.
The barking dog disturbed the neighbors.

Past or Present Participles as Adjectival Nouns

Past or present participles are commonly used as adjectival nouns. As with all adjectival nouns, the past or present participle is capitalized and must have the correct adjective ending.

PAST PARTICIPLE   Man brachte die **Verletzten** ins Krankenhaus.
They brought the injured people to the hospital.

PRESENT PARTICIPLE   Alle Englisch **Sprechenden** müssen hier warten.
All English-speaking people must wait here.

Exercise 8: *Form a past or present participle from the cue verb and add the appropriate adjective ending.*

1. Die Ärztin half dem _____ Kind.   (*injured:* verletzen)
2. Die _____ schauten den Unfall an.   (*people standing around:* herumstehen)
3. Das _____ Haus gehörte meinen Großeltern.   (*ruined:* ruinieren)
4. Die Polizei fand das _____ Geld nie wieder.   (*stolen:* stehlen)
5. Man hört das _____ Kind durch das ganze Wohnhaus.   (*crying:* weinen)
6. Laß den _____ Mann in Ruhe!   (*sleeping:* schlafen)
7. Die _____ Mannschaft verläßt enttäuscht das Spielfeld. (*defeated:* schlagen)
8. Ich habe das Geld für unser _____ Auto bekommen.   (*sold:* verkaufen)
9. Die _____ an der Theke waren schon ziemlich betrunken. (*drinking people:* trinken)
10. Ich habe all die _____ Sachen zum Fundbüro gebracht.   (*found:* finden)

Review Exercises for Adjective Endings

Remember: To supply the correct ending on a **der**-word, **ein**-word, or any adjective, you must answer the three questions noted at the beginning of this chapter:

1. What is the gender/number of the noun being modified: masculine, feminine, neuter, singular or plural?
2. What is the case of the noun being modified: nominative, accusative, dative, or genitive?
3. Which chart is appropriate: the **der**-word chart, the **ein**-word chart, or the unpreceded adjective chart?

Exercise 9: *Supply the correct adjective ending, if necessary.*

1. Alleinstehend__ Mütter haben es schwer.
2. Meine Schwester trägt einen eng__, kurz__, schwarz__ Rock.
3. Du bist ein unausstehlich__ Mensch.
4. Das ist eine dumm__ Idee.
5. Ich konnte den schnell Sprechend__ kaum verstehen.

6. Mein neu__ Kleid ist rot__.
7. In Amerika trinkt man eiskalt__ Wasser.
8. Friederike ist eine gut__ Freundin von mir.
9. Im Juni hatten wir sehr trocken__ Wetter.
10. Die Studenten machten sogar die schwer__ Aufgaben richtig__.
11. Der Fischer hat viele einsam__ Tage am See verbracht.
12. Ich habe nie mit so einem berühmt__ Schauspieler gesprochen.
13. In manchen sehr schwierig__ Fällen wußte die Richterin nicht, was sie tun sollte.
14. In England fährt man auf der link__ Seite der Straße.
15. Bei solchem schrecklich__ Wetter sollen wir etwas Warm__ anziehen.
16. Der Hamburg__ Hafen ist sehr groß.
17. Kompliziert__ Rechenaufgaben mag ich nicht.
18. Das Gut__ und das Schlecht__ liegen manchmal sehr eng beieinander.
19. Wir konnten nichts Neu__ aus der Heimat berichten.
20. Greta Garbo war eine berühmt__ und faszinierend__ Schauspielerin.
21. Mein Vater ist normalerweise ein sehr ruhig__ Mann.
22. Die Studentin interessiert sich sehr für fremd__ Sprachen.
23. Die verunglückt__ Urlauber waren alle leicht verletzt__.
24. Der Unglücklich__ hatte sich beide Arme gebrochen.
25. Wegen des stark__ Windes spielte man nicht mehr Tennis.

Exercise 10: *Select an appropriate adjective from the list for each blank and supply the correct adjective ending, if necessary.*

international	**interessant**	**sauber**	**müde**
spannend	**nett**	**lang**	**neutral**

1. Die Professorin hält _____ Vorträge.
2. Das _____ Mädchen schläft sofort ein.
3. Das Ende des _____ Kriminalromans war eine Enttäuschung.
4. Wien, New York und Genf sind _____ Städte.
5. Österreich ist ein _____ Land.
6. Die Touristen übernachteten in einer _____ Pension.
7. Muß ich wirklich das _____ Formular ausfüllen?
8. Das Geschenk ist für meinen _____ Nachbarn.

gefährlich	**schwierig**	**verliebt**	**verhaftet**
rund	**lecker**	**französisch**	**komisch**

9. Bergsteigen ist manchmal ein sehr _____ Sport.

10. Der Mann hatte wirklich ein _____ Gesicht.
11. Die _____ Frau gab zu, das Geld gestohlen zu haben.
12. Das _____ Paar möchte so schnell wie möglich heiraten.
13. Unser Gast trinkt gern _____ Wein.
14. Ich möchte eine Tüte dieser _____ Schokoladen.
15. Ich hatte große Probleme mit dieser äußerst _____ Klausur.
16. Der Zirkusclown gab eine _____ Vorstellung.

Exercise 11: *Supply the correct ending, if necessary.*

1. D__ Verlobt__ kaufen einander Ringe.
2. Die Lehrerin wünscht ihr__ intelligent__ Schüler__ ein__ gut__ Morgen.
3. Ich muß noch d__ ganz__ Tag arbeiten.
4. Gehört diese Uhr unser__ Zimmerkamerad__?
5. Die Schule kaufte d__ Schüler__ neu__ Computer.
6. Die Katze schläft gern auf d__ weich__ Teppich neben d__ warm__ Heizung.
7. Gehen wir in d__ nächst__ Weinkeller!
8. Es gibt viel__ möglich__ Antworten auf so ein__ ungenau__ Frage.
9. Was für ein__ Student ist er? Er ist ein__ fleißig__ Student.
10. Während d__ kurz__ Pause haben wir Sekt getrunken.
11. Wir haben ein__ neu__ Heizung installiert.
12. D__ Gut__ an dir ist deine Geduld.
13. Wer hat denn dies__ lecker__ Torte gebacken?
14. Kannst du nicht von etwas ander__ erzählen?
15. Ich habe mein__ lieb__ Mutter Blumen gekauft.
16. Man brachte alle Verletzt__ mit dem Hubschrauber in d__ nächst__ Krankenhaus.
17. Ich muß dir unbedingt von den viel__ interessant__ Neuigkeiten berichten.
18. Im letzt__ Jahr haben wir unser__ Urlaub auf d__ griechisch__ Inseln verbracht.

THE COMPARISON OF ADJECTIVES AND ADVERBS

In German and in English, adjectives and adverbs have three degrees of comparison: the positive or base form, the comparative form, and the superlative form.

Formation of the Comparative and Superlative

The comparative form is made by adding **-er** to the base form of the adjective or adverb. The superlative is made by adding **-st** to the base form of the adjective or adverb.

	fast	*possible*	*pretty*	*small*
BASE FORM	schnell	möglich	schön	klein
COMPARATIVE	schnell**er**	möglich**er**	schön**er**	klein**er**
SUPERLATIVE	schnell**st-**	möglich**st-**	schön**st-**	klein**st-**

Note that this is very similar to the comparative and superlative in English. However, in certain cases English forms the comparative and superlative degrees with *more* and *most*, respectively. This is not possible in German. Compare the English and German sentences below.

BASE FORM	*This is a beautiful picture.*
	Das ist ein schönes Bild.
COMPARATIVE	*This picture is **more** beautiful.*
	Dieses Bild ist schön**er**.
SUPERLATIVE	*This picture is the **most** beautiful.*
	Dieses Bild ist das schön**ste**.

VARIATIONS IN THE FORMATION OF THE COMPARATIVE AND SUPERLATIVE

The Superlative Ending *-est*. For the superlative, the ending **-est** is added to adjectives or adverbs ending in **-d**, **-t**, or an **s** sound (**-s**, **-β**, **-z**, or **-sch**).

	round	*far*	*hot*	*pretty*
BASE FORM	rund	weit	heiβ	hübsch
SUPERLATIVE	rund**est-**	weit**est-**	heiβ**est-**	hübsch**est-**

Present participles used as adjectives add **-st** for the superlative, not **-est**, even though they end in **d**.

	charming	*surprising*
BASE FORM	reizend	überraschend
SUPERLATIVE	reizend**st-**	überraschend**st-**

Base Forms Ending in *-el* or *-er*. Base forms ending in **-el** or **-er** usually drop the **e** in the comparative. The superlative form remains regular.

	dark	*expensive*
BASE FORM	dunkel	teuer
COMPARATIVE	dunkler	teurer
SUPERLATIVE	dunkelst-	teuerst-

Umlaut in the Comparative and Superlative. Adjectives or adverbs of one syllable with the vowels **a** or **u** frequently umlaut in the comparative and superlative: **alt/älter/ältest-**, **jung/jünger/jüngst-**. Here is a list of the most common ones.

alt	*old*	kalt	*cold*	scharf	*sharp*
arm	*poor*	klug	*clever*	schwach	*weak*
dumm	*dumb*	krank	*sick*	schwarz	*black*
hart	*hard*	kurz	*short*	stark	*strong*
jung	*young*	lang	*long*	warm	*warm*

Adjectives or adverbs of one syllable with the vowel **o** infrequently umlaut in the comparative and superlative: **grob/gröber**; **oft/öfter**, **rot/röter** or **roter**.

The two-syllable adjective **gesund** also umlauts in the comparative and superlative: **gesünder/gesündest-**.

Irregular Comparative and Superlative Forms. The following adjectives and adverbs have irregular comparative and superlative forms:

	soon	*gladly*	*large*	*good*	*high*	*near*	*much*
BASE FORM	bald	gern	groß	gut	hoch	nah	viel
COMPARATIVE	**eher**	**lieber**	**größer**	**besser**	**höher**	**näher**	**mehr**
SUPERLATIVE	**ehest-**	**liebst-**	**größt-**	**best-**	**höchst-**	**nächst-**	**meist-**

Use of the Comparative and Superlative

Before attempting this section, you are advised to review the difference between attributive adjectives, predicate adjectives, and adverbs as explained at the beginning of this chapter. In brief, an attributive adjective (called simply an adjective in this and many other textbooks) precedes the noun that it modifies and takes an adjective ending. A predicate adjective does not precede the noun it modifies but rather is located after the verb. An adverb modifies a verb, not a noun. Predicate adjectives and adverbs in the base form do not take endings.

ATTRIBUTIVE ADJECTIVES

Comparative and superlative adjectives take normal adjective endings as determined by the guidelines established thus far in this chapter. Do not confuse the comparative or superlative ending with the adjective ending.

BASE FORM	Das ist ein schnell**es** Auto.
	(adjective ending = **es**)
COMPARATIVE	Das ist ein schnell**eres** Auto.
	(comparative = **er**; adjective ending = **es**)
SUPERLATIVE	Das ist das schnell**ste** Auto.
	(superlative = **st**; adjective ending = **e**)

BASE FORM	Das ist ein schnell**er** Wagen.
	(adjective ending = **er**)
COMPARATIVE	Das ist ein schnell**erer** Wagen.
	(comparative = **er**; adjective ending = **er**)
SUPERLATIVE	Das ist der schnell**ste** Wagen.
	(superlative = **st**; adjective ending = **e**)

Exercise 12: *Complete with the correct comparative or superlative form of the cue word. Do not forget to insert the proper adjective endings.*

1. In Ulm gibt es den _____ Kirchturm in der Welt. (hoch: *superlative*)
2. Normalerweise ist Juli der _____ Monat des Jahres. (warm: *superlative*)
3. Sie sieht ihrer _____ Schwester ähnlich. (alt: *comparative*)
4. Das war der _____ Moment meines Lebens. (schlimm: *superlative*)
5. Mein Wagen fährt ziemlich langsam. Ich möchte einen _____ Wagen haben. (schnell: *comparative*)
6. Dieses Kleid ist mir zu teuer. Haben Sie kein _____ Kleid? (billig: *comparative*)
7. Haben Sie _____ Geschwister? (jung: *comparative*) Nein, ich bin das _____ Kind in der Familie. (jung: *superlative*)
8. Das Klavier steht in dem _____ Zimmer des Hauses. (vornehm: *superlative*)
9. Dr. Wagner ist sehr gut, aber Dr. Meyer ist ein noch _____ Arzt. (kompetent: *comparative*)
10. Viele Studenten studieren Politikwissenschaft, aber die _____ Studenten haben Wirtschaftswissenschaft als Hauptfach. (viel: *superlative*)

PREDICATE ADJECTIVES

The comparative form of a predicate adjective does not take an adjective ending in addition to the comparative ending. There are two possible superlative forms for a predicate adjective: either **am** plus the base form of the predicate adjective plus **-sten** or (less frequently) the superlative with the definite article.

BASE FORM	Das Auto ist schnell.
COMPARATIVE	Dieses Auto ist schnell**er**.
SUPERLATIVE	Dieses Auto ist **am** schnell**sten**.
	Dieses Auto ist **das** schnell**ste**.

BASE FORM	Die Studentin ist fleißig.
COMPARATIVE	Die andere Studentin ist noch fleißig**er**.
SUPERLATIVE	Diese Studentin ist **am** fleißig**sten**.
	Diese Studentin ist **die** fleißig**ste**.

The alternate superlative form with the definite article may be used only when the noun that is modified is understood. The definite article and the adjective ending will change according to the modified noun.

Dieses Auto ist **das** schnell**ste**.   (**Auto** is understood.)
Dieser Wagen ist **der** schnell**ste**.   (**Wagen** is understood.)
Diese Autos sind **die** schnell**sten**.   (**Autos** is understood.)

Exercise 13: *Form sentences according to the model.*

der März, der Februar, der Januar: kalt sein
Der März ist kalt. Der Februar ist kälter. Der Januar ist am kältesten.

1. die Rocky Mountains, die Alpen, der Himalaja: hoch sein
2. Spanisch, Deutsch, Russisch: schwer sein
3. Köln, München, Berlin: groß sein
4. ein Zimmer, eine Wohnung, ein Eigenheim: teuer sein
5. die Elbe, der Rhein, die Donau: lang sein
6. Silber, Gold, Platin: wertvoll sein
7. die Heizung, der Backofen, der Hochofen: heiß sein
8. das Papier, die Watte, die Luft: leicht sein
9. der Bodensee, die Nordsee, der Atlantik: tief sein
10. New York, Moskau, Trier: alt sein

ADVERBS

The comparative form of an adverb takes only the comparative ending **-er**. The superlative form of an adverb is **am** plus the base form of the adverb plus **-sten**. Thus, the comparative and superlative forms for adverbs are identical to those for predicate adjectives except that for adverbs there is no alternate superlative form.

BASE FORM	Meine Mutter singt schön.
COMPARATIVE	Der Rock-und-Roll Star singt **schöner**.
SUPERLATIVE	Die Opersängerin singt **am schönsten**.

BASE FORM   Ich fahre schnell.
COMPARATIVE   Meine Schwester fährt **schneller**.
SUPERLATIVE   Mein Vater fährt **am schnellsten**.

A particularly important adverbial construction is **gern** plus a verb, which means *to like to do something*. Note the irregular comparative and superlative forms and their English equivalents in the examples below.

BASE FORM   Ich spiele **gern** Tennis.
                 I like to play tennis.
COMPARATIVE   Ich spiele **lieber** Fußball.
                 I prefer to play soccer.
SUPERLATIVE   Ich spiele **am liebsten** Golf.
                 I like to play golf most/best of all.

Exercise 14: *Form sentences according to the model.*

Ich trinke gern Milch.   (Bier, Wein)
Ich trinke lieber Bier. Ich trinke am liebsten Wein.

1. Matthias lernt fleißig.   (Monika, Günter)
2. Ich spreche gut Deutsch.   (der Austauschstudent, der Deutsche)
3. Das Mädchen schreit laut.   (der Junge, das Baby)
4. Kristin wirft den Ball weit.   (Erika, Jutta)
5. Ich esse gern Gemüse.   (Obst, Schokolade)
6. Klaus raucht viel.   (Peter, Claudia)
7. Ulrike spielt gut Klavier.   (die Musikstudentin, die Pianistin)
8. Ralf telefoniert lange.   (Elfriede, Christoph)

Special Comparative and Superlative Constructions

SO . . . WIE

To express the sameness of two objects or people, German uses **so . . . wie**, frequently in combination with **eben** or **genau**, plus the base form of the adjective or adverb. The English equivalent is *as . . . as*.

Sie sieht **genauso schön** aus **wie** ihre Mutter.
She looks just as pretty as her mother.

Ein Käfer kann nicht **so schnell wie** ein BMW fahren.
A VW Beetle cannot drive as fast as a BMW.

ALS

To express the difference between two objects or people, German uses **als** plus the comparative form of the adjective or adverb. The English equivalent is *than*.

Karotten sind **gesünder als** Schokolade.
Carrots are more healthy than chocolate.

Tina lernt **mehr als** Hans.
Tina studies more than Hans.

IMMER + THE COMPARATIVE

To express increasing degrees of a quality, German uses **immer** plus the comparative form of the adjective or adverb. In English the adjective or adverb is repeated.

Im Frühjahr werden die Tage **immer länger**.
In the spring the days get longer and longer.

Warum sprichst du **immer schneller**?
Why are you speaking faster and faster?

THE ABSOLUTE COMPARATIVE

The comparative may be used without an actual comparison to relativize an adjective.

Trotz eines **längeren** Aufenthalts in Wien kam ich für die Konferenz rechtzeitig an.
In spite of a relatively long/longish stop in Vienna I arrived at the conference punctually.

Der **ältere** Mann kann noch allein wohnen.
The rather old/elderly man can still live alone.

MEHR + THE BASE FORM

When comparing two qualities of the same object or person, German uses **mehr** or **eher** plus the base form of the adjective or adverb plus **als**.

Die Biographie ist **mehr/eher** informativ **als** interessant.
The biography is more informative than interesting.

Die Frau grüßte uns **mehr/eher** kühl als freundlich.
The woman greeted us more cool than friendly.

Review Exercises for the Comparative and Superlative

Exercise 15: *Supply the comparative or superlative form of the cue adjective. Add adjective endings where appropriate.*

1. Das Essen zu Hause schmeckt _____ als in der Mensa.   (gut: *comparative*)
2. Die Kurse bei diesem Professor sind _____.   (lang-weilig: *superlative*)

3. Das rote Auto fährt _____.   (schnell: *superlative*)

4. In der Stadt hat man oft einen _____ Wagen als auf dem Land. (klein: *comparative*)

5. Abends habe ich immer _____ Zeit als morgens.   (viel: *comparative*)

6. Die Studentin lernt _____ zu Hause als in der Bibliothek. (gern: *comparative*)

7. Sebastian ist der _____ Junge in seiner Klasse.   (groß: *superlative*)

8. Dieses Bild ist _____.   (schön: *superlative*)

9. Die _____ Kurse sind oft auch _____. (schwierig: *superlative*; interessant: *superlative*)

10. Freitag war einer der _____ Tage meines Lebens.   (schlecht: *superlative*)

11. Der _____ Mann hat das Spiel verloren.   (dumm: *comparative*)

12. Der _____ Wanderweg dauert eine Stunde.   (kurz: *superlative*)

13. Im Park ist es _____ als in der Innenstadt.   (schön: *comparative*)

14. Wir wollen ein _____ Hotel für den Urlaub finden.   (billig: *comparative*)

15. Sie ist die _____ Frau, die ich jemals kennengelernt habe. (faszinierend: *superlative*)

16. Diese Geschäftsfrau ist die _____ Frau in der Gegend.   (reich: *superlative*)

17. Dieses Angebot ist wesentlich _____ als das andere.   (günstig: *comparative*)

18. Mein _____ Sohn ist mittlerweile 10 Jahre alt.   (jung: *superlative*)

Exercise 16: *Translate into idiomatic German.*

1. She works just as diligently as he does, but she gets worse grades.
2. The party next door is getting louder and louder.
3. I like beer, but I like wine more (I prefer wine).
4. My mother is older than my father.
5. The Rhine is the most important river in Germany.
6. Friday is a better day than Monday!
7. Her parents were more hurt than angry.
8. Berlin is becoming more and more expensive.
9. The bedroom is cooler than the kitchen.
10. Her German is almost as good as her English.

EXTENDED MODIFIERS

An *extended modifier* is an extended description of a noun that substitutes for a relative clause. It precedes the noun that it modifies. There is no equivalent in English; the phrase must be translated into English as a relative clause. Extended modifiers are used primarily in scientific and formal writing.

Extended modifiers can usually be recognized easily by the break in syntax. To the native English speaker, the sentence suddenly makes no sense. Most commonly and most striking, an article is not immediately followed by the noun to which it refers. Usually the extended modifier ends with a present or past participle used as an adjective.

Study the following extended modifiers and their English equivalents:

Der **den Test schreibende** Schüler ist gestreβt.
The student who is taking the test is stressed.

Das **gestern abend nicht gespülte** Geschirr steht immer noch da.
The dishes that weren't washed last night are still there.

Das ist ein **schwer zu entfernender** Fleck.
That is a spot that is difficult to remove.

Exercise 17: *Identify the extended modifier and then translate the sentence.*

1. Der immer dicker werdende Mann nascht gern Schokolade.
2. Der nicht gefeierte Geburtstag war sehr einsam.
3. Er ist ein leicht einzuschüchternder Mensch.
4. Das nicht behandelte Kapitel steht noch aus.
5. Das ist ein schwer zu verstehendes Buch.
6. Es handelt sich um ein leicht zu lösendes Problem.
7. Der erst vor einer Woche veröffentlichte Roman ist schon ein Bestseller.
8. Man zeigte ein vor Hunger laut schreiendes Kind im Fernsehen.
9. Das in der Zeitung empfohlene Buch ist sehr leicht zu lesen.
10. Der im Flugzeug tödlich verunglückte Schauspieler war sehr reich.
11. Diese vor zwei Jahren entdeckte Krankheit ist absolut tödlich.
12. Der vom Wind ungenügend geschützte Baum ist umgefallen.

ANSWERS TO EXERCISES

1.

1. predicate adjective
2. attributive adjective
3. adverb
4. predicate adjective
5. predicate adjective
6. attributive adjective
7. attributive adjective
8. adverb
9. adverb
10. predicate adjective

2.

1. jungen
2. alte
3. schöne
4. großen
5. interessanten
6. unbegrenzten
7. hohen
8. frischen
9. traurigen
10. moderne
11. schmutzigen
12. komplizierte
13. fernen
14. faszinierende
15. riesigen

3.

1. berühmten
2. ganzes
3. tolle
4. abenteuerlichen
5. exklusives
6. verrückten
7. elegantes
8. heiseren
9. berühmten
10. unordentlichen
11. kleines
12. talentierte
13. kleines
14. geniale
15. intelligenter

4.

1. frisches
2. große
3. lauter
4. roten
5. Schmutziges
6. schöne
7. ruhige
8. folgenden
9. geöffnetem
10. schwarzen
11. vorigen
12. ausgezeichnete
13. Zufriedene
14. verschlossenen
15. unglaublichen

5.

1. nette
2. große
3. schwierige
4. lange
5. gute
6. schönen
7. neue
8. unzerstörte

6.

1. Der Verwandte
2. Rothaarige
3. Das Interessante
4. der Ungeduldigen
5. die Deutschen
6. das Alte
7. der Intelligenten
8. Die Reichen; den Armen
9. Das Kleine
10. Eine Deutsche
11. Der Kranke
12. das Gute
13. Die Blinde
14. Das Faszinierende
15. einem Zehnjährigen

7.

1. Gute
2. Besseres
3. Gutes
4. Unverständlichem
5. Amerikanisches
6. Besonderes
7. Überraschendes
8. Erfreulichem
9. Interessantes
10. Schönes

8.

1. verletzten
2. Herumstehenden
3. ruinierte
4. gestohlene
5. weinende
6. schlafenden
7. geschlagene
8. verkauftes
9. Trinkenden
10. gefundenen

9.

1. Alleinstehende
2. engen; kurzen; schwarzen
3. unausstehlicher
4. dumme
5. Sprechenden
6. neues; rot
7. eiskaltes
8. gute
9. trockenes
10. schweren; richtig
11. einsame
12. berühmten
13. schwierigen
14. linken
15. schrecklichen; Warmes
16. Hamburger
17. Komplizierte
18. Gute; Schlechte
19. Neues
20. berühmte; faszinierende
21. ruhiger
22. fremde
23. verunglückten; verletzt
24. Unglückliche
25. starken

10.

1. interessante
2. müde
3. spannenden
4. internationale
5. neutrales
6. sauberen
7. lange
8. netten
9. gefährlicher
10. rundes
11. verhaftete
12. verliebte
13. französischen
14. leckeren

15. schwierigen
16. komische

11.

1. Die Verlobten
2. ihren intelligenten Schülern; einen guten
3. den ganzen
4. unserem Zimmerkameraden
5. den Schülern; neue
6. dem weichen; der warmen
7. den nächsten
8. viele mögliche; eine ungenaue
9. ein; ein fleißiger
10. der kurzen
11. eine neue
12. Das Gute
13. diese leckere
14. anderem
15. meiner lieben
16. Verletzten; das nächste
17. vielen interessanten
18. letzten; unseren; den griechischen

12.

1. höchsten
2. wärmste
3. älteren
4. schlimmste
5. schnelleren
6. billigeres
7. jüngere; jüngste
8. vornehmsten
9. kompetenterer
10. meisten

13.

1. Die Rocky Mountains sind hoch. Die Alpen sind höher. Der Himalaja ist am höchsten.
2. Spanisch ist schwer. Deutsch ist schwerer. Russisch ist am schwersten.
3. Köln ist groß. München ist größer. Berlin ist am größten.
4. Ein Zimmer ist teuer. Eine Wohnung ist teurer. Ein Eigenheim ist am teuersten.
5. Die Elbe ist lang. Der Rhein ist länger. Die Donau ist am längsten.
6. Silber ist wertvoll. Gold ist wertvoller. Platin ist am wertvollsten.
7. Die Heizung ist heiß. Der Backofen ist heißer. Der Hochofen ist am heißesten.
8. Das Papier ist leicht. Die Watte ist leichter. Die Luft ist am leichtesten.
9. Der Bodensee ist tief. Die Nordsee ist tiefer. Der Atlantik ist am tiefsten.
10. New York ist alt. Moskau ist älter. Trier ist am ältesten.

14.

1. Monika lernt fleißiger. Günter lernt am fleißigsten.
2. Der Austauschstudent spricht besser Deutsch. Der Deutsche spricht am besten Deutsch.
3. Der Junge schreit lauter. Das Baby schreit am lautesten.
4. Erika wirft den Ball weiter. Jutta wirft den Ball am weitesten.
5. Ich esse lieber Obst. Ich esse am liebsten Schokolade.
6. Peter raucht mehr. Claudia raucht am meisten.
7. Die Musikstudentin spielt besser Klavier. Die Pianistin spielt am besten Klavier.
8. Elfriede telefoniert länger. Christoph telefoniert am längsten.

15.

1. besser
2. am langweiligsten/die langweiligsten
3. am schnellsten
4. kleineren
5. mehr
6. lieber
7. größte
8. am schönsten/das schönste
9. schwierigsten; am interessantesten/die interessantesten
10. schlechtesten
11. dümmere
12. kürzeste
13. schöner
14. billigeres
15. faszinierendste
16. reichste
17. günstiger
18. jüngster

16.

1. Sie arbeitet genauso fleißig wie er, aber sie bekommt schlechtere Noten.
2. Die Party nebenan wird immer lauter.
3. Ich habe Bier gern, aber (ich habe) Wein (noch) lieber.
4. Meine Mutter ist älter als mein Vater.
5. Der Rhein ist der wichtigste Fluß in Deutschland.
6. Freitag ist ein besserer Tag als Montag!
7. Ihre Eltern waren mehr/eher verletzt als böse.
8. Berlin wird immer teurer.
9. Das Schlafzimmer ist kühler als die Küche.
10. Ihr Deutsch ist fast so gut wie ihr Englisch.

17.

1. Der **immer dicker werdende** Mann nascht gern Schokolade.
The man who is getting fatter and fatter likes to snack on chocolate.
2. Der **nicht gefeierte** Geburtstag war sehr einsam.
The birthday that wasn't celebrated was very lonely.
3. Er ist ein **leicht einzuschüchternder** Mensch.
He is a person who is easy to intimidate.
4. Das **nicht behandelte** Kapitel steht noch aus.
The chapter that wasn't discussed still has to be completed.
5. Das ist ein **schwer zu verstehendes** Buch.
That is a book that is difficult to understand.
6. Es handelt sich um ein **leicht zu lösendes** Problem.
It is a question of a problem that is easy to solve.
7. Der **erst vor einer Woche veröffentlichte** Roman ist schon ein Bestseller.
The novel that was published only a week ago is already a bestseller.

8. Man zeigte ein **vor Hunger laut schreiendes** Kind im Fernsehen.
A child who was screaming loudly from hunger was shown on TV.

9. Das **in der Zeitung empfohlene** Buch ist sehr leicht zu lesen.
The book that was recommended in the newspaper is very easy to read.

10. Der **im Flugzeug tödlich verunglückte** Schauspieler war sehr reich.
The actor who died in the plane accident was very rich.

11. Diese **vor zwei Jahren entdeckte** Krankheit ist absolut tödlich.
This disease, which was discovered two years ago, is absolutely deadly.

12. Der **vom Wind ungenügend geschützte** Baum ist umgefallen.
The tree that was not protected sufficiently from the wind fell down.

6

Numbers and Time Expressions

This chapter presents and practices the expression of numbers and time in German. It includes cardinal numbers, ordinal numbers, the days, months, and seasons of the year, the expression of dates, and telling time.

NUMBERS

Cardinal Numbers

The formation of cardinal numbers in German follows certain patterns.

0 null		
1 **eins**	11 elf	21 einundzwanzig
2 zwei	12 zwölf	22 zweiundzwanzig
3 drei	13 dreizehn	30 **dreißig**
4 vier	14 vierzehn	40 vierzig
5 fünf	15 fünfzehn	50 fünfzig
6 **sechs**	16 sechzehn	60 sechzig
7 **sieben**	17 siebzehn	70 siebzig
8 acht	18 achtzehn	80 achtzig
9 neun	19 neunzehn	90 neunzig
10 zehn	20 zwanzig	100 (ein)hundert

101	hunderteins
102	hundertzwei
199	hundertneunundneunzig
200	zweihundert
201	zweihunderteins
300	dreihundert
400	vierhundert
1 000	(ein)tausend
10 000	zehntausend
100 000	hunderttausend
1 000 000	eine Million
10 000 000	zehn Millionen
100 000 000	hundert Millionen
1 000 000 000	eine Milliarde (*one billion*)
1 000 000 000 000	eine Billion (*one trillion*)

Irregularities in the patterns are in boldface in the chart above and summarized here:

ein**s**	but einundzwanzig (no **s**)
sech**s**	but sechzehn and sechzig (no **s**)
sieb**en**	but siebzehn and siebzig (no **en**)
drei**β**ig	but vierzig, fünfzig, etc.

Note that from 21 on, the ones precede the tens and are connected by **und**—similar to the nursery rhyme line: *"Four and twenty blackbirds. . . ."*

Note that German **eine Milliarde** corresponds to English *one billion*, and that German **eine Billion** corresponds to English *one trillion*.

Note that where English uses a comma to separate numbers, German uses a space (as above) or a period:

1,000 = **1 000** or **1.000**

Note that **Million**, **Milliarde**, and **Billion** are feminine nouns that take -**en** in the plural.

Cardinal numbers do not take adjective endings.

Exercise 1: *Write out the following numbers.*

1. 3	6. 333	11. 8 576
2. 24	7. 417	12. 10 001
3. 77	8. 891	13. 100 608
4. 101	9. 999	14. 1 365 902
5. 189	10. 1 000	15. 13 000 202

OTHER USES OF CARDINAL NUMBERS

Arithmetic. The examples below show how to write and say simple mathematical functions.

$2 + 7 = 9$ zwei plus/und sieben ist neun

$6 - 1 = 5$ sechs minus/weniger eins ist fünf

$5 \cdot 4 = 20$
$5 \times 4 = 20$ } fünf mal vier ist zwanzig

$36 : 3 = 12$ sechsunddreißig (geteilt) durch drei ist zwölf

Exercise 2: *Test your arithmetic! Write out the mathematical statements and provide the answers.*

1. $1 + 1 =$	6. $33 : 3 =$
2. $11 - 8 =$	7. $100 \times 7 =$
3. $13 + 12 =$	8. $88 : 4 =$
4. $4 \times 7 =$	9. $1.705 + 1 =$
5. $176 - 45 =$	10. $500 - 25 =$

Currencies. The currencies for Germany (**D-Mark, Pfennig**) and the United States (**Dollar**) are singular when used in prices. Note that German uses a comma in writing the price. Prices are written and pronounced as follows:

DM 9,30   neun Mark dreißig
$ 2.89   zwei Dollar neunundachtzig

Bill denominations end in **-er** and are masculine.

Ich möchte bitte einen **Fünfziger** und zwei **Zwanziger.**
I would like one fifty-Mark bill and two twenty-Mark bills.

Decades. To express decades, add **-er** to the cardinal number.

In den **sechziger** Jahren gab es viele Studentenunruhen.
In the sixties there was a lot of student unrest.

Anfang der **achtziger** Jahre waren viele Deutsche arbeitslos.
At the beginning of the eighties many Germans were unemployed.

Decimals and Percentages. For decimals and percentages German uses a comma where English uses a period.

7,8   sieben Komma acht
9,2%   neun Komma zwei Prozent

Cardinal Number + -*mal*. Adverbs indicating frequency may be formed by adding the suffix **-mal** to a cardinal number.

einmal	*once*
zweimal	*twice*
dreimal	*three times*
viermal	*four times*
hundertmal	*a hundred times*
etc.	etc.

Das habe ich dir schon **dreimal** gesagt.
I already said that to you three times.

Exercise 3: *Complete with the numbers or words in parentheses in German.*

1. Wieviel kostet dieser Hut? _____.   (DM 15,90)
2. Wie hoch ist die Arbeitslosigkeit in dieser Stadt? _____.
   (10,3%)
3. Das Wirtschaftswunder begann in den _____ Jahren.   (*fifties*)
4. Nach dem Streit haben sie einander nur noch _____ gesehen.
   (*once*)
5. Die Kassiererin hat mir einen _____ zu viel gegeben.   (*50 Mark bill*)
6. Ich jogge _____ die Woche.   (*three times*)

Ordinal Numbers

Ordinal numbers assign rank to something, or, in other words, they are used to order items (*first, second, third,* etc).

To form ordinal numbers, add **-t-** to the cardinal numbers through 19; add **-st-** to numbers 20 and up. The exceptions to this rule are boldface in the chart below.

1–19 : **-t-**

1. (der, das, die) **erste**
2. zweite
3. **dritte**
4. vierte
5. fünfte
6. sechste
7. **siebte** (*less common:* siebente)
8. **achte**
9. neunte
10. zehnte
11. elfte

20– : **-st-**

20. (der, das, die) zwanzigste
21. einundzwanzigste
22. zweiundzwanzigste
30. dreißigste
40. vierzigste
100. hundertste
1000. tausendste

Ordinal numbers are adjectives and therefore take an adjective ending.

Unsere Sitzplätze sind in der neunt**en** Reihe.
Our seats are in the ninth row.

Der erst**e** Tag des Monats ist Zahltag.
The first day of the month is payday.

A period placed immediately after a number indicates an ordinal number.

Unsere Sitzplätze sind in der **9.** Reihe.
Der **1.** Tag des Monats ist Zahltag.

Exercise 4: *Complete with the ordinal number.*

1. (II.)   Nach dem Ende des _____ Weltkriegs wurde
            Deutschland in vier Besatzungszonen geteilt.
2. (8.)   Meine Freundin wohnt im _____ Stock.
3. (17.)   Der 30jährige Krieg fand im _____ Jahrhundert statt.
4. (3.)   Peter ist der _____ Sohn der Familie.
5. (9.)   Beethovens berühmteste Sinfonie ist die _____.

6. (7.)   Die schwangere Frau ist im _____ Monat.
7. (42.) Bill Clinton ist der _____ amerikanische Präsident.
8. (1.)   Die Pyramiden sind das _____ Weltwunder.

OTHER USES OF ORDINAL NUMBERS

Fractions. Fractions are formed by adding **-el** to the ordinal number. They can be used as nouns or adjectives.

NOUNS	ADJECTIVES
1/2 = eine Hälfte	halb-
1/4 = ein Viertel	ein viertel
1/5 = ein Fünftel	ein fünftel
1/20 = ein Zwanzigstel	ein zwanzigstel
3/4 = drei Viertel	dreiviertel
5/8 = fünf Achtel	fünf achtel
2/15 = zwei Fünfzehntel	zwei fünfzehntel

When used as nouns, fractions are neuter, with the exception of **die Hälfte** (*half*).

Ein Viertel der Studenten hat die Grippe.
A quarter of the students have the flu.

Wenn ich so spät aufstehe, ist **die Hälfte** des Tages schon vorbei.
When I get up so late, half of the day is already gone.

When used as adjectives, fractions are not capitalized and, with the exception of **halb-**, do not have adjective endings. Three-quarters is written as one word: **dreiviertel**.

Für den Kuchen braucht man ein **viertel** Pfund Butter und **dreiviertel** Pfund Zucker.
For the cake you need one-quarter of a pound of butter and three-quarters of a pound of sugar.

Das Kind trank eine **halbe** Flasche Apfelsaft.
The child drank a half bottle of apple juice.

In compounds, **halb-** occurs without adjective endings.

1 1/2 = eineinhalb
        anderthalb
2 1/2 = zweieinhalb

3 1/2 = dreieinhalb
  etc.

Ich habe nur **eineinhalb** Wochen Ferien.
I only have a week and a half of vacation.

Das Fieber dauerte **viereinhalb** Tage.
The fever lasted four and a half days.

Ordinal Number + -ens. Adverbs ordering a sequence of points (*first, second, third,* etc.) may be formed by adding **-ens** to the ordinal number.

erstens	*first(ly); in the first place*
zweitens	*second(ly); in the second place*
drittens	*third(ly); in the third place*
viertens	*fourth(ly); in the fourth place*
etc.	etc.

Ich komme heute nicht. Ich habe **erstens** kein Geld und **zweitens** keine Lust.
I'm not coming today. First (first of all; in the first place) I have no money and second no desire.

Ordinal Number + *Mal*. Ordinal numbers may be used as adjectives before **Mal** (*time*) to indicate frequency.

das erste Mal	*the first time*
das zweite Mal	*the second time*
das dritte Mal	*the third time*
etc.	etc.
zum ersten Mal	*for the first time*
zum zweiten Mal	*for the second time*
zum dritten Mal	*for the third time*
etc.	etc.

Zum ersten Mal im Leben muβte sie selbständig sein.
For the first time in her life she had to be independent.

Exercise 5: *Complete with the German equivalent of the cue words.*

 1. Ich lerne seit _____ Jahren Deutsch. (*two and a half years*)
 2. Sie belegt diesen Kurs _____. (*for the second time*)
 3. _____ der Klasse fehlen heute. (*Two-thirds*)
 4. Die Militärtruppen haben _____ der Altstadt zerstört. (*half*)

5. Ich will nicht mit ins Kino, weil ich _____ den Film schon gesehen habe und _____ kein Geld habe.   (*first of all; second of all*)
6. Das war _____, daβ ich im Ausland war.   (*the first time*)
7. Als sie sich _____ trafen, machte mein Groβvater meiner Groβmutter einen Heiratsantrag.   (*for the fourth time*)
8. Die Erben der reichen Dame bekamen alle _____ ihres Vermögens.   (*one-tenth*)

DAYS AND PARTS OF THE DAY

The days of the week and parts of the day (with the exception of **die Nacht** and **die Mitternacht**) are masculine.

der Montag	*Monday*
der Dienstag	*Tuesday*
der Mittwoch	*Wednesday*
der Donnerstag	*Thursday*
der Freitag	*Friday*
der Samstag/der Sonnabend	*Saturday*
der Sonntag	*Sunday*
der Morgen	*morning*
der Vormittag	*morning; before noon*
der Mittag	*noon*
der Nachmittag	*afternoon*
der Abend	*evening*
die Nacht	*night* (after 10:00 P.M.)
die Mitternacht	*midnight*

The Contraction am

To express phrases of time in German, the days of the week and the parts of the day are used with the contraction **am** (**an dem**).

am Montag	*on Monday*
am Dienstag	*on Tuesday*
am Mittwoch	*on Wednesday*
etc.	etc.
am Morgen	*in the morning*
am Vormittag	*in the morning*
am Nachmittag	*in the afternoon*
am Abend	*in the evening*

There are three exceptions.

zu Mittag	*at noon*
in der Nacht	*at night*
um Mitternacht	*at midnight*

As in English, the preposition may be omitted with days of the week.

(Am) Montag muβt du zum Zahnarzt.
(On) Monday you have to go to the dentist.

Day + Time of Day

When combined with a day, times of the day are not capitalized.

(Am) Montag **morgen** muβ ich zum Zahnarzt.
(On) Monday morning I have to go to the dentist.

(Am) Freitag **abend** gehen wir essen.
(On) Friday evening we're going out to eat.

Repeated Time

To form adverbs expressing repeated or habitual occurrences, add -**s** to the day of the week or part of the day. As adverbs, these expressions are not capitalized.

Wir gehen **sonntags** immer in die Kirche.
Sundays we always go to church.

Ich kann **abends** am besten lernen.
I can study best evenings.

Other Adverbs of Time

Here are other common adverbs of time.

vorgestern	*the day before yesterday*
gestern	*yesterday*
heute	*today*
morgen	*tomorrow*
übermorgen	*the day after tomorrow*

Gestern, **heute**, and **morgen** are frequently used together with parts of the day to form new adverbs.

gestern

gestern morgen	*yesterday morning*
gestern vormittag	*yesterday morning*
gestern mittag	*yesterday noon*

gestern nachmittag	*yesterday afternoon*
gestern abend	*yesterday evening; last night*
gestern nacht	*last night*

heute

heute morgen	*this morning*
heute vormittag	*this morning*
heute mittag	*this noon*
heute nachmittag	*this afternoon*
heute abend	*this evening; tonight*
heute nacht	*tonight*

morgen

morgen früh	*tomorrow morning*
morgen vormittag	*tomorrow morning*
morgen mittag	*tomorrow noon*
morgen nachmittag	*tomorrow afternoon*
morgen abend	*tomorrow evening; tomorrow night*
morgen nacht	*tomorrow night*

MONTHS AND SEASONS

The months and seasons are masculine.

der Januar	der Juli
der Februar	der August
der März	der September
der April	der Oktober
der Mai	der November
der Juni	der Dezember

der Winter	*winter*
der Frühling	*spring*
der Sommer	*summer*
der Herbst	*fall*

The Contraction im

To express phrases of time in German, the months and seasons use the contraction **im** (**in dem**).

im Januar	im Winter
im Februar	im Frühling
im März	im Sommer
im April	im Herbst
etc.	

OTHER UNITS OF TIME

Other common units of time include the following:

die Sekunde -n   *second*
die Minute -n   *minute*
die Stunde -n   *hour*
der Tag -e   *day*
der Wochentag -e   *weekday*
die Woche -n   *week*
das Wochenende -n   *weekend*
der Monat -e   *month*
die Jahreszeit -en   *season*
das Jahr -e   *year*

Time + -lang

To express a length of time, the suffix **-lang** may be added to the plural form of many time units. The resulting adverb is not capitalized.

Sie wohnte **jahrelang** in Berlin.
She lived in Berlin for years.

Es regnete **tagelang.**
It rained for days.

Time + -lich

Some time units may add the suffix **-lich** (equivalent to English *-ly*). The resulting adverb or adjective frequently adds an umlaut and is not capitalized.

täglich   *daily*
wöchentlich   *weekly*
monatlich   *monthly*
jährlich   *yearly*

CASE WITH TIME EXPRESSIONS

Time expressions take the accusative, dative, or genitive case. (For additional examples and a more complete review of case with time expressions, see chapter 2.)

Time Expressions with the Accusative Case

The accusative case is used with durative and definite time expressions without a preposition. Common accusative time expressions include the following:

einen ganzen Tag; das ganze Jahr	*a whole day; the whole year*
jeden Sommer; jedes Wochenende	*every summer; every weekend*
jeden zweiten Tag/alle zwei Tage	*every other day*
nächste Woche; nächstes Jahr	*next week; next year*
diese Woche; diesen Herbst	*this week; this fall*
vorige Woche/letzte Woche	*last week*
guten Morgen; guten Tag	*good morning; good day*
übernächste Woche	*the week after next*

Time Expressions with the Dative Case

The dative case is used in time expressions after the prepositions **an** (*on, in*), **in** (*in*), and **vor** (*ago*).

an Wochentagen	*on weekdays*
am Wochenende	*on the weekend*
in einem Jahr; **in** einer Sekunde	*in a year; in a second*
heute **in** acht Tagen	*a week from today*
zweimal **im** Jahr; einmal **im** Monat	*twice a year; once a month*
vor einem Monat; **vor** einer Stunde	*a month ago; an hour ago*
vor kurzem; vor einiger Zeit	*a little while ago; a while ago*

Time Expressions with the Genitive Case

The genitive case is used to denote indefinite time.

eines Tages; **eines** Nachts	*one day; one night*

Exercise 6: *Complete with the German equivalents of the cue phrases.*

1. _____ sind meine Ferien zu Ende. (*On Monday; On Friday*)
2. _____ bekommen wir Besuch aus Deutschland. (*Next week; Next Wednesday; Next summer*)
3. Wir arbeiteten _____ an dem Plan. (*for hours; for weeks; for years*)
4. *Die Zeit* erscheint _____. (*weekly*)
5. _____ möchte ich nach Deutschland zurückfahren. (*One day*)
6. Mein Haus wird _____ geputzt. (*every other week; every other month*)
7. _____ muß ich einkaufen gehen. (*This afternoon; Tomorrow morning; Tomorrow afternoon*)
8. _____ ist ihre Lieblingsjahreszeit. (*The fall; The spring*)
9. Die Studenten bekommen ihre Noten _____. (*twice a year; three times a year*)
10. _____ beginnt das Wetter wieder schön zu werden. (*In March; In April; In May*)
11. Es gibt _____ viele Partys. (*on the weekend; on Saturday night*)

12. Leider muß ich _____ lernen.   (*the whole night; the whole day; the whole weekend*)
13. _____ hast du noch gesagt, du würdest mich nie vergessen.   (*A little while ago*)
14. Ich habe dich _____ zum letzten Mal gesehen.   (*last week; last year; last month*)
15. Sie grüßen sich _____.   (*every morning; every day; every evening*)

DATES

There are two common ways to ask for and give dates in German.

Der wievielte ist heute?   **Den wievielten** haben wir heute?
What's the date today?

Heute ist **der** 21. Januar.   Heute haben wir **den** 21. Januar.
Today is January 21.

Note that the first way to give the date is in the nominative case, the second in the accusative case.

In time phrases, dates are preceded by the dative contraction **am**.

Ich bin **am** 17. September geboren.
I was born on September 17.

Die Ausstellung findet **am** 24. August statt.
The exhibit is taking place on August 24.

Dates on Letters and Forms

Dates on letters and forms are in the accusative case. Unlike English, where the month is given first, in German the day precedes the month. In other words, the German method proceeds from the shortest to the longest unit: day—month—year.

Geboren: 3. 5. 1970   **(den dritten Mai)**
Gestorben: 21. 11. 2060   **(den einundzwanzigsten November)**

For letters, the place often precedes the date.

Freiburg, den 15. Juni 1993
Salzburg, den 30. April 1994

Expressing a Year

There are two ways to express a year in German: either the year alone or the year with the phrase **im Jahre**.

1991 studierte ich in Deutschland.
Im Jahre 1991 studierte ich in Deutschland.

Note that the English method of expressing years *(in 1991)* is not possible in German.

Exercise 7: *Complete with the German equivalents of the cue expressions.*

1. _____ feierten die Deutschen ihren ersten Tag der deutschen Einheit. *(On October 3, 1990)*
2. Sie haben _____ geheiratet. *(in 1990)*
3. Heute haben wir _____. *(January 30)*
4. _____ wird auch in Deutschland dazu benutzt, Leute in den April zu schicken. *(April 1)*
5. Morgen ist _____. *(February 28)*
6. Wir fliegen _____ von New York ab. *(on September 3)*
7. Hier auf diesem Formular mußt du deinen Geburtstag angeben: _____. *(11/27/1972)*
8. Helmut Kohl ist _____ geboren. *(in 1930)*

TELLING TIME

Colloquial Time

In colloquial German, clock time is expressed in the following manner:

WRITTEN	SPOKEN
9.00 Uhr	Es ist neun (Uhr).
9.10 Uhr	Es ist zehn (Minuten) nach neun.
9.15 Uhr	Es ist Viertel nach neun.
	Es ist Viertel zehn. *(Southern German and Austrian)*
9.20 Uhr	Es ist zwanzig (Minuten) nach neun.
9.25 Uhr	Es ist fünfundzwanzig (Minuten) nach neun.
	Es ist fünf vor halb zehn.
9.30 Uhr	Es ist halb zehn.
9.35 Uhr	Es ist fünf nach halb zehn.
	Es ist fünfundzwanzig (Minuten) vor zehn.
9.40 Uhr	Es ist zwanzig (Minuten) vor zehn.
9.45 Uhr	Es ist Viertel vor zehn.
	Es ist drei Viertel zehn. *(Southern German and Austrian)*
9.50 Uhr	Es ist zehn (Minuten) vor zehn.
10.00 Uhr	Es ist zehn (Uhr).

Note that German uses a period instead of a colon to write time.

Note that the following time expressions refer to the hour to come, not the preceding one:

Viertel zehn	*a quarter (of the way) to ten*
halb zehn	*half way to ten*
drei Viertel zehn	*three-quarters (of the way) to ten*

There are two ways to express 1:00 in German.

Es ist ein Uhr.
OR
Es ist eins.

Colloquially, adverbs are used to express A.M. or P.M.

Es ist zwei Uhr **morgens**.	*It's 2:00 in the morning.*
Es ist zwei Uhr **nachmittags**.	*It's 2:00 in the afternoon.*
Es ist elf Uhr **vormittags**.	*It's 11:00 in the morning.*
Es ist elf Uhr **nachts**.	*It's 11:00 at night.*

The preposition **um** means *at* in time expressions.

Um wieviel Uhr kommen die Gäste?

At what time are the guests coming?

Sie kommen **um** acht.
They're coming at 8:00.

Exercise 8: *Express the following times in colloquial German.*

1. It's 4:00.	6. It's 7:45.
2. It's 3:15.	7. It's 2:40.
3. It's 7:25.	8. It's 6:30 P.M.
4. It's 1:00.	9. It's 10:00 P.M.
5. It's 9:30.	10. It's 11:00 A.M.

Official Time

Official time in Germany uses the 24-hour clock. Official time is found in schedules for public transportation, the media, businesses, the government, and so on.

WRITTEN	SPOKEN
18.00	Es ist achtzehn Uhr.
18.10	Es ist achtzehn Uhr zehn.
18.15	Es ist achtzehn Uhr fünfzehn.
18.30	Es ist achtzehn Uhr dreißig.
18.45	Es ist achtzehn Uhr fünfundvierzig.
18.50	Es ist achtzehn Uhr fünfzig.
19.00	Es ist neunzehn Uhr.

Exercise 9: *Express the following in official time.*

1. 9:30 P.M.
2. 2:15 P.M.
3. 3:20 A.M.
4. 7:00 P.M.

5. 10:35 P.M.
6. 6:00 A.M.
7. 4:10 P.M.
8. 8:45 P.M.

ANSWERS TO EXERCISES

1.

1. drei
2. vierundzwanzig
3. siebenundsiebzig
4. (ein)hunderteins
5. hundertneunundachtzig
6. dreihundertdreiunddreißig
7. vierhundertsiebzehn
8. achthunderteinundneunzig
9. neunhundertneunundneunzig
10. (ein)tausend
11. achttausendfünfhundertsechs-undsiebzig
12. zehntausendeins
13. hunderttausendsechshundertacht
14. eine Million dreihundertfünf-undsechzigtausendneunhun-dertzwei
15. dreizehn Millionen zweihun-dertzwei

2.

1. eins plus/und eins ist zwei
2. elf minus/weniger acht ist drei
3. dreizehn plus/und zwölf ist fünf-undzwanzig
4. vier mal sieben ist achtundzwanzig
5. (ein)hundertsechsundsiebzig minus/weniger fünfundvierzig ist (ein)hunderteinunddreißig
6. dreiunddreißig (geteilt) durch drei ist elf
7. (ein)hundert mal sieben ist siebenhundert
8. achtundachtzig (geteilt) durch vier ist zweiundzwanzig
9. (ein)tausendsiebenhundertfünf plus/und eins ist (ein)tausend-siebenhundertsechs

10. fünfhundert minus/weniger fünfundzwanzig ist vierhundert-fünfundsiebzig

3.

1. Fünfzehn Mark neunzig.
2. Zehn Komma drei Prozent.
3. fünfziger
4. einmal
5. Fünfziger
6. dreimal

4.

1. zweiten
2. achten
3. siebzehnten
4. dritte
5. neunte
6. siebten (siebenten)
7. zweiundvierzigste
8. erste

5.

1. zweieinhalb
2. zum zweiten Mal
3. Zwei Drittel
4. die Hälfte
5. erstens; zweitens
6. das erste Mal
7. zum vierten Mal
8. ein Zehntel

6.

1. Am Montag; Am Freitag
2. Nächste Woche; Nächsten Mittwoch; Nächsten Sommer
3. stundenlang; wochenlang; jahrelang
4. wöchentlich
5. Eines Tages

6. jede zweite Woche/alle zwei Wochen; jeden zweiten Monat/alle zwei Monate
7. Heute nachmittag; Morgen früh/Morgen vormittag; Morgen nachmittag
8. (Der) Herbst; (Der) Frühling
9. zweimal im Jahr; dreimal im Jahr
10. Im März; Im April; Im Mai
11. am Wochenende; am Samstag abend
12. die ganze Nacht; den ganzen Tag; das ganze Wochenende
13. Vor kurzem
14. letzte/vorige Woche; letztes/voriges Jahr; letzten/vorigen Monat
15. jeden Morgen; jeden Tag; jeden Abend

7.

1. Am 3. Oktober 1990
2. im Jahre 1990/1990
3. den 30. Januar
4. Der 1. April
5. der 28. Februar
6. am 3. September
7. 27. 11. 1972
8. im Jahre 1930/1930

8.

1. Es ist vier (Uhr).
2. Es ist Viertel nach drei. Es ist Viertel vier.
3. Es ist fünf vor halb acht. Es ist fünfundzwanzig (Minuten) nach sieben.
4. Es ist ein Uhr. Es ist eins.

5. Es ist halb zehn.
6. Es ist Viertel vor acht. Es ist drei Viertel acht.
7. Es ist zwanzig (Minuten) vor drei.
8. Es ist halb sieben abends.
9. Es ist zehn Uhr abends.

10. Es ist elf Uhr morgens. Es ist elf Uhr vormittags.

9.

1. einundzwanzig Uhr dreißig
2. vierzehn Uhr fünfzehn
3. drei Uhr zwanzig

4. neunzehn Uhr
5. zweiundzwanzig Uhr fünfunddreißig
6. sechs Uhr
7. sechzehn Uhr zehn
8. zwanzig Uhr fünfundvierzig

PART TWO:
GERMAN VERBS

7

Verb Tenses

There are six verb tenses in German: the present tense, the simple past tense, the present perfect tense, the past perfect tense, the future tense, and the future perfect tense.

The formation of the verb tenses depends on whether the verb is weak or strong. Weak verbs do not change their stem vowels and follow patterns that, once memorized, can be applied to other weak verbs, even those you have not learned. Strong verbs, on the other hand, change their stem vowel and these changes must be memorized individually. The exercises in this chapter will practice the usage and formation of both weak verbs and the most common strong verbs.

PRESENT TENSE

The Infinitive and the Verb Stem

The *infinitive* of the verb is the form under which it is listed in a dictionary. It is the form before conjugation of any type and usually ends in -**en**, sometimes in -**n**.

spielen	*to play*	tun	*to do*
schreiben	*to write*	sammeln	*to collect*
finden	*to find*		
atmen	*to breathe*		
heiβen	*to be called*		
sitzen	*to sit*		

The *verb stem* is the infinitive without the -**en** or -**n** ending.

spiel-   tu-
schreib-   sammel-
find-
atm-
heiß-
sitz-

Present Tense Endings

To form the present tense, add the following endings to the verb stem:

ich	-e	wir	-en
du	-st	ihr	-t
er/es/sie	-t	sie	-en
	Sie	-en	

spielen		**schreiben**	
ich	spiele	ich	schreibe
du	spielst	du	schreibst
er/es/sie	spielt	er/es/sie	schreibt
wir	spielen	wir	schreiben
ihr	spielt	ihr	schreibt
sie	spielen	sie	schreiben
Sie	spielen	Sie	schreiben

IRREGULARITIES IN PRESENT TENSE ENDINGS

Infinitives ending in -*n*. The **wir**, **sie** (*they*), and **Sie** forms are always identical to the infinitive. This means that if the infinitive ends in **-n**, the **wir**, **sie** (*they*), and **Sie** endings are **-n**, rather than **-en**.

sammeln		**tun**	
ich	sammele	ich	tue
du	sammelst	du	tust
er/es/sie	sammelt	er/es/sie	tut
wir	sammeln	wir	tun
ihr	sammelt	ihr	tut
sie	sammeln	sie	tun
Sie	sammeln	Sie	tun

Frequently, if the verb stem ends in -**el**, the **e** is omitted in the first person singular (the **ich** form): **ich samm(e)le.**

Exercise 1: *Restate using the cue subject.*

1. ich besuche   (du)
2. ihr sammelt   (wir)
3. er lernt   (ich)
4. sie spielen   (Sie)
5. sie kennt   (du)
6. wir tun   (sie [*she*])
7. Sie trinken   (ihr)
8. wir stören   (es)
9. er segelt   (ich)
10. sie bleibt   (sie [*they*])

Verb Stems Ending in -*d*, -*t*, or Consonant Clusters. If the verb stem ends in **-d**, **-t**, or certain consonant clusters, the endings **-st** and **-t** become **-est** and **-et** to facilitate pronunciation.

finden		**atmen**	
ich	finde	ich	atme
du	findest	du	atmest
er/es/sie	findet	er/es/sie	atmet
wir	finden	wir	atmen
ihr	findet	ihr	atmet
sie	finden	sie	atmen
Sie	finden	Sie	atmen

Verb stems ending in **-d** or **-t** are fairly common.

antworten	*to answer*	heiraten	*to marry*
arbeiten	*to work*	kosten	*to cost*
baden	*to bathe*	mieten	*to rent*
bedeuten	*to mean*	reden	*to speak*
bitten	*to ask (for)*	warten	*to wait*
finden	*to find*		

Verb stems ending in **-m** or **-n** preceded by another consonant (except **-l** or **-r**) are less common.

atmen	*to breathe*	regnen	*to rain*
öffnen	*to open*	rechnen	*to calculate*

Verb Stems Ending in an *s* Sound. If the verb stem ends in an **s** sound (**-s**, **-ss**, **-β**, **-tz**, **-z**), the second person singular (the **du** form) adds only **-t**.

heiβen		**sitzen**	
ich	heiβe	ich	sitze
du	heiβt	du	sitzt
er/es/sie	heiβt	er/es/sie	sitzt

wir heißen	wir sitzen
ihr heißt	ihr sitzt
sie heißen	sie sitzen
Sie heißen	Sie sitzen

Note that for these verbs, the **du** form is identical to the **er/es/sie** and the **ihr** forms. This type of verb is fairly common.

grüßen	*to greet*	schließen	*to close*
lassen	*to let, leave*	setzen	*to set*
putzen	*to clean*	tanzen	*to dance*
reisen	*to travel*	wachsen	*to grow*

Exercise 2: *Restate using the cue subject.*

1. Frau Meier arbeitet in einem Büro.   (ich)
2. Ich heiße Bruno.   (er)
3. Wir reisen jedes Jahr nach Österreich.   (sie [*she*])
4. Sie atmen schwer.   (der Sportler)
5. Sammelst du Briefmarken?   (ihr)
6. Ich schließe die Tür.   (du)
7. Wieviel kosten zwei Kassetten?   (eine Kassette)
8. Stefanie und Markus reden zu schnell.   (Stefanie)
9. Hassen Sie mich?   (du)
10. Wann heiraten Alexandra und Tobias?   (ihr)

Vowel Changes in the Verb Stem

Some verbs change the stem vowel in the second and third person singular (the **du** and **er/es/sie** forms). These are all strong verbs and you must learn to identify them. All verbs with stem vowel change used in this text are listed in Appendix B. These verbs fall into two categories according to their stem vowel change.

STEM VOWEL CHANGE: *e* → *i* AND *e* → *ie*

e → i	**e → ie**
geben	**sehen**
ich gebe	ich sehe
du gibst	du siehst
er/es/sie gibt	er/es/sie sieht
wir geben	wir sehen
ihr gebt	ihr seht
sie geben	sie sehen
Sie geben	Sie sehen

e → i		e → ie	
brechen	*to break*	befehlen	*to order*
essen	*to eat*	empfehlen	*to recommend*
geben	*to give*	geschehen	*to happen*
helfen	*to help*	lesen	*to read*
nehmen	*to take*	sehen	*to see*
sprechen	*to speak*	stehlen	*to steal*
sterben	*to die*		
treffen	*to meet*		
treten	*to step*		
vergessen	*to forget*		
werfen	*to throw*		

Two verbs, **nehmen** and **treten**, have a consonant change in addition to changing their stem vowel from **e** to **i**.

nehmen		**treten**	
ich	nehme	ich	trete
du	**nimm**st	du	**tritt**st
er/es/sie	**nimm**t	er/es/sie	**tritt**
wir	nehmen	wir	treten
ihr	nehmt	ihr	tretet
sie	nehmen	sie	treten
Sie	nehmen	Sie	treten

STEM VOWEL CHANGE: *a → ä* AND *au → äu*

a → ä		**au → äu**	
fahren		**laufen**	
ich	fahre	ich	laufe
du	**fähr**st	du	**läuf**st
er/es/sie	**fähr**t	er/es/sie	**läuf**t
wir	fahren	wir	laufen
ihr	fahrt	ihr	lauft
sie	fahren	sie	laufen
Sie	fahren	Sie	laufen

a → ä		**au → äu**	
backen	*to bake*	laufen	*to walk*
fahren	*to drive*		
fallen	*to fall*		
fangen	*to catch*		
halten	*to hold*		

a → ä

laden	*to load*
lassen	*to let, leave*
raten	*to advise*
schlafen	*to sleep*
schlagen	*to hit, strike*
tragen	*to carry; to wear*
wachsen	*to grow*
waschen	*to wash*

Three verbs, **halten**, **laden**, and **raten**, in addition to a stem vowel change from **a** to **ä**, do not add the **e** in the second and third person singular that is expected after verb stems ending in -**d** or -**t**.

	halten	**laden**	**raten**
ich	halte	lade	rate
du	**hältst**	**lädst**	**rätst**
er/es/sie	**hält**	**lädt**	**rät**
wir	halten	laden	raten
ihr	haltet	ladet	ratet
sie	halten	laden	raten
Sie	halten	laden	raten

Only one common verb has a stem vowel change from **o** to **ö**: **stoβen** (to push).

Exercise 3: *Restate using the cue subject.*

1. ihr haltet   (du)
2. ich laufe   (er)
3. wir stehlen (du)
4. es nimmt   (ihr)
5. sie liest   (ich)
6. sie treten   (sie [*she*])
7. Sie sprechen   (du)
8. wir schlafen   (er)
9. ich empfehle   (sie [*she*])
10. sie fährt   (ihr)

Exercise 4: *Complete with the appropriate form of the cue verb.*

1. Karin _____ nie genug.   (schlafen)
2. Ich _____ ein gutes Buch.   (lesen)
3. Herbert _____ jeden Tag 100 Kilometer zur Arbeit.   (fahren)
4. Meine Schwester _____ nur ab und zu.   (laufen)
5. Das Kind _____ unglaublich schnell.   (wachsen)
6. Warum _____ du nie Jeans?   (tragen)
7. Was _____ die Frau dir?   (raten)
8. Ich hoffe, er _____ unsere Verabredung nicht.   (vergessen)
9. Herr Hoffmann _____ gern Kuchen.   (backen)
10. _____ du den Ball, wenn ich ihn _____?   (fangen; werfen)

Present Tense *of* haben, sein, werden, *and* wissen

Because **haben** (*to have*), **sein** (*to be*), and **werden** (*to become*) are used so frequently and because they follow no consistent pattern, their forms should be memorized thoroughly.

	haben	**sein**	**werden**
ich	habe	bin	werde
du	hast	bist	wirst
er/es/sie	hat	ist	wird
wir	haben	sind	werden
ihr	habt	seid	werdet
sie	haben	sind	werden
Sie	haben	sind	werden

Exercise 5: *Complete with the correct form of* **haben, sein,** *or* **werden.**

1. _____ du krank?   (werden)
2. Wie _____ das Wetter heute?   (sein)
3. Den wievielten _____ wir heute?   (haben)
4. Meine Eltern _____ nicht zu Hause.   (sein)
5. Was _____ ihr gegen uns?   (haben)
6. Im Frühling _____ die Tage immer länger.   (werden)
7. Inge _____ Psychiaterin.   (werden)
8. _____ du Zeit?   (haben)
9. Warum _____ du noch hier?   (sein)
10. Tobias _____ bald Geburtstag.   (haben)

The present tense forms of **wissen** are also irregular.

wissen   *to know as a fact*

ich	weiß	wir	wissen
du	weißt	ihr	wißt
er/es/sie	weiß	sie	wissen
		Sie	wissen

Wissen means to know as a fact or to have information about something; it should not be confused with **kennen**, which means to be familiar with something or someone. Compare the following sentences:

Ich **weiß**, wo Berlin liegt.	*I know where Berlin is.*
Ich **kenne** Berlin gut.	*I am well acquainted with Berlin.*
Ich **weiß** ihren Namen.	*I know her name.*
Ich **kenne** sie nicht.	*I don't know her. I'm not acquainted with her.*

Exercise 6: *Complete with the correct form of* **wissen** *or* **kennen**.

1. _____ du, wann das Seminar beginnt?
2. _____ du die Professorin?
3. Ich _____ sie nicht, aber ich _____ ihr Buch ziemlich gut.
4. Er glaubt, er _____ mich gut, aber er _____ nichts von mir.
5. Außer mir _____ alle die Antwort.
6. Nur noch wenige Leute _____, wie man Plattdeutsch spricht.
7. _____ du den Mann, der uns gerade gegrüßt hat?
8. _____ ihr nicht, daß das verboten ist?

Usage of the Present Tense

The present tense is used to express an action occurring in the present time. In contrast to English, which has three possible forms, German has only one present tense form.

Sie arbeitet den ganzen Tag.	*She works all day.*
	She is working all day.
	She does work all day.

Arbeitet sie den ganzen Tag?	*Is she working all day?*
	Does she work all day?

Like English, German frequently uses the present tense to express future time if the context or a time phrase makes it clear that the future is meant.

Sie **arbeitet** morgen.	*She's going to work tomorrow.*
	She's working tomorrow.

Exercise 7: *Translate into German.*

1. She's flying to Germany.
2. He's playing golf next Saturday.
3. They're coming home soon.
4. She's reading a good book.
5. Are you going to help me tomorrow?
6. Do they live here?
7. Why do you sleep so long?
8. They always eat in the dining room.
9. I recommend the red wine.
10. I'm meeting my girlfriend in the restaurant.

If an action began in the past but continues into the present, German uses the present tense plus **schon** or (**schon**) **seit** to introduce the time element. English uses the present perfect tense to express continuing time.

Ich lerne **seit** einem Jahr Deutsch.
I have been studying German for one year.

Wie lange wohnst du **schon** hier?
How long have you been living here?

Exercise 8: *Answer the question in German, using the cue. Then translate your sentence into English.*

1. Wie lange wartest du schon?   (schon eine Stunde)
2. Seit wann seid ihr hier?   (seit Montag)
3. Wie lange regnet es schon?   (seit drei Tagen)
4. Seit wann kennt Robert Inge?   (schon drei Jahre)
5. Seit wann telefonierst du?   (seit zwei Stunden)

IMPERATIVES

Imperatives are verb forms used primarily to express orders, but also suggestions, wishes, and requests. There are three forms for every imperative corresponding to the three forms of address in German: **du**, **ihr**, and **Sie**. Commands usually close with an exclamation point. To make a command or request more polite, **bitte** (*please*) may be added.

The Familiar Singular Imperative: du

The familiar singular imperative consists of the verb stem plus an optional **-e** ending. The pronoun **du** is omitted.

Sag(e) das nicht!   *Don't say that.*
Lauf(e) bitte etwas schneller!   *Please walk a little faster.*
Schreib(e) mir bitte einen Brief!   *Please write me a letter.*

If the present tense verb undergoes a stem vowel change from **e** to **ie** or **i**, this stem vowel change is maintained in the imperative. These imperatives always omit the optional **-e** ending.

Lies das Buch!   *Read the book.*
Gib mir bitte mehr Geld!   *Please give me more money.*
Nimm noch ein Stück Kuchen!   *Take another piece of cake.*

To facilitate pronunciation, the optional **-e** ending must be used when the verb stem ends in **-d**, **-t**, or **-ig**, or **-m** or **-n** unless preceded by **l** or **r**.

Entschuldige mich bitte!   *Please excuse me.*
Bitte warte auf mich!   *Please wait for me.*
Atme langsamer!   *Breathe more slowly.*

Exercise 9: *Give the* **du** *imperatives of the following verbs.*

1. schlafen
2. gehen
3. sprechen
4. stehlen
5. essen

6. waschen
7. helfen
8. heiraten
9. reden
10. sehen

Exercise 10: *Complete with the* **du** *imperative form of the cue verb.*

1. _____ mir die Schlüssel!   (geben)
2. _____ mich bitte nicht wieder!   (beleidigen)
3. _____ deine Hausaufgaben!   (machen)
4. _____ diesen Namen nicht!   (vergessen)
5. _____ ihn bitte im Krankenhaus!   (besuchen)
6. _____ bitte etwas lauter!   (sprechen)
7. _____ nicht immer mit so scharfen Gewürzen!   (kochen)
8. _____ mir bitte, diese Tasche zu tragen!   (helfen)
9. _____ dir die Schuhe aus, bevor du ins Haus gehst!   (ziehen)
10. _____ mich endlich in Ruhe!   (lassen)
11. _____ mal wieder!   (schreiben)
12. _____ es dir nicht so zu Herzen und _____ darüber zu lachen!
    (nehmen; versuchen)

The Familiar Plural Imperative: ihr

The familiar plural imperative is identical to the present tense **ihr** form. For the imperative, however, the pronoun **ihr** is omitted.

Sagt das nicht!   *Don't say that.*
Lest das Buch!   *Read the book.*
Entschuldigt mich bitte! *Please excuse me.*

The Formal Imperative (Singular and Plural): Sie

The formal imperative is identical to the present tense **Sie**-form of the verb except that the word order is inverted: the pronoun subject follows the verb.

Sagen Sie das nicht!   *Don't say that.*
Lesen Sie das Buch!   *Read the book.*
Entschuldigen Sie mich bitte! *Please excuse me.*

The Imperative Forms of sein and werden

The imperative forms of **sein** and **werden** are exceptions to the rules above and must be learned separately.

Sei nicht nervös!   *Don't be nervous.*
Seid nicht nervös!
Seien Sie nicht nervös!

Werde nicht frech!   *Don't get smart.*
Werdet nicht frech!
Werden Sie nicht frech!

Exercise 11: *Change the singular imperatives to plural imperatives, first informal (**ihr** form) and then formal (**Sie**).*

1. Antworte sofort auf die Frage!
2. Trag bitte diesen Koffer für mich!
3. Bleib ruhig!
4. Sei nicht so unfreundlich!
5. Halte bitte mal kurz das Buch für mich!
6. Klag nicht so!
7. Laβ mich allein!
8. Lüg nicht wieder!
9. Lauf nicht so schnell!
10. Erklär mir das noch einmal!

Exercise 12: *Determine the person being addressed and then complete with the appropriate imperative form of the cue verb.*

1. Kinder, _____ bitte brav!   (sein)
2. Jutta, _____ dein Geld!   (sparen)
3. Markus, _____ dich nicht aus dem Fenster!   (lehnen)
4. Herr Koppensteiner, _____ so schnell wie möglich wieder gesund! (werden)
5. Daniel und Jens, _____ nicht miteinander! (streiten)
6. Frau Breuer, _____ mir bitte die Rechnung!   (schicken)
7. Susi, _____ es nicht so ernst!   (nehmen)
8. Herr und Frau Wagner, _____ sich bitte keine Sorgen! (machen)
9. Meine Damen und Herren, _____ nun das berühmte Theaterstück von Bertolt Brecht!   (sehen)
10. Janina, _____ mir bitte deine Telefonnummer!   (geben)

The wir Imperative

The **wir** imperative is identical to the present tense **wir** form of the verb except that the word order is inverted: the pronoun subject follows the verb. The **wir** imperative corresponds to *let's . . .* in English.

Gehen wir!	*Let's go.*
Trinken wir auf unser Wohl!	*Let's drink to our health.*
Machen wir die Hausaufgaben zusammen!	*Let's do the homework together.*

Using Infinitives as Imperatives

Infinitives are used frequently in German to direct commands to the general public.

Bitte nicht rauchen!   *Please don't smoke.*
Rechts fahren!   *Drive on the right.*

VERB PREFIXES

Verb prefixes change the meaning of the verb. They do not, however, change the conjugation of the verb. German has two basic types of verb prefixes: inseparable prefixes and separable prefixes.

Inseparable Prefixes

Inseparable prefixes are never separated from the verb. There are eight common inseparable prefixes.

be-
Was **bedeutet** das?
What does that mean?

emp-
Was **empfehlen** Sie?
What do you recommend?

ent-
Wer **entdeckt** die Antwort des Rätsels?
Who's going to discover the answer to the riddle?

er-
Die Professorin **erklärt** das Problem.
The professor explains the problem.

ge-
Die Stadt **gefällt** uns nicht.
We don't like the city.

miß-
Er **mißversteht** mich immer.
He always misunderstands me.

ver-
Der Junge **vermißt** seine Eltern.
The boy misses his parents.

zer-
Der Sturm **zerstört** das Dorf.
The storm is destroying the village.

With the exception of **miß-**, the inseparable prefixes are unstressed in pronunciation. **Miß-** is unstressed unless it precedes another unstressed prefix. Compare:

mi ́βverstehen   miβd ́euten

Separable Prefixes

Separable prefixes are separated from the verb to stand at the end of a main clause, which may be a statement, a question, or an imperative.

STATEMENT
Ich **bringe** mein Buch über Europa **mit**.
I'm bringing my book about Europe along.

QUESTION
Wann **holst** du deine Schwester vom Bahnhof **ab**?
When are you going to pick up your sister from the train station?

IMPERATIVE
Mach so schnell wie möglich die Tür **zu**!
Close the door as quickly as possible!

If the main verb also stands at the end of the clause, the separable prefix is rejoined to it.

Weißt du, wann der Zug **ankommt**?
Do you know when the train arrives?

Ich muß mein Referat **vorbereiten**.
I have to prepare my oral report.

Separable prefixes are normally adverbs or prepositions and they therefore have an independent meaning that may help you to deduce the meaning of the separable-prefix verb. Listed below are some common separable prefixes that are used in this text.

ab-   *off, down, away*
Man **reißt** das alte Haus **ab**.
They are demolishing (tearing down) the old house.

an-   *on, to, at*
Wann **kommt** der Zug **an**?
When does the train arrive?

auf-   *on, up*
Ich **stehe** jeden Morgen um 8 Uhr **auf**.
I get up every morning at 8 o'clock.

aus-   *out*
Heute abend **geht** sie mit ihrem Freund **aus**.
Tonight she's going out with her boyfriend.

ein-   *in, into*
Treten Sie bitte **ein**!
Please enter.

fort-   *away, forward*
Nach der Pause **setzt** sie ihre Arbeit **fort**.
She continues to work after the break.

los-   *loose, free*
Das Kind **läßt** den Luftballon **los**.
The child lets go (loose) of the balloon.

mit-   *with, along*
Was **nimmst** du **mit**?
What are you taking along?

nach-   *after*
Meine Uhr **geht nach**.
My watch is slow.

vor-   *before, in front of*
Diese Uhr **geht vor**.
This clock is fast.

weg-   *away*
Wirf bitte diese alten Sachen **weg**!
Please throw away these old things!

zu-   *to*
Die Eltern **hören** ihrem Kind nicht **zu**.
The parents aren't listening to their child.

zurück-   *back, behind*
Bring mir das Buch sofort **zurück**!
Bring that book back to me immediately.

zusammen-   *together*
Arbeiten die Kollegen gut **zusammen**?
Do the colleagues work well together?

A few verbs may be used as a separable prefix.

kennenlernen   Man **lernt** neue Leute auf einer Party **kennen**.
                You meet new people at a party.
spazierengehen Ich **gehe** im Wald **spazieren**.
                I'm going for a walk in the woods.

Separable prefixes always receive the stress in pronunciation.

ánkommen   náchholen   zurúcknehmen

Separable-prefix verbs are indicated in the end vocabulary with a period between the prefix and the base verb.

an.ziehen   mit.kommen   weg.gehen

Exercise 13: *Complete with the correct form of the cue verb.*

1. Du _____ zu viel Geld _____. (ausgeben)
2. Kristin, _____ ins Restaurant _____! (mitkommen)
3. Wer _____ deine teuren Wünsche? (bezahlen)
4. Eine Katastrophe _____ die Leute oft _____. (zusammen-bringen)
5. Kinder, _____ eure wärmste Kleidung _____! (anziehen)
6. _____ Sie mich oder nicht? (verstehen)
7. Die Katze _____ den Hund mit Miβtrauen _____. (ansehen)
8. Morgen _____ ich meinen neuen Computer. (bekommen)
9. Wir _____ _____, am Wochenende aufs Land zu fahren. (vorhaben)
10. Joachim _____ zum Auto _____. (zurückgehen)
11. _____ Sie mich bitte, daβ ich so früh anrufe! (entschuldigen)
12. Nicole _____ ihren Freund zum Volleyballspiel _____. (mit-nehmen)
13. Auf dem Internationalen Tanzfest _____ ich einen spanischen Tanz _____. (vortanzen)
14. Warum _____ die Regierung immer unsere Steuern? (erhöhen)
15. Der Wissenschaftler _____, seine Theorie zu beweisen. (ver-suchen)

Exercise 14: *Make complete sentences using the words provided.*

1. Ich / zurückgehen / gern / nach Berlin.
2. Wieviele Gäste / einladen / du?
3. Welchen Film / empfehlen / er?

4. Die Firma / entlassen / Tausende von Arbeitern.
5. Sie (*you*) / mißdeuten / meine Worte.
6. Dieser Reisepaß / gehören / Frau Becker.
7. Aufhören / mit dem Blödsinn, / Katrin!
8. Die Uhr / nachgehen / eine Stunde.
9. Der Pullover / gefallen / ihm / gut.
10. Helga, / zurückrufen / mich / bitte!
11. Sonntags / aufstehen / die Jugendlichen / erst um 11 Uhr.
12. Das Buch / beschreiben / die Kindheit des Autors.

HER AND *HIN* AS SEPARABLE PREFIXES

Her and **hin** are used frequently as separable prefixes. **Her** denotes motion toward the speaker or person concerned; **hin** indicates motion away from the speaker or person concerned.

Kommen Sie bitte **her**!   *Please come here.*
Gehen Sie bitte **hin**!   *Please go there.*

Her and **hin** can be used together with other separable prefixes. In this case, **her** or **hin** is joined to the other prefix.

Kommen Sie bitte **herein**!   *Please come in.*
Gehen wir zusammen **hinein**!   *Let's go in together.*

For some verbs, **her** and **hin** have lost their directional meaning.

herausbringen   *to publish*   hinrichten   *to execute*

Exercise 15: *Complete with* **her** *or* **hin** *as appropriate.*

1. Bleib bitte hier im Keller! Geh die Treppe nicht _____auf!
2. Sie kommt aus dem Haus _____aus und fährt schnell weg.
3. Mein kleiner Bruder klettert den Baum _____auf. Hoffentlich fällt er nicht _____unter.
4. Als Jochen durch die eine Tür in mein Zimmer _____einkam, ging Antje durch die andere Tür _____aus.
5. Komm, laß uns erst mal das Gepäck aus dem Auto _____aus holen.
6. Die Sonne schien durch das Fenster in das Zimmer _____ein. Ich öffnete das Fenster und sah _____aus.
7. Sie stiegen den Berg _____auf. Ich winkte zum Abschied.
8. Am Ende der Wanderung, mit dem Ziel vor Augen, liefen wir immer schneller den Berg _____unter.

MODAL VERBS

Modal auxiliaries, commonly called *modals*, express an attitude or feeling toward an action or event. There are six modal verbs in German.

Present Tense Forms

	dürfen	**können**	**mögen**	**müssen**	**sollen**	**wollen**
ich	darf	kann	mag	muβ	soll	will
du	darfst	kannst	magst	muβt	sollst	willst
er/es/sie	darf	kann	mag	muβ	soll	will
wir	dürfen	können	mögen	müssen	sollen	wollen
ihr	dürft	könnt	mögt	müβt	sollt	wollt
sie	dürfen	können	mögen	müssen	sollen	wollen
Sie	dürfen	können	mögen	müssen	sollen	wollen

Note that the first person singular (**ich**) and third person singular (**er/es/sie**) forms have no ending and are therefore identical.

Note that all of the modals except **sollen** have a stem vowel change throughout the singular.

Meanings of the Modals

Modals are used generally with a second verb in its infinitive form, without **zu**. In main clauses, the infinitive is placed at the end of the sentence.

Warum **muβt** du hier **bleiben**?   *Why do you have to stay here?*
Du **sollst** mehr **arbeiten**.   *You are supposed to work more.*

If the second verb is a separable-prefix verb, the prefix remains attached to the base verb in the infinitive.

Wann muβt du **aufstehen**?   *When do you have to get up?*
Er will nicht **mitkommen**.   *He doesn't want to come along.*

DÜRFEN

The modal **dürfen** expresses permission and means *may, to be allowed to*.

Du **darfst** die Prüfung wiederholen.
You may repeat the test.   You are permitted to repeat the test.

Darf ich bitte eine Katze haben?
May I please have a cat?

KÖNNEN

The modal **können** expresses ability and means *can, to be able to.*

Ich kann sehr viel schlafen.
I can sleep a lot.   I am able to sleep a lot.

Können Sie dieses Buch für mich bestellen?
Can you order this book for me?

Formal German maintains the distinction between **dürfen** (permission) and **können** (ability).

Darfst du schwimmen gehen?
May you go swimming?   Do you have permission to go swimming?

Kannst du schwimmen?
Can you swim?   Are you able to swim?   Do you know how to swim?

Like English, informal German often ignores this difference and uses **können** even where permission is meant.

MÖGEN

The modal **mögen** expresses a liking or personal preference and means *to like, care to.*

Ich **mag** das nicht hören.
I don't care to hear that.   I don't like hearing that.

Mögen is used generally in a negative statement or a question, without an infinitive. It expresses a (dis)like of something or someone.

Magst du diese Musik?	*Do you like this music?*
Ich **mag** ihn nicht	*I don't like him.*
Ich **mag** keinen Alkohol.	*I don't like alcohol.*

Mögen is used most frequently in its subjunctive form (see chapter 9): **möchten**.

möchten	*would like to*
ich möchte	wir möchten
du möchtest	ihr möchtet
er/es/sie möchte	sie möchten
Sie möchten	

Möchten Sie dieses Kleid kaufen?
Would you like to buy this dress?

Ich **möchte** bitte mitkommen.
I'd like to come along, please.

MÜSSEN

The modal **müssen** expresses necessity and means *must, to have to.*

Muβ ich jetzt nach Hause gehen?
Do I have to go home now?   Must I go home now?

Wir **müssen** um zehn zu Hause sein.
We have to be home at ten.

The negative of **müssen** expresses the lack of necessity. The person concerned still has a choice.

Ich **muβ** jetzt **nicht** nach Hause gehen.
I don't have to go home now (if I don't want to).

German uses the negative of **dürfen** to express *must not.* Compare the following sets of sentences:

Sie muβ nicht bleiben.   *She doesn't have to stay.*
Sie darf nicht bleiben.   *She mustn't stay.*
                             She can't stay.

Du muβt nicht mitkommen.   *You don't have to come along.*
Du darfst nicht mitkommen.   *You mustn't come along.*
                             You can't come along.

SOLLEN

The modal **sollen** expresses obligation and means *to be supposed to.*

Du **sollst** jetzt schlafen gehen.
You're supposed to go to bed now.

Wir **sollen** um neun da sein.
We're supposed to be there at nine.

WOLLEN

The modal **wollen** expresses desire or intention and means *to want to.*

Tina **will** nach Deutschland fahren.
Tina wants to go to Germany. Tina intends to go to Germany.

Ich **will** eine neue Wohnung finden.
I want to find a new apartment.

Exercise 16: *Insert the modal and change the sentence as necessary.*

1. Regnet es ausgerechnet jetzt?   (müssen)
2. Sie fahren nach Griechenland.   (wollen)
3. Bei Tests betrügen die Studenten nicht.   (dürfen)
4. Wir machen die Küche sauber.   (sollen)
5. Der Politiker erklärt uns seine Programme.   (müssen)
6. Das Kind telefoniert mit seiner Großmutter.   (dürfen)
7. Herr Hausmann findet den Kellerschlüssel nicht.   (können)
8. Sie geht gleich in die Bücherei.   (wollen)

Exercise 17: *Make complete sentences using the words provided.*

1. Du / müssen / lösen / das Problem.
2. Ich / dürfen / spielen / morgen Tennis.
3. Sie (*they*) / wollen / einladen / ihre Nachbarn.
4. Der Hund / dürfen / herumlaufen / frei.
5. Wir / sollen / lernen / für die Prüfung.
6. Wann / sollen / ankommen / der Zug?
7. Am Samstag / können / aufstehen / wir / spät.
8. Ich / können / kommen / heute erst später.
9. Die Arbeiter / müssen / arbeiten / schwer.
10. Ich / wollen / besuchen / meine Freunde.
11. Martina und Manfred / möchten / verreisen / gerne.
12. Ihr / sollen / reden / nicht immer so laut.

Exercise 18: *Complete with the correct form of the appropriate modal.*

1. Schwangere Frauen _____ nicht trinken.   (*to be supposed to*)
2. _____ du bitte mit dem Lärm aufhören?   (*can*)
3. Die Sekretärin _____ den ganzen Tag vor dem Computer sitzen. (*to have to*)
4. Sie (*she*) _____ lieber draußen arbeiten.   (*to want to*)
5. Man _____ nur im Flur rauchen.   (*may*)
6. Im Zoo _____ man die Tiere nicht füttern.   (*must*)
7. Ich _____ diese Farbe nicht.   (*to like*)
8. _____ Sie die Speisekarte sehen?   (*would like to*)
9. Warum _____ wir so lange warten?   (*must*)
10. _____ du heute abend mit mir essen gehen?   (*would like to*)
11. Silke und Torben _____ zu Hause viel helfen.   (*must*)
12. Wir _____ die Moschee nicht mit Schuhen betreten.   (*to be allowed to*)
13. Die meisten Leute _____ Weihnachten nicht arbeiten.   (*to have to*)
14. Das _____ du doch nicht machen!   (*to be supposed to*)
15. Ich _____ endlich mal wieder wandern gehen.   (*to want to*)

16. Der Tischler _____ den Schrank nicht bauen, weil er kein Holz hat. (*to be able to*)

17. Die Professoren _____ den Studenten erklären, warum die Grammatik so wichtig ist. (*would like to*)

18. Eva und Nina, das _____ ihr nie wieder machen! (*must*)

19. Ich _____ nicht immer Pizza essen. (*to want to*)

20. _____ ihr noch ein bißchen länger auf mich warten? (*can*)

Modals without the Infinitive

Modals can occur without an infinitive if the context makes the meaning of the sentence clear.

Ich **muß** nach Hause (gehen).
I have to go home.

Ich **kann** Deutsch (sprechen, schreiben, usw.).
I know German.   (I can speak it, write it, etc.)

Ich **will** ein neues Auto (haben).
I want (to have) a new car.

Kannst du mitkommen? Nein, ich **kann** nicht.
Can you come along? No, I can't (come along).

SIMPLE PAST TENSE

The *simple past tense* is used to describe connected past events. It is used more frequently in formal writing than in conversation and is therefore sometimes called the *narrative past*.

Weak Verbs in the Simple Past Tense

Weak verbs have no stem changes and follow predictable patterns. The basic pattern for forming the simple past tense of weak verbs is:

> verb stem + **te** + ending

The **te** is the simple past tense marker for weak verbs and is similar to English *-ed* (*walked*, *repaired*). Simple past tense endings are:

ich	—	wir	**-n**
du	**-st**	ihr	**-t**
er/es/sie	—	sie	**-n**
	Sie	**-n**	

INFINITIVE	**machen**			**besuchen**		
	stem + **te** + *ending*			*stem* + **te** + *ending*		
ich	mach	**te**	—	besuch	**te**	—
du	mach	**te**	**st**	besuch	**te**	**st**
er/es/sie	mach	**te**	—	besuch	**te**	—
wir	mach	**te**	**n**	besuch	**te**	**n**
ihr	mach	**te**	**t**	besuch	**te**	**t**
sie	mach	**te**	**n**	besuch	**te**	**n**
Sie	mach	**te**	**n**	besuch	**te**	**n**

If the verb stem ends in -**d**, -**t** or in -**m** or -**n** preceded by another consonant (other than -**l** or -**r**), the tense marker **te** becomes **ete**.

INFINITIVE	**reden**			**arbeiten**		
	stem + **ete** + *ending*			*stem* + **ete** + *ending*		
ich	red	**ete**	—	arbeit	**ete**	—
du	red	**ete**	**st**	arbeit	**ete**	**st**
er/es/sie	red	**ete**	—	arbeit	**ete**	—
wir	red	**ete**	**n**	arbeit	**ete**	**n**
ihr	red	**ete**	**t**	arbeit	**ete**	**t**
sie	red	**ete**	**n**	arbeit	**ete**	**n**
Sie	red	**ete**	**n**	arbeit	**ete**	**n**

For all verbs (not just weak verbs) in the simple past tense, the first and third person singular forms (**ich** and **er/es/sie**) are identical.

In the simple past tense, as in the present tense, the separable prefix stands in final position in a main clause, separated from its base.

Ich **holte** sie um 9 Uhr **ab**.   *I picked her up at 9 o'clock.*
Wir **bereiteten** das Referat **vor**. *We prepared the oral report.*

Exercise 19: *Change into the simple past tense.*

1. sie arbeitet
2. ich liebe
3. wir leben
4. du amüsierst
5. ihr bemerkt
6. es bedeutet
7. sie hören
8. ich danke
9. Sie berichten
10. er sammelt

Exercise 20: *Restate in the simple past tense.*

1. Der Professor fragt immer nur mich.
2. Nur Sport interessiert sie.
3. Der Ausflug macht viel Spaß.
4. Sie lernen einander auf einer Party kennen.

5. Dieser Rock kostet viel Geld.

6. Im Urlaub mieten wir einen Wohnwagen.

7. Im Sommer pflanzen wir Blumen.

8. Die Lehrerin bereitet ihre Stunde vor.

9. Der Kuchen schmeckt gut.

10. Wir baden immer in der Nordsee.

11. Im Malunterricht malen die Kinder ihre Lieblingstiere.

12. Ich mache einen Witz und ihr lacht mich aus.

Strong Verbs in the Simple Past Tense

Strong verbs have vowel changes that cannot be predicted. Therefore their forms must be learned. You will find a list of the strong verbs in Appendix B.

The basic formula for strong verbs in the simple past tense is:

$$\boxed{\text{simple past stem + ending}}$$

Whereas the marker for weak verbs in the simple past tense is **te**, for strong verbs it is a stem vowel change, sometimes together with a consonant change (**gehen** ➝ **ging**; **stehen** ➝ **stand**; **bitten** ➝ **bat**). The endings for strong verbs are the same as for weak verbs except that the -**n** ending expands to -**en**.

ich	—		wi	**-en**
du	**-st**		ihr	**-t**
er/es/sie	—		sie	**-en**
		Sie	**-en**	

INFINITIVE	**fahren**		**gehen**	
	stem + ending		*stem + ending*	
ich	fuhr	—	ging	—
du	fuhr	**st**	ging	**st**
er/es/sie	fuhr	—	ging	—
wir	fuhr	**en**	ging	**en**
ihr	fuhr	**t**	ging	**t**
sie	fuhr	**en**	ging	**en**
Sie	fuhr	**en**	ging	**en**

If the past tense stem ends in -**d** or -**t**, the second person singular and plural (the **du** and **ihr** forms) ending inserts an **e** (du fand**e**st/ihr fand**e**t; du ritt**e**st/ihr ritt**e**t).

If the past tense stem ends in an **s** sound (-**s**, -**ss**, -β, or -**z**), the second person singular (the **du** form) ending inserts an **e** (du las**e**st; du hieβ**e**st).

Exercise 21: *Give the simple past stem of the following verbs. (Consult Appendix B if you have not memorized the form.) Note the similarities between the verb groupings. They may help you to remember the forms.*

1. beginnen, finden, gewinnen, schwimmen, trinken, singen, sitzen, essen, geben, helfen, lesen, sprechen, treten, werfen, tun, kommen
2. bleiben, scheinen, schreiben, fallen, halten, lassen, schlafen
3. gehen, fangen, beißen, reiten, schneiden, leiden
4. fahren, schlagen, tragen, wachsen, waschen
5. fliegen, fliehen, frieren, schließen, verlieren, ziehen

Exercise 22: *Restate in the simple past tense.*

1. Der Lehrer liest den Schülern eine Geschichte vor.
2. Der Traktor zieht den Wagen.
3. Was tust du dann?
4. Das Kind ißt das Gemüse gern.
5. Wir fliegen mit der Concorde.
6. Der Dieb stiehlt alle Schmucksachen.
7. Seht ihr den Vogel im Gebüsch?
8. Auf dem Börsenmarkt verlieren die Geschäftsleute ihr Geld.
9. Wir halten den Lärm nicht mehr aus.
10. Der Apfel fällt vom Baum herunter.
11. Ich singe ein Weihnachtslied.
12. Wer gewinnt das Spiel?

Exercise 23: *Complete with the correct simple past form of the cue verbs.*

1. Helga _____ ihren neuen Job am Montag.   (beginnen)
2. Wir _____ zusammen und _____.   (sitzen; trinken)
3. Ich _____ den Abfall _____.   (wegtragen)
4. Ich _____ 14 Kilometer und _____ dann den restlichen Tag. (gehen; schlafen)
5. Eine Woche lang _____ die Sonne nicht.   (scheinen)
6. Ihr _____ zu leise.   (sprechen)
7. Wann _____ der Bus _____?   (abfahren)
8. Die Sonne _____ hinter den Wolken _____.   (hervorkommen)
9. Meine Großmutter _____ letzten Mai.   (sterben)
10. Maria _____ zu Hause und _____ den ganzen Tag Briefe. (bleiben; schreiben)
11. Wer _____ gestern abend _____?   (abwaschen)
12. Der Pförtner _____ die Tür.   (schließen)

Haben, sein, and werden in the Simple Past Tense

INFINITIVE	**haben**	**sein**	**werden**
ich	hatte	war	wurde
du	hattest	warst	wurdest
er/es/sie	hatte	war	wurde
wir	hatten	waren	wurden
ihr	hattet	wart	wurdet
sie	hatten	waren	wurden
Sie	hatten	waren	wurden

Exercise 24: *Complete with the correct simple past form of the cue verb.*

1. Das Fahrrad _____ kaputt.   (sein)
2. Was _____ du eigentlich gegen ihn?   (haben)
3. Meine Erkältung _____ immer schlimmer.   (werden)
4. Die letzte Übung _____ schwieriger als diese.   (sein)
5. Die Studenten _____ nie genug Geld.   (haben)
6. Wo _____ ihr gestern abend?   (sein)
7. _____ wir gestern Besuch, oder war das vorgestern?   (haben)
8. Mit einem Male _____ mir alles klar.   (werden)
9. _____ Sie gestern im Kino?   (sein)
10. Der Junge _____ mit der Zeit immer größer.   (werden)
11. _____ du letztes Jahr in Deutschland?   (sein)
12. Ihr _____ davon keine Ahnung, oder?   (haben)

Mixed Verbs in the Simple Past Tense

There is a small group of verbs, known as mixed or irregular weak verbs, that takes the **te** tense marker for weak verbs *plus* the vowel change tense marker for strong verbs in the simple past tense.

INFINITIVE	SIMPLE PAST STEM	
brennen	**brannte**	*to burn*
bringen	**brachte**	*to bring*
denken	**dachte**	*to think*
kennen	**kannte**	*to know, be acquainted with*
nennen	**nannte**	*to name, call*
rennen	**rannte**	*to run*
wissen	**wußte**	*to know as a fact*

Note that the vowel changes to **a** for all mixed verbs except **wissen**.
Note that **bringen** and **denken** have a consonant change in addition to the vowel change.

Exercise 25: *Restate in the simple past tense.*

1. Die Gäste bringen Blumen und Schokolade mit.
2. Der Kaufmann weiß den Preis der Stereoanlage nicht.

3. Das kleine Kind rennt nach Hause.

4. Am Anfang nennen alle den Erfinder einen Idioten.

5. Die heiße Suppe verbrennt mir die Zunge.

6. Ich denke jeden Tag an dich.

7. Kennst du die Stadt schon?

8. Das Haus brennt bis auf die Grundmauern ab.

9. Nach drei Jahren erkennen sie sich fast nicht wieder.

10. Wir wissen die Namen der Bundesländer Deutschlands.

11. Denkst du darüber nach?

12. Die Olympiasiegerin rennt allen anderen voran.

Modal Verbs in the Simple Past Tense

FORMS

The simple past tense of modal verbs follows the pattern for weak verbs (stem + **te** + endings) minus all umlauts.

	dürfen	**können**	**mögen**
ich	durfte	konnte	mochte
du	durftest	konntest	mochtest
er/es/sie	durfte	konnte	mochte
wir	durften	konnten	mochten
ihr	durftet	konntet	mochtet
sie	durften	konnten	mochten
Sie	durften	konnten	mochten

	müssen	**sollen**	**wollen**
ich	mußte	sollte	wollte
du	mußtest	solltest	wolltest
er/es/sie	mußte	sollte	wollte
wir	mußten	sollten	wollten
ihr	mußtet	solltet	wolltet
sie	mußten	sollten	wollten
Sie	mußten	sollten	wollten

Note that **mögen** has a consonant change.

MEANINGS

durfte   *was allowed to*

Das Kind **durfte** nur bis 10 Uhr bleiben.

The child was allowed to stay only until 10 o'clock.

konnte   *was able to, could*

Ich **konnte** die kleine Schrift nicht lesen.

I couldn't read the small print.

mochte   *liked, cared to*
Wir **mochten** den Film nicht.
We didn't like the movie.

muβte   *had to*
Wir **muβten** unsere Hausaufgaben machen.
We had to do our homework.

sollte   *was supposed to*
Die Studenten **sollten** dieses Kapitel lesen.
The students were supposed to read this chapter.

wollte   *wanted to*
Ich **wollte** mit dem Zug fahren.
I wanted to go by train.

Exercise 26: *Complete with the correct simple past tense form of each cue modal.*

1. Ich _____ das kleine Auto nicht.   (mögen, wollen)
2. Wir _____ sofort nach Hause gehen.   (müssen, sollen, wollen, dürfen, können)
3. Warum _____ er nicht mitkommen?   (dürfen, können, müssen, sollen, wollen)
4. Warum _____ du das tun?   (müssen, sollen, wollen)
5. Ihr _____ an dem Abend früh weggehen.   (müssen, sollen, wollen, dürfen, können)
6. _____ du deine Arbeit fertig haben?   (müssen, können, wollen, sollen)

Exercise 27: *Complete with the correct simple past form of the appropriate modal.*

1. Er _____ schon gestern nach Hause fahren.   (*was supposed to*)
2. Am Tag vor den Ferien _____ die Schüler nicht mehr arbeiten. (*wanted to*)
3. _____ du sein Deutsch verstehen?   (*could*)
4. Die Sekretärin _____ den neuen Computer nicht.   (*liked*)
5. Selbst die Professorin _____ das Problem nicht lösen.   (*could*)
6. Die Studenten _____ am Wochenende für die Klausur lernen. (*had to*)
7. Man _____ nur in einem einzigen Zimmer rauchen.   (*was allowed to*)

8. Meine Nachbarin _____ die Katze während der Ferien füttern.
   (*was supposed to*)
9. Wir _____ sehr schnell einpacken.   (*had to*)
10. Ich _____ die Landstraβe nehmen.   (*wanted to*)

Review Exercises for the Simple Past Tense

Exercise 28: *Restate in the simple past tense.*

1. Ich treffe meine Freundin Claudia.
2. Der Wald brennt drei Tage lang.
3. Nur Frauen dürfen teilnehmen.
4. Das will ich nicht.
5. Dieser Film bekommt 7 Oskars.
6. Wir müssen Geduld haben.
7. Sie stellt viele Fragen.
8. Alle müssen ihren Paβ zeigen.
9. Wer gewinnt den ersten Preis?
10. Er kennt die Spielregeln nicht.
11. Ich fahre am Wochenende nach Hause.
12. Der Dieb bricht in das Haus ein.
13. Ich mag den Nachtisch nicht.
14. Wir siegen in letzter Zeit immer öfter.
15. Der Schnellzug hält auch in den kleinen Dörfern.

Exercise 29: *Complete with the simple past form of the cue verb.*

1. Als Kind _____ ich bei meinen Eltern im Bett.   (schlafen)
2. Der Arzt _____ mich von früher.   (kennen)
3. Er _____ so schnell, wie er _____.   (rennen; können)
4. Meine Mutter _____ mir das Essen ans Bett.   (bringen)
5. Wir _____ sie eigentlich anrufen.   (sollen)
6. _____ du nicht auf mich warten?   (können)
7. Ich _____ auf gutes Wetter für das Wochenende.   (hoffen)
8. Die zwei _____ ineinander verliebt.   (sein)
9. Meine Zimmergenossin _____ die ganze Nacht durch.   (lernen)
10. Statt Tomaten _____ ihr Gurken.   (kaufen)
11. Die Richterin _____ die Betrüger.   (verurteilen)
12. Die Tänzer _____ die ganze Zeit.   (lächeln)
13. Ich _____ doch keine Ahnung.   (haben)
14. Während wir auf ihn _____, _____ wir die Geduld.   (warten; verlieren)
15. Der Kellner _____ die Gäste des Restaurants.   (bedienen)

Exercise 30: *Make complete sentences in the simple past tense using the words provided.*

1. Meine Mutter / geben / mir / Geld.
2. Die Polizei / wissen / nichts über den Mordfall.

3. Ich / vergessen / unsere Abmachung.
4. Wir / haben / groβes Glück.
5. Was / passieren / hier?
6. Du / müssen / mithelfen / bei der Gartenarbeit.
7. In diesem Moment / eintreten / er.
8. Sie (*she*) / reden / zu schnell.
9. Ich / können / verstehen / sie (*she*) / nicht.
10. Er / müssen / abwaschen / schon wieder.
11. Gestern / schreiben / ich / einen Brief / an meinen Bruder.
12. Rolf / einschenken / sich / ein zweites Glas Wein.
13. Katrin / durchlesen / das Buch.
14. Backen / du / schon wieder / Kuchen?
15. Wann / vorstellen / er / seinen Eltern / seine Freundin?

PRESENT PERFECT TENSE

Formation of the Present Perfect Tense

The basic formula for forming the *present perfect tense* is the present tense of the auxiliary verb **haben** or, less frequently, **sein** plus the past participle of the main verb:

> **haben/sein** + past participle

The auxiliary is conjugated to agree with the subject of the sentence. The past participle is never conjugated and occupies the final position in a main clause.

Ich **habe** dich da nicht **gesehen.**
I didn't see you there.

Meine Eltern **haben** mich **geschickt.**
My parents sent me.

Monika **ist** viel **gereist.**
Monika has traveled a lot.

Wie **hast** du das **gewuβt?**
How did you know that?

THE PAST PARTICIPLE

The formation of the *past participle* differs depending on whether the verb is weak, strong, mixed, or a modal verb.

Past Participles of Weak Verbs. The past participle of weak verbs can be predicted according to the following pattern:

$$\boxed{\textbf{ge} + \text{stem} + \textbf{t}}$$

INFINITIVE	PAST PARTICIPLE		
suchen	ge + such	+ t	*to seek, look for*
reisen	ge + reis	+ t	*to travel*
machen	ge + mach	+ t	*to do, make*
sagen	ge + sag	+ t	*to say*
lernen	ge + lern	+ t	*to study, learn*

To facilitate pronunciation, **-et** is added to stems ending in **-d**, **-t**, or certain consonant clusters.

landen	ge + land	+ et	*to land*
arbeiten	ge + arbeit	+ et	*to work*
atmen	ge + atm	+ et	*to breathe*

Exercise 31: *Give the past participle.*

1. putzen
2. rechnen
3. schauen
4. wohnen
5. lieben
6. bauen
7. leben
8. hassen
9. kochen
10. antworten
11. schätzen
12. hören
13. schütteln
14. fassen
15. starten
16. lachen
17. fasten
18. kämpfen

Past Participles of Strong Verbs. The past participle of strong verbs is formed according to the following pattern:

$$\boxed{\textbf{ge} + \text{stem (usually with vowel change)} + \textbf{(e)n}}$$

INFINITIVE	PAST PARTICIPLE		
sehen	ge + seh	+ en	*to see*
tun	ge + ta	+ n	*to do*
schreiben	ge + schrieb	+ en	*to write*
fahren	ge + fahr	+ en	*to drive*
finden	ge + fund	+ en	*to find*

Note that whereas the past participle of weak verbs ends in **-t**, the past participle of strong verbs always ends in **-(e)n**.

The vowel change in the stem follows no predictable rules and accordingly must be memorized for each verb. You will find a list of common strong verbs in Appendix B.

Exercise 32: *Give the past participle for each infinitive. (Consult Appendix B if you have not memorized the forms.) Note the similarities within the various groupings. They may help you to remember the past participles.*

1. essen, geben, sehen, lesen
2. helfen, treffen, nehmen, sprechen, werfen
3. bleiben, schreiben, meiden
4. fahren, schlafen, tragen, schlagen, laden, waschen, lassen
5. finden, singen, trinken
6. reiten, leiden, schneiden

Past Participles of Mixed Verbs. There is a small group of verbs, known as mixed or irregular weak verbs, that takes the **-t** ending that characterizes the past participle of weak verbs *plus* the vowel change that characterizes the past participle of strong verbs.

INFINITIVE	PAST PARTICIPLE	
brennen	**gebrannt**	*to burn*
bringen	**gebracht**	*to bring*
denken	**gedacht**	*to think*
kennen	**gekannt**	*to know, be acquainted with*
nennen	**genannt**	*to name, call*
rennen	**gerannt**	*to run*
wissen	**gewuβt**	*to know as a fact*

Note that the vowel changes to **a** for all mixed verbs except **wissen**.

Note that **bringen** and **denken** have a consonant change in addition to the vowel change.

Omission of the *ge-* Prefix. The **ge-** prefix normally added to the past participle is omitted in two cases:

1. If the verb infinitive ends in **-ieren**. All such verbs are weak verbs and therefore their past participle ends in **-t**.

INFINITIVE	PAST PARTICIPLE	
studieren	**studiert**	*to study, learn*
reparieren	**repariert**	*to repair*
probieren	**probiert**	*to try*
passieren	**passiert**	*to happen*

2. If the verb has an inseparable prefix. Such verbs may be weak, strong, or mixed.

INFINITIVE	PAST PARTICIPLE	
begegnen	**begegnet**	*to meet*
empfinden	**empfunden**	*to feel*
entscheiden	**entschieden**	*to decide*
erkennen	**erkannt**	*to recognize*
gefallen	**gefallen**	*to be pleasing to*
miβlingen	**miβlungen**	*to fail*
versuchen	**versucht**	*to try*
zerstören	**zerstört**	*to destroy*

Past Participles of Verbs with Separable Prefixes. If the verb has a separable prefix, the **ge-** prefix is inserted between the separable prefix and the main part of the verb. Such verbs may be weak, strong, or mixed.

INFINITIVE	PAST PARTICIPLE	
anfangen	**angefangen**	*to begin*
aufhören	**aufgehört**	*to stop*
losfahren	**losgefahren**	*to drive away*
mitarbeiten	**mitgearbeitet**	*to work with*
nachdenken	**nachgedacht**	*to reflect*

Exercise 33: *Give the past participle.*

1. zerstören
2. mitnehmen
3. bestellen
4. gehören
5. telefonieren
6. aussehen
7. verkaufen
8. anrufen
9. ausgeben
10. spazieren
11. empfangen
12. geschehen
13. aufstehen
14. mitbringen
15. bezahlen

HABEN OR *SEIN*?

The auxiliary verb in the formation of the present perfect tense for both weak and strong verbs may be either **haben** or **sein**.

AUXILIARY **haben**			AUXILIARY **sein**		
ich	**habe**	gesehen	ich	**bin**	gekommen
du	**hast**	gesehen	du	**bist**	gekommen
er/es/sie	**hat**	gesehen	er/es/sie	**ist**	gekommen
wir	**haben**	gesehen	wir	**sind**	gekommen
ihr	**habt**	gesehen	ihr	**seid**	gekommen
sie	**haben**	gesehen	sie	**sind**	gekommen
Sie	**haben**	gesehen	Sie	**sind**	gekommen

Most verbs take **haben** as their auxiliary.

The auxiliary verb **sein** is used with intransitive verbs (verbs that do not take a direct object in the accusative case) that express a change of position (for example, **gehen**, **fahren**, **spazieren**) or a change in condition (for example, **werden**, **aufstehen**, **sterben**).

Some verbs take **sein** as their auxiliary even though they do not meet these conditions. The most common are **bleiben** and **sein**. Because the auxiliary verb is not always predictable, it is best to learn it along with the other principal parts of a verb.

Prefixes, although they do not affect the principal parts of the verb, may affect the choice of an auxiliary verb. Compare the following sets:

kommen   *to come*
Sie **ist** gestern abend sehr spät nach Hause **gekommen**.
She came home very late last night.
bekommen   *to receive*
Ich **habe** noch keinen Brief von meinen Eltern **bekommen**.
I still haven't received a letter from my parents.

stehen   *to stand*
Die Studenten **haben** an der Tafel **gestanden**.
The students stood at the blackboard.
verstehen   *to understand*
Haben Sie mich endlich **verstanden**?
Have you finally understood me?
aufstehen   *to get up*
Heute morgen **ist** er um neun **aufgestanden**.
He got up this morning at nine.

Some verbs that normally take **sein** as their auxiliary will take **haben** if they are used transitively, that is, if they take a direct object. Compare the following sets of sentences:

Das Flugzeug **ist** in Wien **gelandet**.
The plane landed in Vienna.

Der Pilot **hat** das Flugzeug heil in Wien **gelandet**.
The pilot landed the plane safely in Vienna.

Wir **sind** mit dem Wagen nach Hause **gefahren**.
We drove home (by car).

Der Mann **hat** den Mietwagen nach Hause **gefahren**.
The man drove the rental car home.

Exercise 34: *Complete with the correct auxiliary verb.*

1. Die Kinder _____ mit dem Ball gespielt.
2. Ich _____ nicht schnell genug gerannt.
3. Warum _____ du nach Hause gelaufen?
4. Monika _____ dich gerade angerufen.
5. Wie lange _____ ihre Familie geblieben?
6. Der Fahrer _____ den Bus nach Berlin gefahren.
7. Das _____ viel Spaß gemacht.
8. Das Mädchen _____ in den letzten zwei Jahren viel gewachsen.
9. Die Polizei _____ den Mörder gefangen.
10. Ihr _____ heute aber viel gegessen!
11. Die Astronauten _____ auf dem Mond gelandet.
12. Um wieviel Uhr _____ du heute morgen aufgestanden?

HABEN, SEIN, AND *WERDEN* IN THE PRESENT PERFECT TENSE

The past participle and auxiliary verb for **haben**, **sein**, and **werden** should be memorized thoroughly.

INFINITIVE	AUXILIARY + PAST PARTICIPLE
haben	**hat gehabt**
sein	**ist gewesen**
werden	**ist geworden**

REVIEW EXERCISES FOR WEAK, STRONG, AND MIXED VERBS IN THE PRESENT PERFECT TENSE

Exercise 35: *Restate in the present perfect tense.*

1. Er trinkt zu viel.
2. Der Clown hat viel zu große Schuhe an.
3. Sie reist in jedes Land.
4. Ich bleibe in Amerika.
5. Christian liest den ganzen Tag.
6. Es klingelt.
7. Wir essen den Kuchen schnell.
8. Wir liegen den ganzen Tag in der Sonne.
9. Meine Eltern steigen auf jeden Berg.
10. Er besucht mich jeden Tag.
11. Die Werkstatt repariert das Auto.
12. Sie leiht mir genug Geld.
13. Warum fliegt ihr nicht?
14. Jeder regt sich über den Politiker auf.
15. Ich weiß die Antwort.

16. Angela rennt zur Schule.
17. Niemand hört der Zeugin zu.
18. Die Ärztin hilft dem Kranken.
19. Dieser Sommer ist sehr heiß.
20. Das Kind versteht das nicht.
21. Auf einmal macht sie die Augen auf.
22. In der Wüste gibt es nur wenig Wasser.

Exercise 36: *Make complete sentences in the present perfect tense using the words provided.*

1. Das Konzert / anfangen / vor einer halben Stunde.
2. Niemand / kennen / den Toten.
3. Der Talisman / bringen / Glück.
4. Das gelbe Haus / brennen.
5. Meine Mutter / schicken / mich.
6. Monika / Schluß machen / mit ihrem Freund.
7. In diesem Jahr / wir / lernen / viel.
8. Wir / umsteigen / sehr oft.
9. Meine Tante / studieren / Medizin.
10. Gestern / wir / sehen / einen guten Film.
11. Du / sprechen / zu schnell.
12. Ich / telefonieren / mit meinem Freund.
13. Wann / ankommen / der Bus?
14. Der Alkoholiker / sterben / vor kurzem.
15. Das Wetter / werden / wieder kalt.
16. Ich / beantworten / die Frage nicht.
17. Die Vögel / singen / in unserem Garten.
18. In den Ferien / Ski laufen / Tanja.
19. Ich / aufräumen / mein Zimmer.
20. Eva und Friedrich / feiern / ihren 50. Hochzeitstag.

MODAL VERBS IN THE PRESENT PERFECT TENSE

The basic formula for forming the present perfect tense of modal verbs is the same as for all other verbs: auxiliary verb + past participle. *The auxiliary verb for modals is always* **haben**.

Modal verbs have two different past participles, depending on whether they stand alone or together with another infinitive.

Used without a Dependent Infinitive. When the modal verb is used alone, its past participle follows the pattern of weak verbs (**ge** + stem + **t**) minus all umlauts.

INFINITIVE	PAST PARTICIPLE
dürfen	**gedurft**
können	**gekonnt**
mögen	**gemocht**
müssen	**gemußt**
sollen	**gesollt**
wollen	**gewollt**

Note the consonant change for **gemocht**.

Das **habe** ich nicht **gedurft**.
I wasn't allowed to do that.

Wir **haben** nach Hause **gemußt**.
We had to go home.

Used with a Dependent Infinitive. Modal verbs are usually used together with another infinitive. In such a case, an alternate past participle of the modal is used which is identical to the modal infinitive. In a main clause, the modal infinitive stands at the end, immediately following the other infinitive. This construction is therefore known as a *double infinitive*.

Das Orchester **hat** noch einmal **spielen müssen**.
The orchestra had to play again.

Er **hat** den Rasen **mähen sollen**.
He was supposed to mow the lawn.

Ich **habe** nicht **einschlafen können**.
I couldn't go to sleep.

It should be noted that usually the simple past tense of modal verbs is preferred over the present perfect tense.

Exercise 37: *Restate the sentences in the present perfect tense.*

1. Wir dürfen laute Musik nicht spielen.
2. Ich will das nicht!
3. Er muß die ganze Nacht hindurch lernen.
4. Hier kann niemand Englisch verstehen.
5. Sie will nicht von zu Hause wegfahren.
6. Sie mag die Erbsen nicht.
7. Viele können es sofort.
8. Er muß zur Arbeit.
9. Sie wollen noch ein Bier trinken.
10. Der Arzt kann dem Verletzten nicht helfen.

The Present Perfect Tense vs. the Simple Past Tense

In German, the present perfect tense and the simple past tense mean essentially the same thing: they both are used to describe an event in the past and are interchangeable to a certain extent. However, the two tenses tend to be used in different situations.

The present perfect tense is used in conversational exchanges and accordingly is sometimes called the *conversational past*. Conversational exchanges frequently are marked with interruptions, questions, and asides, all of which break the chronology and sequence of the events being related. Thus the present perfect tense is used to describe *isolated events in the past*.

Was **habt** ihr gestern **gemacht**?
Wir **sind** ins Kino **gegangen**.
What did you do yesterday?
We went to the movies.

Compare this to the simple past tense, which is used to narrate *connected past events in a chain* and accordingly is sometimes called the *narrative past*.

Gestern **ging** das Ehepaar ins Kino, **sah** einen lustigen Film, und **trank** nachher ein Bier in der Kneipe.
Yesterday the married couple went to the movies, saw a funny movie, and drank a beer afterwards in the bar.

PRESENT PERFECT VS. SIMPLE PAST WITH *HABEN, SEIN,* AND MODAL VERBS

For the verbs **haben**, **sein**, and all modal verbs the distinction between isolated events and connected events in the past—that is, between the present perfect and the simple past tenses—is not strictly maintained.

Sein is almost always used in the simple past tense, even in conversational situations.

Ich habe dich gestern angerufen. Wo **warst** du?
Ich **war** krank und bin im Bett geblieben.
I called you yesterday. Where were you?
I was sick and stayed in bed.

Haben and the modals are frequently used in the simple past tense in conversational situations.

Warum bist du nicht mitgekommen?

Ich **hatte** eine Erkältung und **mußte** im Bett bleiben.

Why didn't you come along?

I had a cold and had to stay in bed.

PAST PERFECT TENSE

Formation of the Past Perfect Tense

The basic formula for forming the past perfect tense is the simple past tense of the auxiliary verb **haben** or, less frequently, **sein** plus the past participle of the main verb. The auxiliary is conjugated to agree with the subject of the sentence. The past participle is never conjugated and occupies the final position in a main clause.

Note that the past perfect tense is formed like the present perfect tense except that the *simple past tense of the auxiliary verb* is used instead of the present tense. Thus the basic formula for the formation of the past perfect tense is:

$$\boxed{\textbf{hatten/waren} + \text{past participle}}$$

The rules for the formation of the past participle and for using **haben** as opposed to **sein** remain the same as for the present perfect tense.

Compare the following sets of sentences:

PRESENT PERFECT	PAST PERFECT
Sie **hat** das nicht gesagt.	Sie **hatte** das nicht gesagt.
Es **hat** da gelegen.	Es **hatte** da gelegen.
Ich **bin** zu Hause geblieben.	Ich **war** zu Hause geblieben.
Wir **haben** das doch gewollt.	Wir **hatten** das doch gewollt.

Usage of the Past Perfect Tense

The usage of the past perfect tense in German corresponds to its usage in English. In both languages, it usually expresses a relationship between two events in the past, where one of those events took place even further in the past than the other.

Bevor ich nach Italien fuhr, **hatte** ich Bilder **gesehen**.

*Before I went to Italy I **had looked** at pictures.*

Ehe ich das Licht ausmachte, **war** sie schon **eingeschlafen**.

*Before I turned out the light, she **had** already **fallen asleep**.*

Nachdem Maria **aufgelegt hatte**, war sie frustriert.

*After Maria **had hung up** she was frustrated.*

Exercise 38: *Restate the present perfect sentences in the past perfect.*

1. Ich habe den ganzen Sommer gearbeitet.
2. Sie hat die ganze Zeit da gesessen.
3. Die Kinder sind endlich ruhig geworden.
4. Wir haben zu viel gegessen und getrunken.
5. Du hast die Reise gut vorbereitet.
6. Corinna ist schon den ganzen Tag müde gewesen.
7. Ich bin schnell zum Bäcker gelaufen.
8. Die Menschenmenge hat auf den Präsidenten gewartet.

Exercise 39: *Complete with the correct past perfect form of the cue verb.*

1. Sie mußte zurück nach Hause fahren, weil sie ihre Karte _____
   _____.   (vergessen)
2. Wir waren sehr müde, nachdem wir so viel _____ _____.
   (arbeiten)
3. Bevor ich wählte, _____ ich alle Möglichkeiten _____.
   (studieren)
4. Sie hatte Angst. Sie _____ einen seltsamen Lärm _____.
   (hören)
5. Nachdem er vom Flugzeugunglück _____ _____, wollte er
   nicht mehr fliegen.   (lesen)
6. Ich _____ schon alles _____, als meine Gäste anriefen und
   sagten, daß sie nicht kommen konnten.   (vorbereiten)
7. Als wir endlich ankamen, _____ der Zug schon längst _____.
   (abfahren)
8. Man konnte die Rednerin nicht mehr hören, weil sie heiser _____
   _____.   (werden)

FUTURE TENSE

Formation of the Future Tense

The basic formula for the formation of the future tense is:

> werden + infinitive

Werden is conjugated to agree with the subject. The infinitive is placed at the end of a main clause.

Wann **wird** er nach Hause **gehen**?
When will he go home?

Sie **wird** ihre Doktorarbeit **schreiben**.
She will write her dissertation.

Das Kind **wird** müde **werden**.
The child will become tired.

Modal verbs in the future tense require a double infinitive at the end of a main clause, with the modal infinitive in the final position.

Wann **wird** er nach Hause **gehen müssen**?
When will he have to go home?

Sie **wird** ihre Dissertation **schreiben müssen**.
She will have to write her dissertation.

It should be noted that the future tense of modal verbs is usually avoided if future time is clear from the context.

Usage of the Future Tense

The future tense is used to express actions that will take place in the future. It corresponds closely to the English future tense.

PRESENT TENSE FOR FUTURE MEANING

If future time is clear from the context or from an adverb, German frequently will use the present tense instead of the future tense.

Christa **verbringt** den Sommer in Amerika.
Christa will spend the summer in America.

Morgen **regnet** es.
Tomorrow it's going to rain.

FUTURE TENSE TO EXPRESS PRESENT PROBABILITY

German sometimes uses the future tense plus **wohl**, **sicher**, or **schon** to express present probability.

Sie werden wohl kommen.
They are probably coming.

Es wird schon 7 Uhr sein.
It's probably 7 o'clock.

Exercise 40: *Restate in the future tense.*

1. Wir kommen zu spät.
2. Wir schauen uns einen neuen Film an.
3. Nach der Hochzeit gibt es eine große Party.
4. Ich fahre mit zwei Freunden nach Italien.
5. Das macht sicher Spaß.

6. Mußt du viel für die Chemieprüfung lernen?
7. Die Geschäfte machen um sechs zu.
8. Ich rufe meine Familie an.
9. Katjana kommt am Hauptbahnhof an.
10. Der Ausflug findet auch ohne dich statt.

FUTURE PERFECT TENSE

Formation of the Future Perfect Tense

The basic formula for the formation of the future perfect tense is:

> **werden** + past participle + auxiliary (**haben/sein**)

Werden is conjugated to agree with the subject. The past participle with the appropriate auxiliary infinitive remains constant and stands at the end of a main clause.

Sie **werden** das **gemacht haben**.
They will have done that.

Sie **wird** spazieren **gegangen sein**.
She will have gone for a walk.

Usage of the Future Perfect Tense

The future perfect tense is rare in German and in English. It is generally used together with **wohl**, **schon**, or **sicher** to express past probability.

Der Mechaniker **wird wohl** das Motorrad **repariert haben**.
The mechanic probably repaired the motorbike (already).

Der Bus **wird wohl abgefahren sein**!
The bus probably left (already)!

Exercise 41: *Restate the sentences in the future perfect tense, adding* **wohl** *to express past probability.*

1. Er schreibt den Brief.
2. Das Beste ist vorbei.
3. Sie hat keine Zeit.
4. Der Mann trinkt zu viel.
5. Meine Eltern kommen mit dem Flugzeug.
6. Klaus und Silke heiraten im Sommer.

ANSWERS TO EXERCISES

1.

1. du besuchst
2. wir sammeln
3. ich lerne
4. Sie spielen
5. du kennst
6. sie tut
7. ihr trinkt
8. es stört
9. ich seg(e)le
10. sie bleiben

2.

1. Ich arbeite in einem Büro.
2. Er heißt Bruno.
3. Sie reist jedes Jahr nach Österreich.
4. Der Sportler atmet schwer.
5. Sammelt ihr Briefmarken?
6. Du schließt die Tür.
7. Wieviel kostet eine Kassette?
8. Stefanie redet zu schnell.
9. Haßt du mich?
10. Wann heiratet ihr?

3.

1. du hältst
2. er läuft
3. du stiehlst
4. ihr nehmt
5. ich lese
6. sie tritt
7. du sprichst
8. er schläft
9. sie empfiehlt
10. ihr fahrt

4.

1. schläft
2. lese
3. fährt
4. läuft
5. wächst
6. trägst
7. rät
8. vergißt
9. bäckt
10. Fängst; werfe

5.

1. Wirst
2. ist
3. haben
4. sind
5. habt
6. werden
7. wird
8. Hast
9. bist
10. hat

6.

1. Weißt
2. Kennst
3. kenne; kenne
4. kennt; weiß
5. wissen
6. wissen
7. Kennst
8. Wißt

7.

1. Sie fliegt nach Deutschland.
2. Er spielt nächsten Samstag Golf.
3. Sie kommen bald nach Hause.
4. Sie liest ein gutes Buch.
5. Hilfst du/helft ihr/helfen Sie mir morgen?
6. Wohnen sie hier?
7. Warum schläfst du/schlaft ihr/schlafen Sie so lange?
8. Sie essen immer im Eßzimmer.
9. Ich empfehle den Rotwein.
10. Ich treffe meine Freundin im Restaurant.

8.

1. Ich warte schon eine Stunde.
   I have been waiting for an hour.
2. Wir sind seit Montag hier.
   We've been here since Monday.
3. Es regnet seit drei Tagen.
   It's been raining for three days.
4. Robert kennt Inge schon drei Jahre. *Robert has known Inge for three years.*
5. Ich telefoniere seit zwei Stunden. *I've been on the phone for two hours.*

9.

1. Schlaf(e)!
2. Geh(e)!
3. Sprich!
4. Stiehl!
5. Iß!
6. Wasch(e)!
7. Hilf!
8. Heirate!
9. Rede!
10. Sieh!

10.

1. Gib
2. Beleidige
3. Mach(e)
4. Vergiß
5. Besuch(e)
6. Sprich
7. Koch(e)
8. Hilf
9. Zieh(e)
10. Laß (Lasse)
11. Schreib(e)
12. Nimm; versuch(e)

11.

1. Antwortet / Antworten Sie
2. Tragt / Tragen Sie
3. Bleibt / Bleiben Sie
4. Seid / Seien Sie
5. Haltet / Halten Sie
6. Klagt / Klagen Sie
7. Laßt / Lassen Sie
8. Lügt / Lügen Sie
9. Lauft / Laufen Sie
10. Erklärt / Erklären Sie

12.

1. seid
2. spar(e)
3. lehn(e)
4. werden Sie
5. streitet
6. schicken Sie
7. nimm
8. machen Sie
9. sehen Sie
10. gib

13.

1. gibst . . . aus
2. komm . . . mit
3. bezahlt
4. bringt . . . zusammen
5. zieht . . . an
6. Verstehen
7. sieht . . . an
8. bekomme
9. haben vor
10. geht . . . zurück
11. Entschuldigen

12. nimmt . . . mit
13. tanze . . . vor
14. erhöht
15. versucht

14.

1. Ich gehe gern nach Berlin zurück.
2. Wieviele Gäste lädst du ein?
3. Welchen Film empfiehlt er?
4. Die Firma entläßt Tausende von Arbeitern.
5. Sie mißdeuten meine Worte.
6. Dieser Reisepaß gehört Frau Becker.
7. Hör mit dem Blödsinn auf, Katrin!
8. Die Uhr geht eine Stunde nach.
9. Der Pullover gefällt ihm gut.
10. Helga, ruf mich bitte zurück!
11. Sonntags stehen die Jugendlichen erst um 11 Uhr auf.
12. Das Buch beschreibt die Kindheit des Autors.

15.

1. hinauf
2. heraus
3. hinauf; herunter
4. herein; hinaus
5. heraus
6. herein; hinaus
7. hinauf
8. hinunter

16.

1. Muß es ausgerechnet jetzt regnen?
2. Sie wollen nach Griechenland fahren.
3. Bei Tests dürfen die Studenten nicht betrügen.
4. Wir sollen die Küche saubermachen.
5. Der Politiker muß uns seine Programme erklären.
6. Das Kind darf mit seiner Großmutter telefonieren.
7. Herr Hausmann kann den Kellerschlüssel nicht finden.
8. Sie will gleich in die Bücherei gehen.

17.

1. Du mußt das Problem lösen.
2. Ich darf morgen Tennis spielen.

3. Sie wollen ihre Nachbarn einladen.
4. Der Hund darf frei herumlaufen.
5. Wir sollen für die Prüfung lernen.
6. Wann soll der Zug ankommen?
7. Am Samstag können wir spät aufstehen.
8. Ich kann heute erst später kommen.
9. Die Arbeiter müssen schwer arbeiten.
10. Ich will meine Freunde besuchen.
11. Martina und Manfred möchten gerne verreisen.
12. Ihr sollt nicht immer so laut reden.

18.

1. sollen
2. Kannst
3. muß
4. will
5. darf
6. darf
7. mag
8. Möchten
9. müssen
10. Möchtest
11. müssen
12. dürfen
13. müssen
14. sollst
15. will
16. kann
17. möchten
18. dürft
19. will
20. Könnt

19.

1. sie arbeitete
2. ich liebte
3. wir lebten
4. du amüsiertest
5. ihr bemerktet
6. es bedeutete
7. sie hörten
8. ich dankte
9. Sie berichteten
10. er sammelte

20.

1. Der Professor fragte immer nur mich.
2. Nur Sport interessierte sie.
3. Der Ausflug machte viel Spaß.

4. Sie lernten einander auf einer Party kennen.
5. Dieser Rock kostete viel Geld.
6. Im Urlaub mieteten wir einen Wohnwagen.
7. Im Sommer pflanzten wir Blumen.
8. Die Lehrerin bereitete ihre Stunde vor.
9. Der Kuchen schmeckte gut.
10. Wir badeten immer in der Nordsee.
11. Im Malunterricht malten die Kinder ihre Lieblingstiere.
12. Ich machte einen Witz und ihr lachtet mich aus.

21.

1. begann, fand, gewann, schwamm, trank, sang, saß, aß, gab, half, las, sprach, trat, warf, tat, kam
2. blieb, schien, schrieb, fiel, hielt, ließ, schlief
3. ging, fing, biß, ritt, schnitt, litt
4. fuhr, schlug, trug, wuchs, wusch
5. flog, floh, fror, schloß, verlor, zog

22.

1. Der Lehrer las den Schülern eine Geschichte vor.
2. Der Traktor zog den Wagen.
3. Was tatest du dann?
4. Das Kind aß das Gemüse gern.
5. Wir flogen mit der Concorde.
6. Der Dieb stahl alle Schmucksachen.
7. Saht ihr den Vogel im Gebüsch?
8. Auf dem Börsenmarkt verloren die Geschäftsleute ihr Geld.
9. Wir hielten den Lärm nicht mehr aus.
10. Der Apfel fiel vom Baum herunter.
11. Ich sang ein Weihnachtslied.
12. Wer gewann das Spiel?

23.

1. begann
2. saßen; tranken
3. trug . . . weg
4. ging; schlief
5. schien
6. spracht
7. fuhr . . . ab
8. kam . . . hervor
9. starb

10. blieb; schrieb
11. wusch . . . ab
12. schloß

24.

1. war
2. hattest
3. wurde
4. war
5. hatten
6. wart
7. Hatten
8. wurde
9. Waren
10. wurde
11. Warst
12. hattet

25.

1. Die Gäste brachten Blumen und Schokolade mit.
2. Der Kaufmann wußte den Preis der Stereoanlage nicht.
3. Das kleine Kind rannte nach Hause.
4. Am Anfang nannten alle den Erfinder einen Idioten.
5. Die heiße Suppe verbrannte mir die Zunge.
6. Ich dachte jeden Tag an dich.
7. Kanntest du die Stadt schon?
8. Das Haus brannte bis auf die Grundmauern ab.
9. Nach drei Jahren erkannten sie sich fast nicht wieder.
10. Wir wußten die Namen der Bundesländer Deutschlands.
11. Dachtest du darüber nach?
12. Die Olympiasiergerin rannte allen anderen voran.

26.

1. mochte, wollte
2. mußten, sollten, wollten, durften, konnten
3. durfte, konnte, mußte; sollte, wollte
4. mußtest, solltest, wolltest
5. mußtet, solltet, wolltet, durftet, konntet
6. Mußtest, Konntest, Wolltest, Solltest

27.

1. sollte
2. wollten
3. Konntest
4. mochte

5. konnte
6. mußten
7. durfte
8. sollte
9. mußten
10. wollte

28.

1. Ich traf meine Freundin Claudia.
2. Der Wald brannte drei Tage lang.
3. Nur Frauen durften teilnehmen.
4. Das wollte ich nicht.
5. Dieser Film bekam 7 Oskars.
6. Wir mußten Geduld haben.
7. Sie stellte viele Fragen.
8. Alle mußten ihren Paß zeigen.
9. Wer gewann den ersten Preis?
10. Er kannte die Spielregeln nicht.
11. Ich fuhr am Wochenende nach Hause.
12. Der Dieb brach in das Haus ein.
13. Ich mochte den Nachtisch nicht.
14. Wir siegten in letzter Zeit immer öfter.
15. Der Schnellzug hielt auch in den kleinen Dörfern.

29.

1. schlief
2. kannte
3. rannte; konnte
4. brachte
5. sollten
6. Konntest
7. hoffte
8. waren
9. lernte
10. kauftet
11. verurteilte
12. lächelten
13. hatte
14. warteten; verloren
15. bediente

30.

1. Meine Mutter gab mir Geld.
2. Die Polizei wußte nichts über den Mordfall.
3. Ich vergaß unsere Abmachung.
4. Wir hatten großes Glück.
5. Was passierte hier?
6. Du mußtest bei der Gartenarbeit mithelfen.
7. In diesem Moment trat er ein.
8. Sie redete zu schnell.
9. Ich konnte sie nicht verstehen.
10. Er mußte schon wieder

abwaschen.
11. Gestern schrieb ich einen Brief an meinen Bruder.
12. Rolf schenkte sich ein zweites Glas Wein ein.
13. Katrin las das Buch durch.
14. Backtest du schon wieder Kuchen?
15. Wann stellte er seinen Eltern seine Freundin vor?

31.

1. geputzt
2. gerechnet
3. geschaut
4. gewohnt
5. geliebt
6. gebaut
7. gelebt
8. gehaßt
9. gekocht
10. geantwortet
11. geschätzt
12. gehört
13. geschüttelt
14. gefaßt
15. gestartet
16. gelacht
17. gefastet
18. gekämpft

32.

1. gegessen, gegeben, gesehen, gelesen
2. geholfen, getroffen, genommen, gesprochen, geworfen
3. geblieben, geschrieben, gemieden
4. gefahren, geschlafen, getragen, geschlagen, geladen, gewaschen, gelassen
5. gefunden, gesungen, getrunken
6. geritten, gelitten, geschnitten

33.

1. zerstört
2. mitgenommen
3. bestellt
4. gehört
5. telefoniert
6. ausgesehen
7. verkauft
8. angerufen
9. ausgegeben
10. spaziert
11. empfangen
12. geschehen
13. aufgestanden

14. mitgebracht
15. bezahlt

34.

1. haben
2. bin
3. bist
4. hat
5. ist
6. hat
7. hat
8. ist
9. hat
10. habt
11. sind
12. bist

35.

1. Er hat zu viel getrunken.
2. Der Clown hat viel zu große Schuhe angehabt.
3. Sie ist in jedes Land gereist.
4. Ich bin in Amerika geblieben.
5. Christian hat den ganzen Tag gelesen.
6. Es hat geklingelt.
7. Wir haben den Kuchen schnell gegessen.
8. Wir haben den ganzen Tag in der Sonne gelegen.
9. Meine Eltern sind auf jeden Berg gestiegen.
10. Er hat mich jeden Tag besucht.
11. Die Werkstatt hat das Auto repariert.
12. Sie hat mir genug Geld geliehen.
13. Warum seid ihr nicht geflogen?
14. Jeder hat sich über den Politiker aufgeregt.
15. Ich habe die Antwort gewußt.
16. Angela ist zur Schule gerannt.
17. Niemand hat der Zeugin zugehört.
18. Die Ärztin hat dem Kranken geholfen.
19. Dieser Sommer ist sehr heiß gewesen.
20. Das Kind hat das nicht verstanden.
21. Auf einmal hat sie die Augen aufgemacht.
22. In der Wüste hat es nur wenig Wasser gegeben.

36.

1. Das Konzert hat vor einer halben Stunde angefangen.
2. Niemand hat den Toten gekannt.
3. Der Talisman hat Glück gebracht.
4. Das gelbe Haus hat gebrannt.
5. Meine Mutter hat mich geschickt.
6. Monika hat mit ihrem Freund Schluß gemacht.
7. In diesem Jahr haben wir viel gelernt.
8. Wir sind sehr oft umgestiegen.
9. Meine Tante hat Medizin studiert.
10. Gestern haben wir einen guten Film gesehen.
11. Du hast zu schnell gesprochen.
12. Ich habe mit meinem Freund telefoniert.
13. Wann ist der Bus angekommen?
14. Der Alkoholiker ist vor kurzem gestorben.
15. Das Wetter ist wieder kalt geworden.
16. Ich habe die Frage nicht beantwortet.
17. Die Vögel haben in unserem Garten gesungen.
18. In den Ferien ist Tanja Ski gelaufen.
19. Ich habe mein Zimmer aufgeräumt.
20. Eva und Friedrich haben ihren 50. Hochzeitstag gefeiert.

37.

1. Wir haben laute Musik nicht spielen dürfen.
2. Ich habe das nicht gewollt!
3. Er hat die ganze Nacht hindurch lernen müssen.
4. Hier hat niemand Englisch verstehen können.
5. Sie hat nicht von zu Hause wegfahren wollen.
6. Sie hat die Erbsen nicht gemocht.
7. Viele haben es sofort gekonnt.
8. Er hat zur Arbeit gemußt.
9. Sie haben noch ein Bier trinken wollen.
10. Der Arzt hat dem Verletzten nicht helfen können.

38.

1. Ich hatte den ganzen Sommer gearbeitet.
2. Sie hatte die ganze Zeit da gesessen.
3. Die Kinder waren endlich ruhig geworden.
4. Wir hatten zu viel gegessen und getrunken.
5. Du hattest die Reise gut vorbereitet.
6. Corinna war schon den ganzen Tag müde gewesen.
7. Ich war schnell zum Bäcker gelaufen.
8. Die Menschenmenge hatte auf den Präsidenten gewartet.

39.

1. vergessen hatte
2. gearbeitet hatten
3. hatte . . . studiert
4. hatte . . . gehört
5. gelesen hatte
6. hatte . . . vorbereitet
7. war . . . abgefahren
8. geworden war

40.

1. Wir werden zu spät kommen.
2. Wir werden uns einen neuen Film anschauen.
3. Nach der Hochzeit wird es eine große Party geben.
4. Ich werde mit zwei Freunden nach Italien fahren.
5. Das wird sicher Spaß machen.
6. Wirst du viel für die Chemieprüfung lernen müssen?
7. Die Geschäfte werden um sechs zumachen.
8. Ich werde meine Familie anrufen.
9. Katjana wird am Hauptbahnhof ankommen.
10. Der Ausflug wird auch ohne dich stattfinden.

41.

1. Er wird wohl den Brief geschrieben haben.
2. Das Beste wird wohl vorbei gewesen sein.
3. Sie wird wohl keine Zeit gehabt haben.
4. Der Mann wird wohl zu viel getrunken haben.
5. Meine Eltern werden wohl mit dem Flugzeug gekommen sein.
6. Klaus und Silke werden wohl im Sommer geheiratet haben.

8

The Passive Voice

As in English, German sentences are either in the active or the passive voice. The choice between active and passive voice depends on what is emphasized in the sentence. An active sentence focuses on the person or thing performing some activity. A passive sentence focuses on the activity being performed or on the person or thing receiving the action of the verb.

The passive voice can be used in all of the same tenses that are possible for the active voice. It can also be used with modal verbs and in the subjunctive mood. In this chapter the most important indicative tenses in the passive voice will be practiced. Common methods used to avoid the passive voice will also be discussed.

ACTIVE VS. PASSIVE

Compare the following English sentences:

ACTIVE   The student *is writing* the essay.
PASSIVE   The essay *is (being) written* by the student.

In an active sentence, the subject acts. The emphasis of an active sentence is on the subject. Thus in the active sentence above, *the student* is most important. You are focusing on the person writing the essay.

In a passive sentence, the subject does not act, but is acted upon. The emphasis of the passive sentence is on the receiver of the action of the verb. Thus the passive sentence above focuses on the act of writing and its end result, *the essay*, is the most important element of the sentence.

In both English and German, the active voice is used more frequently than the passive voice, especially in the spoken language. The passive voice is found primarily in technical, scientific, and official writing where the process is more important than the subject and where it is important to sound objective.

Exercise 1: *Transform the active sentences into passive sentences.*

1. My brother is washing the car.
2. Storks do not deliver babies.
3. Many people are reading this novel.
4. The barber is shaving the customer.
5. Toads do not cause warts.

FORMATION OF THE PASSIVE VOICE

The basic formula for the passive voice in German is:

> **werden** + the past participle

The auxiliary verb **werden** is conjugated to agree with the subject. The past participle never changes form and stands at the end of a main clause.

Der Rasen **wird gemäht**.
The lawn is (being) mowed.

Der Zaun **wird gestrichen**.
The fence is (being) painted.

Meine Haare **werden** zu kurz **geschnitten**.
My hair is (being) cut too short.

Exercise 2: *Complete with the correct passive forms of the cue verbs.*

1. Das Brot _____ jeden Tag frisch _____.   (backen)
2. Der Verbrecher _____ von der Polizei _____.   (verhaften)
3. Das Manuskript _____ von dem Journal _____. (akzeptieren)
4. Die Bücher _____ von allen Studenten _____.   (lesen)
5. Der Baum _____ vom Förster _____.   (umsägen)
6. Solche Fragen _____ hier nicht _____.   (beantworten)
7. Der Brief _____ bald _____.   (schreiben)

8. Die Handtücher _____ auf die Leine _____.   (hängen)
9. Der heiße Tee _____ in die Tasse _____.   (gießen)
10. Das Geld _____ in die Bank _____.   (einzahlen)
11. Die Weihnachtsgeschenke _____ unter den Baum _____.
    (legen)
12. Das Lied _____ von der Sopranistin _____.   (singen)

The passive voice occurs in all the tenses of the active voice. The future perfect tense, however, is rare and will not be treated here.

To form the tenses of the passive voice, change the tense of **werden.** Note, however, that for the present perfect and past perfect tenses **geworden** becomes **worden.**

	ACTIVE	PASSIVE
PRESENT	Sie **wird** müde.	Sie **wird** gefragt.
SIMPLE PAST	Sie **wurde** müde.	Sie **wurde** gefragt.
PRESENT PERFECT	Sie **ist** müde **geworden.**	Sie **ist** gefragt **worden.**
PAST PERFECT	Sie **war** müde **geworden.**	Sie **war** gefragt **worden.**
FUTURE	Sie **wird** müde **werden.**	Sie **wird** gefragt **werden.**

In English the passive is formed with the auxiliary *to be* plus the past participle.

PRESENT	Sie **wird** gefragt.	*She **is** (being) asked.*
SIMPLE PAST	Sie **wurde** gefragt.	*She **was** (being) asked.*
PRESENT PERFECT	Sie **ist** gefragt **worden.**	*She **has been** asked.*
PAST PERFECT	Sie **war** gefragt **worden.**	*She **had been** asked.*
FUTURE	Sie **wird** gefragt **werden.**	*She **will be** asked.*

Exercise 3: *Restate the present tense passive sentences in the simple past, present perfect, past perfect, and future tenses.*

1. Das Auto wird immer sonntags gewaschen.
2. Das Fenster wird bei schönem Wetter aufgemacht.
3. Die Toten werden auf dem Friedhof begraben.
4. Das Haus wird von meinen Großeltern umgebaut.
5. Das Auto wird vom Chauffeur geparkt.

Exercise 4: *Form passive sentences from the words provided. Use the tense indicated.*

1. (*simple past*)   1961 / bauen / die Berliner Mauer.
2. (*present perfect*)   das Haus / renovieren / neulich.

3. (*present*)   die Tür / zumachen / langsam.

4. (*future*)   das Gesetz / ändern.

5. (*present*)   in diesem Geschäft / sprechen / Deutsch.

6. (*present perfect*)   diese Rechnung / bezahlen / noch nicht.

7. (*simple past*)   das Lied / singen / zu leise.

8. (*future*)   das Problem / lösen / endlich.

9. (*present perfect*)   die Resultate des Experiments / veröffentlichen / in der Zeitung.

10. (*past perfect*)   das Badezimmer / putzen / gerade.

11. (*simple past*)   das Kind / verletzen / beim Spielen.

12. (*present*)   in Deutschland / sparen / mehr / als in den USA.

13. (*simple past*)   das Haar / kämmen / vorsichtig.

14. (*present*)   auf dem Feld / anbauen / Mais.

15. (*present perfect*)   die Juwelenräuber / fangen / von der Polizei.

16. (*past perfect*)   die Äpfel / pflücken / zu spät.

17. (*simple past*)   die Höhle / erforschen / sorgfältig.

18. (*present perfect*)   nach zwei Wochen / reparieren / der Computer / endlich.

19. (*present*)   die Blume / begießen / täglich.

20. (*simple past*)   im Wohnzimmer / tapezieren / die Wände.

Exercise 5: *Translate into German.*

1. How was the problem finally solved?
2. Where will the experiment be published?
3. Why was the Berlin Wall built?
4. English is not spoken here.
5. This bill has not yet been paid.
6. The music is being played too loudly.
7. When will this law be changed?
8. How often does the flower get watered?

MODAL VERBS IN THE PASSIVE VOICE

The passive is used frequently with the modal verbs and may occur in all tenses. The basic formula for the passive with modal verbs is:

> modal verb + past participle + **werden**

The modal verb is conjugated to agree with the subject of the sentence. It also indicates the tense of the passive sentence. The past participle plus

werden, known as the *passive infinitive*, does not change its form and is placed at the end of a main clause.

PRESENT	Es **muß** gemacht werden.
	It must (has to) be done.
SIMPLE PAST	Es **mußte** gemacht werden.
	It had to be done.
PRESENT PERFECT	Es **hat** gemacht werden **müssen**.
	It has had to be done.
PAST PERFECT	Es **hatte** gemacht werden **müssen**.
	It had had to be done.
FUTURE	Es **wird** gemacht werden **müssen**.
	It will have to be done.

Note that the only differences between the sentences above occur in the forms of the modal. *The tense of the modal verb determines the tense of the passive construction.* In this book, we will use only the most common tenses for the modal verbs in passive: the present tense and the simple past tense.

Die Anmeldung **soll** bis zum 10. April **eingeschickt werden.**
The notification is supposed to be sent in by the tenth of April.

Seine Handschrift **konnte** nicht **gelesen werden.**
His handwriting could not be read.

Exercise 6: *Insert the modal into the passive sentence. Be sure to keep the tenses consistent.*

1. Der Aufsatz wurde mit dem Computer geschrieben.   (müssen)
2. Bei diesem Wetter wird ein Mantel getragen.   (sollen)
3. Die Vergangenheit wird nicht vergessen.   (dürfen)
4. Die Ideologie wird ständig in Frage gestellt.   (sollen)
5. Das Gedicht wurde auswendig gelernt.   (müssen)
6. Die Aufgabe wurde leicht vollendet.   (können)
7. Diese Suppe wird kalt gegessen.   (sollen)
8. Das alte Auto wird nicht zu schnell gefahren.   (dürfen)
9. Der Waffenstillstand wird nicht gebrochen.   (dürfen)
10. Das Zelt wurde wegen des starken Windes nicht aufgebaut. (können)
11. Das teure Bild wird verkauft.   (sollen)
12. Die giftigen Pilze werden nicht gegessen.   (dürfen)

Exercise 7: *You're having a party. Using the elements provided, create passive sentences with the modal* **müssen**, *listing everything that has to be done.*

Wir haben am Samstag eine Party.

1. am Dienstag: die Gäste einladen
2. am Freitag: das Wohnzimmer aufräumen
3. das Badezimmer putzen
4. das Geschirr abwaschen
5. am Samstag: das Wohnzimmer dekorieren
6. das Essen vorbereiten
7. die Getränke kaufen
8. die Plätzchen backen
9. auf der Party: Musik spielen
10. alles aufessen und leer trinken

Nach der Party muß geschlafen werden.

EXPRESSION OF THE AGENT IN PASSIVE SENTENCES

The performer, or *agent,* of the action may be expressed in the passive sentence in a prepositional phrase. Compare the following sentences:

	SUBJECT	DIRECT OBJECT
ACTIVE	**Der Student** schreibt	**den Aufsatz.**

	SUBJECT	AGENT
PASSIVE	**Der Aufsatz** wird	**von dem Studenten** geschrieben.
NO AGENT	Der Aufsatz wird geschrieben.	

The direct object of the active sentence becomes the subject of the passive sentence and the subject of the active sentence becomes the agent of the passive sentence or, if unimportant, is omitted.

The agent is expressed in a prepositional phrase preceded by **von**, **durch**, or **mit**, corresponding to the English preposition *by.*

von + *agent*

Usually the personal agent of the passive sentence is introduced by the dative preposition **von**.

Der Wagen wird **von meinem Bruder** gewaschen.
The car is (being) washed by my brother.

Die Vorlesung wird **von dem Gastprofessor** gehalten.
The lecture is being held (given) by the guest lecturer.

durch + agent

If the agent is impersonal, meaning *by means of* or *as the result of*, the accusative preposition **durch** is used to introduce the prepositional phrase.

Das Kind wurde **durch den Lärm** erschreckt.
The child was startled by the noise.

Der Wald wird **durch das Unwetter** zerstört.
The forest is destroyed as a result of the violent storm.

mit + agent

If the agent is an instrument, it is introduced by the dative preposition **mit**.

Der Aufsatz wurde **mit einem roten Stift** korrigiert.
The essay was corrected with a red pencil.

Exercise 8: *Complete with* **von, durch,** *or* **mit** *as appropriate.*

1. Die Schwerverletzte wurde _____ dem Hubschrauber ins Krankenhaus gebracht.
2. Die Medikamente wurden _____ der Ärztin verschrieben.
3. Bruder und Schwester wurden _____ den Krieg von einander getrennt.
4. Die beste Idee ist _____ der Frau dort hinten vorgeschlagen worden.
5. Briefmarken werden _____ vielen gesammelt.
6. Die neuen Waren werden heute _____ dem Zug geliefert.
7. Das Gebäude wurde _____ das Feuer zerstört.
8. Die Nachbarn werden _____ die laute Musik gestört.
9. Die Bergsteiger werden _____ einem Experten geführt.
10. Das Gemüse wurde _____ der Köchin gewaschen und _____ einem Messer kleingeschnitten.
11. Die wichtigen Papiere im Tresor wurden _____ die Hitze des Feuers zerstört.
12. Nicole wurde _____ das Klingeln des Weckers aufgeweckt.
13. Der Tisch wird _____ dem Sohn gedeckt.
14. Die Büsche werden _____ dem Gärtner geschnitten werden.
15. Die Versuche wurden _____ Hilfe der neuesten Technik durchgeführt.

PASSIVE CONSTRUCTIONS WITH IMPERSONAL VERBS

Some passive sentences have neither a subject nor an object. These constructions are used to describe general activities. They are highly idiomatic and have no corresponding English construction. Study the following examples and their English translations carefully:

Auf der Party wurde viel getanzt.
There was a lot of dancing at the party.

An Sylvester wird viel gefeiert.
There's a lot of celebrating on New Year's Eve.

Um zwölf wird gegessen.
We'll eat at noon. Lunch is served at noon.   (There is eating at noon.)

This type of construction may be used for general commands.

Hier wird nicht geraucht.
There is no smoking here. No smoking here!

Because these constructions have no subject, the verb is always in the third person singular.

Es is frequently inserted at the beginning of such sentences to hold the place of the subject.

Es wurde auf der Party viel getanzt.
Es wird an Sylvester viel gefeiert.
Es wird um zwölf gegessen.
Es wird hier nicht geraucht.

Exercise 9: *Translate into English.*

1. Es wird gesungen und gelacht.
2. In der Bibliothek wird gelernt.
3. Heute wird gefeiert.
4. Es wird gegen Atomkraftwerke demonstriert.
5. Jetzt wird gearbeitet.
6. Auf Straßenmärkten wird oft gefeilscht.
7. Während der Lesung wird nicht gesprochen.
8. Während der Kaffeepause wird viel geplaudert.

PASSIVE CONSTRUCTIONS WITH DATIVE OBJECTS

Dative objects remain dative in passive constructions.

Passive with Indirect (Dative) Objects

In English, either the direct object or the indirect object of an active sentence may become the subject of a passive sentence.

DIRECT OBJECT

ACTIVE   The writer sent the editor **his new novel**.

SUBJECT

PASSIVE   **His new novel** was sent to the editor.

INDIRECT OBJECT

ACTIVE   The writer sent **the editor** his new novel.

SUBJECT

PASSIVE   **The editor** was sent his new novel.

In German, on the other hand, only the direct object (accusative) can become the subject of the passive sentence. The indirect object (dative) cannot be used as the subject and remains in the dative case as the indirect object.

DIRECT OBJECT

ACTIVE   Der Autor schickte **dem Lektor** seinen neuen Roman.

SUBJECT

PASSIVE   Sein neuer Roman wurde **dem Lektor** geschickt.

Exercise 10: *Translate into German. Begin the sentence with the dative object. Follow the model.*

> Wem wurde keine Chance gegeben?   (*I wasn't given a chance.*)
> **Mir wurde keine Chance gegeben.**

1. Wem wurde Geld gegeben?   (*The man was given money.*)
2. Wem wurde der Preis nicht gezeigt?   (*My father wasn't shown the price.*)
3. Wem wurde die Rechnung geschickt?   (*I was sent the bill.*)
4. Wem wurde der kleine Hund geschenkt?   (*The boy was given the little dog.*)

5. Wem wurde die Wahrheit nicht gesagt?   (*The woman wasn't told the truth.*)

6. Wem wurde das falsche Paket geschickt?   (*My family was sent the wrong package.*)

Passive with Dative Verbs

The object of a dative verb remains dative in a passive construction.

Den Anfängern wurde gestern abend geholfen.
The beginners were helped yesterday evening.

Gutem Rat soll immer gefolgt werden.
Good advice should always be followed.

Since **den Anfängern** and **gutem Rat** are in the dative case, the German sentences above have no subjects. The verb is third person singular in such cases.

Es may be inserted at the beginning of such sentences to hold the place of the subject. Similarly, another sentence element may be used instead of **es** as a placeholder for the missing subject. The verb remains in the third person singular.

Es wurde den Anfängern gestern abend geholfen.
Gestern abend wurde den Anfängern geholfen.
Es soll gutem Rat immer gefolgt werden.
Immer soll gutem Rat gefolgt werden.

Exercise 11: *Translate into German. Begin the passive sentence with the dative object. Follow the model.*

Wem wird zum Hochzeitstag gratuliert?   (*The married couple is congratulated on their anniversary.*)
Dem Ehepaar wird zum Hochzeitstag gratuliert.

1. Wem wird nicht mehr geglaubt?   (*The politician is no longer believed.*)

2. Wem wird ständig widersprochen?   (*He is constantly being contradicted.*)

3. Wem wird nicht geholfen?   (*The impudent boy is not being helped.*)

4. Wem kann noch geholfen werden?   (*They can still be helped.*)

5. Wem muß für alles gedankt werden?   (*My parents must be thanked for everything.*)

6. Wem wird nicht getraut?   (*The liar is not trusted.*)

REVIEW EXERCISE WITH THE PASSIVE VOICE

Exercise 12: *Form passive sentences from the words provided. Use the tense indicated.*

1. (*present perfect*)   Amerika / entdecken / wirklich / von / Columbus?
2. (*present*)   endlich / dürfen / nehmen / Platz.
3. (*simple past*)   das Problem / besprechen / von / die Experten.
4. (*present*)   die kleinen Kinder / helfen / von niemand.
5. (*future*)   der deutsche Film / zeigen / von / unser Verein.
6. (*present*)   dieses Buch / lesen / in allen Seminaren.
7. (*simple past*)   die Gitarre des Rockmusikers / zerschlagen / während des Konzerts.
8. (*present*)   dieser Artikel / müssen / übersetzen / bis Montag.
9. (*present*)   die Chirurgen / dürfen / stören / bei der Operation / nicht.
10. (*present perfect*)   der Vertrag / unterschreiben / von / die zwei Länder.
11. (*simple past*)   das Fenster / zerbrechen / durch / der Stein.
12. (*present*)   hier / können / einlösen / Reiseschecks / nicht.
13. (*present*)   die Tür / schließen / ganz leise.
14. (*present*)   an der Grenze / kontrollieren.
15. (*simple past*)   der *Messias* / schreiben / von Händel / in einer Woche.
16. (*present perfect*)   die Schuhe / putzen / gestern / von mir.
17. (*present*)   fremde Hunde / sollen / streicheln / nicht.
18. (*simple past*)   der Banküberfall / filmen / von / die Videokamera.
19. (*present*)   Vor dem Essen / müssen / waschen / die Hände.
20. (*present perfect*)   der Sprecher / unterbrechen / während des Vortrags.

TRUE VS. FALSE PASSIVE

The forms we have practiced so far in this chapter are *true passive* forms. The true passive expresses an *action* that is performed by a stated or understood agent. Any passive sentence that includes an agent is true passive.

The *false passive* expresses a *condition*. The action is already completed and no agent is stated or understood. Compare the following sentences:

TRUE PASSIVE	FALSE PASSIVE
Das Haus **wird** verkauft.	Das Haus **ist** verkauft.
The house is being sold.	*The house is sold.*

In the true passive sentence, the house is being sold; it is on the market. Attention is focused on the act of selling the house, and some agent (for example, a real estate agent or the owner of the house), although not explicitly stated, is engaged in the action. In the false passive sentence, the house is already sold. The act of selling the house is completed and the sentence describes the condition of the house.

As you know, true passive is formed with **werden** plus the past participle. The false passive is formed with **sein** plus the past participle. The past participle functions as an adjective describing the house, like any other descriptive adjective.

Das Haus ist **verkauft**.	*The house is sold.*
Das Haus ist **groß**.	*The house is big.*
Das Haus ist **weiß**.	*The house is white.*

In order to form other tenses of the false passive, the tense of **sein** changes. The only tenses of the false passive practiced in this book are the present and simple past tenses.

PRESENT	Das Haus **ist** verkauft.	*The house is sold.*
SIMPLE PAST	Das Haus **war** verkauft.	*The house was sold.*

Note that English does not make this distinction with verb forms. The passive voice is formed with *to be* plus a past participle. To emphasize the idea of action (true passive), English frequently uses the progressive form. To express the idea of condition (false passive), English frequently uses the adverb *already*.

The house is *being* sold.
The house is *already* sold.

Exercise 13: *Complete with the correct form of* **werden** *for true passive or* **sein** *for false passive. Pay attention to the verb tenses.*

1. Das Zimmer ist kalt. Das Fenster _____ geöffnet.
2. Das Zimmer ist zu warm. Das Fenster _____ von dem Studenten geöffnet.
3. Ich habe ein Glas Wein verschüttet. Der Teppich _____ jetzt beschmutzt.
4. Der Teppich _____ gestern durch ein Glas Wein beschmutzt.
5. Das kleine Kind _____ von seiner Mutter angezogen.

6. Ach! Du siehst schön aus! Du _____ so schön angezogen.
7. Wir warten in der Wäscherei, während die Wäsche gewaschen _____.
8. Ich ziehe dieses Kleid an. Es _____ frisch gewaschen.
9. Die Wohnung _____ von einer amerikanischen Familie gemietet.
10. Man darf die Wohnung nicht mehr besichtigen. Sie _____ schon gemietet.

WAYS TO AVOID THE PASSIVE VOICE

In German, especially in the spoken language, the passive voice frequently is avoided. There are four ways to avoid the passive. The first, using the indefinite pronoun **man**, is very common; the other three are used less frequently.

Using man to Avoid the Passive

The most common way to avoid the passive voice is with the indefinite pronoun **man** plus the active voice. **Man** can be used to avoid any passive sentence that does not contain an agent.

PASSIVE	ACTIVE
Es wird hier gearbeitet.	**Man** arbeitet hier.
Das muß gemacht werden.	**Man** muß das machen.

If the passive sentence contains a subject, it becomes the direct object of the **man** construction.

PASSIVE	ACTIVE
Der Ball wird geworfen.	Man wirft **den Ball**.
Der Lehrer wird gefragt.	Man fragt **den Lehrer**.

Exercise 14: *Use **man** to avoid the passive. Keep the tenses consistent.*

1. Ihr wurde keine Chance gegeben.
2. Beim Autofahren soll nicht getrunken werden.
3. Wird in Amerika zu viel ferngesehen?
4. Ein spannender Krimi wird schnell gelesen.
5. Auf der Autobahn wird sehr schnell gefahren.
6. Der Brief ist gestern abgeschickt worden.
7. Nichts konnte gesehen werden.
8. Es soll nicht gelogen werden.
9. Die Betten mußten neu bezogen werden.
10. In Deutschland werden verschiedene Dialekte gesprochen.
11. Der Stuhl ist gestern weiß gestrichen worden.
12. Nachts können schöne Spaziergänge gemacht werden.

Using sein + zu + the Infinitive to Avoid the Passive

The verb **sein** plus **zu** plus the infinitive can be used to avoid passive sentences containing the modal verbs **können**, **müssen**, and **sollen**. The infinitive phrase is placed at the end of a main clause.

PASSIVE	ACTIVE
Das kann nicht gemacht werden.	Das **ist** nicht **zu machen.**
That cannot be done.	
Der Test muß geschrieben werden.	Der Test **ist zu schreiben.**
The test must be written (taken).	

With separable-prefix verbs, the **zu** is placed between the verb and the prefix.

Bei diesem Wetter ist ein Mantel an**zu**ziehen.
A coat should be put on (worn) in this weather.

Exercise 15: *Use* **sein + zu** + *infinitive to avoid the passive. Keep the tenses consistent.*

1. Die Musik soll leiser gespielt werden.
2. Das Geschirr mußte noch abgewaschen werden.
3. Dieser Moment soll möglichst schnell vergessen werden.
4. Die zwei Fälle können leicht verglichen werden.
5. Die Regeln sollen beachtet werden.
6. Die Fenster sollten aufgemacht werden.
7. Die Katze kann nicht im Haus eingesperrt werden.
8. Die Videofilme müssen zurückgebracht werden.

Using sich lassen + the Infinitive to Avoid the Passive

The verb **sich lassen** plus the infinitive can be used to avoid passive sentences containing the modal verb **können**.

PASSIVE	ACTIVE
Die Tür kann leicht geöffnet werden.	Die Tür **läßt sich** leicht **öffnen.**
The door can be opened easily.	
Das kann nicht vermieden werden.	Das **läßt sich** nicht **vermeiden.**
That cannot be avoided.	

Exercise 16: *Use* **sich lassen** + *the infinitive to avoid the passive.*

1. Das Gedicht kann nur schwer gelernt werden.
2. Vom Weltfrieden kann leider nur geträumt werden.
3. Die Kirche kann von hier aus gut gesehen werden.
4. Von der kaputten Telefonzelle kann nicht mehr telefoniert werden.
5. Die Segeltour kann nur bei gutem Wetter gewagt werden.
6. Der Tresor kann nur mit der richtigen Zahlenkombination geöffnet werden.

7. Unfälle können nur durch vorsichtiges Autofahren vermieden werden.
8. Die Wahrheit kann oft nur schwer erkannt werden.

Using a Reflexive Construction to Avoid the Passive

The verb can be made reflexive to avoid the passive. This type of construction excludes any type of agent and is highly idiomatic.

PASSIVE

Das Buch wird leicht gelesen.
The book is easily read.

ACTIVE

Das Buch **liest sich** leicht.

Das Essen wird schnell gekocht.
The meal is cooked quickly.

Das Essen **kocht sich** schnell.

Exercise 17: *Use a reflexive construction to avoid the passive. Translate your sentences into idiomatic English.*

1. Die Muttersprache wird leichter gesprochen als eine Fremdsprache.
2. Der Umweg wird nur schwer gefunden.
3. Die Tür wird langsam geöffnet.
4. Deutsch wird leicht gelernt.
5. Kartoffeln werden am besten mit Soße gegessen.
6. Die weiche Butter wird leicht aufs Brot gestrichen.

SUMMARY OF THE USES OF WERDEN

The verb **werden** is used in a variety of constructions that must not be confused.

Werden *as the* Main Verb

Werden can be used as a main verb meaning *to become* or *to get*.

Im Herbst **werden** die Tage immer länger.
In the fall the days become longer and longer.

Sie **wurde** durch den langen Spaziergang müde.
She became tired because of the long walk.

Werden *in the* Future Tense

Werden is used with the infinitive of the main verb to express the future tense.

Wir **werden** zu spät **ankommen**.
We'll arrive too late.

Er **wird** uns in der Kneipe **treffen**.
He will meet us in the bar.

Werden *in the Passive Voice*

Werden is used together with the past participle of the main verb to express the passive voice.

In Deutschland **wird** viel Kaffee **getrunken**.
People drink a lot of coffee in Germany.

Das Auto **wurde** durch Hagel **beschädigt**.
The car was damaged by hail.

Exercise 18: *Identify the usage of* **werden** *and the tense of the sentence. Then translate the sentence into English.*

1. Wann wirst du zurückkommen?
2. Dieses Haus wurde schnell verkauft.
3. Ich möchte Professor werden.
4. Die Katze wurde von den Kindern eingefangen.
5. Heute wird Mozarts *Jupitersinfonie* in Cleveland gespielt.
6. Die Zahl der Obdachlosen wird immer größer.
7. Den Gesetzen wird nicht mehr gehorcht werden.
8. Der Briefträger wurde von dem Hund gebissen.
9. Du wirst nie wieder einen Anruf von mir bekommen.
10. Der Rasen muß gemäht werden.
11. Vor einer Klausur werden die Studenten nervös.
12. Ich durfte damals kein Maler werden.
13. Werden Astronauten jemals auf dem Jupiter landen?
14. Die Möbel werden auf den Lastwagen geladen.
15. Nachts soll die Musik nicht so laut gespielt werden.
16. Das Baby ist täglich größer geworden.
17. Der Antrag des Präsidenten wurde angenommen.
18. Ich werde dich dieses Wochenende besuchen.

ANSWERS TO EXERCISES

1.

1. The car is (being) washed by my brother.
2. Babies are not delivered by storks.
3. This novel is (being) read by many people.
4. The customer is (being) shaved by the barber.
5. Warts are not caused by toads.

2.

1. wird . . . gebacken
2. wird . . . verhaftet
3. wird . . . akzeptiert
4. werden . . . gelesen
5. wird . . . umgesägt
6. werden . . . beantwortet
7. wird . . . geschrieben
8. werden . . . gehängt
9. wird . . . gegossen
10. wird . . . eingezahlt
11. werden . . . gelegt
12. wird . . . gesungen

3.

1. wurde . . . gewaschen
   ist . . . gewaschen worden
   war . . . gewaschen worden
   wird . . . gewaschen werden
2. wurde . . . aufgemacht
   ist . . . aufgemacht worden
   war . . . aufgemacht worden
   wird . . . aufgemacht werden
3. wurden . . . begraben
   sind . . . begraben worden
   waren . . . begraben worden
   werden . . . begraben werden
4. wurde . . . umgebaut
   ist . . . umgebaut worden
   war . . . umgebaut worden
   wird . . . umgebaut werden
5. wurde . . . geparkt
   ist . . . geparkt worden
   war . . . geparkt worden
   wird . . . geparkt werden

4.

1. 1961 wurde die Berliner Mauer gebaut.
2. Das Haus ist neulich renoviert worden.
3. Die Tür wird langsam zugemacht.
4. Das Gesetz wird geändert werden.
5. In diesem Geschäft wird Deutsch gesprochen.
6. Diese Rechnung ist noch nicht bezahlt worden.
7. Das Lied wurde zu leise gesungen.
8. Das Problem wird endlich gelöst werden.
9. Die Resultate des Experiments sind in der Zeitung veröffentlicht worden.
10. Das Badezimmer war gerade geputzt worden.
11. Das Kind wurde beim Spielen verletzt.
12. In Deutschland wird mehr als in den USA gespart.
13. Das Haar wurde vorsichtig gekämmt.
14. Auf dem Feld wird Mais angebaut.
15. Die Juwelenräuber sind von der Polizei gefangen worden.
16. Die Äpfel waren zu spät gepflückt worden.
17. Die Höhle wurde sorgfältig erforscht.
18. Nach zwei Wochen ist der Computer endlich repariert worden.
19. Die Blume wird täglich begossen.
20. Im Wohnzimmer wurden die Wände tapeziert.

5.

1. Wie wurde das Problem endlich gelöst?
2. Wo wird das Experiment veröffentlicht werden?
3. Warum wurde die Berliner Mauer gebaut?
4. Englisch wird hier nicht gesprochen.
5. Diese Rechnung ist noch nicht bezahlt worden.
6. Die Musik wird zu laut gespielt.
7. Wann wird dieses Gesetz geändert werden?
8. Wie oft wird die Blume begossen?

6.

1. Der Aufsatz mußte mit dem Computer geschrieben werden.
2. Bei diesem Wetter soll ein Mantel getragen werden.
3. Die Vergangenheit darf nicht vergessen werden.
4. Die Ideologie soll ständig in Frage gestellt werden.
5. Das Gedicht mußte auswendig gelernt werden.
6. Die Aufgabe konnte leicht vollendet werden.
7. Diese Suppe soll kalt gegessen werden.
8. Das alte Auto darf nicht zu schnell gefahren werden.
9. Der Waffenstillstand darf nicht gebrochen werden.
10. Das Zelt konnte wegen des starken Windes nicht aufgebaut werden.
11. Das teure Bild soll verkauft werden.
12. Die giftigen Pilze dürfen nicht gegessen werden.

7.

1. Am Dienstag müssen die Gäste eingeladen werden.
2. Am Freitag muß das Wohnzimmer aufgeräumt werden.
3. Das Badezimmer muß geputzt werden.
4. Das Geschirr muß abgewaschen werden.
5. Am Samstag muß das Wohnzimmer dekoriert werden.
6. Das Essen muß vorbereitet werden.
7. Die Getränke müssen gekauft werden.
8. Die Plätzchen müssen gebacken werden.
9. Auf der Party muß Musik gespielt werden.

10. Alles muß aufgegessen und leer getrunken werden.

8.
1. mit
2. von
3. durch
4. von
5. von
6. mit
7. durch
8. durch
9. von
10. von; mit
11. durch
12. durch
13. von
14. von
15. mit

9.
1. There's singing and laughing. (Everyone's singing and laughing.)
2. There's studying (going on) in the library. (The library is for studying.)
3. Today there's celebrating. (Today we're going to celebrate.)
4. There's demonstrating against nuclear power plants. (There is a demonstration against nuclear power plants.)
5. Now it's time to work.
6. You often bargain at street markets.
7. No speaking during the reading!
8. There's a lot of talking during the coffee break.

10.
1. Dem Mann wurde Geld gegeben.
2. Meinem Vater wurde der Preis nicht gezeigt.
3. Mir wurde die Rechnung geschickt.
4. Dem Jungen wurde der kleine Hund geschenkt.
5. Der Frau wurde die Wahrheit nicht gesagt.
6. Meiner Familie wurde das falsche Paket geschickt.

11.
1. Dem Politiker/Der Politikerin wird nicht mehr geglaubt.
2. Ihm wird ständig widersprochen.
3. Dem frechen Jungen wird nicht geholfen.
4. Ihnen kann noch geholfen werden.
5. Meinen Eltern muß für alles gedankt werden.
6. Dem Lügner wird nicht getraut.

12.
1. Ist Amerika wirklich von Columbus entdeckt worden?
2. Endlich darf Platz genommen werden.
3. Das Problem wurde von den Experten besprochen.
4. Den kleinen Kindern wird von niemand geholfen.
5. Der deutsche Film wird von unserem Verein gezeigt werden.
6. Dieses Buch wird in allen Seminaren gelesen.
7. Die Gitarre des Rockmusikers wurde während des Konzerts zerschlagen.
8. Dieser Artikel muß bis Montag übersetzt werden.
9. Die Chirurgen dürfen bei der Operation nicht gestört werden.
10. Der Vertrag ist von den zwei Ländern unterschrieben worden.
11. Das Fenster wurde durch den Stein zerbrochen.
12. Hier können Reiseschecks nicht eingelöst werden.
13. Die Tür wird ganz leise geschlossen.
14. An der Grenze wird kontrolliert.
15. Der *Messias* wurde von Händel in einer Woche geschrieben.
16. Die Schuhe sind gestern von mir geputzt worden.
17. Fremde Hunde sollen nicht gestreichelt werden.
18. Der Banküberfall wurde von der Videokamera gefilmt.
19. Vor dem Essen müssen die Hände gewaschen werden.
20. Der Sprecher ist während des Vortrags unterbrochen worden.

13.
1. ist
2. wird
3. ist
4. wurde
5. wird
6. bist
7. wird
8. ist
9. wird
10. ist

14.
1. Man gab ihr keine Chance.
2. Man soll beim Autofahren nicht trinken.
3. Sieht man in Amerika zu viel fern?
4. Man liest einen spannenden Krimi schnell.
5. Auf der Autobahn fährt man sehr schnell.
6. Man hat den Brief gestern abgeschickt.
7. Man konnte nichts sehen.
8. Man soll nicht lügen.
9. Man mußte die Betten neu beziehen.
10. In Deutschland spricht man verschiedene Dialekte.
11. Gestern hat man den Stuhl weiß gestrichen.
12. Nachts kann man schöne Spaziergänge machen.

15.
1. Die Musik ist leiser zu spielen.
2. Das Geschirr war noch abzuwaschen.
3. Dieser Moment ist möglichst schnell zu vergessen.
4. Die zwei Fälle sind leicht zu vergleichen.
5. Die Regeln sind zu beachten.
6. Die Fenster waren aufzumachen.
7. Die Katze ist nicht im Haus einzusperren.
8. Die Videofilme sind zurückzubringen.

16.
1. Das Gedicht läßt sich nur schwer lernen.

2. Vom Weltfrieden läßt sich leider nur träumen.

3. Die Kirche läßt sich von hier aus gut sehen.

4. Von der kaputten Telefonzelle läßt sich nicht mehr telefonieren.

5. Die Segeltour läßt sich nur bei gutem Wetter wagen.

6. Der Tresor läßt sich nur mit der richtigen Zahlenkombination öffnen.

7. Unfälle lassen sich nur durch vorsichtiges Autofahren vermeiden.

8. Die Wahrheit läßt sich oft nur schwer erkennen.

17.

1. Die Muttersprache spricht sich leichter als eine Fremdsprache.
   One's native language is spoken more easily than a foreign one.

2. Der Umweg findet sich nur schwer.
   It's a lot of trouble to find the detour.

3. Die Tür öffnet sich langsam.
   The door is opened (opens) slowly.

4. Deutsch lernt sich leicht.
   It is easy to learn German.

5. Kartoffeln essen sich am besten mit Soße.
   Potatoes are best eaten with gravy.

6. Die weiche Butter streicht sich leicht aufs Brot.
   Soft butter is easy to spread on bread.

18.

1. Future tense: When will you come back?

2. Passive; simple past tense: This house (was) sold quickly.

3. Main verb with a modal; present tense: I would like to become a professor.

4. Passive; simple past tense: The cat was caught by the children.

5. Passive; present tense: Mozart's *Jupiter Symphony* is being played in Cleveland today.

6. Main verb; present tense: The number of homeless is becoming greater and greater.

7. Passive; future tense: The laws will no longer be obeyed.

8. Passive; simple past tense: The mail carrier was bitten by the dog.

9. Future tense: You will never again get a call from me.

10. Passive with a modal; present tense: The lawn must be mowed.

11. Main verb; present tense: The students become nervous before a test.

12. Main verb with a modal; simple past tense: I wasn't allowed to become a painter at that time.

13. Future tense: Will astronauts ever land on Jupiter?

14. Passive; present tense: The furniture is being loaded onto the truck.

15. Passive with a modal; present tense: At night music is not supposed to be played so loudly.

16. Main verb; present perfect tense: The baby has grown bigger daily.

17. Passive; simple past tense: The president's proposal was accepted.

18. Future tense: I will visit you this weekend.

9

The General Subjunctive

There are two different moods in English and German: the indicative mood and the subjunctive mood. Mood is used to express differing attitudes of the speaker concerning the truth or likelihood of a statement. The indicative mood indicates that a statement is true or likely; it is based on a real situation. The subjunctive mood is used when the speaker wants to express doubt concerning the veracity of a statement. The subjunctive mood indicates that the statement is improbable, unlikely, hypothetical, or unreal.

Until now, we have practiced the indicative mood. This chapter deals with the uses and forms of the general subjunctive, also called subjunctive II or simply the subjunctive. The subjunctive mood is used frequently in both speaking and writing. It occurs in two tenses, the present and the past, and can be used with the modal verbs. (Subjunctive I is a less common mood that will be discussed in chapter 10.)

THE SUBJUNCTIVE IN ENGLISH

The subjunctive mood is used frequently in both English and German, in written texts as well as in everyday spoken language. It is used in essentially the same way in both languages: the subjunctive mood expresses doubt concerning the factuality or reality of a statement. This section attempts to familiarize you with the subjunctive in English. It is essential that you be able to recognize situations that require the subjunctive.

The Subjunctive in Unreal Conditions

The subjunctive is used frequently to express unreal conditions.

If my parents *were coming*, we *would go* out to dinner.
If she *knew* his address, she *would stop by*.

The sentences above describe conditions that are not true in the sense that they cannot be fulfilled. In the first sentence, my parents are not coming so we will not go out to dinner. In the second sentence, she does not know his address and therefore is not able to stop by. Such unreal conditional sentences imply that the opposite is true. They seem to end with an understood "but." Study the following sentences:

If I *had* enough money, I *would go* to Europe this summer.
(BUT I don't have enough money and therefore I will not be going to Europe this summer.)

If I *knew* that, I *wouldn't be asking* you.
(BUT I don't know that and therefore I am asking you.)

Unreal conditional sentences may be in the present or past tense. Compare the following past tense subjunctive sentences to the present tense ones above:

If my parents *had come*, we *would have gone out* to dinner.
If she *had known* his address, she *would have stopped by*.
If I *had had* enough money, I *would have gone* to Europe this summer.
If I *had known* that, I *wouldn't have asked* you.

Not all conditional sentences are unreal. They may be true or untrue, that is, they may be in the indicative as well as the subjunctive mood. Compare the following real conditional sentences to the unreal ones above:

If my parents *come*, we *will go out* to dinner.
If she *knows* his address, she'*ll stop by*.
If I *have* enough money, I'*ll go* to Europe this summer.
If I *know* that, I *won't ask* you.

In the examples above, the conditions are true or real in the sense that they may happen; they are possible. They are therefore in the indicative mood.

The Subjunctive in Wishes, Hypothetical Situations, and Polite Requests

The subjunctive is also used when the speaker wants to express uncertainty or doubt, such as in wishes that cannot be fulfilled and hypothetical statements. It is also used to soften requests or questions, making them less direct and more polite.

WISHES

If only I *were* a little taller!
If only I *had arrived* ten minutes earlier!

HYPOTHETICAL SITUATIONS

What *would* you *do*?
I *wouldn't have said* that to his face.

POLITE REQUESTS

Would you please *come* with me?
Could you please *explain* this example to me?

Forms of the Subjunctive in English

English generally shifts the tense of the verb to mark the subjunctive. Present time subjunctive is built on the simple past indicative tense of the verb, as in the following sentences:

If only I *had* the time (right now)!
If only I *knew* of a solution (today; now)!

Similarly, the past time subjunctive is built on the past perfect indicative tense of the verb:

If only I *had had* the time (yesterday)!
If only I *had known* of a solution (yesterday; in the past)!

Another common way to form the subjunctive is with *would*.

What *would* you *do*?
What *would* you *have done*?

Exercise 1: *Indicate whether the sentences are indicative or subjunctive.*

1. If it's nice outside, we'll go on a picnic.
2. Would you please turn down the radio?
3. If it's already 5 o'clock, then we're late.
4. If you were sick, you would have to stay in bed.
5. If only I could play the guitar!
6. You shouldn't have said that to her.
7. Could you stop by tonight?
8. After they saw the movie they couldn't go to sleep.
9. If you like chocolate, you'll love Vienna's *Sachertorte*.
10. If I flunk another class, my parents will take me out of school.
11. I wish I had known that earlier.
12. If the weather had been nice, I would have gone jogging.
13. If my car weren't broken, I could give you a ride.

14. If I find out the answer, I'll call.
15. You would undoubtedly be a big hit as a comedian.
16. It would be nice if you could help me.
17. If this suit isn't too expensive, I'll buy it.
18. If my apartment complex allowed pets, I would get a cat.

PRESENT TENSE SUBJUNCTIVE IN GERMAN

The subjunctive occurs in two tenses, the present and the past. The present tense subjunctive is used to express unreal or hypothetical statements in present and future time. As in English, there are two ways to express the present tense subjunctive in German: a one-word form and a paraphrase with **würde** plus the infinitive.

The One-Word Form

Like the English one-word form, German present tense subjunctive is derived from the simple past tense of the verb. Present tense subjunctive endings for all verbs are:

ich	**-e**	wir	**-en**
du	**-est**	ihr	**-et**
er/es/sie	**-e**	sie	**-en**
	Sie	**-en**	

WEAK VERBS

The present tense subjunctive for weak verbs is identical to the simple past tense indicative.

	sagen	**arbeiten**
ich	sag**te**	arbeit**ete**
du	sag**test**	arbeit**etest**
er/es/sie	sag**te**	arbeit**ete**
wir	sag**ten**	arbeit**eten**
ihr	sag**tet**	arbeit**etet**
sie	sag**ten**	arbeit**eten**
Sie	sag**ten**	arbeit**eten**

STRONG VERBS

The basic formula for strong verbs in the present subjunctive is:

simple past stem + subjunctive ending + umlaut if possible (**a**, **o**, **u**)

	fahren	**nehmen**	**gehen**	**schlafen**
ich	führe	nähme	ginge	schliefe
du	führest	nähmest	gingest	schliefest
er/es/sie	führe	nähme	ginge	schliefe
wir	führen	nähmen	gingen	schliefen
ihr	führet	nähmet	ginget	schliefet
sie	führen	nähmen	gingen	schliefen
Sie	führen	nähmen	gingen	schliefen

A few strong verbs have present tense subjunctive forms that are old-fashioned and no longer common. Some of these verbs have developed an alternate form. Even more frequently, the **würde** plus infinitive paraphrase is used.

INFINITIVE	PAST STEM	OLD SUBJUNCTIVE	NEW SUBJUNCTIVE
gewinnen	gewann	gewönne	gewänne
helfen	half	hülfe	hälfe
schwimmen	schwamm	schwömme	schwämme
stehen	stand	stünde	stände
sterben	starb	stürbe	
werfen	warf	würfe	

HABEN, SEIN, AND *WERDEN*

	haben	**sein**	**werden**
ich	hätte	wäre	würde
du	hättest	wärest	würdest
er/es/sie	hätte	wäre	würde
wir	hätten	wären	würden
ihr	hättet	wäret	würdet
sie	hätten	wären	würden
Sie	hätten	wären	würden

MIXED VERBS

The mixed or irregular weak verbs **bringen**, **denken**, and **wissen** form the present subjunctive by adding an umlaut to their simple past tense forms.

INFINITIVE	SIMPLE PAST	PRESENT SUBJUNCTIVE
bringen	brachte	**brächte**
denken	dachte	**dächte**
wissen	wuβte	**wüβte**

The other mixed verbs form the present subjunctive by changing the stem vowel of the simple past tense form to **e**. These forms are not common and usually are replaced by the **würde** paraphrase.

INFINITIVE	SIMPLE PAST	PRESENT SUBJUNCTIVE
brennen	brannte	**brennte**
kennen	kannte	**kennte**
nennen	nannte	**nennte**
rennen	rannte	**rennte**

MODAL VERBS

The present subjunctive of modal verbs is also based on the simple past tense. An umlaut is added to the stem vowel if the infinitive of the modal has an umlaut. In other words, **dürfen**, **können**, **mögen**, and **müssen** add an umlaut in the present subjunctive; **sollen** and **wollen** do not.

INFINITIVE	SIMPLE PAST	PRESENT SUBJUNCTIVE
dürfen	durfte	**dürfte**
können	konnte	**könnte**
mögen	mochte	**möchte**
müssen	mußte	**müßte**
sollen	sollte	**sollte**
wollen	wollte	**wollte**

Exercise 2: *Give the simple past tense and then the present subjunctive of the following verbs.*

1. Gabi lebt, arbeitet, wohnt, fragt, bemerkt, kauft, bestellt
2. ich fahre, singe, esse, lese, schreibe, finde, bleibe, komme, spreche, schlafe, sehe
3. wir haben, sind, werden
4. du denkst, weißt, bringst
5. sie können, dürfen, wollen, sollen, mögen, müssen

The würde Paraphrase

The present subjunctive may be paraphrased with:

> **würde** + the infinitive

This is similar to the English paraphrase with *would* plus the infinitive. **Würde** is conjugated to agree with the subject of the sentence. The infinitive stands at the end of a main clause.

An deiner Stelle **würde** ich das nicht **tun**.
I wouldn't do that if I were you.

Würden Sie bitte **mitkommen**?
Would you come along, please?

Sie **würde** lieber mit dem Auto **fahren**.
She would rather go by car.

Exercise 3: *Make subjunctive sentences from the following words, using the* würde *paraphrase.*

1. Wir / fahren / lieber mit dem Zug.
2. Der rote Mantel / gefallen / mir / besser.
3. Das ältere Auto / kosten / natürlich weniger.
4. Ohne deine Hilfe / unternehmen / ich / dieses Projekt / nie.
5. Diese Farbe / aussehen / besser.
6. Mit einem neuen Computer / arbeiten / ich / schneller.
7. Ich / bleiben / dieses Wochenende / lieber zu Hause.
8. An meiner Stelle / tun / du / das gleiche.
9. Helfen / du / mir / mit den Hausaufgaben?
10. Die andere Fete / machen / mehr Spaβ / als diese.

One-Word Form vs. würde Paraphrase

The one-word form and the **würde** paraphrase mean essentially the same thing but are used in different situations.

In written German, it is considered poor style to use the **würde** paraphrase in both clauses of a conditional sentence. As a result, the **würde** paraphrase is usually avoided in the **wenn**-clause.

Wenn er sich besser **fühlte**, würde er mitkommen.
If he felt better, he would come along.

Wenn es mir nicht **gefiele**, würde ich es nicht tun.
If I didn't like it, I wouldn't do it.

Wenn sie nur nicht so viel **tränken**!
If only they didn't drink so much!

In spoken German, on the other hand, it is becoming increasingly common to use the **würde** paraphrase in **wenn**-clauses.

Wenn er sich besser **fühlen würde**, würde er mitkommen.
Wenn es mir nicht **gefallen würde**, würde ich es nicht tun.
Wenn sie nur nicht so viel **trinken würden**!

In both written and spoken German, the one-word form is preferred for **haben**, **sein**, **wissen**, and the modal verbs.

Wenn ich mehr Zeit **hätte**, **könnten** wir einen Spaziergang machen.
If I had more time, we could go on a walk.

Es **wäre** schön, wenn du mehr Zeit **hättest** und mich besuchen **könntest**.
It would be nice, if you had more time and could visit me.

In the exercises that follow, we will assume that we are using written German.

Uses of the Present Subjunctive

UNREAL CONDITIONAL SENTENCES

A conditional sentence consists of a condition, usually introduced by **wenn**, and a conclusion, which may or may not be introduced by **dann** or **so**. Unreal conditions, or conditions that cannot be fulfilled, are expressed in the subjunctive mood.

Wenn du in der Nähe **wohntest**, (dann/so) **würde** ich dich **besuchen**.
If you lived in the area, (then) I would visit you.

Wenn es nicht **regnete**, (dann/so) **könnten** wir draußen **spielen**.
If it weren't raining, (then) we could play outside.

Remember that real conditional sentences, or conditions that can be fulfilled, are in the indicative mood. Compare the following real conditions to the unreal ones above:

Wenn du in der Nähe **wohnst**, (dann/so) **besuche** ich dich.
If you live in the area, (then) I'll come visit you.

Wenn es nicht **regnet**, (dann/so) **können** wir draußen **spielen**.
If it's not raining, (then) we can play outside.

Word Order. Note the word order of the conditional sentences above. The conditional clause, or **wenn**-clause, is a dependent clause and accordingly the verb stands at its end. The conclusion is a main clause and has inverted word order because it is preceded by the dependent clause (see chapter 13).

Exercise 4: *Rewrite as unreal conditional sentences. Use the one-word form in the **wenn**-clause. Use the **würde** paraphrase in the conclusion except for modal verbs and **haben, sein,** and **wissen**.*

1. Wenn es zu warm ist, kann ich nicht schlafen.
2. Wenn ich in eine andere Stadt ziehe, müssen wir uns schreiben.

3. Wenn wir Lust haben, gehen wir ins Kino.
4. Wenn er recht hat, bewundert man ihn.
5. Wenn es nach mir geht, wandern wir nach Kanada aus.
6. Wenn sie pünktlich kommt, machen wir einen Spaziergang.
7. Wenn ich Zeit finde, kann ich dir helfen.
8. Wenn du willst, hole ich dich um acht ab.
9. Wenn ihr darüber lacht, erzählen wir die Geschichte nicht.
10. Wenn ich hier bleiben darf, bin ich dir ewig dankbar.
11. Wenn sie mich anruft, frage ich sie.
12. Wenn das Kind zu schnell trinkt, verschluckt es sich.
13. Wenn das Wasser nicht zu kalt ist, schwimme ich eine Stunde lang.
14. Wenn du lauter sprichst, kann man dich verstehen.
15. Wenn die Katze ins Haus will, kratzt sie an der Tür.

Omission of *wenn*. The **wenn** in the conditional sentence can be omitted. In this case, the condition clause begins with the verb. The conclusion clause has inverted word order and the optional **dann** or **so** becomes mandatory. There is no corresponding structure in English.

Wohntest du in der Nähe, **dann/so würde** ich dich **besuchen**.
If you lived in the area, (then) I would visit you.

Regnete es nicht, **dann/so könnten** wir draußen **spielen**.
If if weren't raining, (then) we could play outside.

Exercise 5: *Omit* **wenn** *and make all other necessary changes.*

1. Wenn meine Verwandten mich einlüden, würde ich sie besuchen.
2. Wenn ihr still bliebet, könnten wir die Vögel hören.
3. Wenn man die Musik leiser stellte, könnten wir uns verstehen.
4. Wenn der Fremde keine Aufenthaltserlaubnis bekäme, dürfte er nicht bleiben.
5. Wenn der Apparat nicht funktionierte, müßte man ihn zurückbringen.
6. Wenn du Kaffee machtest, würden wir ihn trinken.

Conclusion Clause First. The conclusion clause can precede the condition clause. In this case, **dann/so** is omitted.

Ich würde dich besuchen, wenn du in der Nähe wohntest.
I would visit you if you lived in the area.

Wir könnten zu Fuß gehen, wenn es nicht regnete.
We could go by foot if it weren't raining.

Exercise 6: *Put the conclusion clause first.*

1. Wenn ich nicht so müde wäre, dann würde ich weiter arbeiten.
2. Wenn ich meinen Schlüssel finden könnte, würde ich die Tür öffnen.
3. Wenn die Kartoffeln nicht kalt wären, dann würden wir essen.
4. Wenn sie mit den Hausaufgaben fertig wäre, würde sie mitkommen.
5. Wenn du Hunger hättest, würde ich dir Kuchen anbieten.
6. Wenn es anfinge zu schneien, würden wir Schlitten fahren.

WISHES

Wishes are, by their very nature, unreal in the sense that they are not fulfilled. They therefore are in the subjunctive mood. Several common constructions are used to express wishes.

***Wenn*-Clause Alone.** The **wenn**-clause of an unreal conditional sentence may be used to express wishes. Such clauses end with an exclamation mark. They are strengthened by including **nur** or **doch**, which usually stand immediately after the subject and any pronoun objects but before everything else.

Wenn sie **nur** langsamer **führe**!
If only she would drive slower!

Wenn du mich **nur** öfter besuchen **könntest**!
If only you could visit me more often!

Wenn du **doch** hier **wärest**!
If only you were here!

Omission of *wenn*. In a small number of set phrases, **wenn** is omitted. The verb then stands at the beginning of the clause.

Hätte ich mehr Zeit!
Wärest du doch hier!

Exercise 7: *List all of the things that you wish. Use the one-word form, according to the model.*

mitgehen können   **Wenn ich nur mitgehen könnte!**

1. mehr Zeit haben
2. die Geduld nicht immer verlieren
3. nicht so leicht weinen
4. etwas sagen dürfen
5. berühmt sein
6. in New York wohnen

7. nicht jetzt gehen müssen
8. die Antwort wissen
9. mich darüber nicht ärgern
10. mich auf meine Arbeit konzentrieren können
11. noch etwas wachsen
12. besser singen

Wishes with *wollen* and *wünschen*. Wishes may also be introduced with the verbs **wollen** or **wünschen**. Both the introductory phrase and the wish are in the subjunctive.

Ich **wollte/wünschte**, sie **würde** langsamer **fahren**.
Ich **wollte/wünschte**, sie **führe** langsamer.
Ich **wollte/wünschte**, du **könntest** mich öfter **besuchen**.
Ich **wollte/wünschte**, du **wärest** hier.

Exercise 8: *Wish for the opposite of the statements, according to the model. Use the* **würde** *paraphrase except for modals and* **haben, sein,** *and* **wissen.**

Heute ist Montag.   **Ich wünschte, es wäre heute nicht Montag.**

1. Ich sitze in der Klasse.
2. Gleich schreiben wir die Prüfung.
3. Die Prüfung ist so schwer.
4. Ich schreibe so langsam.
5. Ich mache so viele Fehler.
6. Ich falle durch.
7. Das muß ich meinen Eltern sagen.
8. Meine Eltern werden böse.

***Möchten* for Wishes. Möchten** is commonly used to express a wish.

Ich **möchte** einen neuen Computer.
I would like a new computer.

Ich **möchte** eine Tasse Tee.
I would like a cup of tea.

HYPOTHETICAL SITUATIONS

The subjunctive is used to express hypothetical situations. Usually a condition clause is understood, but not stated.

Ich **würde** das nicht **machen** (wenn ich an deiner Stelle wäre).
I wouldn't do that (if I were in your position).

Ich **würde schlafen gehen** (wenn ich nicht lernen müβte).
I would go to sleep (if I didn't have to study).

Exercise 9: *Tell what you would do if you had the time. Use the* **würde**
paraphrase except for modals and **haben, sein,** *and* **wissen**.

1. in der Sonne liegen können
2. eine Weltreise machen
3. den ganzen Tag fernsehen dürfen
4. herumsitzen und faulenzen
5. mit meinen Freunden Spaβ haben
6. meine Familie besuchen
7. viel lesen und mich besser informieren können
8. eine Radtour machen
9. einen Pullover stricken können
10. das Auto waschen

THE SUBJUNCTIVE FOR POLITENESS

The subjunctive expresses tentativeness, caution, hesitation, and modesty. Requests or questions are put in the subjunctive to make them more polite; they sound less direct or blunt. Compare the following sentences:

Lies das bitte vor!	*Please read this out loud.*
Würdest du das bitte **vorlesen**?	*Would you please read this out loud?*

Kannst du das bitte vorlesen?	*Can you please read this out loud?*
Könntest du das bitte **vorlesen**?	*Could you please read this out loud?*

To express politeness, the **würde** paraphrase frequently is used for all verbs except the modals and **haben**. In other words, the **würde** paraphrase is common even for **sein** and **wissen** when using the subjunctive to express politeness.

Würden Sie bitte so nett **sein** und einen Augenblick hier warten?
Would you please be so kind and wait here for a moment?

Exercise 10: *Express as polite requests. Use the* **würde** *paraphrase.*

1. Sprich bitte deutlicher!
2. Seien Sie bitte leiser!
3. Kommt bitte mit!
4. Übersetzen Sie bitte diesen Artikel!
5. Teil mir das Ergebnis bitte mit!
6. Setzen Sie sich bitte neben mich!
7. Leih mir bitte etwas Geld!
8. Bring bitte den Müll raus!

Exercise 11: *Make the following requests more polite. Use the* **würde** *paraphrase except for* **haben** *and the modal verbs.*

1. Darf ich in die Stadt fahren?
2. Holen Sie für mich die Medikamente ab?
3. Tippen Sie diesen Brief?
4. Hast du jetzt Zeit für mich?
5. Können Sie meinen CD-Spieler reparieren?
6. Nimmst du mich heute abend mit?
7. Hilfst du mir bei meinen Hausaufgaben?
8. Räumst du dein Zimmer bald auf?
9. Bringst du die Einkäufe ins Haus?
10. Schließen Sie das Auto ab?

ALS OB (ALS WENN) AND ALS WITH THE SUBJUNCTIVE

Als ob, als wenn, or **als** introduce suppositions, conjectures, or unreal comparisons and therefore require the subjunctive. **Als ob** and **als wenn** send the verb to the end of the clause.

Du siehst aus, **als ob** du krank **wärest**.
You look as if you were sick.

Der Hund bellt, **als wenn** er mich **beißen wollte**.
The dog's barking as if it wanted to bite me.

A construction with **als** alone has the same meaning, although it is considered to be more literary. It inverts the word order.

Du siehst aus, **als wärest** du krank.
Der Hund bellt, **als wollte** er mich **beißen**.

Exercise 12: *Complete with the logical subjunctive verb. Use the* **würde** *paraphrase except for modals and* **haben, sein,** *and* **wissen.**

1. Frau Niessen ist noch jung; aber sie benimmt sich, als ob sie schon tausend Jahre alt _____.
2. Der Tenor kann wunderschön singen; aber er tut so, als ob er es gar nicht _____.
3. Der Mann versteht nichts von Elektrizität; aber er gibt an, als ob er etwas davon _____.
4. Ich will nicht daran teilnehmen; aber ich tue so, als ob ich daran teilnehmen _____.
5. Der Professor weiß die Antwort selber nicht; aber er beantwortet die Frage, als ob er sie _____.

6. Wir haben nicht viel Geld; aber wir geben unser Geld aus, als ob wir viel davon _____.
7. Sie kochen nicht besonders oft; aber das Essen schmeckt, als ob sie jeden Tag _____.
8. Jennifer will nicht mit Philipp reden; deshalb tut sie so, als ob sie mit Björn reden _____.

PAST TENSE SUBJUNCTIVE IN GERMAN

The past tense subjunctive is used to express unreal or hypothetical conditions that occurred in the past.

As in English, the past subjunctive in German is based on the past perfect tense of the verb. The helping verb **haben** or **sein** is in the subjunctive and the past participle stands at the end of a main clause:

> **hätten/wären** + past participle

PAST PERFECT	PAST SUBJUNCTIVE
hatte gefragt	**hätte gefragt**
hatte gesungen	**hätte gesungen**
war gefahren	**wäre gefahren**
war geblieben	**wäre geblieben**

Wenn ich das nur nicht **gesagt hätte**!
If only I hadn't said that!

Sie **wäre** sicher gern **mitgekommen**.
She surely would have liked to come along.

Whereas English can paraphrase the past subjunctive with *would have* plus the past participle, German does not use a **würde** paraphrase for the past subjunctive.

The Past Subjunctive of Modal Verbs

The past subjunctive for modal verbs is formed as it is for all other verbs: it is based on the past perfect tense and the helping verb is in the subjunctive. Remember that the helping verb for modal verbs is always **haben**. Thus the past subjunctive for modal verbs always uses the helping verb **hätten**:

> **hätten** + past participle

Remember that modal verbs have two different past participles, depending on whether they stand alone or together with another infinitive (see chapter 7). When used alone, the past participle follows the pattern of weak verbs (**ge** + stem + **t**) minus any umlaut.

PAST PERFECT

hatte gedurft

hatte gesollt

PAST SUBJUNCTIVE

hätte gedurft

hätte gesollt

Die Tote **hätte** es so **gewollt**.
The dead woman would have wanted it this way.

Das **hätte** ich nie so gut **gekonnt** wie du.
I never could have done that as well as you.

Usually a modal verb is used together with another infinitive. In this case, the past participle construction is a double infinitive.

PAST PERFECT

hatte sehen wollen

hatte kommen sollen

PAST SUBJUNCTIVE

hätte sehen wollen

hätte kommen sollen

Das **hätte** selbst ein Experte nicht besser **machen können**.
Even an expert could not have done that better.

Das **hättest** du nicht **sagen sollen**.
You shouldn't have said that.

WORD ORDER IN DEPENDENT CLAUSES WITH DOUBLE INFINITIVES

In dependent clauses the conjugated verb normally is sent to the end of the clause. However, the double infinitive acts as a kind of "roadblock," preventing the helping verb from reaching the end of the clause. Instead, the helping verb is placed immediately before the double infinitive, in a position third from the end.

Wenn du ins Kino **hättest** mitkommen wollen, hätte ich dich abgeholt.
If you had wanted to come along to the movies, I would have picked you up.

Wenn ich sie vor meiner Abreise nur noch einmal **hätte** sehen können!
If only I had been able to see her one more time before my departure!

Uses of the Past Subjunctive

The past subjunctive is used like the present subjunctive except that it is not common in polite requests.

UNREAL CONDITIONAL SENTENCES

Wenn du in der Nähe **gewohnt hättest**, (dann/so) **hätte** ich dich **besucht**.
If you had lived in the area, (then) I would have visited you.

Wenn es nicht **geregnet hätte**, (dann/so) **hätten** wir drauβen **spielen können**.

If it hadn't rained, (then) we could have played outside.

Exercise 13: *Restate the present subjunctive unreal conditional sentences in the past subjunctive.*

1. Wenn es neun Uhr wäre, würde die Vorlesung beginnen.
2. Wenn du etwas Schöneres fändest, solltest du es kaufen.
3. Wenn ich wettete, würde ich verlieren.
4. Wenn das Kind müde wäre, würde es einschlafen.
5. Wenn ich abnähme, würde ich die engen Jeans tragen.
6. Wenn Sie helfen könnten, wären wir Ihnen dankbar.
7. Wenn du wolltest, könntest du heute abend vorbeikommen.
8. Wenn man an die Konsequenzen dächte, würde man es nicht tun.
9. Wenn der Hund nicht so laut bellte, hätte ich keine Angst.
10. Wenn der Kuchen zu lange im Ofen bliebe, würde er nicht schmecken.

WISHES

Wenn sie nur langsamer **gefahren wäre**!
If only she had driven slower!

Wenn du mich nur öfter **hättest besuchen können**!
If only you could have visited me more often!

Wenn du doch hier **gewesen wärest**!
If only you had been here!

Ich **wollte/wünschte**, sie **wäre** langsamer **gefahren**.
Ich **wollte/wünschte**, du **hättest** mich öfter **besuchen können**.
Ich **wollte/wünschte**, du **wärest** hier **gewesen**.

Exercise 14: *Restate the present subjunctive wishes in the past subjunctive.*

1. Wenn du mir nur die Wahrheit sagtest!
2. Wenn sie nur nicht so viel tränke!
3. Wenn ich nur diese komplizierte Aufgabe lösen könnte!
4. Wenn ich nur diesen Text nicht lesen müβte!
5. Wenn das nur möglich wäre!
6. Wenn wir nur mehr Zeit hätten!
7. Wenn sie mir nur vergäbe!
8. Wenn die Ferien nur heute anfingen!
9. Wenn er nur nicht ins Büro gehen müβte!
10. Wenn der Mückenstich nur nicht so juckte!

HYPOTHETICAL SITUATIONS

Ich **hätte** das nicht **gemacht** (wenn ich an deiner Stelle gewesen wäre).
I wouldn't have done that (if I had been in your position).

Ich **wäre schlafen gegangen** (wenn ich nicht hätte lernen müssen).
I would have gone to sleep (if I hadn't had to study).

Exercise 15: *Restate the present subjunctive sentences in the past subjunctive.*

1. Ich würde in dieser Situation ruhiger bleiben als du.
2. So viel Aufwand wollte sie sicher nicht.
3. Dieser Anzug würde mir nicht passen.
4. Dem Filmkritiker würde so ein Film nicht gefallen.
5. Als Engländer müβte er Englisch verstehen.
6. Normalerweise würde es im Oktober nicht schneien.
7. Es könnte noch schlimmer werden.
8. Wegen des Schnees sollte man langsamer fahren.
9. Die Jugendlichen dürften nichts Alkoholisches trinken.
10. Vor so vielen Leuten würde ich nervös werden.

ALS OB (ALS WENN) AND *ALS* WITH THE PAST SUBJUNCTIVE

Du siehst aus, **als ob** du krank **gewesen wärest**.
You look as if you had been sick.

Der Hund bellte, **als wenn** er mich **hätte beiβen wollen**.
The dog barked as if it had wanted to bite me.

Exercise 16: *Complete with the past subjunctive of the verb in parentheses.*

1. Du siehst aus, als ob du den ganzen Tag _____ _____.
   (arbeiten)
2. Er sprach mit dem Kind, als ob er böse _____ _____.   (sein)
3. Sie spricht Deutsch, als _____ sie jahrelang in Deutschland
   _____.   (wohnen)
4. Die Studenten tun, als ob sie nichts _____ _____.   (verstehen)
5. Sie ist auβer Atem, als ob sie schnell _____ _____.   (laufen)

REVIEW EXERCISES

Exercise 17: *Translate into English.*

1. Wenn du mich nur gefragt hättest!
2. Ich wollte, ich wäre mit diesen Übungen fertig.

3. Sie würde sich freuen, wenn sie etwas Post bekäme.

4. Wenn ich keinen Paß hätte, dürfte ich nicht ins Ausland reisen.

5. Wenn ich Hunger gehabt hätte, hätte ich gegessen.

6. Selbst du hättest das nicht schöner ausdrücken können.

7. Ich hätte das Steak bestellt, wenn es nicht so teuer gewesen wäre.

8. Dürfte ich Sie kurz stören?

9. Würden Sie hier bitte nicht rauchen?

10. Ich bin so müde, als ob ich die ganze Nacht nicht geschlafen hätte.

11. Wäre ich nur ein bißchen früher gekommen!

12. Ich weiß nicht, ob sie das hätten sagen sollen.

13. Die Wohnung ist so kalt, als hätten wir nicht geheizt.

14. Ich dachte, es müßte schon längst Mitternacht sein, aber es ist erst 10 Uhr.

15. Dieser Roman würde die Frau dort interessieren.

16. Wir würden einen Spaziergang machen, wenn es nicht regnete.

17. Könnten Sie die Frage bitte wiederholen?

18. Würden Sie bitte so nett sein und mir die Uhr dort zeigen?

19. Wenn der Ring nicht so viel kostete, würde ich ihn kaufen.

20. Wenn wir gestern nicht so lange aufgeblieben wären, hätte ich heute früher aufstehen können.

21. Wenn es wärmer wäre, würde ich kurze Hosen tragen.

22. Könnten Sie mir sagen, wie spät es ist?

23. Du hättest es ihr schon lange sagen sollen.

24. Die Pommes frites würden mit Salz besser schmecken.

25. Wäre er schneller gelaufen, hätte er den Zug noch erreicht.

Exercise 18: *Translate into German.*

1. She acts as if she had no money.

2. I wish vacation had already started.

3. The essay would have been perfect if she hadn't made this one mistake.

4. Would you please explain this to me, Professor Klein?

5. Would it be possible to call back in an hour?

6. She wishes she didn't have to read this long book.

7. If we had saved some money, we wouldn't have to borrow it now.

8. They shouldn't have been so impolite.

9. Daniel, don't act as if you haven't received my letter!

10. If only they believed me!

11. If she could have stayed longer, she would have met my parents.

12. If I could cook, I would invite him for dinner.

13. May I please leave class ten minutes early?

14. I wish this moment would last forever.

15. The students should respect their professor more.

16. If only you (**du**) were right!
17. Urte laughed as if someone had told a good joke.
18. Could you please write me a letter of recommendation, Professor Helmreich?
19. The woman would look like my aunt if her nose weren't so big.
20. If the trip hadn't been so long, we would have visited you.

ANSWERS TO EXERCISES

1.

1. indicative
2. subjunctive
3. indicative
4. subjunctive
5. subjunctive
6. subjunctive
7. subjunctive
8. indicative
9. indicative
10. indicative
11. subjunctive
12. subjunctive
13. subjunctive
14. indicative
15. subjunctive
16. subjunctive
17. indicative
18. subjunctive

2.

1. Gabi lebte/lebte; arbeitete/arbeitete; wohnte/wohnte; fragte/fragte; bemerkte/bemerkte; kaufte/kaufte; bestellte/bestellte
2. ich fuhr/führe; sang/sänge; aß/äße; las/läse; schrieb/schriebe; fand/fände; blieb/bliebe; kam/käme; sprach/spräche; schlief/schliefe; sah/sähe
3. wir hatten/hätten; waren/wären; wurden/würden
4. du dachtest/dächtest; wußtest/wüßtest; brachtest/brächtest
5. sie konnten/könnten; durften/dürften; wollten/wollten; sollten/sollten; mochten/möchten; mußten/müßten

3.

1. Wir würden lieber mit dem Zug fahren.
2. Der rote Mantel würde mir besser gefallen.
3. Das ältere Auto würde natürlich weniger kosten.
4. Ohne deine Hilfe würde ich dieses Projekt nie unternehmen.
5. Diese Farbe würde besser aussehen.
6. Mit einem neuen Computer würde ich schneller arbeiten.
7. Ich würde dieses Wochenende lieber zu Hause bleiben.
8. An meiner Stelle würdest du das gleiche tun.
9. Würdest du mir mit den Hausaufgaben helfen?
10. Die andere Fete würde mehr Spaß machen als diese.

4.

1. Wenn es zu warm wäre, könnte ich nicht schlafen.
2. Wenn ich in eine andere Stadt zöge, müßten wir uns schreiben.
3. Wenn wir Lust hätten, würden wir ins Kino gehen.
4. Wenn er recht hätte, würde man ihn bewundern.
5. Wenn es nach mir ginge, würden wir nach Kanada auswandern.
6. Wenn sie pünktlich käme, würden wir einen Spaziergang machen.
7. Wenn ich Zeit fände, könnte ich dir helfen.
8. Wenn du wolltest, würde ich dich um acht abholen.
9. Wenn ihr darüber lachtet, würden wir die Geschichte nicht erzählen.
10. Wenn ich hier bleiben dürfte, wäre ich dir ewig dankbar.
11. Wenn sie mich anriefe, würde ich sie fragen.
12. Wenn das Kind zu schnell tränke, würde es sich verschlucken.
13. Wenn das Wasser nicht zu kalt wäre, würde ich eine Stunde lang schwimmen.
14. Wenn du lauter sprächest, könnte man dich verstehen.
15. Wenn die Katze ins Haus wollte, würde sie an der Tür kratzen.

5.

1. Lüden meine Verwandten mich ein, dann/so würde ich sie besuchen.
2. Bliebet ihr still, dann/so könnten wir die Vögel hören.
3. Stellte man die Musik leiser, dann/so könnten wir uns verstehen.
4. Bekäme der Fremde keine Aufenthaltserlaubnis, dann/so dürfte er nicht bleiben.
5. Funktionierte der Apparat nicht, dann/so müßte man ihn zurückbringen.
6. Machtest du Kaffee, dann/so würden wir ihn trinken.

6.

1. Ich würde weiter arbeiten, wenn ich nicht so müde wäre.
2. Ich würde die Tür öffnen, wenn ich meinen Schlüssel finden könnte.
3. Wir würden essen, wenn die Kartoffeln nicht kalt wären.
4. Sie würde mitkommen, wenn sie mit den Hausaufgaben fertig wäre.
5. Ich würde dir Kuchen anbieten, wenn du Hunger hättest.
6. Wir würden Schlitten fahren, wenn es anfinge zu schneien.

7.

1. Wenn ich nur mehr Zeit hätte!
2. Wenn ich nur die Geduld nicht immer verlöre!
3. Wenn ich nur nicht so leicht weinte!
4. Wenn ich nur etwas sagen dürfte!
5. Wenn ich nur berühmt wäre!
6. Wenn ich nur in New York wohnte!
7. Wenn ich nur nicht jetzt gehen müßte!
8. Wenn ich nur die Antwort wüßte!
9. Wenn ich mich nur darüber nicht ärgerte!
10. Wenn ich mich nur auf meine Arbeit konzentrieren könnte!
11. Wenn ich nur noch etwas wüchse!
12. Wenn ich nur besser sänge!

8.

1. Ich wünschte, ich würde nicht in der Klasse sitzen.
2. Ich wünschte, wir würden die Prüfung nicht gleich schreiben.
3. Ich wünschte, die Prüfung wäre nicht so schwer.
4. Ich wünschte, ich würde nicht so langsam schreiben.
5. Ich wünschte, ich würde nicht so viele Fehler machen.
6. Ich wünschte, ich würde nicht durchfallen.
7. Ich wünschte, das müßte ich meinen Eltern nicht sagen.

8. Ich wünschte, meine Eltern würden nicht böse werden.

9.

1. Ich könnte in der Sonne liegen.
2. Ich würde eine Weltreise machen.
3. Ich dürfte den ganzen Tag fernsehen.
4. Ich würde herumsitzen und faulenzen.
5. Ich hätte mit meinen Freunden Spaß.
6. Ich würde meine Familie besuchen.
7. Ich könnte viel lesen und mich besser informieren.
8. Ich würde eine Radtour machen.
9. Ich könnte einen Pullover stricken.
10. Ich würde das Auto waschen.

10.

1. Würdest du bitte deutlicher sprechen?
2. Würden Sie bitte leiser sein?
3. Würdet ihr bitte mitkommen?
4. Würden Sie bitte diesen Artikel übersetzen?
5. Würdest du mir bitte das Ergebnis mitteilen?
6. Würden Sie sich bitte neben mich setzen?
7. Würdest du mir bitte etwas Geld leihen?
8. Würdest du bitte den Müll rausbringen?

11.

1. Dürfte ich in die Stadt fahren?
2. Würden Sie für mich die Medikamente abholen?
3. Würden Sie diesen Brief tippen?
4. Hättest du jetzt Zeit für mich?
5. Könnten Sie meinen CD-Spieler reparieren?
6. Würdest du mich heute abend mitnehmen?
7. Würdest du mir bei meinen Hausaufgaben helfen?
8. Würdest du dein Zimmer bald aufräumen?
9. Würdest du die Einkäufe ins Haus bringen?

10. Würden Sie das Auto abschließen?

12.

1. wäre
2. könnte
3. verstehen würde
4. wollte
5. wüßte
6. hätten
7. kochen würden
8. wollte

13.

1. Wenn es neun Uhr gewesen wäre, hätte die Vorlesung begonnen.
2. Wenn du etwas Schöneres gefunden hättest, hättest du es kaufen sollen.
3. Wenn ich gewettet hätte, hätte ich verloren.
4. Wenn das Kind müde gewesen wäre, wäre es eingeschlafen.
5. Wenn ich abgenommen hätte, hätte ich die engen Jeans getragen.
6. Wenn Sie hätten helfen können, wären wir Ihnen dankbar gewesen.
7. Wenn du gewollt hättest, hättest du heute abend vorbeikommen können.
8. Wenn man an die Konsequenzen gedacht hätte, hätte man es nicht getan.
9. Wenn der Hund nicht so laut gebellt hätte, hätte ich keine Angst gehabt.
10. Wenn der Kuchen zu lange im Ofen geblieben wäre, hätte er nicht geschmeckt.

14.

1. Wenn du mir nur die Wahrheit gesagt hättest!
2. Wenn sie nur nicht so viel getrunken hätte!
3. Wenn ich nur diese komplizierte Aufgabe hätte lösen können!
4. Wenn ich nur diesen Text nicht hätte lesen müssen!
5. Wenn das nur möglich gewesen wäre!

6. Wenn wir nur mehr Zeit gehabt hätten!
7. Wenn sie mir nur vergeben hätte!
8. Wenn die Ferien nur heute angefangen hätten!
9. Wenn er nur nicht ins Büro hätte gehen müssen!
10. Wenn der Mückenstich nur nicht so gejuckt hätte!

15.

1. Ich wäre in dieser Situation ruhiger geblieben als du.
2. So viel Aufwand hätte sie sicher nicht gewollt.
3. Dieser Anzug hätte mir nicht gepaβt.
4. Dem Filmkritiker hätte so ein Film nicht gefallen.
5. Als Engländer hätte er Englisch verstehen müssen.
6. Normalerweise hätte es im Oktober nicht geschneit.
7. Es hätte noch schlimmer werden können.
8. Wegen des Schnees hätte man langsamer fahren sollen.
9. Die Jugendlichen hätten nichts Alkoholisches trinken dürfen.
10. Vor so vielen Leuten wäre ich nervös geworden.

16.

1. gearbeitet hättest
2. gewesen wäre
3. hätte ... gewohnt
4. verstanden hätten
5. gelaufen wäre

17.

1. If only you had asked me!
2. I wish that I were done with these exercises.
3. She would be happy if she got some mail.
4. If I didn't have a passport, I would not be allowed to travel abroad.

5. If I had been hungry, I would have eaten.
6. Even you could not have expressed that more beautifully.
7. I would have ordered steak if it hadn't been so expensive.
8. May/Might I disturb you briefly?
9. Would you please not smoke here?
10. I am so tired it's as if I hadn't slept the whole night.
11. If only I had come a little earlier!
12. I don't know if they should have said that.
13. The apartment is so cold it's as if we had not turned on the heat.
14. I thought it had to be midnight already, but it's just 10 o'clock.
15. This novel would interest that woman (there).
16. We would take a walk if it weren't raining.
17. Could you please repeat the question?
18. Would you please be so kind and show me the watch there?
19. If the ring didn't cost so much, I would buy it.
20. If we hadn't stayed up so late yesterday, I would have been able to get up earlier today.
21. If it were warmer, I would wear shorts.
22. Could you tell me what time it is (how late it is)?
23. You should have told her long ago.
24. The french fries would taste better with salt.
25. Had he run faster, he would have caught the train.

18.

1. Sie tut so, als ob/als wenn sie kein Geld hätte.
2. Ich wünschte/wollte, die Ferien hätten schon angefangen.

3. Der Aufsatz wäre perfekt gewesen, wenn sie diesen einen Fehler nicht gemacht hätte.
4. Würden Sie mir das bitte erklären, Professor Klein?
5. Wäre es möglich, in einer Stunde zurückzurufen/noch einmal anzurufen?
6. Sie wünschte/wollte, daβ sie dieses lange Buch nicht lesen müβte.
7. Wenn wir etwas Geld gespart hätten, müβten wir es jetzt nicht borgen.
8. Sie hätten nicht so unhöflich sein sollen.
9. Daniel, tu(e) nicht so, als ob du meinen Brief nicht bekommen hättest!
10. Wenn sie mir nur glaubten!
11. Wenn sie länger hätte bleiben können, hätte sie meine Eltern kennengelernt.
12. Wenn ich kochen könnte, würde ich ihn zum Abendessen einladen/lüde ich ihn zum Abendessen ein.
13. Dürfte ich die Klasse zehn Minuten früher verlassen?
14. Ich wünschte/wollte, dieser Moment würde ewig dauern/dauerte ewig.
15. Die Studenten sollten ihren Professor mehr respektieren.
16. Wenn du nur recht hättest!
17. Urte lachte, als ob/als wenn jemand einen guten Witz erzählt hätte.
18. Könnten Sie mir bitte einen Empfehlungsbrief schreiben, Professor Helmreich?
19. Die Frau würde wie meine Tante aussehen, wäre ihre Nase nicht so groβ/wenn ihre Nase nicht so groβ wäre.
20. Wenn die Reise nicht so lang gewesen wäre, hätten wir dich/euch/Sie besucht.

10

The Special Subjunctive: Indirect Discourse

*The **special subjunctive** is used primarily for **indirect discourse** in which the speaker reports the words of another person or source indirectly. Like the general subjunctive, it indicates the speaker's attitude toward the truth or likelihood of a situation. However, whereas the general subjunctive expresses uncertainty and unreality, the special subjunctive expresses **neutrality**. In other words, the speaker has no reason to believe or disbelieve the words or situation being reported.*

The special subjunctive, also called subjunctive I, occurs in three tenses: present, past, and future. It is common to replace the special subjunctive with the general subjunctive or with the indicative. This chapter presents the special subjunctive forms and then discusses when the general subjunctive or indicative forms are preferred.

INDIRECT DISCOURSE

To repeat the words of another person, you can quote him/her directly or indirectly. In a direct quote the speaker's words are simply placed in quotation marks. In German the direct quote is introduced with a colon, in English with either a colon or a comma.

Sie sagte: „Ich glaube dem Kind.”
She said, "I believe the child."

In an indirect quote, the speaker's words are not reproduced verbatim. Compare the following indirect quotes to the direct quotes above and note, for example, that the personal pronouns have changed and that in German the indirect quote is introduced by a comma:

Sie sagte, sie glaube dem Kind.
She said she believed the child.

As with English, in German the conjunction **daβ** (*that*) may introduce the indirect quote. Note that the subordinating conjunction **daβ** sends the verb to the end of its clause.

Sie sagte, **daβ** sie dem Kind **glaube**.
She said that she believed the child.

Note that in English there are no special forms used to indicate indirect discourse, although the tense is frequently shifted. In formal German, in contrast, there exist special forms, called the *special subjunctive*, for indirect discourse.

FORMS OF THE SPECIAL SUBJUNCTIVE

Present Tense

The special subjunctive occurs in three tenses: present, past, and future.

To form the present tense of the special subjunctive add the following endings to the infinitive stem:

ich	**-e**	wir	**-en**	
du	**-est**	ihr	**-et**	
er/es/sie	**-e**	sie	**-en**	
		Sie	**-en**	

Note that these endings are the same as those used for the general subjunctive.

	gehen	**lesen**	**geben**	**reisen**	**müssen**
ich	geh**e**	les**e**	geb**e**	reis**e**	müss**e**
du	geh**est**	les**est**	geb**est**	reis**est**	müss**est**
er/es/sie	geh**e**	les**e**	geb**e**	reis**e**	müss**e**
wir	geh**en**	les**en**	geb**en**	reis**en**	müss**en**
ihr	geh**et**	les**et**	geb**et**	reis**et**	müss**et**
sie	geh**en**	les**en**	geb**en**	reis**en**	müss**en**
Sie	geh**en**	les**en**	geb**en**	reis**en**	müss**en**

There is no vowel change in the special subjunctive, even in strong verbs.

Der Reporter berichtet: „Es gibt zwei Tote."
Der Reporter berichtet, es **gebe** zwei Tote.
The reporter reports, "There are two deaths."
The reporter reports there are two deaths.

Die Studentin sagt: „Ich muβ lernen."
Die Studentin sagt, sie **müsse** lernen.
The student says, "I have to study."
The student says she has to study.

There is one exception to the pattern for forming the special subjunctive. **Sein** omits the -**e** ending for the first and third person singular.

ich	**sei**	wir	**seien**
du	**seiest**	ihr	**seiet**
er/es/sie	**sei**	sie	**seien**
	Sie	**seien**	

Past Tense

The past tense of the special subjunctive is formed with the special subjunctive of the helping verb **sein** or **haben** plus the past participle. (When a modal is used with another infinitive, the past participle is a double infinitive construction.)

> **habe/sei** + past participle

Der Reporter berichtet: „Es hat zwei Tote gegeben."
Der Reporter berichtet, es **habe** zwei Tote **gegeben**.

Die Studentin sagt: „Ich muβte lernen."
Die Studentin sagt, sie **habe lernen müssen**.

Future Tense

The future tense of the special subjunctive is formed with the special subjunctive of **werden** plus the infinitive.

> **werde** + infinitive

Here is the conjugation of **werden** in the special subjunctive:

ich	**werde**	wir	**werden**
du	**werdest**	ihr	**werdet**
er/es/sie	**werde**	sie	**werden**
	Sie	**werden**	

Der Reporter berichtet: ,,Es wird zwei Tote geben.''
Der Reporter berichtet, es **werde** zwei Tote **geben**.

Die Studentin sagt: ,,Ich werde lernen müssen.''
Die Studentin sagt, sie **werde lernen müssen**.

Choosing the Tense of the Indirect Discourse

The tense of the indirect quote is determined by the tense of the direct quote. The tense of the introductory phrase is irrelevant in choosing the tense of the indirect quote. In other words, if the original statement is in the present tense, the indirect statement will also be in the present tense.

Der Meteorologe sagte: ,,Heute regnet es überall in Deutschland.''
Der Meteorologe sagte, heute **regne** es überall in Deutschland.

Exercise 1: *Restate the present tense direct quotes as present tense indirect quotes. Make any other necessary changes.*

1. Der Ultrakonservative schrie: ,,Eine Frau soll nicht arbeiten.''
2. Der Selbstmörder schrieb: ,,Ich habe Liebeskummer.''
3. Frau Meier bemerkt: ,,In zwei Monaten reise ich wieder ab.''
4. Der Musikfreund bestätigt: ,,Ich kann vier Musikinstrumente spielen.''
5. Die Tierärztin bedauerte: ,,Es tut mir leid. Das Tier ist nicht zu retten.''
6. Die Gewerkschaft sagte: ,,Man muß das Arbeitsklima verbessern.''
7. Die Studentin behauptet: ,,Dieses Werk gefällt mir am besten. Ich finde es am interessantesten.''
8. Der Papagei sagt dauernd: ,,Ich will einen Cracker.''
9. Patrick fügt hinzu: ,,Weihnachten ist das schönste Fest!''
10. Die Psychologin meint: ,,Es gibt viele Probleme.''

If the original statement is in any one of the three past tenses (simple past, present perfect, or past perfect), the indirect statement will be in the past tense special subjunctive.

Der Meteorologe sagte: ,,Gestern regnete es überhaupt nicht.''
Der Meteorologe sagte: ,,Gestern hat es überhaupt nicht geregnet.''
Der Meteorologe sagte: ,,Gestern hatte es überhaupt nicht geregnet.''
Der Meteorologe sagte, gestern **habe** es überhaupt nicht **geregnet**.

Exercise 2: *Restate the past direct quotes as past tense indirect quotes. Make any other necessary changes.*

1. Die Autorin schrieb: ,,Ich habe immer ein privates Leben geführt.''
2. Der Bäcker beteuerte: ,,Ich habe das Brot heute morgen frisch gebacken.''

3. Der Mechaniker erklärt: „Ich mußte die Bremse reparieren."
4. Die Politikerin erklärte: „Der Skandal war nicht meine Schuld. Ich habe nichts davon gewußt."
5. In der Zeitung stand: „Die wirtschaftliche Lage in der ehemaligen DDR war eigentlich noch schlimmer, als man gedacht hatte."
6. Mein Bruder erklärte: „Ich konnte gestern nicht kommen, weil mein Sohn plötzlich krank wurde."
7. Die Touristin sagte: „Mir gefiel es in den Bergen am besten."
8. Die Chefin gab bekannt: „Im letzten Quartal ist die Produktivität um 2,3% gestiegen."
9. Die Professorin betonte: „Diese Arbeiten habe ich schon berichtigt und zurückgegeben."
10. Die Gärtnerin widersprach: „Die große Hitze war gar nicht gut."

If the original statement is in the future tense, the indirect statement will be in the future tense special subjunctive.

Der Meteorologe sagte: „Es wird auch in Österreich regnen."
Der Meteorologe sagte, es **werde** auch in Österreich **regnen**.

Exercise 3: *Restate the future direct quotes as future tense indirect quotes. Make any other necessary changes.*

1. Der Polizist sagt: „Diese Straße wird eine Woche lang gesperrt sein."
2. Mein Liebhaber schrieb mir: „Ich werde dich ewig lieben."
3. Der Detektiv sagt: „Das wird man noch herausfinden müssen."
4. Die Frau im Reisebüro sagte: „Eine Kreuzfahrt auf diesem Schiff wird sicher Spaß machen."
5. Der Astronom schreibt: „Ein Meteor wird innerhalb von 100 Jahren mit der Erde kollidieren."

INDIRECT DISCOURSE IN FORMAL GERMAN

Special Subjunctive vs. General Subjunctive

In formal German, the special subjunctive forms are used in indirect discourse unless those forms are identical to indicative forms. *If the special subjunctive is identical to the indicative, the general subjunctive is used.* This occurs most frequently in the third person plural. In the following examples, the forms to be used in indirect discourse are in boldface:

	INDICATIVE	SPECIAL SUBJUNCTIVE	GENERAL SUBJUNCTIVE
ich	fahre	fahre	**führe**
du	fährst	**fahrest**	führest
er/es/sie	fährt	**fahre**	führe
wir	fahren	fahren	**führen**
ihr	fahrt	**fahret**	führet
sie	fahren	fahren	**führen**
Sie	fahren	fahren	**führen**

In formal reporting, the general subjunctive does not imply doubt or uncertainty. It implies neutrality, as does the special subjunctive, and is used only because the special subjunctive forms are not recognizably different from the indicative.

This rule applies to all verbs and all tenses. Study the following examples. In each case, the forms to be used in indirect discourse are in boldface.

PRESENT TENSE OF A MODAL VERB

	INDICATIVE	SPECIAL SUBJUNCTIVE	GENERAL SUBJUNCTIVE
ich	kann	**könne**	könnte
du	kannst	**könnest**	könntest
er/es/sie	kann	**könne**	könnte
wir	können	können	**könnten**
ihr	könnt	**könnet**	könntet
sie	können	können	**könnten**
Sie	können	können	**könnten**

PAST TENSE WITH *HABEN* AS THE HELPING VERB

	INDICATIVE	SPECIAL SUBJUNCTIVE	GENERAL SUBJUNCTIVE
ich	habe getan	habe getan	**hätte** getan
du	hast getan	**habest** getan	hättest getan
er/es/sie	hat getan	**habe** getan	hätte getan
wir	haben getan	haben getan	**hätten** getan
ihr	habt getan	**habet** getan	hättet getan
sie	haben getan	haben getan	**hätten** getan
Sie	haben getan	haben getan	**hätten** getan

PAST TENSE WITH *SEIN* AS THE HELPING VERB

If the helping verb is **sein**, the special subjunctive is used throughout the conjugation because it is always different from the indicative.

	INDICATIVE	SPECIAL SUBJUNCTIVE
ich	bin gefahren	**sei** gefahren
du	bist gefahren	**seiest** gefahren
er/es/sie	ist gefahren	**sei** gefahren
wir	sind gefahren	**seien** gefahren
ihr	seid gefahren	**seiet** gefahren
sie	sind gefahren	**seien** gefahren
Sie	sind gefahren	**seien** gefahren

FUTURE TENSE

	INDICATIVE	SPECIAL SUBJUNCTIVE	GENERAL SUBJUNCTIVE
ich	werde gehen	werde gehen	**würde** gehen
du	wirst gehen	**werdest** gehen	würdest gehen
er/es/sie	wird gehen	**werde** gehen	würde gehen
wir	werden gehen	werden gehen	**würden** gehen
ihr	werdet gehen	werdet gehen	**würdet** gehen
sie	werden gehen	werden gehen	**würden** gehen
Sie	werden gehen	werden gehen	**würden** gehen

Exercise 4: *Restate the direct quotes as indirect quotes. Use the general subjunctive when the special subjunctive is identical to the indicative.*

1. In der Zeitung heißt es: „Die Supermächte haben endlich begonnen abzurüsten."
2. Die Politikerin sagt: „Mit dem Ende des Kalten Krieges kommen neue Hoffnungen, aber auch Schwierigkeiten."
3. Man hörte in den Fernsehnachrichten: „Das wirtschaftliche Problem kam erst in den späten 80er Jahren ans Licht, aber seine Ursachen sind früher zu suchen."
4. Die Professorin sagt: „Die Vorlesung findet heute abend um 8 statt."
5. Der Student sagt: „Alle sollen im Ausland studieren. Es ist eine einmalige Erfahrung."
6. Die Künstlerin behauptet: „Es gibt keine Definition von Pornographie, mit der alle übereinstimmen können."
7. Die zwei Angeklagten behaupteten: „Wir sind unschuldig. Wir haben nichts Falsches gemacht."
8. Das Arbeitsamt meldet: „In Zeiten hoher Arbeitslosigkeit leiden Frauen mehr als Männer."
9. Meine Freundin sagt: „Du gehst mir auf die Nerven!"
10. Der Postbote meinte: „Die Briefe werden sich wegen der Feiertage etwas verspäten."

11. Der Müllmann rät: „Man muβ den Müll recyclen, dann hat man weniger."
12. Der Schwarzfahrer beteuerte: „Ich habe mir eine Fahrkarte gekauft."
13. Der Motorradfahrer schrie: „Die Leute sollen mir aus dem Weg gehen!"
14. Der Direktor meint: „Die Gewerkschaft stellt zu hohe Anforderungen."
15. Der Verkäufer sagte dem Kunden: „Sie müssen sich hinten in die Schlange stellen."

Indirect Discourse in Questions

Direct questions can be stated indirectly. All indirect questions are dependent clauses and therefore send the conjugated verb to the end of the clause. Indirect questions begin either with a question word or with the conjunction **ob** (*whether*).

WITH A QUESTION WORD
Der Kunde fragte: „Warum sind die Preise so hoch gestiegen?"
Der Kunde fragte, **warum** die Preise so hoch **gestiegen seien**.
The customer asked, "Why have the prices gone up so much?"
The customer asked why the prices went up so much.

WITHOUT A QUESTION WORD
Der Patient fragte: „Habe ich meinen Termin verpaβt?"
Der Patient fragte, **ob** er seinen Termin **verpaβt habe**.
The patient asked, "Did I miss my appointment?"
The patient asked whether he had missed his appointment.

Exercise 5: *Restate the direct questions as indirect questions. Use the general subjunctive if the special subjunctive is identical to the indicative.*

1. Die Kinder fragen: „Dürfen wir den Nachtisch vor dem Hauptgericht essen?"
2. Der Kellner fragte: „Ist das Steak gut genug durchgebraten?"
3. Die Fremden fragten: „Wo finden wir den Bahnhof?"
4. Der Beamte fragte mich: „Haben Sie das Formular schon ausgefüllt?"
5. Die Professorin fragte die Studenten: „Warum haben Sie den Text noch nicht zu Ende gelesen?"
6. Der Präsidentschaftskandidat fragt seine Zuhörer: „Leben Sie heute besser oder schlechter als vor vier Jahren?"
7. Der Kunde fragt: „Wie kann man dieses Buch bestellen?"
8. Der Telefonist fragt: „Wer bezahlt den Anruf?"

9. Die Tierärztin fragte: „Hat die Katze schon lange Haarausfall?"
10. Der Reporter fragt: „Werden die Zeugen heute aussagen?"

Indirect Discourse in Commands

Direct commands are reported indirectly with the modal verb **sollen**. As always in formal German, the special subjunctive is used unless it is identical to the indicative, in which case the general subjunctive is used.

„Bestellen Sie die Spezialität des Hauses!"
Die Kellnerin sagte uns, wir **sollten** die Spezialität des Hauses **bestellen**.
"Order the specialty of the house."
The waitress said that we should order the specialty of the house.

„Mach das Licht endlich aus und schlaf ein!"
Die Mutter sagte ihrer Tochter, sie **solle** das Licht endlich **ausmachen** und **einschlafen**.
"Turn out the light finally and go to sleep."
The mother said to her daughter that she should finally turn out the light and go to sleep.

Exercise 6: *Restate the direct commands as indirect commands. Use the general subjunctive if the special subjunctive is identical to the indicative.*

1. „Machen Sie die Bücher bitte zu!"
   Der Lehrer sagte den Studenten, . . .
2. „Bezahlen Sie bitte an der Kasse!"
   Die Verkäuferin sagte mir, . . .
3. „Lies eine Geschichte vor!"
   Das Mädchen sagte ihrer Mutter, . . .
4. „Nehmen Sie zweimal am Tag eine Tablette!"
   Die Ärztin sagte dem Kranken, . . .
5. „Mischen Sie sich nicht ein!"
   Unser Nachbar sagte meinem Mann und mir, . . .
6. „Lüg nicht!"
   Der Vater sagte seinem Sohn, . . .
7. „Eßt euer Gemüse!"
   Man sagt den Kindern immer, . . .
8. „Schickt mir mehr Geld!"
   Der Student sagte seinen Eltern, . . .

Lengthy Passages in Indirect Discourse

For lengthy passages in English, it is necessary to remind the reader or listener that the indirect reporting continues with expressions such as "She continued by saying . . . ," "Then she said . . . ," and so on. In German, because the forms for indirect discourse are distinctly recognizable, such reminders are not necessary. The reader or listener assumes indirect discourse as long as the special or general subjunctive is used.

Der Augenzeuge berichtete: „Wegen des Schnees war die Straße glitschig. Man konnte auch fast nichts sehen. Das grüne Auto ist außer Kontrolle geraten und mit dem blauen Auto zusammengestoßen. Beide Autos haben Totalschaden, aber glücklicherweise ist niemand verletzt worden."

Der Augenzeuge berichtete, wegen des Schnees **sei** die Straße glitschig **gewesen**. Man **habe** auch fast nichts **sehen können**. Das grüne Auto **sei** außer Kontrolle **geraten** und mit dem blauen Auto **zusammengestoßen**. Beide Autos **hätten** Totalschaden, aber glücklicherweise **sei** niemand **verletzt worden**.

Exercise 7: *Restate the direct quote passages as indirect discourse.*

1. Die Reporterin gab bekannt: „Neo-Faschisten haben zwei Asylanten gestern abend angegriffen, als die Asylanten vom Einkaufen nach Hause gingen. Die Polizei sucht noch die Täter. Eine Demonstration gegen Übergriffe dieser Art wird in der kommenden Woche stattfinden."

2. Der Sprecher der Firma sagte: „Die Rezession hat die Firma stark getroffen. Die Firma hat im letzten Quartal Schulden in Höhe von fast einer Billiarde. Man erwartet ungefähr das gleiche im nächsten Quartal. Wenn die Lage sich nicht bessert, werden Tausende ihre Stelle verlieren. Die Direktion verhandelt zur Zeit mit der Gewerkschaft. Es gibt gegensätzliche Interessen. Die Arbeitnehmer wollen Jobsicherheit; die Arbeitgeber wollen niedrigere Arbeitskosten. Der Ausgang der Verhandlungen ist noch ungewiß."

3. Der Zoologe berichtet: „Man erkennt den Waschbären an seiner schwarzen Gesichtsmaske und dem hell-dunkel geringelten Schwanz. Der Waschbär hat sehr geschickte Vorderpfoten, die er zum Beispiel dazu benutzt, sein Fressen zu waschen. Oft kann man ihn an Flüssen beobachten. Er fängt zuerst einen Fisch, nimmt ihn dann aus und frißt ihn. Nach jedem Bissen wäscht er sich dabei im Wasser die Pfoten. So hat er den Namen 'Waschbär' bekommen. Der Waschbär ist ein Nachttier und die meisten Bauern haben ihn nicht besonders gern, weil er Hühner stiehlt."

4. Der Museumsführer erzählte uns: „Dieses Schloß ist im 14. Jahrhundert erbaut worden. Es wohnten seitdem vier verschiedene adlige Familien hier. Der letzte Graf ist 1904 gestorben. Das Schloß gehört jetzt dem Staat und es wird als Museum renoviert. Fünf Räume sind schon fertig. Die Restauratoren arbeiten an den letzten drei. Nächstes Jahr sollen auch sie fertig sein. Ich hoffe, die Führung

hat Ihnen gefallen und Sie kommen nächstes Jahr wieder. Ich wünsche Ihnen noch eine gute Fahrt."

INDIRECT DISCOURSE IN INFORMAL GERMAN

In informal German, the special subjunctive is rarely used. Instead the indicative is used if the reporter does not doubt the truth of the original quote or if the reporter agrees with the original quote. The general subjunctive is used if the reporter doubts the truth of the original quote or does not agree with the original statement. Compare the following sentences:

Der Politiker sagte: „Ich habe gar nichts davon gewußt."
The politician said, "I didn't know anything about it at all."

Der Politiker sagte, er **hat** gar nichts davon gewußt.
Der Politiker sagte, er **hätte** gar nichts davon gewußt.
The politician said that he didn't know anything about it at all.

In the first indirect quotation above, the use of the indicative indicates that the speaker believes the politician. In the second indirect quotation, the use of the subjunctive indicates that the speaker strongly doubts that the politician is telling the truth.

GENERAL SUBJUNCTIVE IN INDIRECT DISCOURSE

In both formal and informal German, if the direct quote is in the general subjunctive, the indirect quote will also be in the general subjunctive. In other words, *general subjunctive stays general subjunctive in indirect reporting.*

Die Schriftstellerin sagt: „Ich **wollte**, ich **hätte** das Ende anders geschrieben."
Die Schriftstellerin sagt, sie **wollte**, sie **hätte** das Ende anders geschrieben.

ANSWERS TO EXERCISES

1.

1. Der Ultrakonservative schrie, eine Frau solle nicht arbeiten.
2. Der Selbstmörder schrieb, er habe Liebeskummer.
3. Frau Meier bemerkt, in zwei Monaten reise sie wieder ab.
4. Der Musikfreund bestätigt, er könne vier Musikinstrumente spielen.
5. Die Tierärztin bedauerte, es tue ihr leid. Das Tier sei nicht zu retten.
6. Die Gewerkschaft sagte, man müsse das Arbeitsklima verbessern.
7. Die Studentin behauptet, dieses Werk gefalle ihr am besten. Sie finde es am interessantesten.
8. Der Papagei sagt dauernd, er wolle einen Cracker.
9. Patrick fügt hinzu, Weihnachten sei das schönste Fest!
10. Die Psychologin meint, es gebe viele Probleme.

2.

1. Die Autorin schrieb, sie habe immer ein privates Leben geführt.
2. Der Bäcker beteuerte, er habe das Brot heute morgen frisch gebacken.
3. Der Mechaniker erklärt, er habe die Bremse reparieren müssen.
4. Die Politikerin erklärte, der Skandal sei nicht ihre Schuld gewesen. Sie habe nichts davon gewußt.
5. In der Zeitung stand, die wirtschaftliche Lage in der ehemaligen DDR sei eigentlich noch schlimmer gewesen, als man gedacht habe.
6. Mein Bruder erklärte, er habe gestern nicht kommen können, weil sein Sohn plötzlich krank geworden sei.
7. Die Touristin sagte, ihr habe es in den Bergen am besten gefallen.
8. Die Chefin gab bekannt, im letz-ten Quartal sei die Produktivität um 2,3% gestiegen.
9. Die Professorin betonte, diese Arbeiten habe sie schon berichtigt und zurückgegeben.
10. Die Gärtnerin widersprach, die große Hitze sei gar nicht gut gewesen.

3.

1. Der Polizist sagt, diese Straße werde eine Woche lang gesperrt sein.
2. Mein Liebhaber schrieb mir, er werde mich ewig lieben.
3. Der Detektiv sagt, das werde man noch herausfinden müssen.
4. Die Frau im Reisebüro sagte, eine Kreuzfahrt auf diesem Schiff werde sicher Spaß machen.
5. Der Astronom schreibt, ein Meteor werde innerhalb von 100 Jahren mit der Erde kollidieren.

4.

1. In der Zeitung heißt es, die Supermächte hätten endlich begonnen abzurüsten.
2. Die Politikerin sagt, mit dem Ende des Kalten Krieges kämen neue Hoffnungen, aber auch Schwierigkeiten.
3. Man hörte in den Fernsehnachrichten, das wirtschaftliche Problem sei erst in den späten 80er Jahren ans Licht gekommen, aber seine Ursachen seien früher zu suchen.
4. Die Professorin sagt, die Vorlesung finde heute abend um 8 statt.
5. Der Student sagt, alle sollten im Ausland studieren. Es sei eine einmalige Erfahrung.
6. Die Künstlerin behauptet, es gebe keine Definition von Pornographie, mit der alle übereinstimmen könnten.
7. Die zwei Angeklagten behaupteten, sie seien unschuldig. Sie hätten nichts Falsches gemacht.
8. Das Arbeitsamt meldet, in Zeiten hoher Arbeitslosigkeit litten Frauen mehr als Männer.
9. Meine Freundin sagt, ich ginge ihr auf die Nerven!
10. Der Postbote meinte, die Briefe würden sich wegen der Feiertage etwas verspäten.
11. Der Müllmann rät, man müsse den Müll recyceln, dann habe man weniger.
12. Der Schwarzfahrer beteuerte, er habe sich eine Fahrkarte gekauft.
13. Der Motorradfahrer schrie, die Leute sollten ihm aus dem Weg gehen!
14. Der Direktor meint, die Gewerkschaft stelle zu hohe Anforderungen.
15. Der Verkäufer sagte dem Kunden, er müsse sich hinten in die Schlange stellen.

5.

1. Die Kinder fragen, ob sie den Nachtisch vor dem Hauptgericht essen dürften.
2. Der Kellner fragte, ob das Steak gut genug durchgebraten sei.
3. Die Fremden fragten, wo sie den Bahnhof fänden.
4. Der Beamte fragte mich, ob ich das Formular schon ausgefüllt hätte.
5. Die Professorin fragte die Studenten, warum sie den Text noch nicht zu Ende gelesen hätten.
6. Der Präsidentschaftskandidat fragt seine Zuhörer, ob sie heute besser oder schlechter als vor vier Jahren lebten.
7. Der Kunde fragt, wie man dieses Buch bestellen könne.
8. Der Telefonist fragt, wer den Anruf bezahle.
9. Die Tierärztin fragte, ob die Katze schon lange Haarausfall habe.

10. Der Reporter fragt, ob die Zeugen heute aussagen würden.

6.

1. Der Lehrer sagte den Studenten, sie sollten die Bücher zumachen.
2. Die Verkäuferin sagte mir, ich solle an der Kasse bezahlen.
3. Das Mädchen sagte ihrer Mutter, sie solle eine Geschichte vorlesen.
4. Die Ärztin sagte dem Kranken, er solle zweimal am Tag eine Tablette nehmen.
5. Unser Nachbar sagte meinem Mann und mir, wir sollten uns nicht einmischen.
6. Der Vater sagte seinem Sohn, er solle nicht lügen.
7. Man sagt den Kindern immer, sie sollten ihr Gemüse essen.
8. Der Student sagte seinen Eltern, sie sollten ihm mehr Geld schicken.

7.

1. Die Reporterin gab bekannt, Neo-Faschisten hätten zwei Asylanten gestern abend angegriffen, als die Asylanten vom Einkaufen nach Hause gegangen seien. Die Polizei suche noch die Täter. Eine Demonstration gegen Übergriffe dieser Art werde in der kommenden Woche stattfinden.
2. Der Sprecher der Firma sagte, die Rezession habe die Firma stark getroffen. Die Firma habe im letzten Quartal Schulden in Höhe von fast einer Billiarde. Man erwarte ungefähr das gleiche im nächsten Quartal. Wenn die Lage sich nicht bessere, würden Tausende ihre Stelle verlieren. Die Direktion verhandele zur Zeit mit der Gewerkschaft. Es gebe gegensätzliche Interessen. Die Arbeitnehmer wollten Jobsicherheit; die Arbeitgeber wollten niedrigere Arbeitskosten. Der Ausgang der Verhandlungen sei noch ungewiß.
3. Der Zoologe berichtet, man erkenne den Waschbären an seiner schwarzen Gesichtsmaske und dem hell-dunkel geringelten Schwanz. Der Waschbär habe sehr geschickte Vorderpfoten, die er zum Beispiel dazu benutze, sein Fressen zu waschen. Oft könne man ihn an Flüssen beobachten. Er fange zuerst einen Fisch, nehme ihn dann aus und fresse ihn. Nach jedem Bissen wasche er sich dabei im Wasser die Pfoten. So habe er den Namen „Waschbär" bekommen. Der Waschbär sei ein Nachttier und die meisten Bauern hätten ihn nicht besonders gern, weil er Hühner stehle.
4. Der Museumsführer erzählte uns, dieses Schloß sei im 14. Jahrhundert erbaut worden. Es hätten seitdem vier verschiedene adlige Familien hier gewohnt. Der letzte Graf sei 1904 gestorben. Das Schloß gehöre jetzt dem Staat und es werde als Museum renoviert. Fünf Räume seien schon fertig. Die Restauratoren arbeiteten an den letzten drei. Nächstes Jahr sollten auch sie fertig sein. Er hoffe, die Führung habe uns gefallen und wir kämen nächstes Jahr wieder. Er wünsche uns noch eine gute Fahrt.

11

Special Problems with Verbs

This chapter treats a number of verbs and constructions that cause frequent problems for speakers of English. The chapter starts with a discussion of four verbs that, like the modals, may be used together with a dependent infinitive. It continues with a discussion of infinitive phrases, anticipatory **da**-*compounds, reflexive verbs, and transitive and intransitive verbs. It concludes with an explanation of the subjective usage of modals.*

THE VERBS HELFEN, HÖREN, LASSEN, *AND* SEHEN

The verbs **helfen**, **hören**, **lassen**, and **sehen** function structurally like the modal verbs (see chapter 7). They may occur by themselves or together with another infinitive, without **zu**. For the perfect tenses, these verbs have two past participles, depending on whether they are used alone (**geholfen**, **gehört**, **gelassen**, **gesehen**) or together with another infinitive (double infinitive). Study the following synopsis of **lassen** for all tenses used alone and with another infinitive:

USED ALONE	TOGETHER WITH ANOTHER INFINITIVE
Ich **lasse** dich hier.	Ich **lasse** es hier **stehen**.
Ich **ließ** dich hier.	Ich **ließ** es hier **stehen**.
Ich **habe** dich hier **gelassen**.	Ich **habe** es hier **stehen lassen**.
Ich **hatte** dich hier **gelassen**.	Ich **hatte** es hier **stehen lassen**.
Ich **werde** dich hier **lassen**.	Ich **werde** es hier **stehen lassen**.

245

hören and *sehen*

Infinitive constructions with **hören** and **sehen** frequently correspond to the English present participle, or *-ing* form.

Ich **höre** den Hund **bellen**.	*I hear the dog barking.*
Ich **sehe** sie **kommen**.	*I see her coming.*

In the perfect tenses, the double infinitive is usually used.

Ich **habe** den Hund **bellen hören**.	*I heard the dog barking.*
Ich **habe** sie **kommen sehen**.	*I saw her coming.*

In spoken German, it is increasingly common to hear **gehört** instead of the double infinitive.

Ich **habe** den Hund **bellen gehört**.

helfen

In fairly short sentences, **helfen** is used without **zu**.

Ich **helfe** ihnen **umziehen**.   *I help them move.*

In the perfect tenses, the double infinitive is preferred in formal German.

Ich **habe** ihnen **umziehen helfen**.
I helped them move.

In spoken German, **geholfen** is common.

Ich habe ihnen umziehen **geholfen**.

In lengthier sentences, **helfen** is usually used with the infinitive plus **zu**.

Ich **helfe** ihnen, alles hinunter**zu**tragen und in das Auto ein**zu**packen.
I help them carry everything down and pack it into the car.

lassen

The verb **lassen** has different meanings and forms depending on whether it stands alone or together with another infinitive.

LASSEN WITHOUT ANOTHER INFINITIVE

Standing alone, **lassen** means *to leave*. The past participle is **gelassen**.

Ich **lasse** meine Reiseschecks im Hoteltresor.
I'm leaving my traveler's checks in the hotel safe.

Ich **habe** meine Reiseschecks im Hoteltresor gelassen.
I left my traveler's checks in the hotel safe.

LASSEN WITH ANOTHER INFINITIVE

Together with another infinitive, **lassen** expresses either permission or causation. The context of the sentence will determine the intended meaning. The past participle is always a double infinitive and **zu** is omitted.

Permission. Lassen is frequently used to mean *to let* or *to allow*.

Die Mutter **läßt** ihren Sohn nicht auf der Straße **spielen**.
The mother doesn't allow her son to play in the street.

Die Mutter **hat** ihren Sohn nicht auf der Straße **spielen lassen**.
The mother didn't allow her son to play in the street.

Causation. Lassen is frequently used causatively to express the idea that someone is having something done, causing something to be done, or sending for something or someone.

Ich **lasse** das Haus **streichen**.
I'm having the house painted.

Ich **habe** das Haus **streichen lassen**.
I had the house painted.

The person actually performing the task is expressed as an accusative object. Thus such sentences may have two accusative objects.

Ich lasse meinen Bruder mein Auto reparieren.
I'm having my brother repair my car.

If the person performing the task is not expressed, English uses a past participle for the verb whereas German uses the infinitive.

Ich lasse mein Auto **reparieren**.
*I'm having my car **repaired**.*

Exercise 1: *Restate in the present perfect tense.*

1. Sie hört ein komisches Geräusch.
2. Sie hört nur den Regen herunterprasseln.
3. Wir sehen uns in der Klasse.
4. Wir sehen euch kommen.
5. Ich helfe ihr am Montag.
6. Ich helfe ihr den Aufsatz schreiben.
7. Er läßt seinen Regenschirm zu Hause.
8. Der Sturm läßt uns nicht einschlafen.

Exercise 2: *Translate into English.*

1. Die Professorin läßt den Studenten nie genug Zeit für die Prüfungen.
2. Wir lassen ein Taxi kommen.
3. In der Stille hörte man nur die Uhr ticken.
4. Ich habe mir gestern die Haare schneiden lassen.
5. Wir müssen sofort einen Arzt kommen lassen.
6. Sie lassen die Kinder jeden Abend abwaschen.
7. Der Polizist sah das Auto bei Rot über die Kreuzung fahren.
8. Für ihre Aufsätze ließ der Professor die Studenten zusammen arbeiten.
9. Ich lasse dich nicht gerne bei Nacht nach Hause fahren.
10. Ich lasse dich morgen wissen, ob ich mitfahren darf oder nicht.
11. Wir lassen den Steuerberater immer unsere Steuern berechnen.
12. Die Verkäuferin im Tante-Emma-Laden kannte mich. Deshalb ließ sie mich die Waren anschreiben.
13. Hast du den Deutschen die Goldmedaille gewinnen sehen?
14. Ich hörte auf einmal den Ballon zerplatzen.
15. Die Kinder helfen immer den Tisch decken.

Exercise 3: *Translate into German, using the present perfect tense for the English past.*

1. We only heard her sing once.
2. He sees the child playing.
3. I hear the telephone ringing.
4. I don't like seeing her cry.
5. She had her dress cleaned.
6. I left my keys at home.
7. We're having a house built.
8. She helped me write the letter.
9. I heard the door close behind me.
10. They sent for the ambulance.

INFINITIVE PHRASES

Infinitive phrases in English and German are constructed in essentially the same way. Compare the following:

Ich habe vor, dieses Wochenende nach Hause **zu fahren**.
*I'm planning **to go** home this weekend.*

Es macht Spaß, ins Kino **zu gehen**.
*It's fun **to go** to the movies.*

As you can see from these examples, the main difference between German and English infinitive phrases is that in German the **zu** plus infinitive stands *at the end of the infinitive phrase*, whereas in English the infinitive introduces the phrase.

Infinitive phrases of more than two words follow the main clause and are set off by a comma.

Das Orchester fängt an, **ein Stück von Arnold Schönberg zu spielen**.
The orchestra is beginning to play a piece by Arnold Schönberg.

Infinitive phrases of just two words (**zu** + infinitive) are considered part of the entire sentence and therefore may or may not be incorporated into the main clause.

Das Orchester **fängt an zu spielen**.
OR
Das Orchester **fängt zu spielen an**.
The orchestra is beginning to play.

If the infinitive phrase includes a separable-prefix verb, the **zu** is inserted between the prefix and the main part of the verb.

Ich habe den ganzen Tag versucht, dich an**zu**rufen.
I tried to call you the whole day.

Man darf nicht vergessen, den Text im Computer ein**zu**speichern.
You mustn't forget to save your text in the computer.

Exercise 4: *Complete by translating the infinitive clauses into German.*

1. Habt ihr einen Kompromiß geschlossen?
   Du weißt, wie schwer es ist, _____.   (*to find a compromise*)
2. Wer füttert die Katze, während du weg bist?
   Ich habe meinen Nachbarn gebeten, _____.   (*to feed her*)
3. Willst du einen Spaziergang machen?
   Es ist zu spät, _____.   (*to take a walk*)
4. Welche Kurse belegst du dieses Semester?
   Mein Vertrauenslehrer empfahl mir, _____.   (*to take these courses*)
5. Warum hast du sie noch nicht gefragt?
   Ich finde es dumm, _____.   (*to ask her*)

6. Ich kann dieses Problem nicht lösen.
Aber es ist äußerst wichtig, _____.   (*to solve the problem*)
7. Hast du das Essen mitgebracht?
Nein, ich habe leider vergessen, _____.   (*to bring it along*)
8. Erzähl bitte niemandem von der Affäre!
Ich verspreche dir, _____.   (*to tell no one about it*)
9. Darf ich in diesem Restaurant rauchen?
Nein, es ist nicht erlaubt, _____.   (*to smoke here*)
10. Ich muß den Tisch in das andere Zimmer tragen.
Kannst du mir helfen, _____?   (*to carry it into the other room*)
11. Die Kinder wollen bis 5 morgens aufbleiben, aber die Mutter
verbietet ihnen, _____.   (*to stay up so long*)
12. Kannst du bitte das Fenster aufmachen?
Ich habe vergessen, _____.   (*to open it*)

Infinitive Phrases with um, ohne, and (an)statt

The prepositions **um**, **ohne**, and **(an)statt** frequently introduce infinitive phrases.

UM . . . ZU + INFINITIVE: *IN ORDER TO*

An infinitive phrase introduced by **um** expresses purpose or intent.

Sie geht ins Büro, **um** am Manuskript **zu arbeiten**.
She's going to the office (in order) to work on the manuscript.

Der Fahrer trinkt Kaffee, **um** wach **zu bleiben**.
The driver is drinking coffee (in order) to stay awake.

Contrary to English, which frequently omits *in order*, in German the preposition **um** is necessary to express purpose. Thus whenever the English sentence *could* mean *in order to*, the **um . . . zu** + infinitive construction *must* be used in German.

OHNE . . . ZU + INFINITIVE: *WITHOUT . . . -ING*

Sie schauten einander an, **ohne** ein Wort **zu sagen**.
They looked at each other without saying a word.

Sie ist weggefahren, **ohne** sich **zu verabschieden**.
She left without saying goodbye.

Note that the English equivalent is usually a gerund.

AN(STATT) . . . ZU + INFINITIVE: *INSTEAD . . . -ING*

Sie kämpfen immer gegen einander, **statt** miteinander **zu arbeiten**.
They're always fighting each other instead of working with each other.

Die Kinder wollten lieber drinnen fernsehen, **statt** draußen **zu spielen**.
The children wanted to watch TV inside instead of playing outside.

Note that the English equivalent is usually a gerund.

Frequently the infinitive phrase with **statt** stands at the beginning of the sentence. This means that the main clause will have inverted word order.

Statt miteinander zu arbeiten, kämpfen sie immer gegen einander.
Statt draußen zu spielen, wollten die Kinder lieber drinnen fernsehen.

Anstatt is more formal than **statt**.

Exercise 5: *Translate into German using infinitive phrases.*

1. Sie hat angerufen. Sie wollte mich zur Party einladen.
   She called (in order) to invite me to the party.
2. Wir gehen oft zu Fuß. Wir wollen gesund bleiben.
   We often go on foot (in order) to stay healthy.
3. Er handelte. Er dachte nicht an die Konsequenzen.
   He acted without thinking of the consequences.
4. Sie singt nicht im Chor, sondern spielt ein Instrument im Orchester.
   Instead of singing in the choir she plays an instrument in the orchestra.
5. Die Schriftstellerin zieht aufs Land. Sie will in Ruhe schreiben.
   The writer is moving to the country (in order) to work in peace.
6. Sie lernen nicht für die Prüfung, sondern sie gehen trinken.
   Instead of studying for the test they're going drinking.
7. Ich arbeite während der Ferien. Ich muß Geld verdienen.
   I'm working during the vacation (in order) to earn money.
8. Ich sprach ihn an. Ich kannte ihn nicht.
   I spoke to him without knowing him.
9. Meine Schwiegereltern kommen oft vorbei. Sie rufen nicht vorher an.
   My in-laws frequently stop by without calling first.
10. Wir finden uns in der Stadt zurecht. Wir haben keinen Stadtplan.
    We find our way around the city without having a city map.
11. Sie fuhr nicht mit ihrem Auto, sondern ging zu Fuß.
    Instead of driving her car, she walked.
12. Ich wollte mit ihr reden. Ich wollte bestimmte Themen besprechen.
    I wanted to talk to her (in order) to discuss certain topics.
13. Sie gingen nicht nach Hause. Sie blieben noch eine Stunde im Park.
    Instead of going home they stayed in the park for another hour.
14. Sie hat es gesagt. Sie dachte dabei nicht nach.
    She said it without thinking.

15. Ich fahre in die Stadt. Ich muβ einkaufen gehen.
I'm going to town (in order) to go shopping.

English Infinitive Phrases vs. German Subordinate Clauses

There are a number of cases in which English uses an infinitive phrase but German must use a subordinate clause.

WITH A QUESTION WORD

In German, a question word can only introduce a subordinate clause. In English, a question word may introduce an infinitive phrase or a subordinate clause. Compare the following German and English sentences:

Ich weiβ nicht, **was** ich tun soll.
I don't know what to do.
I don't know what I am supposed to do.

Sag mir, **wohin** ich gehen soll!
Tell me where to go.
Tell me where I am supposed to go.

Weiβt du, **wie** man dahin kommt?
Do you know how to get there?
Do you know how one gets there?

WITH VERBS OF SAYING, WANTING, AND EXPECTING

Verbs of Saying. In German, the verb **sagen** (*to tell, to say*) is followed by a subordinate clause introduced by **daβ**. English may use either an infinitive phrase or a subordinate clause. Compare the following German and English sentences:

Sie sagte, **daβ** ich sofort nach Hause gehen sollte.
She told me to go home immediately.
She told me that I should go home immediately.

Verbs of Wanting and Expecting. In German, verbs of wanting (**wollen** and **möchten**) and the verb **erwarten** (*to expect*) are followed by a subordinate clause introduced by **daβ** if the sentence involves two different subjects. English uses an infinitive phrase.

Wir wollen, **daβ** du mitkommst.
We want you to come along.
Meine Mutter möchte, **daβ** ich weiter zu Hause wohne.
My mother would like me to continue living at home.

Er erwartete, **daβ** sie seine Arbeit tippen würde.
He expected her to type his paper for him.

Exercise 6: *Translate into German.*

1. I don't know when to come.
2. My mother doesn't want me to read this book.
3. The teacher expects her students to know everything.
4. Would you like me to show you this vase, Mr. Ruprecht?
5. He doesn't know when to stop.
6. Does she want me to help her?
7. They told us to be quiet.
8. Who knows how to say this in German?
9. Tell me what to bring to the party, Astrid.
10. I want the evening to be perfect.

ANTICIPATORY da-*COMPOUNDS*

In English, prepositions may precede nouns, pronouns, or whole clauses. In German, prepositions may only precede nouns or pronouns. If the preposition refers to a phrase or an entire clause, it must be used in a **da**-compound (see chapter 4) that anticipates the clause to come. Compare the following German and English sentences:

Er hat groβes Interesse **daran**, seine Ferien in den Alpen zu verbringen.
He's very interested in spending his vacation in the Alps.

Wir waren alle **darüber** erstaunt, daβ er so etwas sagte.
We were all astonished about his saying such a thing.

Note that the anticipatory **da**-compound is not expressed in English. Instead, English frequently uses a gerund.

If identical subjects are used in both parts of the sentence (as in the first example above), an infinitive phrase is usually used in German. If the subjects are different (as in the second example), a subordinate clause must be used. Compare the following sentences:

SUBJECTS IDENTICAL: INFINITIVE PHRASE
Hast du Interesse daran, im **Chor zu singen**?
Are you interested in singing in the choir?

SUBJECTS DIFFERENT: SUBORDINATE CLAUSE
Hast du Interesse daran, **daβ** ich im **Chor singe**?
Are you interested in my singing in the choir?

Exercise 7: *Translate into English. (You may have to consult the glossary or review the idiomatic meanings of prepositions in chapter 4.)*

1. Die Eltern sind stolz darauf, daβ ihre Tochter so schön Klavier spielen kann.
2. Mein Freund wartet darauf, daβ ich um neun anrufe.
3. Ich bin stolz darauf, eine Fremdsprache zu können.
4. Ich habe oft daran gedacht, so etwas zu machen.
5. Bist du damit zufrieden, diese Note in dem Kurs zu bekommen?
6. Meine Mutter ist absolut dagegen, daβ ich mit dir ausgehe.
7. Die Kinder waren davon begeistert, eine Nacht bei den Groβeltern zu verbringen.
8. Mein Kollege ist darauf eifersüchtig, daβ ich, und nicht er, die Beförderung bekam.
9. Meine Sehnsucht danach, dich wiederzusehen, wird immer gröβer.
10. Ich habe Angst davor, daβ die Schluβprüfung sehr schwer sein wird.

Exercise 8: *Translate into German.*

1. The students were enthusiastic about studying in Germany.
2. I'm waiting for my roommate to get home.
3. I'm against buying another car.
4. He's jealous that his neighbors have such a big house.
5. The married couple is interested in adopting a child.
6. My parents are proud of my working in the Peace Corps.
7. I'm afraid of taking the final exam.
8. They're talking about buying a house together.

REFLEXIVE VERBS

In chapter 3 we learned that many verbs may be used reflexively or nonreflexively. When used reflexively, the action of the verb refers back to the subject of the sentence. Compare the following sentence pairs:

NONREFLEXIVE USAGE	REFLEXIVE USAGE
Sie sieht ihn an.	Sie sieht sich an.
She looks at him.	*She looks at herself.*

Er kauft mir ein Auto.	Er kauft sich ein Auto.
He buys me a car.	*He buys himself a car.*
Ich ziehe das Kind an.	Ich ziehe mich an.
I dress the child.	*I dress myself.*

Remember that reflexive pronouns may be accusative or dative, depending on whether they function as the direct or indirect object in the sentence. Here is a review of the reflexive pronouns:

ACCUSATIVE REFLEXIVES	DATIVE REFLEXIVES
Ich wasche **mich**.	Ich kaufe **mir** ein Auto.
Du wäschst **dich**.	Du kaufst **dir** ein Auto.
Er wäscht **sich**.	Er kauft **sich** ein Auto.
Es wäscht **sich**.	Es kauft **sich** ein Auto.
Sie wäscht **sich**.	Sie kauft **sich** ein Auto.
Wir waschen **uns**.	Wir kaufen **uns** ein Auto.
Ihr wascht **euch**.	Ihr kauft **euch** ein Auto.
Sie (*they*) waschen **sich**.	Sie (*they*) kaufen **sich** ein Auto.
Sie (*you*) waschen **sich**.	Sie (*you*) kaufen **sich** ein Auto.

The usage of the reflexive pronouns above is fairly logical and corresponds to English usage for the most part. However, there are many German verbs that use reflexives idiomatically. For these verbs, called *reflexive verbs*, there is no corresponding English reflexive construction.

Common Reflexive Verbs

Here is a list of some common reflexive verbs.

sich amüsieren	*to have a good time*
sich ärgern über + *acc.*	*to be angry about*
sich beeilen	*to hurry up*
sich benehmen	*to behave*
sich bewerben um	*to apply for*
sich (*dat.*) denken	*to imagine*
sich erholen von	*to recover from*
sich erinnern an + *acc.*	*to remember; to recall*
sich erkälten	*to catch a cold*
sich freuen auf + *acc.*	*to look forward to*
sich freuen über + *acc.*	*to be happy about*
sich fühlen	*to feel*
sich fürchten vor + *dat.*	*to be afraid of*
sich gewöhnen an + *acc.*	*to become accustomed to*
sich interessieren für	*to be interested in*
sich irren	*to be mistaken*

sich konzentrieren auf + *acc.*	*to concentrate on*
sich kümmern um	*to care for; to concern oneself with*
sich (*dat.*) leisten	*to afford*
sich sehnen nach	*to long for*
sich (*dat.*) Sorgen machen um	*to worry about; to be concerned about*
sich verlassen auf + *acc.*	*to depend on*
sich (*dat.*) vorstellen	*to imagine*
sich wundern über + *acc.*	*to be surprised about*

Reflexive Verbs with Prepositions

As you can tell from the list above, many reflexive verbs in German are accompanied by a preposition. If the preposition is an either-or preposition, the case cannot be predicted and must be learned.

sich erinnern an + acc.   *to remember; to recall*

Ich erinnere mich nicht an den Namen des Filmes.

I don't remember the name of the film.

sich fürchten vor + dat.   *to be afraid of*

Fürchtest du dich wirklich vor dieser kleinen Spinne?

Are you really afraid of this little spider?

Accusative vs. Dative Reflexive Verbs

As you can tell from the list above, most reflexive verbs are accusative.

sich erkälten   *to catch cold*

Ich erkälte **mich** immer im Winter.

I always get a cold in the winter.

sich irren   *to be mistaken*

Du irrst **dich**.

You're mistaken.

However, if there is already an accusative object in the sentence, then the reflexive pronoun must be dative.

sich (dat.) **vorstellen**   *to imagine*

Solches Glück konnte ich **mir** kaum vorstellen.

I could scarcely imagine such good fortune.

sich (dat.) **leisten**   *to afford*

Kannst du **dir** so ein Auto wirklich leisten?

Can you really afford such a car?

Reflexive Verbs in the Perfect Tenses

The auxiliary verb for reflexive verbs in the present perfect or past perfect tenses is always **haben**.

Der Vater **hat** sich um sein krankes Kind Sorgen gemacht.
The father worried about his sick child.

Sie **hat** sich noch nicht an dieses Klima gewöhnt.
She still hasn't gotten used to this climate.

Reflexive Verbs in Commands

Reflexive verbs used in commands require the appropriate reflexive pronoun, depending on the person being addressed.

ACCUSATIVE REFLEXIVES
Sylvia, beeil **dich** bitte!
Sylvia und Winfried, beeilt **euch** bitte!
Frau Konrad, beeilen Sie **sich** bitte!

DATIVE REFLEXIVES
Sylvia, stell **dir** das mal vor!
Sylvia und Winfried, stellt **euch** das mal vor!
Frau Konrad, stellen Sie **sich** das mal vor!

Exercise 9: *Translate into German, using the list of common reflexives earlier in this section.*

1. I feel sick.
2. Did she apply for the job?
3. We had a good time at the party.
4. I'm looking forward to the holidays.
5. He can't get used to the cold.
6. Hurry up, Franz! It's already 9 o'clock.
7. I'm not afraid of anything.
8. They never remember my name.
9. You can depend on me, Karin.
10. Children, behave yourselves!

Exercise 10: *Translate into German, using the list of common reflexives earlier in this section and an anticipatory* **da**-*compound.*

1. She's interested in studying German.
2. I'm looking forward to finally meeting you, Ms. Wilhelm.
3. We can depend on their coming on time.
4. I can't get used to taking the bus.
5. She doesn't remember his saying that.
6. He's afraid of being alone.

THE VERBS LEGEN/LIEGEN, SETZEN/SITZEN, STELLEN/STEHEN, AND HÄNGEN

The verbs **legen/liegen**, **setzen/sitzen**, **stellen/stehen**, and **hängen** are paired depending on whether the verb is transitive or intransitive. A *transitive verb* requires a direct object; an *intransitive verb* cannot take a direct object.

The Verbs legen, setzen, stellen

Legen, **setzen**, and **stellen** are weak verbs.

	to lay; to put	*to set; to put*	*to place; to put*
INFINITIVE	legen	setzen	stellen
SIMPLE PAST	legte	setzte	stellte
PAST PARTICIPLE	gelegt	gesetzt	gestellt

All three verbs are transitive. When used with an either-or preposition they denote a change of position and therefore take the accusative case:

> verb + acc. object + either-or preposition + acc.

Ich lege das Buch auf den Tisch.
I put the book on the table.

Wir setzen das Kind auf den Stuhl.
We set the child on the chair.

Sie stellt die Lampe in die Ecke.
She's putting the lamp in the corner.

Note that all three verbs correspond to English *to put*. In general, **legen** is used for objects that lie flat, **setzen** for living beings, and **stellen** for objects that stand upright. All three verbs may be used reflexively.

Sie legt sich auf das Bett.
She lies down on the bed.

Setz dich neben mich!
Sit down next to me!

Stellt euch in die Schlange!
Go stand in line!

The Verbs liegen, sitzen, stehen

Liegen, **sitzen**, and **stehen** are strong verbs.

	to lie	*to sit*	*to stand*
INFINITIVE	liegen	sitzen	stehen
SIMPLE PAST	lag	saβ	stand
PAST PARTICIPLE	gelegen	gesessen	gestanden

All three verbs are intransitive. When used with an either-or preposition they denote no change of position and therefore take the dative case. Compare the following basic pattern to the one above for the transitive verbs:

> verb + either-or preposition + dat.

Das Buch liegt auf dem Tisch.
The book is lying on the table.

Das Kind sitzt auf dem Stuhl.
The child is sitting on the chair.

Die Lampe steht in der Ecke.
The lamp is standing in the corner.

The Verb hängen

Hängen is both a transitive and an intransitive verb. Like the verb pairs above, if used transitively **hängen** is weak, denotes a change of position, and therefore takes the accusative case with an either-or preposition. If used intransitively, **hängen** is strong, denotes no change of position, and therefore takes the dative case with an either-or preposition.

TRANSITIVE USAGE

	to hang
INFINITIVE	hängen
SIMPLE PAST	hängte
PAST PARTICIPLE	gehängt

Er hängt seinen Mantel in den Schrank.
He's hanging his coat in the closet.

Sie haben das Bild an die Wand gehängt.
They hung the picture on the wall.

INTRANSITIVE USAGE

	to be hanging
INFINITIVE	hängen
SIMPLE PAST	hing
PAST PARTICIPLE	gehangen

Der Mantel hängt im Schrank.
The coat is hanging in the closet.

Das Bild hat an der Wand gehangen.
The picture was hanging on the wall.

Exercise 11: *Restate in the simple past and the present perfect tenses.*

1. Meine Mutter legt sich jeden Nachmittag hin.
2. Die Katze liegt den ganzen Tag in der Sonne.
3. Die hungrigen Gäste setzen sich schnell an den Tisch.
4. Die Informatikerin sitzt acht Stunden am Computer.
5. Wir stellen den Videorecorder neben den Fernseher.
6. Warum stehen diese Leute hier herum?
7. Warum hängen Sie das Bild nicht über den Kamin?
8. Der Weihnachtsschmuck hängt am Tannenbaum.

Exercise 12: *Translate into German.*

1. The tourists lie on the beach.
2. On December 6th children put their shoes in front of the door.
3. The church stands next to the city hall.
4. The key is hanging on the hook.
5. She puts the milk into the refrigerator.
6. Moritz and Peter, sit down next to us!
7. Put the newspaper on the desk, Wolf.
8. Martin, please put the dirty dishes into the dishwasher.
9. Everyone's sitting at the table already.
10. Students frequently hang posters on the walls of their room.

THE SUBJECTIVE USE OF MODAL VERBS

Until now, you have used the modal verbs *objectively* to describe a situation factually. The speaker has no opinion concerning that situation. In addition, modal verbs are sometimes used to express an assumption or judgment made by the speaker. The speaker *surmises* something based on the evidence presented, or the speaker *doubts* the truth of a statement. This is called the *subjective use of modal verbs*. Compare the following two situations:

OBJECTIVE USE
Heidi hat morgen eine Schlußprüfung. **Sie muß viel lernen**.
Heidi has a final exam tomorrow. She has to study a lot.

SUBJECTIVE USE

Heidi bekommt immer die beste Note in der Klasse. **Sie muβ viel lernen**.

Heidi always gets the best grade in the class. She must study a lot.

The first sentence above is objective because it describes a fact: Heidi has to study because she has an exam. The second sentence is subjective because it is an assumption made by the speaker based on the evidence: it is safe to assume that Heidi studies a lot because she always gets such good grades.

Tenses of Modals Used Subjectively

The modals may be used subjectively in only two tenses: the present tense and the past tense.

PRESENT TENSE OF MODALS USED SUBJECTIVELY

In the present tense, the subjective use of modals is identical in form to the objective use of modals. The only way to know the meaning of the sentence is through the context.

OBJECTIVE USE   Sie muβ viel lernen.
She has to study a lot.

SUBJECTIVE USE   She muβ viel lernen.
She must study a lot.

PAST TENSE OF MODALS USED SUBJECTIVELY

In the past tense, the subjective use of modals differs in form from the objective use of modals. Compare the following sentences:

OBJECTIVE USE

Heidi hatte gestern eine Schluβprüfung. Sie **muβte** viel **lernen**.

Heidi had a final exam yesterday. She had to study a lot.

SUBJECTIVE USE

Heidi bekam die beste Note in der Klasse. Sie **muβ** viel **gelernt haben**.

Heidi got the best grade in the class. She must have studied a lot.

The past tense of modal verbs used subjectively is formed with a conjugated form of the modal plus the perfect infinitive, which consists of the past participle and the infinitive of the appropriate auxiliary verb.

MODAL	PERFECT INFINITIVE
muβ	**gelernt haben**
muβ	**gewesen sein**

Note that the English construction is very similar: *must have learned; must have been.*

The Subjunctive of Modals Used Subjectively

Modals used subjectively may be in the subjunctive mood to express that the assumption of the speaker is tentative and uncertain or to express politeness. Compare:

Sie **kann** schon fertig sein.
She may be done already.

Sie **könnte** schon fertig sein.
Sie might/could be done already.

The second assumption is in the subjunctive and therefore more speculative than the first assumption.

Subjective Meanings of the Modal Verbs

All six modal verbs may be used subjectively. Study the examples below in the present and past tenses.

DÜRFEN

When used subjectively, **dürfen** is usually made subjunctive. It expresses an uncertain and tentative assumption on the part of the speaker, similar to **können** in the subjunctive.

PRESENT   Sie dürfte schon fertig sein.
Sie könnte schon fertig sein.
She might/could be done already.

PAST   Sie dürfte schon fertig gewesen sein.
Sie könnte schon fertig gewesen sein.
She might/could have been done already.

KÖNNEN

When used subjectively, **können** expresses a fairly safe assumption on the part of the speaker. It expresses a possibility.

PRESENT   Sie kann schon fertig sein.
She may be done already.

PAST   Sie kann schon fertig gewesen sein.
She may have been done already.

MÖGEN

The subjective use of **mögen** is similar to that of **können**: it too expresses a fairly safe assumption on the part of the speaker. The situation described is a definite possibility.

PRESENT   Sie mag schon fertig sein.
She may be done already.

PAST   Sie mag schon fertig gewesen sein.
She may have been done already.

MÜSSEN

When used subjectively, **müssen** expresses an assumption made by the speaker on the basis of considerable evidence or after considerable thought.

PRESENT   Sie muβ schon fertig sein.
She must be done already.

PAST   Sie muβ schon fertig gewesen sein.
She must have been done already.

SOLLEN

Sollen is used subjectively to report hearsay. The speaker has the information from another source and does not want to vouch for its accuracy.

PRESENT   Der Präsident soll davon nichts wissen.
The president is said to know nothing about it.

PAST   Der Präsident soll davon nichts gewuβt haben.
The president is said to have known nothing about it.

WOLLEN

When used subjectively, **wollen** indicates serious doubt on the part of the speaker concerning an allegation or claim made by another person.

PRESENT   Der Präsident will davon nichts wissen.
The president claims to know nothing about it.

PAST   Der Präsident will davon nichts gewuβt haben.
The president claims to have known nothing about it.

Exercise 13: *Translate into English.*

1. Das Konzert soll sehr gut gewesen sein.
2. Ich sehe sonst niemand. Du mußt wohl der letzte sein.
3. Sie will viel lernen, aber ich sehe sie nie in der Bibliothek.
4. Er mag das Buch zwar gelesen haben, aber er versteht die Situation trotzdem nicht.
5. Es klopft! Wer kann das nur so spät in der Nacht sein?
6. Er ist sehr verärgert. Er muß den Brief schon gelesen haben.
7. Ich habe den neuen Nachbarn noch nicht kennengelernt, aber er soll sehr gut aussehen.
8. Der Spion will von der Affäre keine Ahnung haben.
9. Das kann doch nicht die Wahrheit sein!
10. Wie wissen sie davon? Jemand muß es ihnen gesagt haben.
11. Die Assistentin will viel mit dem Erfinder zusammen gearbeitet haben, aber sie kannte seine Erfindungen nicht.
12. Der Unfall soll gestern abend um 22 Uhr passiert sein.

Exercise 14: *Translate the English cues into German.*

1. Das Baby weint. _____.   (*It might be hungry.*)
2. Niemand ist hier. _____.   (*They must have left already.*)
3. Das Haus ist noch ganz still. _____.   (*She must still be sleeping.*)
4. _____.   (*She claims to have been home.*) Aber ich habe drei- oder viermal angerufen.
5. Die Ergebnisse stimmen nicht. _____.   (*They must have made a mistake.*)
6. _____.   (*The student claims to be 21.*) Aber er sieht ziemlich jung aus.
7. Ich lese in der Zeitung über die Demonstration. _____. (*Thousands are said to have participated.*)
8. Hier ist es 9 Uhr morgens. _____.   (*It must be 3 in the afternoon already in Germany.*)
9. Es war ihre Handschrift. _____.   (*She must have written it.*)
10. Obwohl der chemische Versuch länger dauern sollte, _____ (*she may be done already*).

The Past Subjective vs. the Past Subjunctive of können

Compare the following two sentences:

PAST SUBJECTIVE

Du warst auf derselben Party wie er. Du **könntest** es ihm **gesagt haben**.

You were at the same party that he was at. You could have told him.

PAST SUBJUNCTIVE

Wenn du da gewesen wärest, **hättest** du es ihm **sagen können**.

If you had been there, you could have told him.

Do not confuse the past subjective of **können**, which expresses an assumption, with the past subjunctive of **können**, which expresses a contrary-to-fact condition.

Exercise 15: *Translate into German.*

1. She is an author. She could have written this book.
2. She only could have written this book if she were an author.
3. I haven't seen him for weeks. He could have gone on vacation.
4. If he had had more free time, he could have gone on vacation.
5. It's very quiet. Everyone could have fallen asleep.
6. If it had been quiet, they could have fallen asleep.

ANSWERS TO EXERCISES

1.

1. Sie hat ein komisches Geräusch gehört.
2. Sie hat nur den Regen herunterprasseln hören.
3. Wir haben uns in der Klasse gesehen.
4. Wir haben euch kommen sehen.
5. Ich habe ihr am Montag geholfen.
6. Ich habe ihr den Aufsatz schreiben helfen.
7. Er hat seinen Regenschirm zu Hause gelassen.
8. Der Sturm hat uns nicht einschlafen lassen.

2.

1. The professor never lets the students have enough time for the exams.
2. We are sending for a taxi.
3. In the silence one only heard the clock ticking.
4. I had my hair cut yesterday.
5. We have to send for a doctor immediately.
6. They have the children wash the dishes every evening.
7. The policeman saw the car run the red light.
8. The professor let the students work together on their essays.
9. I don't like letting you drive home at night.
10. I'll let you know tomorrow whether I can come along or not.
11. We always have the accountant do our taxes.
12. The saleswoman in the corner store knew me. Therefore she let me charge the goods.
13. Did you see the German win the gold medal?
14. Suddenly I heard the balloon burst.
15. The children always help set the table.

3.

1. Wir haben sie nur einmal singen hören.
2. Er sieht das Kind spielen.
3. Ich höre das Telefon klingeln.
4. Ich sehe sie nicht gern weinen.
5. Sie hat ihr Kleid reinigen lassen.
6. Ich habe meine Schlüssel zu Hause gelassen.
7. Wir lassen uns ein Haus bauen.
8. Sie hat mir den Brief schreiben helfen.
9. Ich habe die Tür hinter mir schließen hören.
10. Sie haben den Krankenwagen kommen lassen.

4.

1. Du weißt, wie schwer es ist, einen Kompromiß zu schließen.
2. Ich habe meinen Nachbarn gebeten, sie zu füttern.
3. Es ist zu spät, einen Spaziergang zu machen.
4. Mein Vertrauenslehrer empfahl mir, diese Kurse zu belegen.
5. Ich finde es dumm, sie zu fragen.
6. Aber es ist äußerst wichtig, das Problem zu lösen.
7. Nein, ich habe leider vergessen, es mitzubringen.

8. Ich verspreche dir, niemandem davon zu erzählen.

9. Nein, es ist nicht erlaubt, hier zu rauchen.

10. Kannst du mir helfen, ihn in das andere Zimmer zu tragen?

11. Die Kinder wollen bis 5 morgens aufbleiben, aber die Mutter verbietet ihnen, so lange aufzubleiben.

12. Ich habe vergessen, es aufzumachen.

5.

1. Sie hat angerufen, um mich zur Party einzuladen.

2. Wir gehen oft zu Fuβ, um gesund zu bleiben.

3. Er handelte, ohne an die Konsequenzen zu denken.

4. Statt im Chor zu singen, spielt sie ein Instrument im Orchester.

5. Die Schriftstellerin zieht aufs Land, um in Ruhe zu schreiben.

6. Statt für die Prüfung zu lernen, gehen sie trinken.

7. Ich arbeite während der Ferien, um Geld zu verdienen.

8. Ich sprach ihn an, ohne ihn zu kennen.

9. Meine Schwiegereltern kommen oft vorbei, ohne vorher anzurufen.

10. Wir finden uns in der Stadt zurecht, ohne einen Stadtplan zu haben.

11. Statt mit ihrem Auto zu fahren, ging sie zu Fuβ.

12. Ich wollte mit ihr reden, um bestimmte Themen zu besprechen.

13. Statt nach Hause zu gehen, blieben sie noch eine Stunde im Park.

14. Sie hat es gesagt, ohne dabei nachzudenken.

15. Ich fahre in die Stadt, um einkaufen zu gehen.

6.

1. Ich weiβ nicht, wann ich kommen soll.

2. Meine Mutter will nicht, daβ ich dieses Buch lese.

3. Die Lehrerin erwartet, daβ ihre Studenten alles wissen.

4. Möchten Sie, daβ ich Ihnen

diese Vase zeigen, Herr Ruprecht?

5. Er weiβ nicht, wann er aufhören soll.

6. Will sie, daβ ich ihr helfe?

7. Sie sagten uns, daβ wir ruhig sein sollten.

8. Wer weiβ, wie man das auf deutsch sagt?

9. Sag mir, was ich zur Party mitbringen soll, Astrid!

10. Ich will, daβ der Abend schön (perfekt) ist.

7.

1. The parents are proud that their daughter can play the piano so beautifully.

2. My friend is waiting for me to call at nine.

3. I'm proud of knowing a foreign language.

4. I have often thought of doing such a thing.

5. Are you satisfied with getting this grade in the course?

6. My mother is absolutely against my going out with you.

7. The children were enthusiastic about staying a night with their grandparents.

8. My colleague is jealous that I, not he, got the promotion.

9. My longing to see you again is becoming greater and greater.

10. I'm afraid that the final exam will be very difficult.

8.

1. Die Studenten waren davon begeistert, in Deutschland zu studieren.

2. Ich warte darauf, daβ mein Zimmergenosse/meine Zimmergenossin nach Hause kommt.

3. Ich bin dagegen, noch ein Auto zu kaufen.

4. Er ist eifersüchtig darauf, daβ seine Nachbarn so ein groβes Haus haben.

5. Das Ehepaar hat Interesse daran, ein Kind zu adoptieren.

6. Meine Eltern sind stolz darauf, daβ ich für das Peace Corps arbeite.

7. Ich habe Angst davor, die Schluβprüfung zu schreiben.

8. Sie sprechen darüber, zusammen ein Haus zu kaufen.

9.

1. Ich fühle mich krank.

2. Hat sie sich um den Job/die Stelle beworben?

3. Wir haben uns auf der Party amüsiert.

4. Ich freue mich auf die Ferien.

5. Er kann sich an die Kälte nicht gewöhnen.

6. Beeil dich, Franz! Es ist schon 9 Uhr.

7. Ich fürchte mich vor nichts.

8. Sie erinnern sich nie an meinen Namen.

9. Du kannst dich auf mich verlassen, Karin.

10. Kinder, benehmt euch!

10.

1. Sie interessiert sich dafür, Deutsch zu studieren.

2. Ich freue mich darauf, Sie endlich kennenzulernen, Frau Wilhelm.

3. Wir können uns darauf verlassen, daβ sie rechtzeitig kommen.

4. Ich kann mich nicht daran gewöhnen, mit dem Bus zu fahren.

5. Sie erinnert sich nicht daran, daβ er das gesagt hat.

6. Er fürchtet sich davor, allein zu sein.

11.

1. Meine Mutter legte sich jeden Nachmittag hin. Meine Mutter hat sich jeden Nachmittag hingelegt.

2. Die Katze lag den ganzen Tag in der Sonne. Die Katze hat den ganzen Tag in der Sonne gelegen.

3. Die hungrigen Gäste setzten sich schnell an den Tisch. Die hungrigen Gäste haben sich schnell an den Tisch gesetzt.

4. Die Informatikerin saβ acht Stunden am Computer. Die

Informatikerin hat acht Stunden am Computer gesessen.

5. Wir stellten den Videorecorder neben den Fernseher. Wir haben den Videorecorder neben den Fernseher gestellt.

6. Warum standen diese Leute hier herum?Warum haben diese Leute hier herumgestanden?

7. Warum hängten Sie das Bild nicht über den Kamin? Warum haben Sie das Bild nicht über den Kamin gehängt?

8. Der Weihnachtsschmuck hing am Tannenbaum. Der Weihnachtsschmuck hat am Tannenbaum gehangen.

12.

1. Die Touristen liegen am Strand.
2. Am 6. Dezember stellen die Kinder ihre Schuhe vor die Tür.
3. Die Kirche steht neben dem Rathaus.
4. Der Schlüssel hängt am Haken.
5. Sie stellt die Milch in den Kühlschrank.
6. Moritz und Peter, setzt euch neben uns (hin)!
7. Leg die Zeitung auf den Schreibtisch, Wolf!
8. Martin, stell das schmutzige Geschirr bitte in den Geschirrspüler!

9. Alle sitzen schon am Tisch.
10. Studenten hängen oft Posters an die Wände ihres Zimmers.

13.

1. The concert is said to have been very good.
2. I don't see anyone else. You must be the last one.
3. She claims to study a lot, but I never see her in the library.
4. He may have read the book, but he doesn't understand the situation anyway.
5. Someone's knocking! Who can that be so late at night?
6. He's very angry. He must have already read the letter.
7. I haven't met the new neighbor yet, but he is said to be very good-looking.
8. The spy claims to have no idea about the affair.
9. That simply cannot be the truth!
10. How do they know about that? Someone must have told them about it.
11. The assistant claims to have worked a lot with the inventor, but she wasn't familiar with his inventions.
12. The accident is said to have happened last (yesterday) evening at 10 o'clock.

14.

1. Es dürfte/könnte Hunger haben.
2. Sie müssen schon weggegangen sein/abgefahren sein.
3. Sie muß noch schlafen.
4. Sie will zu Hause gewesen sein.
5. Sie müssen einen Fehler gemacht haben.
6. Der Student will 21 sein.
7. Tausende sollen teilgenommen haben.
8. Es muß schon 3 Uhr nachmittags in Deutschland sein.
9. Sie muß es geschrieben haben.
10. . . . mag/kann sie schon fertig sein.

15.

1. Sie ist Schriftstellerin. Sie könnte dieses Buch geschrieben haben.
2. Sie hätte dieses Buch nur schreiben können, wenn sie Schriftstellerin wäre.
3. Ich habe ihn seit Wochen nicht gesehen. Er könnte Urlaub gemacht haben.
4. Wenn er mehr Freizeit gehabt hätte, hätte er Urlaub machen können.
5. Es ist sehr still. Alle könnten eingeschlafen sein.
6. Wenn es still gewesen wäre, hätten sie einschlafen können.

PART THREE: GERMAN WORD ORDER

_____

12

Principles of German Word Order

In general, German word order is more flexible than English word order. In English, the function of a particular noun within a sentence is determined by its position within that sentence or, in other words, by its word order. In German, on the other hand, it is the case system (chapter 2) that indicates the function of a noun within the sentence, and this allows for greater freedom in the word order.

You have already practiced various word-order rules in previous chapters. In this chapter we will study some basic principles of German word order not yet covered, including the position of the verb, of adverbs, and of **nicht.** The chapter concludes with a brief discussion of the influence of emphasis on German word order.

POSITION OF THE VERB

The position of the verb will vary depending on whether it is found in a statement as opposed to a question, or in a main as opposed to a dependent clause.

The Verb in a Statement

One of the most fundamental word-order rules in German is that *the conjugated verb occupies the second position in a main clause.* This is true regardless of what occupies the first position in the clause, as the examples below illustrate. Note that the grammatical unit occupying the first position may consist of more than one word.

  1   2

Die Jugend von heute hört immer noch gern Rock.
The youth of today still likes to listen to rock music.

  1   2

Am Montag beginnt die Schule wieder.
School starts again on Monday.

  1   2

Den Jungen da habe ich noch nie gesehen.
I have never before seen the boy over there.

  1   2

Dir schenke ich gar nichts.
I'm not giving you anything at all.

  1   2

Aus diesem Grund war das Experiment unerfolgreich.
The experiment was unsuccessful for this reason.

Many texts differentiate between normal word order and inverted word order. In a sentence with *normal word order*, the subject occupies the first position, with the verb standing second. Thus normal word order means that the subject precedes the verb: subject-verb. Normal word order corresponds to English word order.

Der Mantel **ist** zu groß für ihn.
The coat is too big for him.

Sie **fahren** morgen wieder nach Hause.
They're going back home again tomorrow.

Ich **kann** dir das leider nicht sagen.
I can't tell you that, unfortunately.

In a sentence with *inverted word order*, some element other than the subject is in the first position. Thus the subject follows the verb: verb-subject. English has no such flexibility; the subject always precedes the verb. In German, inverted word order is very common and is used for stylistic reasons or to emphasize certain elements. Compare the following sentences to those above:

Für ihn **ist** der Mantel zu groß.
Morgen **fahren** sie wieder nach Hause.
Das **kann** ich dir leider nicht sagen.
Leider **kann** ich dir das nicht sagen.

Note that both normal word order and inverted word order follow the rule that *the verb occupies the second position in a main clause, regardless of what is in the first position.*

In German you cannot separate an element from the rest of the sentence with a comma, as is frequently done in English.

Leider kann ich dir das nicht sagen.
Unfortunately, I can't tell you that.

Für mich ist es nicht nur eine Frage des Geldes.
For me, it's not only a question of money.

EXCEPTIONS

A few words or parts of speech do not count as the first element of a clause.

Interjections. Common interjections such as **ja**, **nein**, and **ach** followed by a comma do not count as the first element of the clause.

   0   1   2
Nein, ich komme heute abend nicht.
No, I'm not coming tonight.

The Coordinating Conjunctions. The coordinating conjunctions **aber**, **denn**, **oder**, **sondern**, and **und** connect two main clauses and do not count as the first element of their clause.

                        0   1   2
Sie liest das Diktat vor, und die Studenten schreiben mit.
She reads the dictation and the students write along.

The coordinating conjunctions will be treated in detail in chapter 13.

Exercise 1: *Restate, beginning with the boldface word.*

1. Das Museum schließt **montags** immer eine Stunde früher.
2. Wir fuhren **trotz des schlechten Wetters** an den Strand.

3. Sie hören mit der Arbeit **um 5 Uhr** auf.
4. Es gibt **nur diese letzte Möglichkeit**.
5. Sie hat **außer mir** nur 10 Leute eingeladen.
6. Ich möchte **den Rock dahinten** anprobieren.
7. Die Enkelin bleibt **heute abend** bei ihren Großeltern.
8. Wir haben unsere Nachbarn **erst auf der Party** kennengelernt.
9. Ich kann **diese Erkältung** einfach nicht loswerden.
10. Sie fühlt sich **heute** viel besser als gestern.
11. Sie besuchten ihre Verwandten **während der Winterferien**.
12. Die Familie aß die Torte **zum Nachtisch**.

The Verb in Direct and Indirect Questions

A question may be either direct or indirect. Most questions are direct. *Direct questions* stand alone, whereas *indirect questions* are preceded by an introductory phrase.

DIRECT QUESTIONS

Direct questions have inverted word order. In other words, the verb always precedes the subject. This is true of direct questions with or without a question word.

With a Question Word. In questions introduced with a question word, the verb occupies the second position and is followed by the subject.

Wann **gehen wir** nach Hause?
When are we going home?

Warum **machen wir** alles in der Gruppe?
Why do we do everything with the group?

Wem **schreibst du** so einen langen Brief?
To whom are you writing such a long letter?

Without a Question Word. In questions not introduced by a question word, the verb occupies the first position and is followed by the subject.

Kannst du bitte ein bißchen langsamer sprechen?
Can you please speak a little more slowly?

Schläft das Baby noch?
Is the baby still sleeping?

Essen wir heute abend zu Hause oder in einem Restaurant?
Are we eating at home tonight or in a restaurant?

Exercise 2: *Make questions using the question words in parentheses.*

1. Der Spaziergang dauert eine Stunde.   (Wie lange?)
2. Die Studentin arbeitet am besten in der Bibliothek.   (Wo?)
3. Der Hund wartet geduldig vor der Tür.   (Wie?)
4. Wegen des zu starken Windes kenterte das Segelboot.   (Warum?)
5. Frau Wilheimer kommt nicht mit.   (Wer?)
6. Am Montag beginnt die Arbeit wieder.   (Wann?)
7. Mozart kam aus Salzburg.   (Woher?)
8. Der Junge hat einen Frosch in der Hand.   (Was?)
9. Sie muß ihre kleine Schwester zum Zahnarzt bringen.   (Wen?)
10. Die Krawatte des Moderators gefällt ihm gut.   (Wessen?)

Exercise 3: *Turn the statements into questions.*

1. Es hat den ganzen Tag geschneit.
2. Dieses Beispiel ist richtig.
3. In diesem Reisebüro kann man Englisch sprechen.
4. Der Kaffee riecht gut.
5. Dieser Krimi ist langweilig.
6. Schnitzel steht auf der Speisekarte.
7. Der Radfahrer verlor das Gleichgewicht.
8. Der Arzt war selber krank.
9. Die Tiefseetaucher sollen vorsichtig sein.
10. Das hat wirklich niemand gewußt.

INDIRECT QUESTIONS

An indirect question is a question that is preceded by an introductory phrase such as "I don't know" or "Please tell me." It begins with a question word. The conjugated verb of the indirect question occupies the final position in that clause.

Ich weiß nicht, um wieviel Uhr der Zug ankommen **soll**.
I don't know what time the train is supposed to arrive.

Kannst du mir sagen, wie der Mann dort **heißt**?
Can you tell me what that man's name is?

Exercise 4: *Restate the direct questions as indirect questions, completing the introductory phrase provided.*

1. Wo kann ich ein bißchen Ruhe finden?
   Ich möchte wissen, _____.

2. In welchem Restaurant essen wir heute abend?
   Vater entscheidet, _____.
3. Um wieviel Uhr beginnt die Oper?
   Sagen Sie mir bitte, _____!
4. Wieviele Kaninchen gibt es im Käfig?
   Können Sie sehen, _____?
5. Aus welchem Land kommen Sie?
   Hier müssen Sie angeben, _____.
6. Was für Haustiere darf man in dieser Wohnung halten?
   Hier steht, _____.
7. Wie kommen wir zum Hauptplatz?
   Können Sie mir bitte sagen, _____?
8. Was ist die Geschwindigkeitsbegrenzung auf dieser Straße?
   Der Polizist hinter uns weiß sicher, _____.
9. Wann kommt der nächste Zug aus Bern an?
   Unter „Ankunft" steht, _____.
10. Warum ist das Pferd so nervös?
    Der Reiter überlegt, _____.

POSITION OF DIRECT AND INDIRECT OBJECTS

Direct and indirect objects usually stand directly after the subject-verb unit. As we learned in chapter 3, if the objects are both nouns, the indirect object (IO) precedes the direct object (DO).

     IO   DO

Ich schreibe meinen Eltern einen Brief.
I'm writing my parents a letter.

If the objects are both pronouns, the order is reversed and the direct object (DO) precedes the indirect object (IO).

     DO   IO

Ich schreibe ihn (einen Brief) ihnen (meinen Eltern).
I'm writing it (a letter) to them (my parents).

If one object is a noun and the other object a pronoun, the pronoun precedes the noun, regardless of case.

Ich schreibe **ihn** meinen Eltern.
Ich schreibe **ihnen** einen Brief.

Exercise 5: *Insert the cue nouns and pronouns into the sentence in the correct order.*

1. Ich möchte _____ _____ zeigen.   (meine neue Bluse; dir)
2. Die Studentin schuldet _____ _____.   (viel Geld; der Universität)
3. Kannst du _____ bitte _____ reichen?   (das Salz; mir)
4. Der Autor liest _____ _____ vor.   (Kurzgeschichten; seinem Publikum)
5. Die Kinder wollen, daß der Vater _____ _____ kauft.   (ein Eis; ihnen) Kauft er _____ _____?   (es; ihnen)
6. Verrate _____ _____!   (dein Geheimnis; mir) Es tut mir leid, aber ich kann _____ _____ noch nicht verraten.   (dir; es)
7. Hast du _____ _____ geschickt?   (eine Postkarte; mir) Nein, ich habe _____ _____ geschickt!   (sie; deiner Schwester)
8. Weißt du, ob man in Deutschland _____ _____ gibt?   (dem Kellner; ein Trinkgeld)
9. Der Räuber sagte: „Geben Sie _____ _____!"   (Ihr Geld und Ihren Schmuck; mir)
10. Die Rechtsanwältin sollte _____ _____ beweisen.   (die Unschuld ihrer Klientin; der Jury)
11. Hatte der Autofahrer _____ _____ genommen?   (die Vorfahrt; dem Radfahrer)
12. Der Zeitungsartikel von gestern hat _____ _____ nicht gut genug beschrieben. (den Unfall; mir)

POSITION OF ADVERBS

Position of Adverbs within the Sentence

Adverbs may be single words or phrases. Adverbs express when, how, or where something takes place and are categorized as adverbs of time, manner, and place, respectively. Some typical examples of each category are listed below.

ADVERBS OF TIME	ADVERBS OF MANNER	ADVERBS OF PLACE
gestern	schnell	dort
heute	langsam	hier
am Samstag	mit Geduld	am Bahnhof
in einer Woche	mit dem Auto	in der Stadt

Adverbs frequently stand at the beginning of a sentence.

Heute machen wir einen langen Spaziergang.
Today we're going to take a long walk.

In der Schweiz gibt es viele hohe Berge.
In Switzerland there are many high mountains.

If not at the beginning of a sentence, adverbs follow the subject, verb, and any pronouns. Adverbs of time are generally positioned toward the beginning of the sentence, immediately following pronouns.

Ich kann dir **heute abend** das Problem erklären.
I can explain the problem to you this evening.

Adverbs of place are generally positioned toward the end of the sentence, following pronouns and nouns.

Ich kann dir das Problem nur **zu Hause** erklären.
I can only explain the problem to you at home.

In German, adverbs cannot stand between the subject and the verb, as is common in English.

Sie kommt **oft** zu spät in die Klasse.
She frequently comes to class late.

WORD ORDER WITH MORE THAN ONE ADVERB

Time–Manner–Place. If a sentence contains more than one type of adverb, the adverbs occur in the following order: *Time–Manner–Place.* Note that this word order differs from English word order, where adverbs of place often precede adverbs of time.

       TIME   MANNER   PLACE
Ich bin heute mit dem Auto zur Uni gekommen.
I came to the university today by car.

           TIME   MANNER   PLACE
Wir sahen ihn gestern ganz kurz im Supermarkt.
We saw him in the supermarket yesterday very briefly.

General to Specific. If more than one adverb of time occurs in a sentence, *the general time precedes the specific time.*

                GENERAL   SPECIFIC
Die Karnevalssaison beginnt am 11. November um 11 Uhr 11.
The season of Fasching begins on November 11th at 11:11.

Exercise 6: *Restate with the cue adverbs in the correct position.*

1. Sie ist auf der Straße stehengeblieben. (plötzlich)
2. Man darf mit dieser Karte fahren. (überall in der Stadt)
3. Er sitzt heute in der ersten Reihe. (ausnahmsweise)
4. Ich möchte dich morgen sprechen. (gleich nach der Klasse)
5. Es gab einen guten Film im Fernsehen. (gestern)
6. Das Farbband der Schreibmaschine klemmte. (zweimal; gestern)
7. Der Professor kommt in die Klasse. (15 Minuten zu spät; immer)
8. Ich bringe dir eine Tasse Tee. (bald)
9. Das Kind spielte im Sandkasten. (den ganzen Nachmittag; mit den Nachbarskindern)
10. Sie wartete eine Stunde. (vor dem Bahnhof; ungeduldig)

POSITION OF NICHT

The placement of **nicht** depends on whether the entire sentence or a specific sentence unit is being negated.

Negation of the Entire Sentence

To negate an entire sentence, **nicht** is placed after the subject-verb unit, after pronouns and nouns, and after most adverbs of time. It is placed before most adverbs of manner and place and before most prepositional phrases. **Nicht** precedes those sentence elements that complete the meaning of the verb, such as predicate adjectives and nouns, separable prefixes, past participles, and infinitives. These word-order rules also apply to questions and commands. Study the following examples carefully:

AFTER THE SUBJECT-VERB UNIT
Meine Freundin kommt **nicht**.
My girlfriend isn't coming.

Morgen kommt meine Freundin **nicht**.
My girlfriend isn't coming tomorrow.

AFTER PRONOUNS AND MOST NOUNS
Ich sehe ihn **nicht**.
I don't see him.

Leider weiß ich die Antwort **nicht**.
Unfortunately I don't know the answer.

AFTER MOST ADVERBS OF TIME
Wir machen das heute **nicht**.
We aren't doing that today.

BEFORE MOST ADVERBS OF MANNER AND PLACE
Sie macht das **nicht** schnell genug.
She isn't doing that fast enough.

Er fährt **nicht** mit dem Auto.
He's not going by car.

Wir fahren **nicht** in die Stadt.
We aren't driving into town.

BEFORE MOST PREPOSITIONAL PHRASES
Der Student antwortete **nicht** auf die Frage.
The student didn't answer the question.

BEFORE SENTENCE ELEMENTS THAT COMPLETE VERB MEANING
Sei mir bitte **nicht** böse! (*predicate adjective*)
Please don't be angry at (with) me.

Sie nehmen ihre Freunde diesmal **nicht** mit. (*separable prefix*)
They aren't taking their friends along this time.

Ich habe meine Hausaufgaben noch **nicht** gemacht. (*past participle*)
I haven't yet done my homework.

Ich will meinem Bruder die neue Kneipe **nicht** zeigen. (*infinitive*)
I don't want to show my brother the new bar.

Exercise 7: *Negate the statements, commands, or questions.*

1. Warum bist du gestern mitgekommen?
2. Der Schluß des Filmes war sehr dramatisch.
3. Dieser Kuchen ist zu süß für mich.
4. Ich habe den schrecklichen Unfall gesehen.
5. Sie hörte den Beschwerden der Kinder zu.
6. Machen Sie die Arbeit zusammen!
7. Sie erinnerte sich an seinen Namen.
8. Der Asylant kam aus Rumänien.
9. Sie schreibt an ihren Freund.
10. Die Expedition konnte rechtzeitig aufbrechen.
11. Wir lachten über den Scherz.
12. Das Baby hat die Flasche Milch ausgetrunken.
13. Er hat das ernst gemeint, oder?
14. Der Mensch kann Hitze gut ertragen.
15. Sie hat deine Worte absichtlich mißdeutet.
16. Die kleine Modelleisenbahn war besonders teuer.
17. Hat dir der Nachtisch geschmeckt?
18. Die liberale Partei vereinigt sich mit den Konservativen.

Negation of a Specific Sentence Unit

Nicht may be used to negate a specific sentence unit for emphasis or contrast. In this case, **nicht** is placed immediately before the particular sentence unit being negated.

Ich will **nicht** allein zu Hause bleiben.
I don't want to stay home all by myself.

The emphasis here is placed on being alone. The speaker would presumably have no objection to staying home if someone else were there.

Frequently **sondern** (*but rather*) is added to sentences where specific elements are negated in order to emphasize the contrast even more.

Sie will nicht ihren Vater, **sondern** ihre Mutter sehen.
She doesn't want to see her father, but rather her mother.

Exercise 8: *Negate the specific sentence unit that is in boldface, setting up a contrast with* **sondern**. *Follow the model.*

Wir wollen **Tennis** spielen.   (Volleyball)
Wir wollen nicht Tennis, sondern Volleyball spielen.

1. Meine Eltern sollen mich **heute** besuchen.   (morgen)
2. Ich habe **meine Kreditkarte** auf der Reise verloren.   (meinen Paß)
3. Sie schenkt **ihrem Mann** ihr Vertrauen.   (ihrer Freundin)
4. Ich brauche **den Bleistift**.   (den Kugelschreiber)
5. Er fährt **in einer Woche** nach Paris.   (in zwei Wochen)

VARIATIONS IN GERMAN WORD ORDER

The rules discussed and practiced thus far are the most basic of German word order. However, as we mentioned at the beginning of this chapter, German word order is quite flexible. This section attempts to give you a feel for German word order in general and then discusses when and why a speaker may want to vary that word order.

Basic Sentence Structure

The structure of a basic German sentence may be diagrammed as follows:

```
    1         2             3                4
_____/_____/\_
```

As you know, position 1 is frequently occupied by the subject of the sentence, but may also be occupied by other sentence elements such as objects, adverbs, or prepositional phrases.

Position 2 is always occupied by the conjugated verb.

Position 4 is reserved for those sentence elements that complete the meaning of the verb. It is therefore frequently occupied by a predicate adjective, a predicate noun, an infinitive, a past participle, or a separable prefix. Sometimes it remains empty.

The middle field of the sentence, designated as position 3, contains all elements not occupying other positions and may include the subject, indirect and direct objects, adverbs, or prepositional phrases.

News Value

A German sentence is arranged according to the principle of increasing importance. *This means that the sentence element with the greatest news value will be put at the end of the sentence*.

The principle of news value explains many of the word-order rules you have already learned. It is for this reason that position 4 is occupied by a sentence element that completes the meaning of the verb: the verb conveys the most important information of the sentence. This is also the reason that noun objects follow pronoun objects. Pronouns refer back to something already known or mentioned and therefore have less news value than nouns.

Most of the flexibility in German word order occurs in the middle field (position 3). *Stressed sentence elements are frequently shifted to the end of the middle field because they have greater news value*.

In the examples below, the first sentence represents word order as you have learned it. However, word order changes as the speaker confirms various items of information through emphasis.

Ich rufe meine Tante mindestens einmal im Monat an.
I call my aunt at least once a month.
Wen rufst du mindestens einmal im Monat an? Deine Mutter?
Nein, ich rufe mindestens einmal im Monat **meine Tante** an.

Die Polizei hat den netten, alten Butler wegen des Mordes in Verdacht.
The police suspect the nice old butler of the murder.
Wen hat die Polizei wegen des Mordes in Verdacht?
Die Polizei hat wegen des Mordes **den netten, alten Butler** in
    Verdacht.
Und warum?
Sie hat den Butler in Verdacht **wegen des Mordes**.

Exercise 9: *Stress the information asked for by changing the word order of the original sentence. Underline the stressed information in your new sentence.*

1. Wir sollen kurz nach Mitternacht dort ankommen.
   Wann sollen wir dort ankommen?
2. Der Chef hat meiner faulen Kollegin die Beförderung gegeben.
   Wem hat der Chef die Beförderung gegeben?
3. Ich bin wegen dieser anstrengenden Arbeit erschöpft.
   Warum bist du so erschöpft?
4. Sie haben ihre Flugtickets irgendwo im Flughafen verloren.
   Was haben sie irgendwo im Flughafen verloren?
5. Der Fahrer ist sehr schnell auf der Autobahn gefahren.
   Wie ist der Fahrer auf der Autobahn gefahren?
6. Ich habe niemandem unser Geheimnis verraten.
   Wem hast du unser Geheimnis verraten?

ANSWERS TO EXERCISES

1.

1. Montags schließt das Museum immer eine Stunde früher.
2. Trotz des schlechten Wetters fuhren wir an den Strand.
3. Um 5 Uhr hören sie mit der Arbeit auf.
4. Nur diese letzte Möglichkeit gibt es.
5. Außer mir hat sie nur 10 Leute eingeladen.
6. Den Rock dahinten möchte ich anprobieren.
7. Heute abend bleibt die Enkelin bei ihren Großeltern.
8. Erst auf der Party haben wir unsere Nachbarn kennengelernt.
9. Diese Erkältung kann ich einfach nicht loswerden.
10. Heute fühlt sie sich viel besser als gestern.
11. Während der Winterferien besuchten sie ihre Verwandten.
12. Zum Nachtisch aß die Familie die Torte.

2.

1. Wie lange dauert der Spaziergang?
2. Wo arbeitet die Studentin am besten?
3. Wie wartet der Hund vor der Tür?
4. Warum kenterte das Segelboot?
5. Wer kommt nicht mit?
6. Wann beginnt die Arbeit wieder?
7. Woher kam Mozart?
8. Was hat der Junge in der Hand?
9. Wen muß sie zum Zahnarzt bringen?
10. Wessen Krawatte gefällt ihm gut?

3.

1. Hat es den ganzen Tag geschneit?
2. Ist dieses Beispiel richtig?
3. Kann man in diesem Reisebüro Englisch sprechen?
4. Riecht der Kaffee gut?
5. Ist dieser Krimi langweilig?
6. Steht Schnitzel auf der Speisekarte?
7. Verlor der Radfahrer das Gleichgewicht?
8. War der Arzt selber krank?
9. Sollen die Tiefseetaucher vorsichtig sein?
10. Hat das wirklich niemand gewußt?

4.

1. Ich möchte wissen, wo ich ein bißchen Ruhe finden kann.
2. Vater entscheidet, in welchem Restaurant wir heute abend essen.
3. Sagen Sie mir bitte, um wieviel Uhr die Oper beginnt!
4. Können Sie sehen, wieviele Kaninchen es im Käfig gibt?
5. Hier müssen Sie angeben, aus welchem Land Sie kommen.
6. Hier steht, was für Haustiere man in dieser Wohnung halten darf.
7. Können Sie mir bitte sagen, wie wir zum Hauptplatz kommen?
8. Der Polizist hinter uns weiß sicher, was die Geschwindigkeitsbegrenzung auf dieser Straße ist.
9. Unter „Ankunft" steht, wann der nächste Zug aus Bern ankommt.
10. Der Reiter überlegt, warum das Pferd so nervös ist.

5.

1. Ich möchte dir meine neue Bluse zeigen.
2. Die Studentin schuldet der Universität viel Geld.
3. Kannst du mir bitte das Salz reichen?
4. Der Autor liest seinem Publikum Kurzgeschichten vor.
5. Die Kinder wollen, daß der Vater ihnen ein Eis kauft. Kauft er es ihnen?
6. Verrate mir dein Geheimnis! Es tut mir leid, aber ich kann es dir noch nicht verraten.
7. Hast du mir eine Postkarte geschickt? Nein, ich habe sie deiner Schwester geschickt!
8. Weißt du, ob man in Deutschland dem Kellner ein Trinkgeld gibt?
9. Der Räuber sagte: „Geben Sie mir Ihr Geld und Ihren Schmuck!"
10. Die Rechtsanwältin sollte der Jury die Unschuld ihrer Klientin beweisen.
11. Hatte der Autofahrer dem Radfahrer die Vorfahrt genommen?
12. Der Zeitungsartikel von gestern hat mir den Unfall nicht gut genug beschrieben.

6.

1. Sie ist plötzlich auf der Straße stehengeblieben.
2. Man darf mit dieser Karte überall in der Stadt fahren.
3. Er sitzt heute ausnahmsweise in der ersten Reihe.
4. Ich möchte dich morgen gleich nach der Klasse sprechen.
5. Es gab gestern einen guten Film im Fernsehen.
6. Das Farbband der Schreibmaschine klemmte gestern zweimal.
7. Der Professor kommt immer 15 Minuten zu spät in die Klasse.
8. Ich bringe dir bald eine Tasse Tee.
9. Das Kind spielte den ganzen Nachmittag mit den Nachbarskindern im Sandkasten.
10. Sie wartete eine Stunde ungeduldig vor dem Bahnhof.

7.

1. Warum bist du gestern nicht mitgekommen?
2. Der Schluß des Filmes war nicht sehr dramatisch.
3. Dieser Kuchen ist nicht zu süß für mich.
4. Ich habe den schrecklichen Unfall nicht gesehen.
5. Sie hörte den Beschwerden der Kinder nicht zu.
6. Machen Sie die Arbeit nicht zusammen!
7. Sie erinnerte sich nicht an seinen Namen.
8. Der Asylant kam nicht aus Rumänien.
9. Sie schreibt nicht an ihren Freund.
10. Die Expedition konnte nicht rechtzeitig aufbrechen.
11. Wir lachten nicht über den Scherz.
12. Das Baby hat die Flasche Milch nicht ausgetrunken.
13. Er hat das nicht ernst gemeint, oder?

14. Der Mensch kann Hitze nicht gut ertragen.
15. Sie hat deine Worte nicht absichtlich mißdeutet.
16. Die kleine Modelleisenbahn war nicht besonders teuer.
17. Hat dir der Nachtisch nicht geschmeckt?
18. Die liberale Partei vereinigt sich nicht mit den Konservativen.

8.

1. Meine Eltern sollen mich nicht heute, sondern morgen besuchen.
2. Ich habe nicht meine Kreditkarte, sondern meinen Paß auf der Reise verloren.
3. Sie schenkt nicht ihrem Mann, sondern ihrer Freundin ihr Vertrauen.
4. Ich brauche nicht den Bleistift, sondern den Kugelschreiber.
5. Er fährt nicht in einer Woche, sondern in zwei Wochen nach Paris.

9.

1. Wir sollen dort **kurz nach Mitternacht** ankommen.
2. Der Chef hat die Beförderung **meiner faulen Kollegin** gegeben.
3. Ich bin erschöpft **wegen dieser anstrengenden Arbeit**.
4. Sie haben irgendwo im Flughafen **ihre Flugtickets** verloren.
5. Der Fahrer ist auf der Autobahn **sehr schnell** gefahren.
6. Ich habe unser Geheimnis **niemandem** verraten.

13

Conjunctions

Conjunctions are words that connect sentence units: one word to another word, phrases to phrases, clauses to clauses. There are two types of conjunctions: coordinating conjunctions and subordinating conjunctions. Coordinating conjunctions combine units of equal status and therefore do not affect word order. Subordinating conjunctions combine units of unequal status; one unit depends on another and therefore requires dependent word order. In this chapter, we will present and discuss the meanings and word order of the various conjunctions.

COORDINATING CONJUNCTIONS AND INDEPENDENT CLAUSES

Coordinating conjunctions are used to combine a variety of sentence elements that have equal status. Clauses combined by coordinating conjunctions are called independent, or main, clauses. An independent clause is a clause that can stand on its own.

Word Order with Coordinating Conjunctions

Coordinating conjunctions do not affect word order. The conjunction does not count as a sentence element. Remember that, as we saw in chapter 12, the conjugated verb always occupies the second position in a main, or independent, clause. This is the case whether the clause precedes or follows the coordinating conjunction.

<pre>
  1   2   0   1   2
</pre>
Ich **muß** in die Bibliothek, denn meine Seminararbeit **ist** fällig.
I have to go to the library because my seminar paper is due.

<pre>
     1   2   0   1   2
</pre>
Zu Hause **kocht** mein Vater, und meine Mutter **wäscht** danach ab.
At home my father cooks and my mother washes the dishes afterwards.

Note that a comma is used to separate the clauses.

Meanings of the Coordinating Conjunctions

There are five common coordinating conjunctions: **aber**, **sondern**, **denn**, **oder**, and **und**.

ABER   *BUT, HOWEVER*

Ich studiere Wirtschaftswissenschaften, **aber** es macht mir keinen Spaß.
I'm studying economics, but I don't enjoy it.

SONDERN   *BUT RATHER; BUT ON THE CONTRARY*

Ich habe diese Bluse nicht gekauft, **sondern** ich habe sie von meiner Schwester bekommen.
I didn't buy this blouse, but rather I got it from my sister.

The conjunction **sondern** always follows a clause that is negated with **nicht**, **kein**, **nie**, and so on. It combines mutually exclusive ideas and expresses a contrast or contradiction. **Sondern** is not interchangeable with **aber**. The conjunction **aber** may also follow a negative clause, but the ideas are not mutually exclusive. Compare the following two sentences:

Das Auto war nicht neu, **sondern** gebraucht.
The car wasn't new, but (rather, on the contrary) used.

Das Auto war nicht neu, **aber** trotzdem schön.
The car wasn't new, but nice nevertheless.

The conjunction **sondern** is frequently used in the expression **nicht nur . . . sondern auch** (*not only . . . but also*).

Hier gibt es **nicht nur** im Sommer, **sondern auch** im Winter viel zu tun.
There's a lot to do here not only in the summer but also in the winter.

DENN   *BECAUSE, FOR*

Jutta ist schlecht gelaunt, **denn** sie hat sich mit ihren Eltern gestritten.
Jutta is in a bad mood because she quarreled with her parents.

ODER   *OR*

Du kannst es alleine versuchen, **oder** jemand kann dir helfen.
You can try it on your own or someone can help you.

The conjunction **oder** is frequently used together with **entweder** to express the meaning *either . . . or.* Word order in the **entweder** clause may vary, as may the position of **entweder** itself.

Entweder kannst du es alleine versuchen, **oder** jemand kann dir helfen.

Entweder du kannst es alleine versuchen, **oder** jemand kann dir helfen.

Du kannst es **entweder** alleine versuchen, **oder** jemand kann dir helfen.

Either you can try it on your own or someone can help you.

UND   *AND*

Wir sind zu spät angekommen, **und** der Bus ist ohne uns abgefahren.
We arrived too late and the bus left without us.

Omission of Redundant Information

Information from the first clause that is repeated in the second clause is frequently omitted in German as in English.

Wir essen heute abend Spaghetti und (wir) trinken dazu eine Flasche Rotwein.
We're eating spaghetti tonight and (we're) having a bottle of red wine with it.

Trägt er eine Brille oder (trägt er) Kontaktlinsen?
Does he wear glasses or (does he wear) contacts?

If repeated information is omitted after the conjunctions **und** and **oder**, the comma separating clauses is dropped. Compare the following two sentences:

Trägt er eine Brille, oder trägt er Kontaktlinsen?
Trägt er eine Brille oder Kontaktlinsen?

Exercise 1: Aber *or* sondern?

1. Der Film war zu lang, _____ er war trotzdem interessant.
2. Ich werde nicht dieses Kleid, _____ meine Jeans tragen.
3. Christine hat nicht lockige Haare, _____ sie hat glatte Haare.
4. Nicht nur die Kinder, _____ auch die Erwachsenen haben mitge-spielt.
5. Sie treibt gar keinen Sport, _____ sie bleibt irgendwie schlank.
6. Die Jacke ist eigentlich nicht seine Größe, _____ sie paßt ihm trotzdem.
7. Wir essen kein Rindfleisch mehr, _____ nur noch Hühnchen.
8. Die alten Schulfreunde hatten sich seit 20 Jahren nicht gesehen, _____ sie haben sich trotzdem gleich wiedererkannt.
9. Nein, wir hatten uns nicht für 15 Uhr, _____ für 16 Uhr verabre-det.
10. Er ist mein Zwillingsbruder, _____ wir sehen uns gar nicht ähn-lich.

Exercise 2: *Combine the sentences with the German equivalent of the cue conjunction.*

1. (*but*)   Wir haben eine ganze Stunde gewartet. Nichts ist passiert.
2. (*but*)   Ich würde gerne ausgehen. Ich habe kein Geld.
3. (*because*)   Wir gehen nicht einkaufen. Es regnet.
4. (*or*)   Benehmt euch anständig! Ihr müßt ins Bett gehen.
5. (*and*)   Er hat mit dem Rauchen aufgehört. Dann hat er viel zugenommen.
6. (*or*)   Sollen wir tanzen gehen? Willst du hier bleiben und fernse-hen?
7. (*because*)   Ich fahre mit dem Lift. Ich habe mir den Fuß gebrochen.
8. (*but rather*)   Wir durften dem Spiel nicht einfach zuschauen. Wir mußten selber daran teilnehmen.
9. (*because*)   Ich mache jetzt Schluß. Ich habe in einer halben Stunde eine Verabredung.
10. (*and; and*)   Sie erzählte die furchtbare Wahrheit. Alle waren sehr erschrocken. Einige weinten sogar.

SUBORDINATING CONJUNCTIONS AND DEPENDENT CLAUSES

Subordinating conjunctions introduce clauses that are "dependent" in that they cannot stand alone. They depend on, or are subordinate to, a main clause. Dependent clauses are sometimes called *subordinate clauses*.

Word Order with Subordinating Conjunctions

The subordinating conjunction sends the conjugated verb to the end of its clause.

Es ist wichtig, **daβ** man die Größe des Problems **erfaβt**.
It is important that one comprehends the magnitude of the problem.

Die Party war zu Ende, **weil** die Nachbarn sich beschwert **hatten**.
The party ended because the neighbors had complained.

If a separable prefix stands at the end of the clause, the conjugated verb is rejoined to it.

Du kannst mitkommen, wenn du dich **umziehst**.
You can come along if you change your clothes.

Note that a comma is used in German to separate the clauses.

DEPENDENT CLAUSE FIRST

A dependent clause may begin the sentence. In this case, the word order of the main clause is inverted (verb-subject). This word order is consistent with the rules learned in chapter 12: the entire dependent clause counts as the first element of the sentence and the verb occupies the second position.

         1   2
Weil er zuviel getrunken hatte, geriet er in eine Schlägerei.
Because he had drunk too much he got into a brawl.

        1   2
Ehe die Geschäfte schlieβen, muβ ich Milch kaufen.
Before the stores close I have to buy milk.

Meanings of the Subordinating Conjunctions

Here are some common subordinating conjunctions and their English equivalents.

als	*when*
bevor	*before*
bis	*until*
da	*because, since* (cause)
dadurch, daβ	*by doing* (something)
damit	*so that*
daβ	*that*
ehe	*before*
falls	*in case*
indem	*by doing* (something)

je . . . desto	*the . . . the*
nachdem	*after*
ob	*whether*
obgleich	*although*
obwohl	*although*
seit	*since* (time)
seitdem	*since* (time)
sobald	*as soon as*
solange	*as long as*
während	*while, during; whereas*
weil	*because*
wenn	*when, whenever, if*

THE DIFFERENCE BETWEEN *ALS*, *WENN*, AND *WANN*

Als, **wenn**, and **wann** all correspond to *when*; however, they are not interchangeable.

Als is used for a single event in the past.

Als ich neun Jahre alt war, bekam ich meine erste Klavierstunde.
When I was nine years old I received my first piano lesson.

Wenn is used for present and future events, as well as for repeated events in the past. It frequently means *whenever.*

Wenn ich Zeit habe, übe ich Klavier.
When(ever) I have time, I practice the piano.

Wenn ich Zeit hatte, übte ich Klavier.
When(ever) I had time, I practiced the piano.

Wann is used for direct and indirect questions and corresponds to *at what time*. Remember that indirect questions require dependent, or verb-last, word order.

Wann ist meine Klavierstunde?
When is my piano lesson?

Ich habe vergessen, **wann** meine Klavierstunde ist.
I've forgotten when my piano lesson is.

Exercise 3: Als, *wenn*, or **wann**?

1. _____ es dir wieder besser geht, können wir weiter fahren.
2. Sie war nur 19 Jahre alt, _____ sie heiratete.

3. Wer weiß, _____ der Empfang beginnen soll?
4. _____ ich meine Großmutter besuchte, backte sie immer Kuchen.
5. Man soll es zugeben, _____ man im Irrtum ist.
6. _____ ich ihn um Hilfe bat, war er jedesmal für mich da.
7. Ich kenne dich schon so lange, daß ich vergesse, _____ wir uns kennengelernt haben.
8. _____ ich das Auto kaufte, war es schon total verrostet.
9. Alexander freute sich immer, _____ er Lisa traf. Aber _____ er sie gestern sah, wechselte er die Straßenseite!
10. Sasha ist immer so beschäftigt. Man weiß nie, _____ man ihn mal treffen kann.

THE DIFFERENCE BETWEEN *WENN* AND *OB*

Do not confuse **wenn** and **ob**. **Ob** means *whether* and frequently introduces an indirect question. **Wenn** means *if* in the sense of *when* or *in the event that*. It is frequently used in conditional sentences. Compare the following sentences:

Ich weiß nicht, **ob** ich den Streß aushalten kann.
I don't know whether I can stand the stress.

Wenn ich gestreßt bin, esse ich oft.
If (when; in the event that) I'm under pressure, I'll often eat.

Exercise 4: Wenn *or* ob?

1. Kannst du mir sagen, _____ du mich vom Bahnhof abholen kannst? _____ du mich abholst, muß ich nämlich kein Taxi bestellen.
2. Wir finden um 6 Uhr heraus, _____ wir in der Lotterie gewonnen haben. _____ wir gewinnen, dann kaufen wir uns einen neuen Wagen.
3. Mir ist es egal, _____ du kommst oder nicht.
4. _____ ich älter bin, lasse ich mir einen Bart wachsen.
5. Wir müssen flexibel bleiben, _____ wir einen Kompromiß finden wollen.
6. _____ man in der Innenstadt wohnt, kann man überall zu Fuß gehen.
7. Die Kellnerin fragte, _____ der Kunde essen oder nur trinken wollte.
8. Man kann von hier aus nicht sehen, _____ es im Haus Licht gibt.
9. Ich weiß nicht, _____ man mit der Straßenbahn dorthin kommt.
10. _____ du dich beeilst, kommst du noch rechtzeitig an.

DA VS. *WEIL*

Da and **weil** are both used to express causal relationships and correspond to *since* or *because*. **Da** is the less common conjunction and is found more often in the written language. It is used to express a reason or condition that is already known; it is usually located at the beginning of the sentence.

Da ihre Vorfahren aus Deutschland kamen, wollte sie Deutsch lernen.
Since her ancestors came from Germany she wanted to learn German.

Ich will Deutsch lernen, **weil** ich nächstes Jahr nach Deutschland fahre.
I want to learn German because I'm going to Germany next year.

DA AND *WEIL* VS. *SEITDEM/SEIT*

As we just saw, **da** and **weil** mean *since* in a causal sense. The conjunction **seitdem** (sometimes shortened to **seit**) means *since* in a temporal sense. Compare the following sentences:

Da (**weil**) es regnet, spielen wir nicht drauβen.
Since (because) it's raining, we're not playing outside.

Seitdem/seit es regnet, spielen wir nicht drauβen.
Since (the time) it's been raining, we haven't played outside.

Note that if the action of the sentence began in the past but is still continuing, the *present tense* plus **seitdem** is usually used in German, whereas English uses the present perfect tense.

DAβ

daβ vs. *das*. Do not confuse the conjunction **daβ** with the demonstrative or relative pronoun **das**. They all correspond to *that* in English. However, the demonstrative and relative pronouns replace nouns—that is, they point at or refer back to something previously mentioned (see chapter 3). Compare the following sentences:

SUBORDINATING CONJUNCTION
Man hat uns nicht gesagt, **daβ** es so teuer war.
They didn't tell us that it was so expensive.

DEMONSTRATIVE PRONOUN
Man hat uns **das** nicht gesagt.
They didn't tell us that.

RELATIVE PRONOUN

Wie heißt das Buch, **das** du liest?

What is the name of the book that you are reading?

Exercise 5: daß *or* **das**?

1. Ich habe _____ mit eigenen Augen gesehen.
2. Ich hatte keine Ahnung, _____ dir das alte Bild so wichtig war.
3. Das Poster, _____ an der Wand hängt, ist häßlich.
4. _____ werde ich doch nie verstehen.
5. Warum hast du mir _____ nicht vorher gesagt?
6. Das Obst, _____ schlecht ist, haben wir erst gestern gekauft.
7. Sie glaubt nicht, _____ _____ möglich ist.
8. Es freut mich, _____ du morgen kommst.

daß **Plus a Second Subordinating Conjunction.** In English, especially in the spoken language, it is common to combine the conjunction *that* with other subordinating conjunctions.

I heard that although she wanted to come she couldn't.

It's important that as soon as you arrive you call.

In German this is also possible, but awkward. It is better to separate the clauses.

Ich habe gehört, **daß** sie nicht kommen konnte, **obwohl** sie wollte.
I heard that she couldn't come, although she wanted to.

Es ist wichtig, **daß** du anrufst, **sobald** du ankommst.
It's important that you call as soon as you arrive.

Omission of *daß*. In German, **daß** (like English *that*) is sometimes omitted. In this case, both clauses are main clauses and take normal word order with the verb in second position.

   1   2   1 2
Wir haben gehört, es soll heute regnen.

   1   2   1 · 2
Wir haben gehört, heute soll es regnen.
We heard it's supposed to rain today.

Omission of **daß** is particularly common in indirect discourse (chapter 10).

Der Meteorologe sagte, morgen gebe es Schnee.
The weatherman said it will snow tomorrow.

INDEM AND DADURCH, DAβ

Use either **indem** or **dadurch, da**β to express means or, in other words, to express how something is done. Both conjunctions correspond to English *by doing* (*something*).

Sie beruhigte das Kind, **indem** sie ihm ein Wiegenlied sang.

Sie beruhigte das Kind **dadurch, da**β sie ihm ein Wiegenlied sang.

She calmed the child by singing it a lullaby.

JE . . . DESTO/UMSO

Je . . . desto/umso is a two-part conjunction used together with comparatives. It corresponds to *the . . . the . . .* with English comparatives. Note the word order in the following examples:

Je später ich ins Bett gehe, **desto** müder bin ich am Morgen.
The later I go to bed the more tired I am in the morning.

Je länger ich in der Schlange stehen muβte, **umso** ungeduldiger wurde ich.
The longer I had to wait in line the more impatient I became.

NACHDEM

A dependent clause introduced with **nachdem** expresses an action or event that happened prior to the action of the main clause. If the main clause is in the present or future tense, the dependent clause is in the present perfect tense. If the main clause is in the simple past tense, the dependent clause is in the past perfect tense.

PRESENT	PRESENT PERFECT
Sie küssen sich,	**nachdem** sie sich versöhnt haben.

They kiss after they make up.

FUTURE	PRESENT PERFECT
Sie werden sich küssen,	**nachdem** sie sich versöhnt haben.

They'll kiss after they make up.

SIMPLE PAST	PAST PERFECT
Sie küβten sich,	**nachdem** sie sich versöhnt hatten.

They kissed after they made up.

CONJUNCTIONS AS OPPOSED TO PREPOSITIONS AND ADVERBS

Be careful not to confuse the conjunctions corresponding to *before*, *after*, and *since* with the prepositions and adverbs of similar meaning.

CONJUNCTION	PREPOSITION	ADVERB
bevor	vor	vorher
nachdem	nach	nachher
seitdem/seit	seit	seither/seitdem

Whereas subordinating conjunctions combine sentences, prepositions precede nouns or pronouns and adverbs stand on their own. Study the following sentences carefully:

bevor, vor, vorher

Stefanie ist immer nervös, **bevor** sie eine Prüfung hat.
Stefanie is always nervous before she has a test.

Vor Prüfungen ist Stefanie immer nervös.
Stefanie is always nervous before tests.

Stefanie hat eine Prüfung. **Vorher** ist sie nervös.
Stefanie has a test. Beforehand she is nervous.

nachdem, nach, nachher

Herr Meier schläft immer, **nachdem** er gegessen hat.
Mr. Meier always sleeps after he has eaten.

Herr Meier schläft immer **nach** dem Essen.
Mr. Meier always sleeps after eating.

Herr Meier ißt. **Nachher** schläft er.
Mr. Meier is eating. Afterwards he'll sleep.

seitdem/seit, seit, seither/seitdem

Sie haben sich nicht mehr gesehen, **seitdem/seit** er das Land verlassen hat.
They haven't seen each other since he left the country.

Sie haben sich **seit** vier Monaten nicht mehr gesehen.
They haven't seen each other for four months.

Er hat das Land verlassen. **Seither** haben sie sich nicht mehr gesehen.
He left the country. They haven't seen each other since.

Exercise 6: *Complete with the German conjunction, preposition, or adverb that corresponds to the English cue.*

1. (*Since the time that*) _____ sie in den Bergen wohnt, hat sie weniger Allergien.
2. (*after*) Sie verließ ihn, _____ er sein Geld verspielt hatte.
3. (*after*) Gleich _____ dem Gewitter schien die Sonne wieder.
4. (*before*) Der Junge mußte sein Zimmer aufräumen, _____ er draußen spielen durfte.
5. (*beforehand*) Das Mädchen wollte schwimmen gehen, aber _____ mußte sie ihre Hausaufgaben machen.
6. (*afterwards*) Im Juni bin ich mit dem Studium fertig. Ich hoffe _____ eine Stelle zu finden.
7. (*before*) Jeden Abend, _____ ich ins Bett gehe, putze ich mir die Zähne.
8. (*before*) Habe ich _____ dem Anfang des Filmes noch Zeit, ein Getränk zu holen?
9. (*since*) Er hat letzte Woche mit seiner Freundin Schluß gemacht und fühlt sich _____ sehr einsam.
10. (*After*) _____ Silke eine halbe Stunde lang versucht hatte, ihren Freund anzurufen, gab sie auf.
11. (*since*) Das kranke Kind hat _____ vorgestern ein gefährlich hohes Fieber.
12. (*After*) _____ dem gestrigen Tag war ich sehr erschöpft.

Exercise 7: *Combine the sentences with the English equivalent of the cue subordinating conjunction.*

1. (*so that*) Ich muß den Wecker stellen. Ich stehe rechtzeitig auf.
2. (*whether*) Die Studentin wollte wissen. Der Kurs wird in diesem Semester angeboten.
3. (*before*) Entschuldige dich bei ihr! Es ist zu spät.
4. (*although*) Sie lächelte ihn an. Sie war böse auf ihn.
5. (*until*) Wir blieben. Das Licht wurde angemacht.
6. (*by doing*) Die Studenten lernten viel. Sie machten alle Übungen.
7. (*the . . . the*) Du schiebst es länger auf. Es wird schwieriger.
8. (*if, in the case that*) Wie lange dauert es? Ich schicke das Paket mit Luftpost.
9. (*as soon as*) Wir können losfahren. Du bist mit dem Packen fertig.
10. (*as long as*) Man kann keine Hilfsgüter in das Land einfliegen. Der Bürgerkrieg hält an.

Exercise 8: *Combine the sentences. Begin your sentence with the German equivalent of the cue subordinating conjunction.*

1. (*As soon as*) Ich hörte ihre Stimme. Ich legte auf.
2. (*Since the time that*) Sie raucht nicht mehr. Sie kann ausdauernder joggen.
3. (*Since, Because*) Sie hatten sich nichts mehr zu sagen. Sie haben ihre Beziehung beendet.
4. (*That*) Es wird Eintritt kosten. Man hat (es) uns nicht gesagt.
5. (*In case*) Er will dir nicht helfen. Wir sind dazu bereit.
6. (*While*) Wir machten Urlaub. Jemand ist ins Haus eingebrochen.
7. (*As long as*) Du wohnst in diesem Haus. Du machst, was ich dir sage.
8. (*If*) Du hast dazu Lust. Wir können durch die Stadt bummeln.
9. (*Although*) Sie kannten sich nicht. Sie waren sich gleich sympathisch.
10. (*Whereas, While*) Es schneite in Alaska. Die Touristen lagen in Hawaii in der Sonne.

REVIEW EXERCISES FOR CONJUNCTIONS

Exercise 9: *Complete with the appropriate word from the lists. Each word may be used only once.*

wenn   wann   als   aber   sondern

1. In Deutschland mußte ich letztes Jahr jedes Mal zur Post, _____ ich telefonieren wollte.
2. Die Familie wohnt nicht in einer Mietwohnung, _____ in einer Eigentumswohnung.
3. Ihre Erkältung war nicht mehr schlimm, _____ sie ging trotzdem nicht zur Arbeit.
4. In Deutschland regelt das Ladenschlußgesetz, _____ die Läden schließen müssen.
5. Wir gingen ins Haus, _____ es zu tröpfeln anfing.

wenn   ob   daß   das   bis

6. In diesen Nachtklub darf man nur gehen, _____ man ledig ist.
7. Einige Menschen denken, _____ Amerikaner nur Hamburger essen.
8. Geh bitte nicht in die Küche, _____ der Fußboden trocken ist!

9. Fahr hier nicht um die Ecke! _____ ist eine Einbahnstraße.

10. Auf dem Führerschein steht, _____ man eine Brille tragen muß.

seit   seither   nachdem   vor   bevor

11. _____ wir alles in den Wagen eingepackt hatten, sind wir losgefahren.

12. Die Austauschstudentin wohnte ein Jahr in Nürnberg. _____ ißt
sie gern Lebkuchen.

13. Erst _____ 1971 haben Frauen in der Schweiz das Wahlrecht.

14. Verträge soll man lesen, _____ man sie unterschreibt.

15. Wir stehen jetzt _____ dem ältesten Fachwerkhaus der Stadt.

Exercise 10: *Combine the sentences with the English equivalent of the cue
conjunction. Watch the word order. If the cue conjunction is capitalized
(#6, 8, 14, 16), begin the sentence with it.*

1. (*so that*)   Manche Stars tragen auf der Straße eine Perücke. Sie
werden nicht erkannt.

2. (*or*)   Wollen wir eine Pension suchen? Sollen wir in der
Jugendherberge übernachten?

3. (*whether*)   Frag den Fahrer! Ist das die richtige Haltestelle?

4. (*that*)   Hast du (es) gewußt? Graz ist die zweitgrößte Stadt in
Österreich.

5. (*whereas*)   Im Norden von Deutschland ist es flach. Es ist im
Süden bergiger.

6. (*If*)   Wir haben Glück. Wir finden noch ein freies Zimmer.

7. (*since*)   Ich habe Gerda nicht gesehen. Sie hat sich die Haare
geschnitten.

8. (*Although*)   Natalie genießt die Ruhe auf dem Land. Sie vermißt
das kulturelle Leben einer Großstadt.

9. (*as soon as*)   Ruf mich an! Du kannst (es).

10. (*that*)   Ich glaube (es) schon. Mein Geburtstagswunsch erfüllt
sich.

11. (*but*)   Ich habe angerufen. Niemand war zu Hause.

12. (*and*)   Zuerst müssen die zwei Seiten zusammenkommen. Dann
kann man verhandeln.

13. (*but rather*)   Die negative Aussicht ist leider nicht übertrieben.
(Sie ist) realistisch.

14. (*In case*)   Du glaubst es mir nicht. Frag doch Dirk!

15. (*by doing*)   Regine verschönert ihr Haus. Sie stellt frische Blumen
auf den Tisch.

16. (*After*)   Arne beendet seinen Zivildienst. Er fängt an zu studieren.

ANSWERS TO EXERCISES

1.

1. aber
2. sondern
3. sondern
4. sondern
5. aber
6. aber
7. sondern
8. aber
9. sondern
10. aber

2.

1. Wir haben eine ganze Stunde gewartet, aber nichts ist passiert.
2. Ich würde gerne ausgehen, aber ich habe kein Geld.
3. Wir gehen nicht einkaufen, denn es regnet.
4. Benehmt euch anständig, oder ihr müßt ins Bett gehen!
5. Er hat mit dem Rauchen aufgehört, und dann hat er viel zugenommen.
6. Sollen wir tanzen gehen, oder willst du hier bleiben und fernsehen?
7. Ich fahre mit dem Lift, denn ich habe mir den Fuß gebrochen.
8. Wir durften dem Spiel nicht einfach zuschauen, sondern wir mußten selber daran teilnehmen.
9. Ich mache jetzt Schluß, denn ich habe in einer halben Stunde eine Verabredung.
10. Sie erzählte die furchtbare Wahrheit, und alle waren sehr erschrocken, und einige weinten sogar.

3.

1. Wenn
2. als
3. wann
4. Wenn
5. wenn
6. Wenn
7. wann
8. Als
9. wenn; als
10. wann

4.

1. ob; Wenn
2. ob; Wenn
3. ob
4. Wenn
5. wenn
6. Wenn
7. ob
8. ob
9. ob
10. Wenn

5.

1. das
2. daß
3. das
4. Das
5. das
6. das
7. daß; das
8. daß

6.

1. Seitdem/Seit
2. nachdem
3. nach
4. bevor
5. vorher
6. nachher
7. bevor
8. vor
9. seither/seitdem
10. Nachdem
11. seit
12. Nach

7.

1. Ich muß den Wecker stellen, damit ich rechtzeitig aufstehe.
2. Die Studentin wollte wissen, ob der Kurs in diesem Semester angeboten wird.
3. Entschuldige dich bei ihr, bevor/ehe es zu spät ist!
4. Sie lächelte ihn an, obwohl/obgleich sie böse auf ihn war.
5. Wir blieben, bis das Licht angemacht wurde.
6. Die Studenten lernten viel dadurch, daß sie alle Übungen machten. Die Studenten lernten viel, indem sie alle Übungen machten.
7. Je länger du es aufschiebst, desto/umso schwieriger wird es.
8. Wie lange dauert es, wenn ich das Paket mit Luftpost schicke?
9. Wir können losfahren, sobald du mit dem Packen fertig bist.
10. Man kann keine Hilfsgüter in das Land einfliegen, solange der Bürgerkrieg anhält.

8.

1. Sobald ich ihre Stimme hörte, legte ich auf.
2. Seitdem/Seit sie nicht mehr raucht, kann sie ausdauernder joggen.
3. Da/Weil sie sich nichts mehr zu sagen hatten, haben sie ihre Beziehung beendet.
4. Daß es Eintritt kosten wird, hat man uns nicht gesagt.
5. Falls er dir nicht helfen will, sind wir dazu bereit.
6. Während wir Urlaub machten, ist jemand ins Haus eingebrochen.
7. Solange du in diesem Haus wohnst, machst du, was ich dir sage.
8. Wenn du dazu Lust hast, können wir durch die Stadt bummeln.
9. Obwohl/Obgleich sie sich nicht kannten, waren sie sich gleich sympathisch.
10. Während es in Alaska schneite, lagen die Touristen in Hawaii in der Sonne.

9.

1. wenn
2. sondern
3. aber
4. wann
5. als
6. wenn
7. daß
8. bis
9. Das
10. ob

11. Nachdem
12. Seither
13. seit
14. bevor
15. vor

10.

1. Manche Stars tragen auf der Straße eine Perücke, damit sie nicht erkannt werden.
2. Wollen wir eine Pension suchen, oder sollen wir in der Jugendherberge übernachten?
3. Frag den Fahrer, ob das die richtige Haltestelle ist!
4. Hast du gewußt, daß Graz die zweitgrößte Stadt in Österreich ist?
5. Im Norden von Deutschland ist es flach, während es im Süden bergiger ist.
6. Wenn wir Glück haben, finden wir noch ein freies Zimmer.
7. Ich habe Gerda nicht gesehen, seitdem/seit sie sich die Haare geschnitten hat.
8. Obwohl/Obgleich Natalie die Ruhe auf dem Land genießt, vermißt sie das kulturelle Leben einer Großstadt.
9. Ruf mich an, sobald du kannst!
10. Ich glaube schon, daß mein Geburtstagswunsch sich erfüllt.
11. Ich habe angerufen, aber niemand war zu Hause.
12. Zuerst müssen die zwei Seiten zusammenkommen, und dann kann man verhandeln.
13. Die negative Aussicht ist leider nicht übertrieben, sondern (sie ist) realistisch.
14. Falls du es mir nicht glaubst, frag doch Dirk!
15. Regine verschönert ihr Haus dadurch, daß sie frische Blumen auf den Tisch stellt. Regine verschönert ihr Haus, indem sie frische Blumen auf den Tisch stellt.
16. Nachdem Arne seinen Zivildienst beendet, fängt er an zu studieren.

Vocabulary

GERMAN-ENGLISH

The following list contains all German words used in the exercises and examples of this book, with the exception of pronouns, possessive adjectives, numbers, days of the week, months, and some obvious cognates. The meanings given are specific to the usage of the word in this book.

Nouns are listed with both singular and plural forms.

    der **Abend**, -e = der Abend
                die Abende

Weak nouns are designated with the genitive and plural ending.

    der **Mensch**, -en, -en = der Mensch
                    des Menschen
                    die Menschen

    der **Name**, -ens, -en = der Name
                   des Namens
                   die Namen

Adjectival nouns are designated as follows:

    der/die **Fremde** (*adj. noun*)
    der/die **Verwandte** (*adj. noun*)

Separable prefixes are indicated by a period.

    ab·holen
    ein·mischen

All strong and irregular weak verbs are listed with their principal parts.

    fahren (fährt), fuhr, ist gefahren

haben (hat), hatte, gehabt

For weak verbs the infinitive alone is usually given. If the weak verb takes **sein** as its auxiliary, it is noted in parentheses.

machen

passieren (ist)

Those adjectives and adverbs that umlaut in the comparative and superlative are indicated as follows:

alt (ä)

jung (ü)

The following abbreviations are used in this vocabulary:

acc.	accusative
adj.	adjective
adj. noun	adjectival noun
coor. conj.	coordinating conjunction
dat.	dative
gen.	genitive
nom.	nominative
pl.	plural
prep.	preposition
sub. conj.	subordinating conjunction

ab und zu   now and then

ab·brennen, brannte ab, abgebrannt   to burn away, burn down

der **Abend, -e**   evening

das **Abendessen, -**   evening meal, dinner

die **Abendkasse, -n**   evening box office

abenteuerlich   adventurous, fantastic

aber (*coor. conj.*)   but, however

ab·fahren (fährt ab), fuhr ab, ist abgefahren   to depart, drive away

der **Abfall, ⁀e**   garbage

ab·hängen, hing ab, abgehangen (von)   to depend (on)

abhängig (von)   dependent (on)

ab·holen   to pick up

die **Abmachung, -en**   agreement

ab·nehmen (nimmt ab), nahm ab, abgenommen   to lose weight

die **Abreise, -n**   departure

ab·reißen, riß ab, abgerissen   to tear down, demolish

ab·rüsten   to disarm

der **Absatz, ⁀e**   heel of a shoe; paragraph

ab·schicken   to send off

der **Abschied, -e**   departure;   **zum Abschied**   at departure

ab·schließen, schloß ab, abgeschlossen   to lock, shut; to conclude

ab·schreiben, schrieb ab, abgeschrieben   to copy

absolut   absolute

die **Abtreibung, -en**   abortion

ab·waschen (wäscht ab), wusch ab, abgewaschen   to wash (the dishes)

adlig   noble

der **Advokat, -en, -en**/die **Advokatin, -nen**   lawyer

die **Affäre, -n**   affair

der **Affe, -n, -n**   ape

der **Agent, -en, -en**/die **Agentin, -nen**
  agent

ähnlich   similar

die **Ahnung: keine Ahnung haben**
  to have no idea

aktiv   active

der **Akzent, -e**   accent

akzeptieren   to accept

der **Alkohol**   alcohol

der **Alkoholiker, -/**die **Alkoholikerin,
  -nen**   alcoholic person

all-   all

die **Allergie, -n**   allergy

alles   everything

die **Alpen**   Alps

als   than

als (*sub. conj.*)   when

alt (ä)   old

die **Altstadt, ⁻e**   old section of the city

der **Amerikaner, -/**die **Amerikanerin,
  -nen**   American person

amerikanisch   American

die **Ampel, -n**   traffic light

sich amüsieren   to have a good time,
  amuse oneself

an + *acc./dat.*   on (vertical surfaces);
  at; to

analysieren   to analyze

an·bauen   to grow, plant

an·bieten, bot an, angeboten
  to offer

ander-   other; different

ändern   to change

anders   differently

der **Anfang, ⁻e**   beginning;   **am
  Anfang**   in the beginning

**an·fangen (fängt an), fing an, ange-
  fangen**   to begin

der **Anfänger, -/**die **Anfängerin, -nen**
  beginner

an·fassen   to touch

an·fertigen   to make, produce; to
  prepare

die **Anforderung, -en**   demand;
  Anforderungen stellen   to make
  demands

an·geben (gibt an), gab an, angegeben
  to indicate, give; to brag

angeboren   inborn, hereditary

das **Angebot, -e**   offer

der/die **Angeklagte** (*adj. noun*)
  accused person

angenehm   pleasant

der/die **Angestellte** (*adj. noun*)
  employee

an·greifen, griff an, angegriffen
  to attack

die **Angst, ⁻e**   fear

an·haben (hat an), hatte an, angehabt
  to have on, wear

**an·halten (hält an), hielt an,
  angehalten**   to last; to stop; to hold

**an·kommen, kam an, ist angekom-
  men**   to arrive

die **Ankunft, ⁻e**   arrival

die **Anmeldung, -en**   notification

**an·nehmen (nimmt an), nahm an,
  angenommen**   to accept; to assume

an·probieren   to try on

der **Anruf, -e**   telephone call

an·rufen, rief an, angerufen
  to telephone

an·schauen   to look at

sich an·schnallen   to fasten one's seat
  belt

**an·schreiben, schrieb an,
  angeschrieben**   to charge

an·sehen (sieht an), sah an, angesehen
  to look at

die **Ansichtskarte, -n**   postcard

**an·sprechen (spricht an), sprach an,
  angesprochen**   to speak to

anständig   respectable, decent

(an)statt + *gen.*   instead of

an·steigen, stieg an, ist angestiegen
  to go up, increase

anstrengend   strenuous

die **Antenne, -n**   antenna

der **Antrag, ⁻e**   proposal

die **Antwort, -en**   answer

antworten (*dat.*)   to answer (with
  people);   **antworten (auf** + *acc.*)
  to answer

die **Anweisung, -en** direction, instruction

die **Anwesenheit** presence

an·ziehen, zog an, angezogen to get dressed

der **Anzug, ¨e** suit, clothes

der **Apfel, ¨** apple

der **Apfelsaft** apple juice

das **Aquarell, -e** watercolor

das **Aquarium,** die **Aquarien** aquarium

arabisch Arabian

die **Arbeit, -en** work, job

arbeiten (an + *dat.***)** to work (on)

der **Arbeiter, -/**die **Arbeiterin, -nen** worker

der **Arbeitgeber, -/**die **Arbeitgeberin, -nen** employer

der **Arbeitnehmer, -/**die **Arbeitnehmerin, -nen** employee

das **Arbeitsamt, ¨er** employment office

die **Arbeitserlaubnis** permit to work

das **Arbeitsklima** working climate

die **Arbeitslosigkeit** unemployment

ärgern to annoy; **sich ärgern (über + ** *acc.***)** to be annoyed (about)

arm (ä) poor

der **Arm, -e** arm

die **Art, -en** type, kind

der **Artikel, -** article

der **Arzt, ¨e/**die **Ärztin, -nen** doctor, physician

der **Assistent, -en, -en/**die **Assistentin, -nen** assistant

der **Asylant, -en, -en/**die **Asylantin, -nen** asylum seeker

der **Atem** breath; **außer Atem** out of breath

atmen to breathe

das **Atomkraftwerk, -e** nuclear plant

auch too, also

auf + *acc./dat.* on (horizontal surfaces), upon

auf·bauen to set up, erect

auf·bleiben, blieb auf, ist aufgeblieben to stay up

auf·brechen (bricht auf), brach auf, aufgebrochen to get going, start; to break open

der **Aufenthalt, -e** stay

die **Aufenthaltserlaubnis** residency permit

auf·essen (ißt auf), aß auf, aufgegessen to eat up

auf·fordern to order, command

die **Aufgabe, -n** assignment, task

auf·geben (gibt auf), gab auf, aufgegeben to give up

auf·hören to stop

auf·legen to hang up (a phone)

auf·machen to open

auf·räumen to clean up, straighten up

sich auf·regen (über + *acc.***)** to get excited (about)

aufregend exciting

der **Aufsatz, ¨e** essay, composition

auf·schieben, schob auf, aufgeschoben to postpone

auf·stehen, stand auf, ist aufgestanden to get up

der **Aufwand** expense, expenditure; **viel Aufwand** a lot of trouble, a lot of expense

auf·wecken to wake (someone) up

das **Auge, -n** eye

der **Augenzeuge, -n, -n/**die **Augenzeugin, -nen** eyewitness

aus + *dat.* out of; from

ausdauernd persistent, persevering

aus·drücken to express

aus·fallen (fällt aus), fiel aus, ist ausgefallen to fall out; to be canceled

der **Ausflug, ¨e** excursion

aus·füllen to fill out

der **Ausgang, ¨e** exit, departure

aus·geben (gibt aus), gab aus, ausgegeben to spend (money)

aus·gehen, ging aus, ist ausgegangen to go out

ausgerechnet just; precisely

ausgezeichnet excellent

aus·halten (hält aus), hielt aus, ausgehalten to stand, endure

die **Auskunft, ¨e** information

aus·lachen to laugh at

das **Ausland** foreign country

der **Ausländer, -/**die **Ausländerin, -nen** foreigner

aus·machen to turn off

ausnahmsweise as an exception, for a change

aus·nehmen (nimmt aus), nahm aus, ausgenommen to gut (a fish); to take out

aus·sagen to testify

aus·sehen (sieht aus), sah aus, ausgesehen to look (like), appear

die **Außenpolitik** foreign policy

außer + *dat.* except for; besides; other than

äußerst extremely

die **Aussicht, -en** view; perspective

aus·stehen, stand aus, ausgestanden to endure; to be owed, outstanding

die **Ausstellung, -en** exhibit

der **Austauschstudent, -en, -en/**die **Austauschstudentin, -nen** exchange student

aus·trinken, trank aus, ausgetrunken to drink up

aus·wandern (ist) to emigrate

auswendig by heart, by memory; **auswendig lernen** to memorize

aus·ziehen, zog aus, ausgezogen to undress; **aus·ziehen (ist)** to move out

das **Auto, -s** car

die **Autobahn, -en** expressway

der **Autofahrer, -/**die **Autofahrerin, -nen** car driver

der **Autohändler, -/**die **Autohändlerin, -nen** car dealer

der **Autor, -en/**die **Autorin, -nen** author

das **Baby, -s** baby

babysitten to babysit

backen (bäckt), backte, gebacken to bake

der **Bäcker, -/**die **Bäckerin, -nen** baker

die **Bäckerei, -en** bakery

der **Backofen, ¨** oven

baden to bathe; to go swimming

das **Badezimmer, -** bathroom

der **Bahnhof, ¨e** train station

bald (eher, ehest-) soon

der **Ball, ¨e** ball

der **Ballon, -s** or **-e** balloon

der **Band, ¨e** volume (book)

das **Band, ¨er** tape; ribbon

die **Bank, ¨e** bench

die **Bank, -en** bank

bankrott bankrupt

der **Banküberfall, ¨e** bank robbery

der **Bart, ¨e** beard

basteln to putter; to work at a hobby

der **Bauarbeiter, -/**die **Bauarbeiterin, -nen** construction worker

bauen to build

der **Bauer, -n, -n/**die **Bäuerin, -nen** farmer

der **Baum, ¨e** tree

beachten to observe

der **Beamte, -n, -n/**die **Beamtin, -nen** official

beantworten to answer

bedauern to regret

bedeuten to mean

bedienen to serve; to use

sich beeilen to hurry

beenden to end, conclude

befehlen (befiehlt), befahl, befohlen (*dat.*) to order, command

sich befinden, befand, befunden to be located

die **Beförderung, -en** promotion

begegnen (ist) (*dat.*) to meet, encounter

begeistert (von) enthusiastic (about)

begießen, begoß, begossen to water

beginnen, begann, begonnen to begin

begraben (begräbt), begrub, begraben to bury

behandeln to treat; to handle

behaupten to maintain

bei + *dat.* at; near; with

beide both

das **Bein, -e** leg

der **Beinbruch, ̈-e** broken leg

beißen, biß, gebissen to bite

das **Beispiel, -e** example; **zum Beispiel** for example

bekannt well-known; familiar

bekommen, bekam, bekommen to receive

belegen to take (a course)

beleidigen to insult

beliebt popular

bellen to bark

bemerken to notice; to observe

sich benehmen (benimmt), benahm, benommen to act, behave

benutzen to use

beobachten to observe

berechnen to calculate, compute

der **Berg, -e** mountain

bergig mountainous, hilly

der **Bergsteiger, -/die Bergsteigerin, -nen** mountain climber

der **Bericht, -e** report

berichten to report

berichtigen to correct, mark

der **Beruf, -e** profession

beruhen (auf + *dat.*) to be based (on)

beruhigen to quiet, calm

berühmt famous

die **Besatzungszone, -n** occupation zone

beschäftigt busy

beschmutzen to dirty

beschreiben, beschrieb, beschrieben to describe

die **Beschwerde, -n** complaint

sich beschweren (über + *acc.*) to complain (about)

besichtigen to view

besitzen, besaß, besessen to possess, own

besonders especially

besprechen (bespricht), besprach, besprochen to discuss

besser better

bestätigen to confirm

bestellen to order

bestimmt certain

der **Besuch, -e** visit

besuchen to visit

beteuern to assert

betonen to emphasize, stress

betreten (betritt), betrat, betreten to walk onto, enter

der **Betrieb, -e** operation, plant, firm; **außer Betrieb** out of order

betrügen, betrog, betrogen to cheat; to deceive

betrunken drunk

das **Bett, -en** bed

der **Bettler, -/die Bettlerin, -nen** beggar

bevor (*sub. conj.*) before

beweisen, bewies, bewiesen to prove

sich bewerben (bewirbt), bewarb, beworben (um) to apply (for)

der **Bewerbungsbrief, -e** letter of application

bewundern to admire

bezahlen to pay for

beziehen, bezog, bezogen: ein Bett beziehen to make a bed

die **Beziehung, -en** relationship

die **Bibliothek, -en** library

das **Bier** beer

der **Biergarten, ̈** open-air restaurant

bieten, bot, geboten to offer

das **Bild, -er** picture

das **Bilderbuch, ̈-er** picturebook

der **Bildhauer, -/die Bildhauerin, -nen** sculptor

billig inexpensive

die **Biographie, -n** biography

die **Birne, -n** pear; light bulb

bis + *acc.* until; as far as

bis (*sub. conj.*) until

bißchen: ein bißchen a little

der **Bissen, -** bite, morsel
bitte please; you're welcome
bitten, bat, gebeten (um) to ask (for)
blau blue
bleiben, blieb, ist geblieben to remain, stay
der **Bleistift, -e** pencil
blind blind
der **Blödsinn** nonsense
die **Blume, -n** flower
die **Bluse, -n** blouse
der **Boden, ⸚** ground, floor
der **Bodensee** Lake Constance
bohren to drill, bore
die **Bohrmaschine, -n** drilling machine
das **Boot, -e** boat
borgen to borrow; to lend
der **Börsenmarkt, ⸚e** stock market
böse (auf + *acc.*) angry (at)
braun brown
die **Braut, ⸚e** bride
der **Bräutigam, -e** bridegroom
das **Brautpaar, -e** bride and bridegroom
brav well-behaved
brechen (bricht), brach, gebrochen to break
die **Bremse, -n** brake
brennen, brannte, gebrannt to burn
der **Brief, -e** letter
die **Briefmarke, -n** stamp
die **Briefmarkensammlung, -en** stamp collection
die **Brieftasche, -n** pocketbook, wallet
der **Briefträger, -/die Briefträgerin, -nen** mail carrier
die **Brille, -n** (eye)glasses
bringen, brachte, gebracht to bring
das **Brot, -e** bread; sandwich
das **Brötchen, -** roll
die **Brücke, -n** bridge
der **Bruder, ⸚** brother
der **Brunnen, -** fountain; well
das **Buch, ⸚er** book

buchen to book
die **Bücherei, -en** library
der **Buchstabe, -ns, -n** letter (of the alphabet)
bummeln to stroll
der **Bundeskanzler** federal chancellor
das **Bundesland, ⸚er** federal state
bunt many-colored, colorful
die **Burg, -en** castle
der **Bürgerkrieg, -e** civil war
der **Bürgermeister, -/die Bürgermeisterin, -nen** mayor
das **Büro, -s** office
der **Busch, ⸚e** bush, shrub
die **Butter** butter

der **CD-Spieler, -** CD player
der **Champagner** champagne
die **Chance, -n** opportunity, chance
der **Chef, -s/die Chefin, -nen** boss, head, chief
die **Chemikalien (*pl.*)** chemicals
chemisch chemical
der **Chirurg, -en, -en/die Chirurgin, -nen** surgeon
der **Chor, ⸚e** choir
der **Computer, -** computer

da there
da (*sub. conj.*) because, since (causally)
das **Dach, ⸚er** roof
das **Dachgeschoβ, -(ss)e** attic
dahinten back there
damals at that time
damit (*sub. conj.*) so that
danach afterwards
(das) Dänemark Denmark
Dank: Vielen Dank! Many thanks!
dankbar thankful
danken (*dat.*) to thank
dann then
daβ (*sub. conj.*) that
die **Dauer** duration, length
dauern to last, endure
dauernd all the time, continually

decken   to cover; **den Tisch decken**
  to set the table
die **Definition, -en**   definition
dekorieren   to decorate
demolieren   to demolish, tear down
der **Demonstrant, -en, -en**/die
  Demonstrantin, -nen
  demonstrator
demonstrieren   to demonstrate
denken, dachte, gedacht (an + *acc*.)
  to think (of, about); **sich denken**
  to imagine
das **Denkmal, ̈er**   monument
denn (*coor. conj.*)   because, for
deshalb   therefore
deutlich   clear
der/die **Deutsche** (*adj. noun*)   German
  person
(das) **Deutschland**   Germany
der **Dialekt, -e**   dialect
der **Diamantring, -e**   diamond
  ring
die **Diät, -en**   diet
dick   fat
der **Dieb, -e**/die **Diebin, -nen**   thief
dies-   this; these
das **Diktat, -e**   dictation
das **Diplom, -e**   diploma
die **Direktion**   management
der **Direktor, -en**/die **Direktorin, -nen**
  manager
der **Dirigent, -en, -en**/die **Dirigentin,
  -nen**   conductor
die **Diskussion, -en**   discussion
diskutieren   to discuss
die **Doktorarbeit, -en**   doctoral
  thesis
der **Dom, -e**   cathedral
das **Dorf, ̈er**   village
dramatisch   dramatic
drauβen   outside
dreimal   three times
drinnen   inside
die **Drogerie, -n**   drugstore
dumm (ü)   dumb
dunkel   dark
die **Dunkelheit**   darkness

durch + *acc*.   through
das **Durcheinander**   confusion,
  disorder
**durch·fallen (fällt durch), fiel durch,
  ist durchgefallen**   to flunk
durch·führen   to accomplish, carry
  through; to lead through
durchgebraten   well done (of meat)
**durch·lesen (liest durch), las durch,
  durchgelesen**   to read through
durch·suchen   to search through
dürfen (darf), durfte, gedurft   to be
  allowed to

die **Ecke, -n**   corner
egal   equal; **Das ist mir egal.**
  It's all the same to me.
ehe *(sub. conj.)*   before
ehemalig   former
das **Ehepaar, -e**   married couple
das **Ehrenzeichen, -**   medal,
  decoration
das **Ei, -er**   egg
eifersüchtig (auf + *acc*.)   jealous (of)
das **Eigenheim, -e**   privately owned
  house
eigentlich   actually
die **Eigentumswohnung, -en**
  privately owned apartment
einander   each other
die **Einbahnstraβe, -n**   one-way
  street
der **Einbrecher, -/**die **Einbrecherin,
  -nen**   burglar
einfach   simple
**ein·fangen (fängt ein), fing ein,
  eingefangen**   to catch
ein·fliegen, flog ein, ist eingeflogen
  to fly in
der **Eingang, ̈e**   entrance
die **Einheit, -en**   unity; union
einig   in agreement
einiges   several things
der **Einkauf, ̈e**   something purchased
ein·kaufen   to buy, purchase
das **Einkaufszentrum, -zentren**
  shopping center

ein·laden (lädt ein), lud ein, einge-laden to invite
ein·lösen to cash
einmalig unique, one-time
sich ein·mischen to interfere
ein·packen to pack
einsam lonely
ein·schenken to pour in, fill
ein·schicken to send in
ein·schlafen (schläft ein), schlief ein, ist eingeschlafen to fall asleep
ein·schüchtern to intimidate
ein·speichern to save (in a computer)
ein·sperren to lock in
ein·stellen to stop; to hire
ein·treten (tritt ein), trat ein, ist eingetreten to enter
einverstanden in agreement
ein·zahlen to pay in
einzig only, sole, single
das **Eis** ice; ice cream
eiskalt ice cold
der **Elefant, -en, -en** elephant
elegant elegant
die **Elektrizität** electricity
die **Eltern** (*pl.*) parents
der **Empfang, ⸚e** reception
empfehlen (empfiehlt), empfahl, empfohlen to recommend
der **Empfehlungsbrief, -e** letter of recommendation
empfinden, empfand, empfunden to feel
das **Ende, -n** end
endlich finally
eng tight
der **Engländer, -/die Engländerin, -nen** English person
englisch English
der **Enkel, -/die Enkelin, -nen** grandson/granddaughter
entdecken to discover
entfernen to remove
entlang + *acc.* along
entlassen (entläßt), entließ, entlassen to fire, dismiss; to release

entscheiden, entschied, entschieden to decide
die **Entschuldigung, -en** excuse; **Entschuldigung!** Pardon me!
entsetzt (über + *acc.*) terrified (about)
entspringen, entsprang, ist entsprungen to arise, spring from; to escape
enttäuschen to disappoint
entwaffnen to disarm
erbauen to build, construct
der **Erbe, -n, -n/die Erbin, -nen** heir
die **Erbse, -n** pea
die **Erdbeere, -n** strawberry
die **Erde, -n** earth, world
die **Erfahrung, -en** experience
erfassen to comprehend
der **Erfinder, -/die Erfinderin, -nen** inventor
die **Erfindung, -en** discovery, invention
der **Erfolg, -e** success
erforschen to explore
erfreulich delightful
erfüllen to fulfill, come true
das **Ergebnis, -se** result
erhalten (erhält), erhielt, erhalten to receive; to maintain
erhöhen to raise
die **Erhöhung, -en** rise; increase
sich erholen (von) to recover (from)
sich erinnern (an + *acc.*) to remember, recall
sich erkälten to catch a cold
die **Erkältung, -en** cold
erkennen, erkannte, erkannt to recognize
erklären to explain
die **Erklärung, -en** explanation
erlauben to permit
erläutern to explain, illustrate
ernst serious; **ernst nehmen** to take (something) seriously
erreichen to reach, obtain, get
erscheinen, erschien, ist erschienen to appear
erschöpft exhausted

erschrecken   to startle, frighten
erschrecken (erschrickt), erschrak, ist erschrocken   to be terrified, frightened, startled
erst   just, only, not until
erstaunt (über + *acc.*)   surprised, astonished (about)
erstellen   to produce, make
ertragen (erträgt), ertrug, ertragen   to stand, endure
erwähnen   to mention
erwarten   to expect
erwischen   to catch
erzählen   to tell
es gibt   there is; there are
das **Essen, -**   meal
essen (iβt), aβ, gegessen   to eat
etwas   something
(das) **Europa**   Europe
ewig   eternal
exklusiv   exclusive
die **Exkursion, -en**   excursion
die **Expedition, -en**   expedition
das **Experiment, -e**   experiment
der **Experte, -n, -n/**die **Expertin, -nen**   expert

die **Fabrik, -en**   factory
das **Fach, ⸚er**   field, subject
das **Fachwerkhaus, ⸚er**   half-timbered house
fahren (fährt), fuhr, ist gefahren   to drive; to travel
der **Fahrer, -/**die **Fahrerin, -nen**   driver
das **Fahrrad, ⸚er**   bicycle
die **Fahrt, -en**   trip, tour
der **Fall, ⸚e**   case
fallen (fällt), fiel, ist gefallen   to fall
fällig   due; payable
falls (*sub. conj.*)   in case
falsch   false
die **Familie, -n**   family
fangen (fängt), fing, gefangen   to catch, capture
das **Farbband, ⸚er**   typewriter ribbon
die **Farbe, -n**   color

fassen   to grasp; to contain
fast   almost
fasten   to fast
faszinierend   fascinating
faul   lazy
faulenzen   to lounge about, laze about
fehlen (*dat.*)   to be absent, be missing
der **Fehler, -**   mistake
feiern   to celebrate
der **Feiertag, -e**   holiday
das **Feld, -er**   field
das **Fenster, -**   window
die **Ferien** (*pl.*)   vacation, holidays
fern   distant
fern·sehen (sieht fern), sah fern, ferngesehen   to watch TV
der **Fernseher, -**   television set
die **Fernsehnachricht, -en**   television news
fertig   done, completed
fest·stellen   to establish, confirm
die **Fete, -n**   party
das **Feuer, -**   fire; light (for a cigarette)
das **Fieber, -**   fever
der **Film, -e**   movie
filmen   to film
finanziell   financial
finden, fand, gefunden   to find
die **Firma,** die **Firmen**   company, firm
der **Fisch, -e**   fish
der **Fischer, -/**die **Fischerin, -nen**   fisher
flach   flat
die **Flasche, -n**   bottle
der **Fleck, -e**   spot
das **Fleisch**   meat
fleiβig   industrious, diligent
flexibel   flexible
fliegen, flog, ist geflogen   to fly
fliehen, floh, ist geflohen   to flee
die **Flöte, -n**   flute
der **Flug, ⸚e**   flight
die **Fluggesellschaft, -en**   airline company
der **Flughafen, ⸚**   airport

das **Flugticket, -s** airline ticket
das **Flugzeug, -e** plane
das **Flugzeugunglück** airplane crash, accident
der **Flur, -e** hallway
der **Fluβ, ̈(ss)e** river
folgen (*dat.*) to follow, obey
folgend following
die **Förderung, -en** support, assistance, advancement
das **Formular, -e** form
der **Forscher, -/**die **Forscherin, -nen** researcher, investigator
der **Förster, -/**die **Försterin, -nen** forester
fort·setzen to continue
das **Foto, -s** photograph, picture
die **Frage, -n** question
fragen (nach) to ask (about)
der **Franzose, -n, -n/**die **Französin, -nen** French person
französisch French
die **Frau, -en** woman
frech smart, impudent
frei free
fremd strange, foreign
der/die **Fremde** (*adj. noun*) stranger
die **Fremdsprache, -n** foreign language
fressen (friβt), fraβ, gefressen to eat (of animals)
die **Freude, -n** joy, delight, happiness
freuen to make happy; **sich freuen (auf + *acc.*)** to look forward (to); **sich freuen (über + *acc.*)** to be happy (about)
der **Freund, -e/**die **Freundin, -nen** friend
freundlich friendly
die **Freundlichkeit** friendliness
der **Friede, -ns, -n** peace
der **Friedhof, ̈e** cemetery
frieren, fror, gefroren to freeze
frisch fresh
der **Friseur, -e/**die **Friseuse, -n** barber/hairdresser
froh (über + *acc.*) happy (about)

der **Frosch, ̈e** frog
früh early
das **Frühjahr, -e** spring
der **Frühling, -e** spring
das **Frühstück, -e** breakfast
fühlen to feel; **sich (wohl) fühlen** to feel (good)
führen to lead
der **Führerschein, -e** driver's license
die **Führung, -en** tour
der **Füller, -** ink pen
das **Fundbüro, -s** lost and found agency
funktionieren to work, function
für + *acc.* for
furchtbar terrible
sich fürchten (vor + *dat.*) to be afraid (of)
der **Fuβball** soccer
die **Fuβballmannschaft, -en** soccer team
die **Fuβballsaison, -s** soccer season
die **Fuβgängerzone, -n** pedestrian zone
füttern to feed

die **Gabel, -n** fork
die **Gänseblume, -n** daisy
ganz complete, total, whole
die **Garage, -n** garage
die **Garderobe, -n** (clothes) closet, wardrobe
der **Garten, ̈** garden
die **Gartenarbeit, -en** garden work
der **Gärtner, -/**die **Gärtnerin, -nen** gardener
der **Gast, ̈e** guest
die **Gastfamilie, -n** homestay family
der **Gastgeber, -/**die **Gastgeberin, -nen** host/hostess
der **Gastprofessor, -en/**die **Gastprofessorin, -nen** guest professor
das **Gebäude, -** building
geben (gibt), gab, gegeben to give; **es gibt + *acc.*** there is, there are

gebraucht used

die **Geburt, -en** birth

der **Geburtstag, -e** birthday; **zum Geburtstag** for (one's) birthday

das **Gebüsch, -e** bushes, shrubs

der **Gedanke, -ns, -n** thought

das **Gedicht, -e** poem

die **Geduld** patience

geduldig patient

die **Gefahr, -en** danger

gefährlich dangerous

gefallen (gefällt), gefiel, gefallen (*dat.*) to be pleasing to

das **Gefühl, -e** feeling, emotion

gegen + *acc.* against

die **Gegend, -en** area, region

gegensätzlich contrary, opposite

der **Gegenspieler, -/**die **Gegenspielerin, -nen** opponent

gegenüber + *dat.* across from, opposite

der **Gegner, -/**die **Gegnerin, -nen** opponent, adversary

das **Gehalt, ̈er** salary

das **Geheimnis, -se** secret

gehen, ging, ist gegangen to go

gehören (*dat.*) to belong to

gelaunt disposed, humored; **gut/schlecht gelaunt sein** to be in a good/bad mood

gelb yellow

das **Geld** money

der/die **Geliebte** (*adj. noun*) lover, beloved

gelingen, gelang, ist gelungen (*dat.*) to succeed

das **Gemüse, -** vegetable

genial ingenious

genießen, genoß, genossen to enjoy

genug enough

das **Gepäck** luggage

gepflegt well-groomed, cared for

gerade just

geraten (gerät), geriet, ist geraten (in + *acc.*) to get into

das **Geräusch, -e** noise

geringelt ringed

gern (lieber, liebst-) + *verb* to like to do something

gesamt entire, total

das **Geschäft, -e** store; business; deal

der **Geschäftsführer, -/**die **Geschäftsführerin, -nen** manager

die **Geschäftsleute** (*pl.*) business people

der **Geschäftsmann, ̈er/**die **Geschäftsfrau, -en** businessman/businesswoman

geschehen (geschieht), geschah, ist geschehen (*dat.*) to happen

das **Geschenk, -e** present

die **Geschichte, -n** story; history

geschickt coordinated

geschieden divorced

das **Geschirr** dishes

die **Geschwindigkeit, -en** speed

die **Geschwindigkeitsbegrenzung, -en** speed limit

die **Geschwister** (*pl.*) siblings, brothers and sisters

die **Gesellschaft, -en** society; company

das **Gesetz, -e** law

die **Gesichtsmaske, -n** face mask

gespalten divided

gesperrt closed

gestern yesterday

gestreßt stressed

gestrig yesterday

gesund (ü) healthy

die **Gesundheit** health

das **Getränk, -e** drink, beverage

die **Gewalt** force, violence

die **Gewerkschaft, -en** union

gewinnen, gewann, gewonnen to win

das **Gewitter, -** thunderstorm

sich gewöhnen (an + *acc.*) to become accustomed (to)

das **Gewürz, -e** spice

gießen, goß, gegossen to pour

giftig poisonous

die **Gitarre, -n** guitar

die **Gitarrenmusik** guitar music

das **Glas, ̈er** glass
glatt straight
der **Glaube, -ns** belief
glauben (*dat.*) to believe (a person);
  glauben (**an** + *acc.*) to believe (in)
gleich equal; soon
das **Gleichgewicht** balance
glitschig slippery
das **Glück** luck, good fortune
glücklich (**über** + *acc.*) happy
  (about)
glücklicherweise fortunately
das **Gold** gold
die **Goldmedaille, -n** gold medal
das **Golf** golf
gönnen to allow, grant; to not envy,
  not begrudge; to wish
der **Gott, ̈er** God
der **Graf, -en, -en**/die **Gräfin, -nen**
  count/countess
die **Grafik, -en** graphic
die **Grammatik** grammar
grammatikalisch grammatical
gratulieren (*dat.*) (**zu**)
  to congratulate (on)
grau gray
grell glaring, harsh, shrill
die **Grenze, -n** border
grenzen (**an** + *acc.*) to border (on)
(das) **Griechenland** Greece
griechisch Greek
die **Grippe, -n** flu, cold
grob (**ö**) uncouth, coarse
groß (**größer, größt-**) big
die **Größe, -n** size (clothing);
  magnitude
die **Großeltern** (*pl.*) grandparents
die **Großmutter, ̈** grandmother
die **Großstadt, ̈e** large city
grün green
der **Grund, ̈e** reason; **aus diesem**
  Grund for this reason
die **Grundmauer, -n** foundation wall
der **Grundsatz, ̈e** principle
das **Grundstück, -e** property, piece
  of land
die **Gruppe, -n** group

der **Gruß, ̈e** greeting
grüßen to greet
die **Gurke, -n** cucumber
gut (**besser, best-**) good
das **Gymnasium, die Gymnasien**
  German high school

das **Haar, -e** hair
der **Haarausfall** loss of hair
haargenau precisely, exactly
haben (**hat**), **hatte, gehabt** to have
der **Hafen, ̈** harbor
der **Hagel** hail
der **Halbkreis, -e** half circle
die **Hälfte, -n** half
halten (**hält**), **hielt, gehalten** to hold;
  halten von to think of, be of an
  opinion; (**jemand**) **halten für**
  to regard (someone) as; to take
  (someone) for
die **Haltestelle, -n** (bus) stop
die **Hand, ̈e** hand
handeln to act; **handeln von**
  to deal with, be about; **sich han-**
  deln um to concern, be a matter of
der **Händler, -**/die **Händlerin, -nen**
  dealer, trader
die **Handlung, -en** action; plot
die **Handschrift, -en** handwriting
die **Handtasche, -n** pocketbook,
  purse
das **Handtuch, ̈er** towel
hängen to hang (something) up
hängen, hing, gehangen to be
  hanging
hart (**ä**) hard; difficult
hassen to hate
häßlich ugly
der **Hauptbahnhof, ̈e** main train
  station
das **Hauptfach, ̈er** major (in
  college)
das **Hauptgericht, -e** main course
der **Hauptplatz, ̈e** main (market)
  square
die **Hauptstadt, ̈e** capital (city)
die **Hauptstraße, -n** main street

das **Haus, ⸚er** house; **nach Hause gehen** to go home; **zu Hause sein** to be at home

die **Hausarbeit, -en** housework; homework

das **Haushaltsgerät, -e** household utensil, household item

der **Hausmeister, -/**die **Hausmeisterin, -nen** caretaker

das **Haustier, -e** pet

die **Hauswand, ⸚e** wall of the house

das **Heft, -e** notebook

die **Heilquelle, -n** medicinal spring

die **Heimat, -en** native country, homeland

heiraten to marry

der **Heiratsantrag, ⸚e** marriage proposal; **einen Heiratsantrag machen** to propose marriage

heiser hoarse

heiß hot

heißen, hieß, geheißen to be called, be named

heizen to heat

die **Heizung, -en** heating

der **Held, -en, -en/**die **Heldin, -nen** hero

helfen (hilft), half, geholfen (*dat.*) to help

hell light; bright

das **Hemd, -en** shirt

herab·fallen (fällt herab), fiel herab, ist herabgefallen to fall down

heraus·bringen, brachte heraus, herausgebracht to bring out; to publish

heraus·finden, fand heraus, herausgefunden to find out, discover

heraus·geben (gibt heraus), gab heraus, herausgegeben to edit; to publish

der **Herausgeber, -/**die **Herausgeberin, -nen** publisher; editor

der **Herbst, -e** autumn, fall

der **Herr, -n, -en** master; gentleman; Mr.

her·stellen to produce, manufacture

herum around; about

herum·laufen (läuft herum), lief herum, ist herumgelaufen to walk around, walk about

herum·sitzen, saß herum, herumgesessen to sit around

herunter down

herunter·prasseln to patter down (rain or hail)

hervor·kommen, kam hervor, ist hervorgekommen to come out, come forth

hervorragend excellent

das **Herz, -ens, -en** heart

herzlich hearty; heartfelt

heute today

heutzutage nowadays

hier here

die **Hilfe, -n** help

das **Hilfsgut, ⸚er** relief freight; (*pl.*) relief supplies

hindern to prevent, hinder

das **Hindernis, -se** obstacle, hindrance

hin·fallen (fällt hin), fiel hin, ist hingefallen to fall down

sich **hin·legen** to lie down

hin·richten to execute

hinter + *acc./dat.* behind, in back of

hinunter down; below

hinunter·laufen (läuft hinunter), lief hinunter, ist hinuntergelaufen to run down

hinunter·tragen (trägt hinunter), trug hinunter, hinuntergetragen to carry down

hinzu·fügen to add, append

die **Hitze** heat

hoch (höher, höchst-) high

das **Hochhaus, ⸚er** skyscraper

der **Hochofen, ⸚** blast furnace

höchst highest; extreme

die **Hochzeit, -en** wedding

die **Hochzeitsparty, -s** wedding celebration

der **Hochzeitstag, -e** wedding
anniversary
hoffen (auf + *acc.*) to hope (for)
die **Hoffnung, -en** hope
die **Höhe, -n** height; **in Höhe von**
at a height of
der **Höhepunkt, -e** high point, climax
die **Höhle, -n** cave
holen to fetch, get
das **Holz, ̈er** wood
horchen (*dat.*) to obey
hören to hear
die **Hose, -n** pair of pants
der **Hoteltresor, -e** hotel safe
hübsch pretty
der **Hubschrauber, -** helicopter
das **Huhn, ̈er** chicken
der **Hund, -e** dog
der **Hunger** hunger
der **Hut, ̈e** hat

ideal ideal
die **Idee, -n** idea
die **Ideologie, -n** ideology
der **Idiot, -en, -en**/die **Idiotin, -nen**
idiot
immer always; **immer noch** still
in + *acc./dat.* in, into
indem (*sub. conj.*) by doing
(something)
(das) **Indien** India
der **Informatiker, -**/die
Informatikerin, -nen computer
programmer
informativ informative
informieren to inform
der **Ingenieur, -e**/die **Ingenieurin,
-nen** engineer
der **Inhalt, -e** content; contents
die **Innenstadt, ̈e** inner city, center
of the city
innerhalb + *gen.* within, inside
die **Insel, -n** island
installieren to install
das **Instrument, -e** instrument
intelligent intelligent
interessant interesting

das **Interesse, -n** interest; **Interesse
haben (an** + *dat.*) to be interested
(in)
interessieren to interest; **sich interessieren (für)** to be interested (in)
international international
die **Interpretation, -en** interpretation
der **Irak** Iraq
der **Iran** Iran
irgendwie somehow
irgendwo somewhere
sich irren to be mistaken
der **Irrtum, ̈er** error
(das) **Italien** Italy

die **Jacke, -n** jacket
das **Jahr, -e** year
jahrelang for years
der **Jahrestag, -e** anniversary
die **Jahreszeit, -en** season
das **Jahrhundert, -e** century
jährlich yearly
je . . . desto (*sub. conj.*) the . . . the
die **Jeans** (*pl.*) jeans
jed- each, every
jedesmal every time
jemals ever
jemand someone, somebody
jen- that
jetzt now
der **Job, -s** job
die **Jobsicherheit** job security
jodeln to yodel
joggen to jog
das **Journal, -e** journal; newspaper
jucken to itch
die **Jugend** youth
die **Jugendherberge, -n** youth
hostel
der/die **Jugendliche** (*adj. noun*)
young person
jung (ü) young
der **Junge, -n, -n** boy
die **Jury, -s** jury
der **Juwelenräuber, -**/die
Juwelenräuberin, -nen jewel
thief

der **Juwelier, -e**/die **Juwelierin, -nen**
  jeweler

der **Käfer, -** bug; VW beetle
der **Kaffee** coffee
die **Kaffeepause, -n** coffee break
der **Käfig, -e** cage
der **Kaiser, -**/die **Kaiserin, -nen**
  emperor/empress
das **Kalb, ̈er** calf
kalt (ä) cold
der **Kamerad, -en, -en**/die
  Kameradin, -nen comrade
der **Kamin, -e** fireplace
kämmen to comb
kämpfen to fight
(das) **Kanada** Canada
der **Kandidat, -en, -en**/die
  Kandidatin, -nen candidate
das **Kaninchen, -** rabbit
das **Kapitel, -** chapter
kaputt broken
die **Karnevalssaison** season of Mardi
  Gras or Fasching
die **Karotte, -n** carrot
die **Karte, -n** ticket
die **Kartoffel, -n** potato
die **Kasse, -n** checkout counter, cash
  register
die **Kassette, -n** cassette
der **Kassierer, -**/die **Kassiererin, -nen**
  cashier
die **Katastrophe, -n** catastrophe
der **Katholik, -en, -en**/die **Katholikin,**
  -nen Catholic person
das **Kätzchen, -** kitten
die **Katze, -n** cat
kaufen to buy
der **Kaufmann, ̈er**/die **Kauffrau, -en**
  salesman/saleswoman
kaum scarcely
der **Kellner, -**/die **Kellnerin, -nen**
  waiter/waitress
kennen, kannte, gekannt to know,
  be familiar with
kennen·lernen to become
  acquainted, get to know

kentern to capsize, heel over
der **Kilometer, -** kilometer
das **Kind, -er** child
das **Kinderbett, -en** baby crib
die **Kindheit** childhood
das **Kino, -s** movie theater
der **Kiosk, -e** kiosk
die **Kirche, -n** church
der **Kirchturm, ̈e** church steeple
die **Kirschtorte, -n** cherry torte
klagen to complain
klar clear
die **Klasse, -n** class
die **Klassenarbeit, -en** in-class exam
das **Klassenzimmer, -** classroom
die **Klausur, -en** examination
das **Klavier, -e** piano
die **Klavierstunde, -n** piano lesson
das **Kleid, -er** dress; (*pl.*) clothes
der **Kleiderschrank, ̈e** clothes
  closet
klein small
der **Kleinbus, -se** small bus
klemmen to get jammed
klettern (ist) to climb
der **Klient, -en, -en**/die **Klientin, -nen**
  client (of a lawyer)
das **Klima** climate
klingeln to ring
klingen, klang, geklungen
  to sound
klopfen to knock; **es klopft**
  there's a knock at the door
klug (ü) clever
die **Kneipe, -n** tavern, bar
das **Knie, -** knee
kochen to boil; to cook
der **Koffer, -** suitcase
der **Kollege, -n, -n**/die **Kollegin, -nen**
  colleague
kollidieren to collide
der **Kolonist, -en, -en**/die **Kolonistin,**
  -nen colonist, colonial settler
komisch strange; funny
kommen, kam, ist gekommen
  to come
kompetent competent

der **Komplex, -e** complex
kompliziert complicated
der **Komponist, -en, -en**/die
  Komponistin, -nen composer
der **Kompromiß, -(ss)e** compromise;
  einen Kompromiß schließen
  to find a compromise
die **Konferenz, -en** conference
der **König, -e**/die **Königin, -nen**
  king/queen
können (kann), konnte, gekonnt
  to be able to
die **Konsequenz, -en** consequence,
  result
konservativ conservative
die **Kontaktlinse, -n** contact lens
die **Kontrolle, -n** control; **außer**
  Kontrolle geraten to go out of
  control
kontrollieren to control
sich **konzentrieren (auf +** *acc.***)**
  to concentrate (on)
das **Konzert, -e** concert
die **Kopie, -n** copy
der **Kopf, ̈e** head
korrekt correct
korrigieren to correct
die **Kosten** (*pl.*) costs, expenses
kosten to cost
krank (ä) sick
das **Krankenhaus, ̈er** hospital
die **Krankenschwester, -n** nurse
der **Krankenwagen, -** ambulance
die **Krankheit, -en** illness, sickness
kratzen to scratch
die **Krawatte, -n** tie
die **Kreditkarte, -n** credit card
die **Kreuzfahrt, -en** cruise
die **Kreuzung, -en** intersection; **bei**
  Rot über die Kreuzung fahren
  to run a red light
das **Kreuzworträtsel, -** crossword
  puzzle
der **Krieg, -e** war
der **Kriminalkommissar, -e**/die
  Kriminalkommissarin, -nen
  criminal inspector

der **Kritiker, -/**die **Kritikerin, -nen**
  critic
kritisch critical
kritisieren to criticize
die **Küche, -n** kitchen
der **Kuchen, -** cake
der **Kugelschreiber, -** ballpoint pen
kühl cool
der **Kühlschrank, ̈e** refrigerator
der **Kuli, -s** ballpoint pen
die **Kultur, -en** culture
kulturell cultural
sich **kümmern (um)** to care (for),
  concern oneself (with)
der **Kunde, -n, -n**/die **Kundin, -nen**
  customer
die **Kunst, ̈e** art
der **Künstler, -/**die **Künstlerin, -nen**
  artist
das **Kunstmuseum, -museen** art
  museum
das **Kunstwerk, -e** work of art
die **Kur, -en** treatment, cure
der **Kurort, -e** health resort, spa
der **Kurs, -e** course
kurz (ü) short
küssen to kiss
die **Küste, -n** coast

lachen (über + *acc.*) to laugh (about)
laden (lädt), lud, geladen to load
der **Laden, ̈** shop, store
der **Ladendieb, -e**/die **Ladendiebin,**
  -nen shoplifter
das **Ladenschlußgesetz** German law
  regulating store closing time
die **Lage, -n** situation; condition
das **Lamm, ̈er** lamb
die **Lampe, -n** lamp
das **Land, ̈er** state; country; **auf**
  dem Land wohnen to live in the
  country
landen (ist) to land
die **Landkarte, -n** map
die **Landschaft, -en** landscape
die **Landstraße, -n** main road
lang (ä) long

langsam slow
langweilig boring
der **Lärm** noise
lassen (läßt), ließ, gelassen to let; to leave
der **Lastwagen, -** truck
das **Laub** foliage
laufen (läuft), lief, ist gelaufen to run
laut loud
das **Leben** life
leben to live
der **Lebenslauf, ⁻e** curriculum vitae
der **Lebkuchen** gingerbread
lecker delicious
ledig single, unmarried
leer empty
legen to put, lay
lehnen to lean
der **Lehrer, -/**die **Lehrerin, -nen** teacher
leicht easy; slightly
leid tun, tat, getan (*dat.*) to be sorry
leiden, litt, gelitten to suffer
leider unfortunately
leihen, lieh, geliehen to lend
die **Leine, -n** clothesline; leash
leise soft
sich **leisten** to afford
die **Leistung, -en** achievement
der **Leiter, -/**die **Leiterin, -nen** leader
die **Leiter, -n** ladder
der **Lektor, -en/**die **Lektorin, -nen** editor; reader
lernen to learn; to study
lesen (liest), las, gelesen to read
die **Lesung, -en** reading
letzt last
die **Leute** (*pl.*) people
liberal liberal
das **Licht, -er** light; **ans Licht kommen** to come to light
lieb dear
die **Liebe** love
lieben to love
lieber rather
der **Liebesbrief, -e** love letter

die **Liebesgeschichte, -n** love story
der **Liebeskummer** lover's grief
der **Liebhaber, -/**die **Liebhaberin, -nen** lover; admirer; amateur
die **Lieblingsjahreszeit, -en** favorite season of the year
der **Lieblingstag, -e** favorite day
das **Lied, -er** song
liefern to deliver
liegen, lag, gelegen to lie, be situated
lila pale violet
die **Literatur** literature
loben to praise
lockig curly
der **Löffel, -** spoon
der **Lohn, ⁻e** wages
lösen to solve
los·fahren (fährt los), fuhr los, ist losgefahren to drive away
los·lassen (läßt los), ließ los, losgelassen to let go
los·werden (wird los), wurde los, ist losgeworden to get rid of
die **Lösung, -en** solution
die **Lotterie, -n** lottery
das **Lotto, -s** lottery
der **Löwe, -n, -n** lion
die **Luft** air
der **Luftballon, -s** or **-e** balloon
die **Luftpost** airmail; **mit Luftpost** by airmail
lügen, log, gelogen to lie, tell a lie
die **Lust** pleasure, desire; **Lust haben** to feel like, be in the mood
lustig funny, amusing

machen to do, make
das **Mädchen, -** girl
der **Magen, ⁻** stomach
mähen to mow
der **Mais** corn
der **Makler, -/**die **Maklerin, -nen** broker, agent
das **Mal, -e** time; **zum (ersten) Mal** for the (first) time
mal once; **(zwei) mal** (two) times
malen to paint

der **Maler, -**/die **Malerin, -nen** painter

man one, you, they

manch- many a; (*pl.*) some

manch ein many a

manchmal sometimes

der **Mann, ¨-er** man

der **Mantel, ¨-** coat

das **Manuskript, -e** manuscript

das **Märchen, -** fairy tale

der **Marktplatz, ¨-e** marketplace

die **Maschine, -n** machine

die **Mathematik** mathematics

der **Mathematiker, -**/die **Mathematikerin, -nen** mathematician

die **Mauer, -n** wall

die **Maus, ¨-e** mouse

der **Mechaniker, -**/die **Mechanikerin, -nen** mechanic

das **Medikament, -e** medicine, drug

die **Medizin** science of medicine

mehr more

meiden, mied, gemieden to avoid

meinen to have the opinion; to mean

meinetwegen for all I care, as far as I'm concerned

die **Meinung, -en** opinion; **(meiner) Meinung nach** in (my) opinion

meistens usually, mostly

melden to announce

die **Mensa,** die **Mensen** student cafeteria

der **Mensch, -en, -en** human being

die **Menschenmenge, -n** crowd of people

das **Messer, -** knife

das **Meteor, -e** meteor

der **Meteorologe, -n, -n**/die **Meteorologin, -nen** meteorologist

der **Meter, -** meter

die **Methode, -n** method

mieten to rent

die **Mietwohnung, -en** rented apartment

der **Mikrowellengrill, -s** microwave

die **Milch** milk

die **Militärtruppe, -n** military unit

mindestens at least

die **Minute, -n** minute

miβdeuten to misinterpret

miβlingen, miβlang, ist miβlungen (*dat.*) to be unsuccessful at

das **Miβtrauen** mistrust

das **Miβverständnis, -se** misunderstanding

miβverstehen, miβverstand, miβverstanden to misunderstand

mit + *dat.* with

mit·arbeiten to work with

der **Mitarbeiter, -**/die **Mitarbeiterin, -nen** coworker

mit·bringen, brachte mit, mitgebracht to bring along

das **Mitglied, -er** member

mit·kommen, kam mit, ist mitgekommen to come along

das **Mitleid** pity, compassion

mit·nehmen (nimmt mit), nahm mit, mitgenommen to take along

mit·spielen to play with

der **Mittag, -e** noon

die **Mittagspause, -n** lunch hour, midday break

mit·teilen to communicate; to inform

die **Mitternacht** midnight

mittlerweile in the meantime

das **Möbel** furniture

das **Mobile, -s** mobile

möchten would like to

die **Modelleisenbahn** model train set

der **Moderator, -en**/die **Moderatorin, -nen** (TV) anchor, moderator

modern modern

mögen (mag), mochte, gemocht to like

möglich possible

die **Möglichkeit, -en** possibility

der **Moment, -e** moment

der **Monat, -e** month

monatlich monthly

der **Mond, -e** moon

der **Mord, -e** murder

der **Mörder, -/**die **Mörderin, -nen**
  murderer
der **Mordfall, ⁻e** murder case
morgen tomorrow
der **Morgen, -** morning
morgens in the morning
die **Moschee, -n** mosque
der **Motor, -en** motor
das **Motorrad, ⁻er** motorcycle
der **Mückenstich, -e** mosquito bite
müde tired
der **Müll** rubbish, trash
das **Museum,** die **Museen** museum
der **Museumsführer, -/**die
  Museumsführerin, -nen museum
  guide
die **Musik** music
der **Musiker, -/**die **Musikerin, -nen**
  musician
das **Musikinstrument, -e** musical
  instrument
der **Musikstudent, -en, -en/**die
  Musikstudentin, -nen music
  student
müssen (muβ), muβte, gemuβt
  to have to, must
die **Mutter, ⁻** mother
die **Muttersprache, -n** native language

nach + *dat.* after; to; according to
der **Nachbar, -n, -n/**die **Nachbarin,**
  -nen neighbor
die **Nachbarschaft, -en** neighbor-
  hood
nachdem (*sub. conj.*) after
nach·denken, dachte nach,
  nachgedacht (über + *acc.*)
  to think (about), to reflect (on)
nach·gehen, ging nach, ist
  nachgegangen to be slow (clock)
nachher afterwards
die **Nachhilfestunde, -n** private
  tutoring
nach·holen to make up, catch up
der **Nachmittag, -e** afternoon
der **Nachrichtensprecher, -/**die

Nachrichtensprecherin, -nen
  news broadcaster
nächst next
die **Nacht, ⁻e** night
der **Nachtisch, -e** dessert
der **Nachtklub, -s** nightclub
die **Nachtschicht, -en** night shift
das **Nachttier, -e** night animal
nah (näher, nächst-) close, near
die **Nähe** proximity; **in der Nähe**
  in the vicinity
der **Name, -ns, -n** name
nämlich namely; of course
naschen to snack
die **Nase, -n** nose
die **Natur** nature
neben + *acc./dat.* next to, beside
der **Neffe, -n, -n** nephew
negativ negative
nehmen (nimmt), nahm, genommen
  to take
nennen, nannte, genannt to name;
  to call
der **Neo-Faschist, -en, -en/**die **Neo-**
  Faschistin, -nen neofascist
der **Nerv, -en** nerve; **(mir) auf die**
  Nerven gehen to get on (my)
  nerves
nervös nervous
nett nice
neu new
die **Neuigkeit, -en** news, piece of
  news
das **Neujahr** New Year's (Day)
neulich recently
neutral neutral
nicht not
die **Nichte, -n** niece
nichts nothing
nie never
nieder·brennen, brannte nieder,
  niedergebrannt to burn down
die **Niederlande** (*pl.*) Netherlands
niedrig low
niemand nobody
noch still; **noch nicht** not yet
der **Norden** North

die **Nordsee** North Sea
normalerweise normally, usually
die **Note, -n** grade
nur only
nützlich useful, of use

ob (*sub. conj.*) whether
obgleich (*sub. conj.*) although
obdachlos homeless
oben above, at the top, upstairs
der **Oberarzt, ⸚e**/die **Oberärztin, -nen** head physician
das **Obst** fruit
obwohl (*sub. conj.*) although
oder (*coor. conj.*) or
der **Ofen, ⸚** oven
offiziell official
öffnen to open
oft (ö) often
ohne + *acc.* without
ohnmächtig unconscious
der **Ohrring, -e** earring
der **Olympiasieger, -/**die **Olympiasiegerin, -nen** Olympic champion
die **Oma, -s** grandma
der **Onkel, -** uncle
der **Opa, -s** grandpa
die **Operation, -en** operation
operieren to operate
das **Opernhaus, ⸚er** opera house
die **Opposition, -en** opposition
der **Optimismus** optimism
das **Orchester, -** orchestra
die **Organisation, -en** organization
der **Ort, -e** place
der **Osten** East
der **Osterhase, -n, -n** Easter bunny
die **Ostern** Easter
(das) **Österreich** Austria

paar: ein paar a few
das **Paar, -e** couple, pair
das **Paket, -e** package
die **Panne, -n** breakdown (car)
das **Panorama,** die **Panoramen** panorama

der **Papagei, -en** parrot
das **Papier** paper
der **Papierdrache, -n, -n** paper kite
der **Park, -s** park
parken to park
die **Partei, -en** political party
die **Party, -s** party
der **Paß, ⸚(ss)e** passport
der **Passagier, -e**/die **Passagierin, -nen** passenger
passen (*dat.*) to fit
passieren (ist) (*dat.*) to happen
der **Patient, -en, -en**/ die **Patientin, -nen** patient
der **Patriotismus** patriotism
die **Pause, -n** pause, break
die **Pension, -en** retirement; small hotel
pensioniert retired
der **Persische Golf** Persian Gulf
die **Person, -en** person
die **Perücke, -n** wig
der **Pfadfinder, -/**die **Pfadfinderin, -nen** Boy Scout/Girl Scout
der **Pfeffer** pepper
das **Pferd, -e** horse
pflanzen to plant
pflücken to pluck, pick
der **Pförtner, -/**die **Pförtnerin, -nen** doorkeeper
die **Pfote, -n** paw
der **Philosoph, -en, -en**/die **Philosophin, -nen** philosopher
das **Photo, -s** photograph, picture
der **Photograph, -en, -en**/die **Photographin, -nen** photographer
der **Pianist, -en, -en**/die **Pianistin, -nen** pianist
das **Picknick, -s** or **-e** picnic
der **Pilot, -en, -en**/die **Pilotin, -nen** pilot
der **Pilz, -e** mushroom
die **Pistole, -n** pistol
der **Plan, ⸚e** plan
planen to plan
das **Platin** platinum
platt flat, level

Plattdeutsch   North German dialect
der **Plattenspieler, -**   record player
der **Platz, ⁻e**   seat; place;   **Platz nehmen**   to take one's seat
das **Plätzchen, -**   cookie
plaudern   to chat, gossip
plötzlich   suddenly
die **Politik**   politics
der **Politiker, -/**die **Politikerin, -nen** politician
die **Politikwissenschaft**   political science
politisch   political
die **Polizei**   police
der **Polizist, -en, -en/**die **Polizistin, -nen**   police officer
Pommes frites (*pl.*)   french fries
populär   popular
die **Pornographie**   pornography
positiv   positive
die **Post**   mail
der **Postbote, -n, -n/**die **Postbotin, -nen**   mail carrier
die **Postkarte, -n**   postcard
der **Präsident, -en, -en/**die **Präsidentin, -nen**   president
der **Präsidentschaftskandidat, -en, -en/**die **Präsidentschaftskandidatin, -nen**   candidate for president
der **Preis, -e**   prize; price
die **Presse, -n**   the press
privat   private
die **Probe, -n**   rehearsal
probieren   to try; to test
das **Problem, -e**   problem
problematisch   problematic
die **Produktivität, -en**   productivity
produzieren   to produce
der **Professor, -en/**die **Professorin, -nen**   professor
das **Programm, -e**   program (TV) (political)
das **Projekt, -e**   project
das **Protokoll, -e**   record
die **Prüfung, -en**   test
der **Psychiater, -/**die **Psychiaterin, -nen**   psychiatrist

der **Psycholog, -en, -en/**die **Psychologin, -nen**   psychologist
die **Psychologie**   psychology
das **Publikum**   audience, public
der **Pullover, -**   sweater, pullover
der **Punkt, -e**   point
pünktlich   punctual
putzen   to clean

das **Quartal, -e**   quarter (of a year)

der **Radfahrer, -/**die **Radfahrerin, -nen**   bike rider
das **Radio, -s**   radio
der **Rasen**   lawn;   **den Rasen mähen** to mow the lawn
der **Rasenmäher, -**   lawn mower
rasieren   to shave
der **Rat**   advice
raten (rät), riet, geraten (*dat.*) to advise
das **Rathaus, ⁻er**   city hall
das **Rätsel, -**   puzzle
der **Räuber, -/**die **Räuberin, -nen** robber
rauchen   to smoke
der **Raum, ⁻e**   room
räumen   to clean up, put away; to clear away, remove
reagieren (auf + *acc.*)   to react (to)
realistisch   realistic
die **Rechenaufgabe, -n**   math problem
rechnen   to calculate
die **Rechnung, -en**   bill
recht: recht haben   to be right;   **das ist (mir) recht**   that's OK with (me)
das **Recht, -e**   right; law
rechts: rechts fahren   to drive on the right
der **Rechtsanwalt, ⁻e/**die **Rechtsanwältin, -nen**   lawyer
rechtzeitig   promptly, on time
recyclen   to recycle
reden   to speak
der **Redner, -/**die **Rednerin, -nen** speaker

regeln   to regulate, put in order
der **Regen**   rain
der **Regenmantel, ⸚**   raincoat
der **Regenschirm, -e**   umbrella
der **Regenwald, ⸚er**   rain forest
die **Regierung, -en**   government
der **Regisseur, -e**/die **Regisseurin,
   -nen**   producer
reich   rich
reichen   to pass, reach
der **Reifen, -**   tire
die **Reihe, -n**   row; **in der (ersten)
   Reihe**   in the (first) row
die **Reise, -n**   trip
das **Reisebüro, -s**   travel agency
der **Reiseleiter, -**/die **Reiseleiterin,
   -nen**   travel guide
reisen (ist)   to travel
der **Reisepaß, ⸚(ss)e**   passport
der **Reisescheck, -s**   traveler's
   checks
der **Reiter, -**/die **Reiterin, -nen**
   (horse) rider
reizend   charming
der **Rektor, -en**/die **Rektorin, -nen**
   school principal
die **Religion, -en**   religion
rennen, rannte, ist gerannt   to run
renoviert   renovated
reparieren   to repair
der **Reporter, -**/die **Reporterin, -nen**
   reporter
die **Reservierung, -en**   reservation
der **Respekt**   respect
das **Restaurant, -s**   restaurant
der **Restaurator, -en**/die
   Restauratorin, -nen   restorer (of
   art, buildings)
restlich   remaining
das **Resultat, -e**   result
retten   to save
die **Rezession, -en**   recession
der **Rhein**   Rhine (river)
der **Rhythmus**   rhythm
der **Richter, -**/die **Richterin, -nen**
   judge
richtig   correct, right

riechen, roch, gerochen (nach)
   to smell (of, like)
riesengroß   gigantic
riesig   gigantic, vast
das **Rindfleisch**   beef
der **Ring, -e**   ring
der **Rock, ⸚e**   skirt
der **Rockmusiker, -**/die
   Rockmusikerin, -nen   rock
   musician
rollen   to roll
der **Roman, -e**   novel
die **Rose, -n**   rose
rot (o or ö)   red
rothaarig   red-haired
der **Rotwein**   red wine
die **Ruhe**   peace; **laß mich in Ruhe**
   leave me alone
ruhig   calm, quiet
(das) **Rumänien**   Rumania
rund   round
russisch   Russian

die **Sache, -n**   thing
die **Saison, -s**   season
der **Salat, -e**   salad
das **Salz**   salt
salzig   salty
sammeln   to collect
der **Sammler, -**/die **Sammlerin, -nen**
   collector
der **Sandkasten, -**   sandbox
der **Sänger, -**/die **Sängerin, -nen**
   singer
satt   satiated, full
der **Satz, ⸚e**   sentence
sauber   clean
sauber·machen   to clean
das **Schach**   chess
schädigen   to damage
der **Schäferhund, -e**   sheepdog
schaffen   to accomplish, manage,
   make do
der **Schal, -e**   shawl, scarf
die **Schallplatte, -n**   record
sich schämen (über + *acc.*)   to be
   ashamed (about)

scharf (ä)   sharp, hot
schätzen   to value, appreciate;
   to guess
schauen   to look
das **Schauspiel, -e**   play
der **Schauspieler, -/**die
   Schauspielerin, -nen   actor/actress
scheinen, schien, geschienen
   to shine; to appear
schenken   to give as a gift
die **Schere, -n**   pair of scissors
der **Scherz, -e**   joke
schicken   to send
das **Schiff, -e**   ship
der/die **Schizophrene** (*adj. noun*)
   schizophrenic person
schlafen (schläft), schlief, geschlafen
   to sleep
die **Schlaftablette, -n**   sleeping pill
schlagen (schlägt), schlug, geschlagen
   to hit, strike; to defeat
die **Schlägerei, -en**   brawl, fight
die **Schlange, -n**   snake; line;   **sich in
   die Schlange stellen**   to get in line
schlank   slim, slender
schlecht   bad
schließen, schloß, geschlossen
   to close
der **Schlitten, -**   sled;   **Schlitten
   fahren**   to go sledding
das **Schloß, ¨(ss)er**   castle
der **Schluß, ¨(ss)e**   conclusion;
   Schluß machen   to end, call off
der **Schlüssel, -**   key
schmecken (*dat.*)   to taste
schminken   to put on makeup
der **Schmuck, -e**   jewelry; ornament
die **Schmucksache, -n**   piece of
   jewelry; ornament
schmutzig   dirty
der **Schnee**   snow
schneiden, schnitt, geschnitten
   to cut
schnell   fast
der **Schnellzug, ¨e**   express train
das **Schnitzel**   cutlet
schockiert   shocked

die **Schokolade, -n**   chocolate
schon   already
schön   pretty, beautiful
der **Schrank, ¨e**   closet
schrecklich   terrible
schreiben, schrieb, geschrieben
   (**an** + *acc.*)   to write (to)
die **Schreibmaschine, -n**   typewriter
der **Schreibtisch, -e**   desk
schreien, schrie, geschrie(e)n   to cry
   out, scream
die **Schrift, -en**   handwriting; print
der **Schriftsteller, -/**die
   Schriftstellerin, -nen   writer,
   author
der **Schuh, -e**   shoe
die **Schuld, -en**   debt; guilt
schulden   to owe
die **Schule, -n**   school
der **Schüler, -/**die **Schülerin, -nen**
   pupil
die **Schulzeit**   school years
schütteln   to shake
schützen   to protect
schwach (ä)   weak
schwanger   pregnant
der **Schwanz, ¨e**   tail
schwarz (ä)   black
der **Schwarzfahrer, -/**die
   Schwarzfahrerin, -nen   rider
   without a ticket
der/die **Schwarzhaarige** (*adj. noun*)
   black-haired person
die **Schweiz**   Switzerland
der **Schweizer, -/**die **Schweizerin, -nen**
   Swiss person
schwer   difficult; heavy
die **Schwester, -n**   sister
die **Schwiegereltern** (*pl.*)   parents-
   in-law
die **Schwiegermutter, ¨**   mother-
   in-law
der **Schwiegervater, ¨**   father-in-law
schwierig   difficult
die **Schwierigkeit, -en**   difficulty
das **Schwimmbad, ¨er**   swimming
   pool

schwimmen, schwamm, ist geschwommen to swim
der **See, -n** lake
die **See, -n** ocean, sea
das **Segelboot, -e** sailboat
segeln to sail
die **Segeltour, -en** sailing trip
der **Segler, -/**die **Seglerin, -nen** person who sails
sehen (sieht), sah, gesehen to see
die **Sehenswürdigkeit, -en** tourist attraction, object worth seeing
sich sehnen (nach) to long (for)
die **Sehnsucht, ⁓e** longing, yearning; **Sehnsucht haben (nach)** to have a longing (for)
sehr very
die **Seife, -n** soap
sein (ist), war, ist gewesen to be
seit + *dat.* since, for (with time)
seit/seitdem (*sub. conj.*) since (the time that)
seitdem since then
die **Seite, -n** side
der **Sekretär, -e/**die **Sekretärin, -nen** secretary
der **Sekt** champagne
die **Sekunde, -n** second
selbständig independent
der **Selbstmörder, -/**die **Selbstmörderin, -nen** suicide (person)
selten seldom
seltsam strange
das **Semester, -** semester
das **Seminar, -e** seminar
die **Seminararbeit, -en** seminar paper
sentimental sentimental
servieren to serve
der **Sessel, -** armchair
setzen to put, set; **sich setzen** to sit down
sicher safe; certain
siegen to win, be victorious
das **Silber** silver
die **Sinfonie, -n** symphony

die **Sirene, -n** siren
die **Situation, -en** situation
sitzen, saβ, gesessen to be sitting
der **Sitzplatz, ⁓e** seat
der **Skandal, -e** scandal
Ski laufen (läuft), lief, ist gelaufen to go skiing
so ein- such a
so . . . wie as . . . as
sobald (*sub. conj.*) as soon as
sofort immediately
sogar even
der **Sohn, ⁓e** son
solange (*sub. conj.*) as long as
solch- such
solch ein- such a
der **Soldat, -en, -en/**die **Soldatin, -nen** soldier
sollen to be supposed to
der **Sommer, -** summer
die **Sonne, -n** sun
der **Sonnenbrand, ⁓e** sunburn
sonst otherwise
die **Sopranistin, -nen** soprano
die **Sorge, -n** care; sorrow; **sich Sorgen machen (um)** to worry (about), be concerned (about)
sorgfältig careful
die **Soβe, -n** gravy; sauce
der **Sozialismus** socialism
spanisch Spanish
spannend gripping, thrilling
sparen to save
der **Spaβ** fun; **es macht (mir) Spaβ** that's fun to (me), I enjoy it
spät late
spazieren (ist) to walk
spazieren·führen to take on a walk
spazieren·gehen, ging spazieren, ist spazierengegangen to go on a walk
der **Spaziergang, ⁓e** walk
die **Speisekarte, -n** menu
der **Spezialist, -en, -en/**die **Spezialistin, -nen** specialist
die **Spezialität, -en** specialty
der **Spiegel, -** mirror

das **Spiel, -e**   game
spielen   to play
das **Spielfeld, -er**   playing field
die **Spielregel, -n**   playing rule, rule of the game
das **Spielzeug, -e**   plaything, toy
die **Spinne, -n**   spider
der **Spion, -e**/die **Spionin, -nen**   spy
die **Spitze, -n**   top; point
der **Sport**   sport;   **Sport treiben** to play sports
die **Sportart, -en**   specific type of sports
der **Sportler, -**/die **Sportlerin, -nen** athlete
der **Sportwagen, -**   sports car
das **Sportzentrum, -zentren**   sports center
die **Sprache, -n**   language
sprechen (spricht), sprach, gesprochen (über + *acc.*)   to speak (about)
der **Sprecher, -**/die **Sprecherin, -nen** speaker
spülen   to wash dishes
der **Staat, -en**   state; country
die **Stadt, ¨e**   city
stadtbekannt   known citywide
der **Stadtplan, ¨e**   city map
die **Stahlindustrie, -n**   steel industry
ständig   constant
stark (ä)   strong
starten   to start
die **Statistik, -en**   statistics
statt + *gen.*   instead of
statt·finden, fand statt, stattgefunden to take place
stehen, stand, gestanden   to stand
stehen·bleiben, blieb stehen, ist stehengeblieben   to stop
stehlen (stiehlt), stahl, gestohlen to steal
steigen, stieg, ist gestiegen   to climb, go up
der **Stein, -e**   stone
die **Stelle, -n**   job; position;   **an (deiner) Stelle**   in (your) position

stellen   to put, place;   **in Frage stellen**   to question
sterben (stirbt), starb, ist gestorben to die
die **Stereoanlage, -n**   stereo
steril   sterile
das **Steuer, -**   steering wheel
die **Steuer, -n**   tax
der **Steuerberater, -**/die **Steuerberaterin, -nen**   accountant, tax consultant
der **Stift, -e**   pencil
still   quiet, still
die **Stimme, -n**   voice
stimmen   to be correct
das **Stipendium, -ien**   scholarship
der **Stock**, die **Stockwerke**   story (of a house)
stolz   proud
stören   to disturb
der **Strand, ¨e**   beach
die **Straße, -n**   street
die **Straßenbahn, -en**   streetcar
der **Straßenlärm**   street noise
der **Straßenmarkt, ¨e**   street market
die **Straßenseite, -n**   side of the street
streicheln   to pet
streichen, strich, gestrichen   to paint; to spread (on bread)
der **Streit, -e**   fight, quarrel
streiten, stritt, gestritten   to fight, quarrel
der **Streß**   stress
stricken   to knit
der **Strom, ¨e**   stream; electrical current
das **Stück, -e**   piece
der **Student, -en, -en**/die **Studentin, -nen**   student
die **Studentenorganisation, -en** student organization
die **Studentenunruhe, -n**   student unrest
die **Studienzeit, -en**   college years
studieren   to study
das **Studium**   university education
der **Stuhl, ¨e**   chair

die **Stunde, -n** hour
der **Sturm, ⸚e** storm
suchen to look for, seek
der **Süden** South
die **Supermacht, ⸚e** superpower
der **Supermarkt, ⸚e** supermarket
die **Suppe, -n** soup
süß sweet
die **Süßigkeiten** (*pl.*) sweets
Sylvester (or **Silvester**) New Year's Eve
sympathisch likable

die **Tablette, -n** tablet, pill
die **Tafel, -n** blackboard
der **Tag, -e** day
täglich daily
talentiert talented
der **Talisman, -e** charm, talisman
der **Tannenbaum, ⸚e** Christmas tree
die **Tante, -n** aunt
tanzen to dance
das **Tanzfest, -e** dance festival
tapezieren to wallpaper
die **Tasche, -n** pocket; purse
die **Tasse, -n** cup
der **Täter, -/**die **Täterin, -nen** perpetrator
die **Tätigkeit, -en** activity
der **Tatort, -e** site of the deed, place where something is done
die **Tatsache, -n** fact
der **Taxifahrer, -/**die **Taxifahrerin, -nen** taxi driver
die **Technik** technology
der **Techniker, -/**die **Technikerin, -nen** technician, engineer
der **Tee** tea
der **Teil, -e** part
teilen to divide
teil·nehmen (nimmt teil), nahm teil, teilgenommen (an + *dat.***)** to participate (in)
das **Telefon, -e** telephone
der **Telefonanruf, -e** telephone call

telefonieren to telephone
der **Telefonist, -en, -en/**die **Telefonistin, -nen** phone operator
die **Telefonnummer, -n** telephone number
die **Telefonzelle, -n** telephone booth
die **Temperatur, -en** temperature
das **Tennis** tennis
der **Tennisschläger, -** tennis racket
der **Tenor, ⸚e** tenor
der **Teppich, -e** rug, carpet
der **Termin, -e** appointment; deadline
die **Terrasse, -n** terrace, balcony
der **Test, -s** test
teuer expensive
der **Teufel, -** devil
der **Text, -e** text
das **Theater, -** theater
die **Theatersaison, -s** theater season
das **Theaterstück, -e** theater piece, drama
die **Theke, -n** counter; bar counter
das **Thema,** die **Themen** theme, topic
die **Theorie, -n** theory
das **Thermometer, -** thermometer
ticken to tick
tief deep
der **Tiefseetaucher, -/**die **Tiefseetaucherin, -nen** deep-sea diver
das **Tier, -e** animal
der **Tierarzt, ⸚e/**die **Tierärztin, -nen** veterinarian
das **Tierheim, -e** animal shelter
der **Tip, -s** tip, advice
tippen to type
der **Tisch, -e** table
der **Tischler, -/**die **Tischlerin, -nen** carpenter
die **Tochter, ⸚** daughter
der **Tod** death
tödlich deadly
toll great, fantastic
die **Tomate, -n** tomato
das **Tor, -e** gate; goal (in a game)
der **Tor, -en, -en/**die **Törin, -nen** fool
tot dead

total   total, entire
der **Totalschaden**   total loss, damage
  beyond repair
töten   to kill
der **Tourist, -en, -en/**die **Touristin,
  -nen**   tourist
tragen (trägt), trug, getragen
  to carry; to wear
der **Trainer, -/**die **Trainerin, -nen**
  trainer, coach
trainieren   to train, go into training
der **Traktor, -en**   tractor
die **Träne, -n**   tear
trauen (*dat.*)   to trust
träumen   to dream
die **Traumrolle, -n**   dream role, role
  of a lifetime
traurig   sad
treffen (trifft), traf, getroffen
  to meet; to affect
treiben, trieb, getrieben   to push; to
  engage in;   **Sport treiben**   to do
  sports
die **Treppe, -n**   stairs
der **Tresor, -e**   treasury; safe, vault
treten (tritt), trat, ist getreten
  to step
treu   true, faithful
trinken, trank, getrunken   to drink
das **Trinkgeld, -er**   gratuity, tip
trocken   dry
tröpfeln   to drip, fall in drops
trotz + *gen.*   in spite of
trotzdem   in spite of that,
  nevertheless
tun, tat, getan   to do
die **Tür, -en**   door
die **Türkei**   Turkey
die **Tüte, -n**   bag
typisch   typical

übel   bad, evil;   **übel nehmen**
  to take amiss, resent
üben   to practice
über + *acc./dat.*   over, above
überall   everywhere
überein·stimmen   to agree with

der **Übergriff, -e**   encroachment,
  infringement
überhaupt   at all; generally
übernachten   to stay overnight
überragend   overlooking; towering
  above
die **Überraschung, -en**   surprise
übersetzen   to translate
übertreiben, übertrieb, übertrieben
  to exaggerate
überwinden, überwand, überwunden
  to overcome
überzeugen   to persuade, convince
übrig   left over, remaining
die **Übung, -en**   exercise, practice
die **Uhr, -en**   clock
der/die **Ultrakonservative** (*adj. noun*)
  ultraconservative person
um + *acc.*   around; at
um·bauen   to remodel, reconstruct
**um·fallen (fällt um), fiel um, ist
  umgefallen**   to fall over
die **Umgebung, -en**   surroundings
um·sägen   to saw down
umständlich   involved; troublesome
um·steigen, stieg um, ist umgestiegen
  to change (trains)
der **Umweg, -e**   detour
um·ziehen, zog um, umgezogen   to
  change clothes;   **um·ziehen (ist)**
  to move (change residence)
unausstehlich   unbearable; hateful
unbedingt   absolutely, without
  question
unbegreiflich   incomprehensible
unbegrenzt   unlimited
unbeliebt   unpopular
unbezahlbar   priceless
und (*coor. conj.*)   and
unehrlich   dishonest
unentbehrlich   indispensable
unerfolgreich   unsuccessful
der **Unfall, ̈e**   accident
die **Unfallstelle, -n**   accident site
ungeduldig   impatient
ungeheuer   monstrous, huge;
  extremely

ungenau inexact
ungenügend insufficient
ungewiß uncertain
ungewöhnlich unusual
unglaublich unbelievable
unglücklich unhappy
ungültig invalid
die **Universität, -en** university
unmöglich impossible
unordentlich messy
unrealistisch unrealistic
unruhig uneasy, troubled
die **Unschuld** innocence
unschuldig innocent
unten downstairs; at the bottom
unter + *acc./dat.* under
**unterbrechen (unterbricht), unter-
brach, unterbrochen** to interrupt
**unterhalten (unterhält), unterhielt,
unterhalten** to entertain, amuse;
sich unterhalten (über + acc.)
to talk with someone (about)
**unternehmen (unternimmt), unter-
nahm, unternommen** to under-
take
der **Unterricht** instruction
**unterschreiben, unterschrieb,
unterschrieben** to sign
unterstützen to support
untersuchen to examine, investigate
unverständlich unintelligible,
incomprehensible
unvorsichtig careless
das **Unwetter** violent storm
unzerstört not destroyed
der **Urlaub, -e** vacation
die **Ursache, -n** reason, cause
die **USA** (*pl.*) United States of
America

die **Vase, -n** vase
der **Vater, ⸚** father
die **Verabredung, -en** meeting,
date
sich verabschieden to say good-bye
veraltet old, obsolete
verantwortlich responsible

die **Verantwortung, -en**
responsibility
verärgert angry, irritated
verbieten, verbot, verboten to forbid
verbrennen, verbrannte, verbrannt
to burn
verbringen, verbrachte, verbracht
to spend (time)
der **Verdacht** suspicion
verdienen to earn
der **Verein, -e** club
vereinigen to unite, join
vereinigt united, unified
die **Vereinigten Staaten** (*pl.*) United
States
vereint united
die **Vereinten Nationen** (*pl.*) United
Nations
die **Vergangenheit, -en** past
vergeben (vergibt), vergab, vergeben
to forgive
**vergessen (vergißt), vergaß,
vergessen** to forget
vergleichen, verglich, verglichen
to compare
verhaften to arrest
verhandeln to negotiate
die **Verhandlung, -en** negotiation
verheiratet married; **verheiratet
sein mit** to be married to
der **Verkäufer, -/die Verkäuferin,
-nen** salesperson
der **Verkehr** traffic
verlassen (verläßt), verließ, verlassen
to leave, depart; **sich verlassen
(auf** + *acc.*) to depend (on)
verletzen to injure
verliebt in love; **verliebt sein in** +
acc. to be in love with
verlieren, verlor, verloren to lose
verloben to get engaged
**verloren·gehen, ging verloren, ist
verlorengegangen** to become lost
vermeiden, vermied, vermieden
to avoid
vermissen to miss (a person)
das **Vermögen** wealth, fortune

veröffentlichen   to publish

verpassen   to miss

verraten (verrät), verriet, verraten   to betray, disclose

verreisen (ist)   to set out on a journey

verrostet   rusted

verrückt   crazy;   **verrückt sein auf + acc.**   to be crazy about

verschieden   different

verschlossen   locked; closed, taciturn

sich verschlucken   to swallow the wrong way, choke

verschönern   to make pretty

verschreiben, verschrieb, verschrieben   to prescribe

verschütten   to spill

versichern   to assure, make certain

versöhnen   to make up, reconcile

sich verspäten   to be late

die **Verspätung, -en**   delay, lateness

verspielen   to lose in betting

versprechen (verspricht), versprach, versprochen   to promise

verstecken   to hide

verstehen, verstand, verstanden   to understand

der **Versuch, -e**   experiment, attempt

der **Vertrag, ⁻e**   contract; treaty

das **Vertrauen**   trust, confidence

vertrauen (*dat.*)   to trust

der **Vertrauenslehrer, -/**die **Vertrauenslehrerin, -nen**   academic adviser

verunglücken   to have an accident

verurteilen   to condemn, convict

verwandt   related;   **verwandt sein mit**   to be related to

der/die **Verwandte** (*adj. noun*)   relative

die **Videokamera, -s**   video camera

der **Videorecorder, -**   video recorder

viel (mehr, meist-)   much, a lot

vieles   much, a lot

die **Villa,** die **Villen**   villa, country home

der **Vogel, ⁻**   bird

vollenden   to complete

vollkommen   perfect, complete

von + *dat.*   from; by

vor + *acc./dat.*   in front of, before; ago;   **vor kurzem**   a little while ago

voran·rennen, rannte voran, ist vorangerannt   to run ahead of, run faster than

vor·bereiten   to prepare

die **Vorderpfote, -n**   front paw

vor·fahren (fährt vor), fuhr vor, ist vorgefahren   to overtake

die **Vorfahrt**   right-of-way

der **Vorfall, ⁻e**   incident, occurrence

vor·gehen, ging vor, ist vorgegangen   to be fast (clock)

vorgestern   day before yesterday

vor·haben (hat vor), hatte vor, vorgehabt   to plan, intend

der **Vorhang, ⁻e**   curtain

vorher   beforehand

vorig   previous, former

vor·lesen (liest vor), las vor, vorgelesen   to read out loud; to lecture

die **Vorlesung, -en**   lecture

der **Vormittag, -e**   morning

vornehm   formal, elegant

der **Vorschlag, ⁻e**   suggestion, proposal

vor·schlagen (schlägt vor), schlug vor, vorgeschlagen   to propose, suggest

vorsichtig   careful

vor·stellen   to introduce;   **sich vor·stellen**   to imagine

die **Vorstellung, -en**   performance; introduction; imagination

vor·tanzen   to demonstrate a dance

der **Vorteil, -e**   advantage

der **Vortrag, ⁻e**   lecture

wach·bleiben, blieb wach, ist wachgeblieben   to stay awake

wachsen (wächst), wuchs, ist gewachsen   to grow

der **Waffenstillstand, ⁻e**   armistice

der **Wagen, -** car
wagen to dare
wählen to choose; to vote
das **Wahlrecht** right to vote
während + *gen.* during; (*sub. conj.*) while, during; whereas
die **Wahrheit** truth
wahrscheinlich probably
der **Wald, "er** forest
die **Wand, "e** wall
der **Wanderer, -/die Wanderin, -nen** hiker
wandern (ist) to hike
die **Wanderung, -en** hike
der **Wanderweg, -e** hiking path
die **Wange, -n** cheek
wann when
die **Ware, -n** article; (*pl.*) goods, merchandise
warm (ä) warm
warnen to warn
die **Warnung, -en** warning
warten (auf + *acc.*) to wait (for)
warum why
was für (ein) what kind of (a)
was what
der **Waschbär, -en, -en** raccoon
das **Waschbecken, -** sink
die **Wäsche** laundry
waschen (wäscht), wusch, gewaschen to wash
die **Wäscherei, -en** laundromat
das **Wasser** water
der **Wasserhahn, "e** faucet
die **Watte, -n** cotton
wechseln to change
der **Wecker, -** alarm clock; **den Wecker stellen** to set the alarm
der **Weg, -e** path, way, road
wegen + *gen.* because of
weg·gehen, ging weg, ist weggegangen to go away
weg·werfen (wirft weg), warf weg, weggeworfen to throw away
weh tun, tat weh, weh getan (*dat.*) to hurt
weich soft

Weihnachten Christmas; **zu Weihnachten** at Christmas
der **Weihnachtsschmuck, -e** Christmas ornament
weil (*sub. conj.*) because
der **Wein, -e** wine
weinen to cry
das **Weingebiet, -e** wine area
der **Weinkeller, -** wine cellar
weiß white
weit far
die **Weite, -n** distance
weiter further; additional
welch- which
die **Welt, -en** world
weltbekannt world-known
der **Weltfriede, -ns, -n** world peace
der **Weltkrieg, -e** world war
die **Weltreise, -n** trip around the world
das **Weltwunder, -** wonder of the world
sich wenden, wandte, gewandt (**an** + *acc.*) to turn (to)
wenig little
wenn (*sub. conj.*) when, whenever, if
wer who
werden (wird), wurde, ist geworden to become, get
werfen (wirft), warf, geworfen to throw
das **Werk, -e** book, work; factory
die **Werkstatt, "e** workshop, place of work
wert worth, of value to
wertvoll valuable
wesentlich significant, substantial
wessen whose
der **Westen** West
wetten to bet
das **Wetter** weather
wichtig important
widersprechen (widerspricht), widersprach, widersprochen (*dat.*) to contradict
widmen to dedicate

wie how; as
wieder again
wiederholen to make up; to repeat
**wieder·sehen (sieht wieder), sah
  wieder, wiedergesehen** to see
  again
das **Wiegenlied, -er** lullaby
die **Wiese, -n** field, meadow
wieviel how much; **wie viele**
  how many
der **Wille, -ns, -n** will
willkommen welcome
der **Wind, -e** wind
winken to wave
der **Winter, -** winter
wirklich really
wirtschaftlich economic
die **Wirtschaftswissenschaften** (*pl.*)
  economics
das **Wirtschaftswunder, -** economic
  miracle
wissen (weiβ), wuβte, gewuβt
  to know as a fact
der **Wissenschaftler, -/**die
  Wissenschaftlerin, -nen scientist
der **Witwer, -/**die **Witwe, -n**
  widower/widow
der **Witz, -e** joke
wo where
die **Woche, -n** week
das **Wochenende, -n** weekend
wochenlang for weeks
der **Wochentag, -e** weekday
wöchentlich weekly
wohl probably; well, good
das **Wohl** health, well-being,
  welfare
wohnen to live
das **Wohnhaus, ⁻er** house
die **Wohnung, -en** apartment
der **Wohnwagen, -** trailer home
die **Wolke, -n** cloud
wollen (will), wollte, gewollt to want
  to, intend to
das **Wort, -e** connected word
das **Wort, ⁻er** individual word

das **Wörterbuch, ⁻er** dictionary
wunderbar wonderful
sich wundern (über + *acc.*) to be
  surprised (about)
wunderschön wonderfully beautiful,
  very beautiful
der **Wunsch, ⁻e** wish
wünschen to wish
würzig spicy
die **Wüste, -n** desert

die **Zahl, -en** number
zahlen to pay for
zählen to count
die **Zahlenkombination, -en**
  combination (of a safe)
der **Zahltag, -e** payday
der **Zahn, ⁻e** tooth
der **Zahnarzt, ⁻e/**die **Zahnärztin, -nen**
  dentist
der **Zaun, ⁻e** fence
das **Zedernholz** cedar wood
zehnjährig ten-year-old
zeigen to show
die **Zeit, -en** time; **zur Zeit** at this
  time
die **Zeitung, -en** newspaper
der **Zeitungsartikel, -** newspaper
  article
das **Zelt, -e** tent
**zerfallen (zerfällt), zerfiel, ist
  zerfallen** to fall apart
zerplatzen to burst
**zerschlagen (zerschlägt), zerschlug,
  zerschlagen** to smash to pieces
zerstören to destroy
der **Zeuge, -n, -n/**die **Zeugin, -nen**
  witness
ziehen, zog, gezogen to pull;
  ziehen (ist) to move, change one's
  residency
das **Ziel, -e** goal
ziemlich quite
die **Zigarette, -n** cigarette
das **Zimmer, -** room
der **Zimmerkamerad, -en, -en/**die der

der **Zimmerkollege, -n, -n**/die
Zimmerkollegin, -nen   roommate
der **Zirkus, -se**   circus
der **Zirkusclown, -s**   circus clown
zittern   to tremble
der **Zivildienst**   civil service
der **Zoo, -s**   zoo
der **Zoologe, -n, -n**/die **Zoologin, -nen**
zoologist
der **Zorn**   anger, wrath
zu   too;   **zu** + *dat.*   to, at
der **Zucker**   sugar
zuerst   at first
der **Zufall, ⁻e**   chance, coincidence;
durch Zufall   by accident
zufrieden (mit)   contented, satisfied
(with)
der **Zug, ⁻e**   train
zu·geben (gibt zu), gab zu, zugegeben
to admit
zu·hören (*dat.*)   to listen to
der **Zuhörer, -**/die **Zuhörerin, -nen**
listener
die **Zukunft**   future
zu·machen   to close, shut
zunächst   first of all, to begin with
die **Zunge, -n**   tongue
**sich zurecht·finden, fand zurecht,
zurechtgefunden**   to find one's
way around
**zurück·bringen, brachte zurück,
zurückgebracht**   to bring back
zurück·fahren (fährt zurück), fuhr

zurück, ist zurückgefahren
to drive back, return
**zurück·geben (gibt zurück), gab
zurück, zurückgegeben**   to give
back, return
**zurück·gehen, ging zurück, ist
zurückgegangen**   to go back,
return
**zurück·nehmen (nimmt zurück),
nahm zurück, zurückgenommen**
to take back
**zurück·rufen, rief zurück,
zurückgerufen**   to call back
zusammen   together
zusammen·arbeiten   to work together
**zusammen·brechen (bricht
zusammen), brach zusammen, ist
zusammengebrochen**   to collapse,
break
**zusammen·kommen, kam zusammen,
ist zusammengekommen**   to come
together
**zusammen·stoßen (stößt zusammen),
stieß zusammen, ist zusammengestoßen**   to collide
zu·schauen (*dat.*)   to look at, watch
**zu·schlagen (schlägt zu), schlug zu,
zugeschlagen**   to hit, strike out; to
slam shut
zweideutig   ambiguous
der **Zwillingsbruder, ⁻**   twin brother
zwischen + *acc./dat.*   between

ENGLISH-GERMAN

The explanations and abbreviations at the beginning of the German-English vocabulary also apply to the English-German vocabulary. This vocabulary contains words necessary for the English into German translation exercises.

to be able to können (kann), konnte, gekonnt

according to nach + *dat.*

to act (so) tun, tat, getan; handeln

address die Adresse, -n

to adopt adoptieren

afraid: to be afraid (of) sich fürchten (vor + *dat.*); Angst haben (vor + *dat.*)

after (*prep.*) nach + *dat.*; (*sub. conj.*) nachdem

afternoon der Nachmittag, -e

again wieder

against gegen + *acc.*

to be allowed to dürfen (darf), durfte, gedurft

alone allein

already schon

always immer

ambulance der Krankenwagen, -

America (das) Amerika

American (*adj.*) amerikanisch; (*noun*) der Amerikaner, - /die Amerikanerin, - nen

angry böse, verärgert

another noch ein-

answer die Antwort, -en

to answer antworten (auf + *acc.*);
    to answer a person antworten (*dat.*)

apartment die Wohnung, -en

to apply for sich bewerben (bewirbt), bewarb, beworben um

to arrest verhaften

to arrive an·kommen, kam an, ist angekommen

as . . . as so . . . wie

to be ashamed (of) sich schämen (über + *acc.*)

to ask fragen

at (someone's house) bei + *dat.*

at (time) um + *acc.*

aunt die Tante, -n

author der Autor, -en/die Autorin, -nen

to babysit babysitten

bad luck das Pech

to be sein (ist), war, ist gewesen

beach der Strand, ¨e

to become werden (wird), wurde, ist geworden

bedroom das Schlafzimmer, -

beer das Bier

to behave sich benehmen (benimmt), benahm, benommen

behind hinter + *acc./dat.*

to believe glauben (*dat.*)

besides außer + *dat.*

big groß (größer, größt-)

bill die Rechnung, -en

black schwarz (ä)

bone der Knochen, -

book das Buch, ¨er

boring langweilig

to borrow borgen

boy der Junge, -n, -n

brand new ganz neu

breakable zerbrechlich

to bring bringen, brachte, gebracht;
    to bring along mit·bringen

broken gebrochen; kaputt

brother der Bruder, ¨

to build bauen

burglar der Einbrecher, -/die
Einbrecherin, -nen
but aber (*coor. conj.*); **but rather**
sondern (*coor. conj.*)
to buy kaufen

to be called heißen, hieß, geheißen
to call an·rufen, rief an, angerufen;
to call back zurück·rufen, rief
zurück, zurückgerufen
can, to be able to können (kann),
konnte, gekonnt
car das Auto, -s; der Wagen, -
to carry tragen (trägt), trug,
getragen
castle das Schloß, ¨(ss)er
cat die Katze, -n
certain bestimmt
to change (sich) ändern
child das Kind, -er
choir der Chor, ¨e
church die Kirche, -n
city hall das Rathaus, ¨er
city map der Stadtplan, ¨e
class die Klasse, -n
to clean reinigen
to close schließen, schloß,
geschlossen
cold (*noun*) die Kälte; **cold** (*adj.*)
kalt (ä)
to come kommen, kam, ist gekommen
compromise: to find a compromise
einen Kompromiß schließen, schloß,
geschlossen
computer der Computer, -
consequence die Konsequenz,
-en
contents der Inhalt, -e
to cook kochen
cool kühl
correct richtig
country das Land, ¨er; **to the
country** aufs Land; **in the
country** auf dem Land
crazy verrückt
to cry weinen

day der Tag, -e
to depend on sich verlassen (verläßt), verließ, verlassen auf + *acc.*
dependent (on) abhängig (von)
desk der Schreibtisch, -e
dining room das Eßzimmer, -
dinner das Abendessen, -
dirty schmutzig
to discuss besprechen (bespricht),
besprach, besprochen
dishes das Geschirr
dishwasher der Geschirrspüler, -
to do tun, tat, getan; machen
doctor der Arzt ¨e/die Ärztin, -nen
dog der Hund, -e
done fertig
door die Tür, -en
dress das Kleid, -er
to dress an·ziehen, zog an,
angezogen
to drink trinken, trank, getrunken
to drive fahren (fährt), fuhr, ist
gefahren
during während + *gen.*
early früh
to earn verdienen
to eat essen (ißt), aß, gegessen;
to eat out im Restaurant essen
English (*adj.*) englisch; (*noun*)
der Engländer, -/die Engländerin,
-nen
enough genug
enthusiastic enthusiastisch
essay der Aufsatz, ¨e
Europe (das) Europa
ever je
every jed-
everything alles
exam die Prüfung, -en
except außer + *dat.*
exchange student der
Austauschstudent, -en, -en/die
Austauschstudentin, -nen
to expect erwarten
expensive teuer
experiment das Experiment, -e
to explain erklären

fall   der Herbst

family   die Familie, -n

fast   schnell

father   der Vater, ⸚

to feed   füttern

to feel   sich fühlen

film   der Film, -e

finally   endlich

to find   finden, fand, gefunden;
to find one's way around   sich
zurecht·finden

finished   fertig

to fit   passen (*dat.*)

flower   die Blume, -n

to fly   fliegen, flog, ist geflogen

food   das Essen

foot   der Fuβ, ⸚e; **on foot**   zu
Fuβ

frequently   oft

Friday   der Freitag

friend   der Freund, -e/die Freundin,
-nen

from   von + *dat.*

furniture   das Möbel

German (language)   Deutsch; **in
German**   auf deutsch

Germany   (das) Deutschland

to get, become   werden (wird), wurde,
ist geworden

to get, receive   bekommen, bekam,
bekommen

to get to know, become acquainted
kennen·lernen

to get used to   sich gewöhnen an +
acc.

girl   das Mädchen, -

girlfriend   die Freundin, -nen

to give   geben (gibt), gab, gegeben

glasses   die Brille, -n

to go   gehen, ging, ist gegangen

good   gut (besser, best-)

grade   die Note, -n

to hang   hängen

to be hanging   hängen, hing,
gehangen

to have   haben (hat), hatte, gehabt

to have a good time   sich amüsieren

to have to   müssen (muβ), muβte,
gemuβt

health insurance   die
Krankenversicherung, -en

healthy   gesund (ü)

to hear (about)   hören (von)

to help   helfen (hilft), half, geholfen
(*dat.*)

here   hier

holidays, vacation   die Ferien (*pl.*)

home: to go home   nach Hause
gehen; **to be at home**   zu Hause
sein

hook   der Haken, -

hour   die Stunde, -n

house   das Haus, ⸚er

how   wie; **how often**   wie oft

hungry   hungrig

to hurry up   sich beeilen

hurt   verletzt

impolite   unhöflich

important   wichtig

in front of   vor + *acc./dat.*

in order to   um . . . zu

incomprehensible   unverständlich

instrument   das Instrument, -e

intelligent   intelligent

to be interested in   sich interessieren
für; Interesse haben an + *dat.*

to invite   ein·laden (lädt ein), lud ein,
eingeladen

jealous (of)   eifersüchtig (auf + *acc.*)

job   der Job, -s; die Stelle, -n

joke   der Witz, -e; der Scherz, -e

key   der Schlüssel, -

kitchen   die Küche, -n

to know as a fact   wissen (weiβ),
wuβte, gewuβt

large   groβ (gröβer, gröβt-)

to last   dauern

to laugh   lachen

law   das Gesetz, -e

to leave   lassen (läßt), ließ, gelassen;
   to leave class   die Klasse verlassen
leg   das Bein, -e
letter   der Brief, -e
letter of recommendation   der
   Empfehlungsbrief, -e
liar   der Lügner, -/die Lügnerin, -nen
to lie   liegen, lag, gelegen
to like   mögen (mag), mochte,
   gemocht;   **to like something**
   gefallen (gefällt), gefiel, gefallen;
   to like to do something   etwas
   gern machen;   **would like to**
   möchten
to live   leben, wohnen
long   lang (ä)
to long (for)   sich sehnen (nach)
longing: to have a longing (for)
   Sehnsucht haben (nach)
to look forward to   sich freuen auf +
   acc.
to look like   aus·sehen (sieht aus), sah
   aus, ausgesehen;   **to look like someone**   jemandem ähnlich sehen
to lose   verlieren, verlor, verloren
loud   laut
love   die Liebe
to love   lieben

mad   böse; verärgert
mail   die Post
to make   machen;   **to make dinner**
   das Essen kochen
man   der Mann, ¨-er
many a   manch-
married couple   das Ehepaar, -e
mathematics   die Mathematik
may, to be allowed to   dürfen (darf),
   durfte, gedurft
to meet   kennen·lernen
mistake   der Fehler, -
moment   der Moment, -e
Monday   der Montag
money   das Geld
more   mehr
morning   der Morgen, -
mother   die Mutter, ¨-

to move to a new residence
   um·ziehen, zog um, ist umgezogen
museum   das Museum, die Museen
music   die Musik

name   der Name, -ns, -n
neighbor   der Nachbar, -n, -n/die
   Nachbarin, -nen
never   nie
new   neu
next door   nebenan
next to   neben + *acc./dat.*
no one   niemand
nose   die Nase, -n
now   jetzt

old   alt (ä)
on   an + *acc./dat.* (*vertical surface*);
   auf + *acc./dat.* (*horizontal surface*);
   on time   rechtzeitig
once   einmal
only   nur
to open   auf·machen
opinion   die Meinung, -en;   **in my
   opinion**   meiner Meinung nach
orchestra   das Orchester, -
other   ander-
pants (pair of)   die Hose, -n
parents   die Eltern (*pl.*)
parents-in-law   die Schwiegereltern
   (*pl.*)
park   der Park, -s
part   der Teil, -e
to participate (in)   teilnehmen
   (nimmt teil), nahm teil,
   teilgenommen (an + *dat.*)
party   die Party, -s
to pay   bezahlen
peace: leave me in peace   laß mich in
   Ruhe
pencil   der Bleistift, -e
people   die Leute (*pl.*)
perfect   perfekt
person   die Person, -en
to pick up   ab·holen
picture   das Bild, -er
to play   spielen

player　der Spieler, -/die Spielerin, -nen

Poland　(das) Polen

police　die Polizei

possible　möglich

poster　das Poster, -

to prefer something　lieber haben; **to prefer doing something**　lieber + *verb*

problem　das Problem, -e

professor　der Professor, -en/die Professorin, -nen

proud (of)　stolz (auf + *acc.*)

to publish　heraus·geben (gibt heraus), gab heraus, herausgegeben; veröffentlichen

to put　stellen; stecken; setzen

question　die Frage, -n

quiet　ruhig

rain　der Regen

to rain　regnen

to read　lesen (liest), las, gelesen

really　wirklich

to receive　bekommen, bekam, bekommen

to recommend　empfehlen (empfiehlt), empfahl, empfohlen

red　rot (o *or* ö)

red wine　der Rotwein

to remember　sich erinnern an + *acc.*

to repair　reparieren

to respect　respektieren

restaurant　das Restaurant, -s

Rhine　der Rhein

to ring　klingeln

river　der Fluß, ̈(ss)e

road　die Straße, -n

room　der Raum, ̈e

Saturday　der Samstag; der Sonnabend

to save　sparen

to say　sagen

scissors　die Schere, -n

to see　sehen (sieht), sah, gesehen

to sell　verkaufen

to send for　kommen lassen

sentence　der Satz, ̈e

to set　setzen

sharp　scharf (ä)

shirt　das Hemd, -en

shoe　der Schuh, -e

to shop　einkaufen gehen

should, to be supposed to　sollen

to show　zeigen

to shower　sich duschen

sick　krank (ä)

to sing　singen, sang, gesungen

sister　die Schwester, -n

to sit　sitzen, saβ, gesessen; **to sit down**　sich setzen

to sleep　schlafen (schläft), schlief, geschlafen

to smoke　rauchen

to solve　lösen

some　etwas

someone　jemand

soon　bald

South　der Süden; **to the South of**　südlich von

to speak　sprechen (spricht), sprach, gesprochen; **to speak to**　an·sprechen; **to speak with**　reden mit

stairs　die Treppe, -n

to stand　stehen, stand, gestanden

to start　an·fangen (fängt an), fing an, angefangen

statistics　die Statistik

to stay　bleiben, blieb, ist geblieben; **to stay up**　auf·bleiben, blieb auf, ist aufgeblieben

still　noch

to stop　auf·hören; **to stop by**　vorbei·kommen, kam vorbei, ist vorbeigekommen

student　der Student, -en, -en/die Studentin, -nen

to study　studieren; lernen

such　solch- ; **such a**　solch ein-

Sunday　der Sonntag

to be supposed to   sollen
Switzerland   die Schweiz

to take   nehmen (nimmt), nahm, genommen
to take a course   einen Kurs belegen
to take an exam   eine Prüfung schreiben, schrieb, geschrieben
to take a walk   einen Spaziergang machen
to take the bus   mit dem Bus fahren (fährt), fuhr, ist gefahren
to talk (about)   sprechen (spricht), sprach, gesprochen (über + *acc.*)
to taste   schmecken (*dat.*)
teacher   der Lehrer, -/die Lehrerin, -nen
telephone   das Telefon, -e
to tell   erzählen
test   die Prüfung, -en
than   als
that   daβ (*sub. conj.*)
there   da
there is, there are   es gibt + *acc.*
to think (of)   denken, dachte, gedacht (an + *acc.*);   **to think about** nach·denken über + *acc.*
this, these   dies-
thousand   das Tausend, -e
Thursday   der Donnerstag
ticket   die Karte, -n
time   die Zeit
together   zusammen
tomorrow   morgen
too   auch; zu
topic   das Thema, die Themen
tourist   der Tourist, -en, -en/die Touristin, -nen
trip   die Reise, -n
Tuesday   der Dienstag

to understand   verstehen, verstand, verstanden
to use   benutzen; gebrauchen

vacation   die Ferien (*pl.*); der Urlaub;   **to go on vacation**   Urlaub machen
vase   die Vase, -n
to visit   besuchen

to wait   warten
wall   die Wand, ⸚e; die Mauer, -n
to want to   wollen (will), wollte, gewollt
war   der Krieg, -e
to water   begieβen, begoβ, begossen
to wear   tragen (trägt), trug, getragen
Wednesday   der Mittwoch
week   die Woche, -n;   **for weeks** wochenlang
what   was;   **what a**   welch ein-;   **what kind of**   was für ein-
when   wann, wenn, als
where   wo
which   welch-
who   wer
why   warum
window   das Fenster, -
wine   der Wein
to wish   wünschen; wollen
without   ohne + *acc.*
woman   die Frau, -en
word (*in a connected sequence*)   das Wort, -e; (*unconnected*)   das Wort, ⸚er
work   die Arbeit; (*of an author*)   das Werk, -e
to work   arbeiten
worker   der Arbeiter, -/die Arbeiterin, -nen
worse   schlechter
would like to   möchten
to write (to)   schreiben, schrieb, geschrieben (an + *acc.*)
writer   der Schriftsteller, -/die Schriftstellerin, -nen
wrong   falsch

APPENDIX A: GRAMMATICAL TABLES

A. Definite Article and **der**-Words

	MASC.	NEUT.	FEM.	PLURAL
NOM.	der	das	die	die
ACC.	den	das	die	die
DAT.	dem	dem	der	den (n)
GEN.	des (s, es)	des (s, es)	der	der

The endings in parentheses are noun endings. Here are the most common **der**- words.

all-	*all*
dies-	*this*
jed-	*each, every*
jen-	*that, that one*
manch-	singular: *many a;* plural: *several, some*
solch-	*such*
welch-	*which*

B. Indefinite Article and **ein**-Words

	MASC.	NEUT.	FEM.	PLURAL
NOM.	ein	ein	eine	keine
ACC.	einen	ein	eine	keine

	MASC.	NEUT.	FEM.	PLURAL
DAT.	einem	einem	einer	keinen (n)
GEN.	eines (s, es)	eines (s, es)	einer	keiner

The endings in parentheses are noun endings. The **ein**-words include **kein** and the possessive adjectives. Here are the possessive adjectives.

mein	*my*
dein	*your*
sein	*his*
sein	*its*
ihr	*her*
unser	*our*
euer	*your*
ihr	*their*
Ihr	*your*

C. Adjective Endings after **der**-Words

	MASCULINE	NEUTER	FEMININE	PLURAL
NOM.	der groβe Mann	das groβe Kind	die groβe Frau	die groβen Häuser
ACC.	den groβen Mann	das groβe Kind	die groβe Frau	die groβen Häuser
DAT.	dem groβen Mann	dem groβen Kind	der groβen Frau	den groβen Häusern
GEN.	des groβen Mannes	des groβen Kindes	der groβen Frau	der groβen Häuser

D. Adjective Endings after **ein**-Words

	MASCULINE	NEUTER	FEMININE	PLURAL
NOM.	ein groβer Mann	ein groβes Kind	eine groβe Frau	keine groβen Häuser
ACC.	einen groβen Mann	ein groβes Kind	eine groβe Frau	keine groβen Häuser
DAT	einem groβen Mann	einem groβen Kind	einer groβen Frau	keinen groβen Häusern
GEN.	eines groβen Mannes	eines groβen Kindes	einer groβen Frau	keiner groβen Häuser

E. Unpreceded Adjective Endings

	MASCULINE	NEUTER	FEMININE	PLURAL
NOM.	guter Kaffee	gutes Bier	gute Limonade	gute Freunde
ACC.	guten Kaffee	gutes Bier	gute Limonade	gute Freunde
DAT.	gutem Kaffee	gutem Bier	guter Limonade	guten Freunden
GEN.	guten Kaffees	guten Bieres	guter Limonade	guter Freunde

F.   Personal Pronouns

NOMINATIVE	ACCUSATIVE	DATIVE
ich	mich	mir
du	dich	dir
er	ihn	ihm
es	es	ihm
sie	sie	ihr
wir	uns	uns
ihr	euch	euch
sie	sie	ihnen
Sie	Sie	Ihnen

G. Reflexive Pronouns

NOMINATIVE	ACCUSATIVE	DATIVE
ich	mich	mir
du	dich	dir
er, es, sie	sich	sich
wir	uns	uns
ihr	euch	euch
sie	sich	sich
Sie	sich	sich

H. Relative Pronouns and Demonstrative Pronouns

	MASC.	NEUT.	FEM.	PLURAL
NOM.	der	das	die	die
ACC.	den	das	die	die
DAT.	dem	dem	der	denen
GEN.	dessen	dessen	deren	deren

I. Prepositions

ACCUSATIVE	DATIVE	EITHER-OR	GENITIVE
bis	aus	an	(an)statt
durch	außer	auf	trotz
für	bei	hinter	während
entlang	gegenüber	in	wegen
gegen	mit	neben	
ohne	nach	über	
um	seit	unter	
	von	vor	
	zu	zwischen	

J. Dative Verbs

antworten	gefallen	helfen	trauen
befehlen	gehören	leid tun	vertrauen
begegnen	gelingen	passen	weh tun
danken	geschehen	passieren	widersprechen
fehlen	glauben	raten	zuhören
folgen	gratulieren	schmecken	zuschauen

APPENDIX B: PRINCIPAL PARTS OF STRONG AND IRREGULAR WEAK VERBS

Here is a list of the principal parts of the most common strong and irregular weak verbs. Present tense vowel changes are listed in parentheses after the infinitive. For verbs with separable and inseparable prefixes not listed, look under the main verb.

INFINITIVE	SIMPLE PAST	PAST PARTICIPLE	GENERAL SUBJUNCTIVE	MEANING
backen (bäckt)	backte	gebacken	backte	to bake
befehlen (befiehlt)	befahl	befohlen	befähle/beföhle	to command
beginnen	begann	begonnen	begänne/begönne	to begin
beißen	biß	gebissen	bisse	to bite
betrügen	betrog	betrogen	betröge	to deceive
beweisen	bewies	bewiesen	bewiese	to prove
biegen	bog	gebogen	böge	to bend
bieten	bot	geboten	böte	to offer
binden	band	gebunden	bände	to bind, tie
bitten	bat	gebeten	bäte	to ask for, request
bleiben	blieb	ist geblieben	bliebe	to remain
brechen (bricht)	brach	gebrochen	bräche	to break
brennen	brannte	gebrannt	brennte	to burn
bringen	brachte	gebracht	brächte	to bring
denken	dachte	gedacht	dächte	to think
empfehlen (empfiehlt)	empfahl	empfohlen	empfähle/empföhle	to recommend
erschrecken (erschrickt)	erschrak	ist erschrocken	erschräke	to be frightened
essen (ißt)	aß	gegessen	äße	to eat
fahren (fährt)	fuhr	ist gefahren	führe	to drive
fallen (fällt)	fiel	ist gefallen	fiele	to fall
fangen (fängt)	fing	gefangen	finge	to catch
finden	fand	gefunden	fände	to find

344

fliegen	flog	ist geflogen	flöge	to fly
fliehen	floh	ist geflohen	flöhe	to flee
fließen	floß	ist geflossen	flösse	to flow
fressen (frißt)	fraß	gefressen	fräße	to eat (of animals)
frieren	fror	gefroren	fröre	to freeze
geben (gibt)	gab	gegeben	gäbe	to give
gehen	ging	gegangen	ginge	to go
gelingen	gelang	gelungen	gelänge	to succeed
gelten (gilt)	galt	gegolten	gälte/gölte	to be valid, be worth
genießen	genoß	genossen	genösse	to enjoy
geschehen (geschieht)	geschah	ist geschehen	geschähe	to happen
gewinnen	gewann	gewonnen	gewänne/gewönne	to win
gießen	goß	gegossen	gösse	to pour
gleichen	glich	geglichen	gliche	to resemble
gleiten	glitt	ist geglitten	glitte	to glide
graben (gräbt)	grub	gegraben	grübe	to dig
greifen	griff	gegriffen	griffe	to grasp, seize
haben (hat)	hatte	gehabt	hätte	to have
halten (hält)	hielt	gehalten	hielte	to hold; to stop
hängen	hing	gehangen	hinge	to hang (intransitive)
heben	hob	gehoben	höbe	to lift
heißen	hieß	geheißen	hieße	to be called
helfen (hilft)	half	geholfen	hälfe/hülfe	to help
kennen	kannte	gekannt	kennte	to know, be acquainted with
klingen	klang	geklungen	klänge	to sound
kommen	kam	ist gekommen	käme	to come
kriechen	kroch	ist gekrochen	kröche	to crawl
laden (lädt)	lud	geladen	lüde	to load
lassen (läßt)	ließ	gelassen	ließe	to leave, let, allow
laufen (läuft)	lief	ist gelaufen	liefe	to run
leiden	litt	gelitten	litte	to suffer
leihen	lieh	geliehen	liehe	to lend
lesen (liest)	las	gelesen	läse	to read
liegen	lag	gelegen	läge	to lie
lügen	log	gelogen	löge	to tell a lie
meiden	mied	gemieden	miede	to avoid
messen (mißt)	maß	gemessen	mäße	to measure
nehmen (nimmt)	nahm	genommen	nähme	to take
nennen	nannte	genannt	nennte	to name
pfeifen	pfiff	gepfiffen	pfiffe	to whistle
raten (rät)	riet	geraten	riete	to advise
reiben	rieb	gerieben	riebe	to rub
reißen	riß	gerissen	risse	to tear
reiten	ritt	ist geritten	ritte	to ride
rennen	rannte	ist gerannt	rennte	to run
riechen	roch	gerochen	röche	to smell
ringen	rang	gerungen	ränge	to struggle, wrestle
rufen	rief	gerufen	riefe	to call
saufen (säuft)	soff	gesoffen	söffe	to drink (of animals)
schaffen	schuf	geschaffen	schüfe	to create
scheiden	schied	geschieden	schiede	to separate
scheinen	schien	geschienen	schiene	to shine; to seem
schelten (schilt)	schalt	gescholten	schölte	to scold
schieben	schob	geschoben	schöbe	to shove
schießen	schoß	geschossen	schösse	to shoot
schlafen (schläft)	schlief	geschlafen	schliefe	to sleep
schlagen (schlägt)	schlug	geschlagen	schlüge	to hit, strike

schleichen	schlich	ist geschlichen	schliche	to sneak about
schließen	schloß	geschlossen	schlösse	to close
schmeißen	schmiß	geschmissen	schmisse	to fling, throw
schmelzen (schmilzt)	schmolz	geschmolzen	schmölze	to melt
schneiden	schnitt	geschnitten	schnitte	to cut
schreiben	schrieb	geschrieben	schriebe	to write
schreien	schrie	geschrie(e)n	schriee	to shout, scream
schreiten	schritt	ist geschritten	schritte	to stride
schweigen	schwieg	geschwiegen	schwiege	to be silent
schwimmen	schwamm	ist geschwommen	schwämme/schwömme	to swim
schwören	schwor	geschworen	schwöre	to swear (an oath)
sehen (sieht)	sah	gesehen	sähe	to see
sein (ist)	war	ist gewesen	wäre	to be
senden	sandte	gesandt	sendete	to send
singen	sang	gesungen	sänge	to sing
sinken	sank	ist gesunken	sänke	to sink
sitzen	saß	gesessen	säße	to sit
sprechen (spricht)	sprach	gesprochen	spräche	to speak
springen	sprang	ist gesprungen	spränge	to spring
stechen (sticht)	stach	gestochen	stäche	to sting, prick
stehen	stand	gestanden	stände/stünde	to stand
stehlen (stiehlt)	stahl	gestohlen	stähle	to steal
steigen	stieg	ist gestiegen	stiege	to climb
sterben (stirbt)	starb	ist gestorben	stürbe	to die
stinken	stank	gestunken	stänke	to stink
stoßen (stößt)	stieß	gestoßen	stieße	to push
streichen	strich	gestrichen	striche	to paint; to stroke
streiten	stritt	gestritten	stritte	to argue
tragen (trägt)	trug	getragen	trüge	to carry; to wear
treffen (trifft)	traf	getroffen	träfe	to meet
treiben	trieb	getrieben	triebe	to set in motion
treten (tritt)	trat	ist getreten	träte	to step
trinken	trank	getrunken	tränke	to drink
tun	tat	getan	täte	to do
verderben (verdirbt)	verdarb	verdorben	verdürbe	to ruin
vergessen (vergißt)	vergaß	vergessen	vergäße	to forget
verlieren	verlor	verloren	verlöre	to lose
verschwinden	verschwand	ist verschwunden	verschwände	to disappear
verzeihen	verzieh	verziehen	verziehe	to forgive
wachsen (wächst)	wuchs	ist gewachsen	wüchse	to grow
waschen (wäscht)	wusch	gewaschen	wüsche	to wash
weichen	wich	ist gewichen	wiche	to yield
wenden	wandte	gewandt	wendete	to turn
werben (wirbt)	warb	geworben	würbe	to recruit
werden (wird)	wurde	ist geworden	würde	to become
werfen (wirft)	warf	geworfen	würfe	to throw
wiegen	wog	gewogen	wöge	to weigh
wissen (weiß)	wußte	gewußt	wüßte	to know as a fact
ziehen	zog	gezogen	zöge	to pull
zwingen	zwang	gezwungen	zwänge	to force

Index

ab-, as separable prefix,
159
aber, use of, 286–87
Absolute comparative,
122
Abstract concepts, definite
article with, 15–16
Accusative case, 30–33
either-or prepositions in,
86–87
forms of, 30
reflexive pronouns and,
55
relative pronouns in, 65
time expressions with,
138–39
usage of
after certain preposi-
tions, 32
direct object, 30
with **es gibt,** 32
measurement, expres-
sions of, 31–32
time expressions, 31,
41
Accusative prepositions,
32. *See also* Either-
or (accusative-
dative) prepositions
bis, 78
contractions with, 94
da-compounds and,
98–99
durch, 78–79
entlang, 79
für, 79

gegen, 79
ohne, 79
relative pronouns with,
67–68
special meanings for,
92
um, 79–80
Accusative reflexive verbs,
256
Active voice, passive voice
vs., 192–93
Adjectival nouns, 110–12
past participles as,
113–14
present participles as,
113–14
superlative, **was** used to
refer to, 71
Adjective endings, 105–16.
See also Compar-
ative; Superlative
adjectival nouns, 110–12
of adjectives in a
sequence, 113
after **ein-**words, 107–8
after indefinite pronouns,
112
of **der-**words, 106–7
indefinite numerals,
109–10
with names of cities,
113
past participles and pre-
sent participles used
as adjectival nouns,
113–14

past participles and pre-
sent participles used
as adjectives, 113
unpreceded, 108–9
Adjectives
comparative and superla-
tive, 116–23
attributive adjectives,
118–19
formation of, 117–18
irregular, 118
predicate adjectives,
119–20
special constructions,
121–22
dative with, 36–37
ordinal numbers as,
132–34
past participles as, 113
possessive, 20–22
inanimate objects and,
20–21
present participles as,
113
in a sequence
endings of, 113
Adverbs, 104
cardinal numbers plus
-mal, 131
comparative and superla-
tive, 116–23,
120–21
formation of, 117–18
irregular, 118
special constructions,
121–22

Adverbs (*cont.*)
conjunctions opposed to,
295
definition of, 105
of manner, 277, 278
ordinal numbers plus
-ens, 134
of place, 277, 278
position of, 277–79
more than one adverb,
278–79
time, 135–37, 277, 278
Agent in passive sentence,
197–98
all-, use of, 19
als
with past subjunctive,
227
plus comparative,
121–22
with present subjunctive,
223
use of, 290
als ob
with past subjunctive,
227
with present subjunctive,
223
als wenn
with past subjunctive,
227
with present subjunctive,
223
am, with days of the week
and parts of day,
135–36
an, use of, 88
special meanings, 92
an-, as separable prefix,
159
(an)statt, infinitive phrases
with, 250–51
anstatt, use of, 95
Antecedent, 63
Anticipatory **da-**com-
pounds, infinitive
phrase or subordi-
nate clause follow-
ing, 253–54
antworten, use of, 35
Appositives, case in, 45
Arithmetic, 130

Articles, 15–18. *See also*
Definite article;
Gender; Indefinite
article
Attributive adjectives, 104
comparative and superla-
tive, 118–19
definition of, 105
außer, use of, 81
auf, use of, 88
special meanings, 92
auf-, as separable prefix,
159
aus, use of, 80–81
aus-, as separable prefix,
160
Auxiliary verbs, present
perfect tense and,
178–79

be-, as inseparable prefix,
158
bei, use of, 81–82
bevor, vor, vorher, 295
bis, use of, 78
bleiben
indefinite article
ommited after, 17
nominative as predicate
noun after, 29
Body parts
definite article with, 17
reflexive pronouns with,
55
bringen, in simple past
tense, 171

Capitalization
of nouns, 3–5
of proper names, 4–5
Cardinal numbers, 128–31
arithmetic and, 130
currencies and, 130
decades and, 130–31
decimals and percent-
ages, 131
-mal and, 131
separating, 129
Case(s), 27–48. *See also*
specific cases
accusative, 30–33
in appositves, 45

in English, 27–28
nominative, 28–30
principle of, 27–28
of reflexive pronouns, 55
in sentence fragments,
44–45
Causation, **lassen** used to
express, 247
-chen, gender of nouns
ending in, 7
Cities, names of
adjective endings with,
113
definite article with, 16
gender of, 7
Clothing
definite article with, 17
reflexive pronouns with,
55
Commands. *See also*
Imperatives
indirect discourse in,
240
reflexive verbs in, 257
Comparative, 116–23
absolute, 122
als plus, 121–22
formation of, 117
immer plus, 122
irregular, 118
mehr plus base form,
122
use of, 118–21
Compass points, gender of,
7
Compound nouns, 14–15
Conditional clause. *See*
wenn clause
Conditional sentences, 218.
See also Unreal
conditions
word order in, 218
Conjunctions, 285–300.
*See also specific
conjunctions*
coordinating
meanings of, 286–87
omission of redundant
information and,
287–88
word order and, 273,
285–86

prepositions and adverbs
opposed to, 295
subordinating, 288–97
meanings of, 289–90
word order and, 289
Continents, gender of, 7–8
Contractions, with prepositions, 94–95
Coordinating conjunctions
meanings of, 286–87
omission of redundant
information and,
287–88
word order and, 285–86
position of verb, 273
Countries, names of
definite article with, 16
gender of, 7
Currencies, 130

da
demonstrative pronouns
combined with,
60
use of, 292
daβ
das vs., 292–93
to express means, 294
omission of, 293–94
with second subordinat-
ing conjunction,
293
subordinate clause intro-
duced by, 252
da-compounds, 98–99
anticipatory, infinitive
phrase or subordi-
nate clause follow-
ing, 253–54
dadurch, 294
dann, conclusion of conditional sentence
introduced by, 218,
219
das
daβ vs., 292–93
was used to refer to, 71
Dates, 140–41
Dative case, 33–38
either-or prepositions in,
86–87
forms of, 33

reflexive pronouns and,
55
relative pronouns in, 65
time expressions with,
139
usage of
after certain preposi-
tions, 38
with certain adjec-
tives, 36–37
with dative verbs,
34–36
indirect object, 33
time expressions,
37–38, 41
Dative objects, passive
constructions with,
200–201
Dative prepositions, 80–86.
See also Either-or
(accusative-dative)
prepositions
auβer, 81
aus, 80–81
bei, 81–82
contractions with, 94–95
da-compounds and,
98–99
gegenüber, 82
mit, 82–83
nach, 83–84
relative pronouns with,
68
seit, 84
special meanings for, 92
von, 84–85
zu, 85
Dative reflexive verbs, 256
Dative verbs, 34–36
passive constructions
with, 201
Days, parts of, 135–36
Days of the week, 135–36
gender of, 6–7
Decades, 130–31
Decimals, 131
Definite article, 15
chart of, 28
use of, 15–17
Demonstrative pronouns,
59–61
forms of, 59–60

denken, in simple past
tense, 171
denn, use of, 287
Dependent clauses. *See
also* Subordinating
conjunctions
with double infinitives,
word order in, 225
der-words, 19–20. *See also
specific words*
accusative form of, 30
adjective endings after,
106–7
dative form of, 33
genitive form of, 38
nominative forms of,
28–29
as pronouns, 61–62
die, as article for all plural
nouns, 9
dies, as demonstrative pronoun, 60
dies-, use of, 19
Direct object
accusative as, 30
indirect object compared
to, 34
position of, 276–77
Direct questions, position
of verb in, 274–75
doch, in wishes, 220
dort, demonstrative pronouns combined
with, 60
Double infinitives, word
order in dependent
clauses with, 225
du, 50
durch
agent in passive sentence
introduced by, 198
usage of, 78–79
dürfen, 163–65
simple past tense of, 172
subjective use of, 262
durfen, present tense subjunctive of, 216

-e
plural formed with, 10
unstressed, gender of
nouns ending in, 8

eher plus base form of adjective or adverb, 122

-ei, gender of nouns ending in, 8

ein-, as separable prefix, 160

einander, 55

ein-words, 20–25. *See also specific words*
  accusative form of, 30
  adjective endings after, 107–8
  dative form of, 33
  genitive form of, 38
  kein, 22
  nicht, 22–23
  nominative forms of, 28–29
  possessive adjectives, 20–22
  as pronouns, 62–63

Either-or (accusative-dative) prepositions, 86–91
  in, 89, 93
  accusative of, 32
  an, 88, 92
  auf, 88, 92
  contractions with, 95
  da-compounds and, 98–99
  dative or accusative, 86–87
  hinter, 88–89
  neben, 89
  relative pronouns with, 68
  special meanings for, 92–93
  über, 89–90, 93
  unter, 90
  vor, 90, 93
  zwischen, 90–91

emp-, as inseparable prefix, 158

-(e)n, plural formed with, 11

English
  case in, 27–28
  subjunctive in, 211–14

-ens, ordinal numbers with, 134

ent-, as inseparable prefix, 158

entlang, use of, 79

er-, as inseparable prefix, 158

-er, plural formed with, 10–11

es gibt, accusative with, 32

Expecting, verbs of, subordinate clause following, 252

Extended modifiers, 124

False passive, 202–3

Familiar plural imperative, 156

Familiar singular imperative, 155–56

Feminine gender groups, 8–9

Feminine nouns, 8–9

Formal form of address, 50

Formal German, indirect discourse in, 236–42
  commands, 240
  future tense, 238
  lengthy passages, 240–42
  questions, 239
  sein as helping verb in past tense, 237–38
  special subjunctive vs. general subjunctive, 236–40, 244

Formal imperative, 156

Forms, dates on, 140

Forms of address, 50

fort-, as separable prefix, 160

Fractions, 133–34

für, use of, 79

Future perfect tense
  formation of, 187
  passive voice in, 194
  use of, 187

Future tense, 185–87
  formation of, 185–86
  modal verbs in, 186
  passive voice in, 194
  use of, 186

gefallen, use of, 35–36

gegen, use of, 79

gegenüber, use of, 82

Gender, 5–9
  feminine, 8
  for human beings, 5–6
  masculine, 6–7
  neuter, 7–8
  nouns with two genders, 9
  of personal pronouns, 51–52
  prediction of, 6–9

gender-, as inseparable prefix, 158

General subjunctive. *See* Subjunctive (general subjunctive)

Genitive case, use of, 38–42
  after certain prepositions, 42
  forms of, 38–39
  indefinite time expressions, 41
  with names of people, 41
  noun endings and, 39
  for possession, 39
  relative pronouns in, 65–66
  time expressions with, 139

Genitive prepositions
  anstatt, statt, 95
  trotz, 95
  während, 95
  wegen, 96

glauben, use of, 35

haben
  future perfect tense formed with, 187
  past perfect tense formed with, 184
  past tense of special subjunctive formed with, 234, 237–38
  in present perfect tense, 180

present perfect tense
formed with, 175,
178–79, 181
present tense of, 153
present tense subjunctive
of, 215, 217–18
to express politeness,
222
in simple past tense, 171,
183–84
halten, present tense of,
152
hängen, 259–60
-heit, gender of nouns
ending in, 8
helfen, 245, 246
her, as separable prefix,
162
hier, demonstrative
pronouns combined
with, 60
hin, as separable prefix,
162
hinter, use of, 88–89
hören, 245, 246
Hypothetical situations,
subjunctive in
English, 212, 213
German
past tense, 227
present tense, 221–22

-ie, gender of nouns ending
in, 8
ihr, 50
im, with months and
seasons, 137
immer plus comparative,
122
Imperatives, 155–58. *See
also* Commands
bitte and, 155
familiar plural, 156
familiar singular, 155–56
formal, 156
infinitives as, 157–58
of **sein** and **werden,**
156–57
wir imperative, 157
Impersonal verbs, passive
constructions with,
199

in, use of, 89
special meaning, 93
-in
gender of nouns ending
in, 8
plural of nouns ending
in, 11–12
Inanimate objects, possessive adjectives and,
20–21
Indefinite article, 15
omission of, 17–18
Indefinite numerals, as
adjectives, 109–10
Indefinite pronouns
adjective endings after,
112
man, 58
was used as a relative
pronoun to refer
back to, 70–71
Indefinite time expressions,
genitive with, 41
indem, 294
Independent clauses, coordinating conjunc-
tions and, 285–88
Indirect discourse, 232–33.
See also Special
subjunctive
choosing tense of,
235–36
in formal German,
236–42
commands, 240
future tense, 238
lengthy passages,
240–42
questions, 239
sein as helping verb in
past tense, 237–38
special subjunctive vs.
general subjunctive,
236–40, 244
general subjunctive in,
236–40, 244
in informal German, 242
Indirect object
dative as, 33
direct object compared
to, 34
passive constructions

with, 200–201
position of, 276–77
Indirect questions, position
of verb in, 275–76
Infinitive, 147
Infinitive phrases, 248–53
English, German subor-
dinate clauses vs.,
252–53
following anticipatory
da-compounds,
253–54
of more than two words,
249
with separable-prefix
verb, 249
of two words only, 249
um, ohne and **(an)statt,**
249–50
Infinitives
avoiding passive voice
with, 205
double, word order in
dependent clauses
with, 225
as imperatives, 157–58
as nouns
gender of, 7
passive, 196
Informal form of address,
50
Informal German, indirect
discourse in, 242
Inseparable prefixes,
158–59
past participles and, 178
Interjections, as first element of a clause,
position of verb
and, 273
Interrogative pronouns,
57–58
prepositions and, 100
as relative pronouns,
70–73
Intransitive verbs, 258
Inverted word order, difference between nor-
mal word order and,
272–73
-ion, gender of nouns ending in, 8

je...desto/umso, 294
jen-, use of, 19
    as pronoun, 61–62

kein, nicht vs., 22
-keit, gender of nouns end-
        ing in, 8
kennen, 153–54
können, 164
    past subjective vs. past
        subjective of,
        264–65
    present tense subjunctive
        of, 216
    simple past tense of,
        172
    subjective use of, 262

laden, present tense of,
        152
lassen, 245–47
legen, 258
-lein, gender of nouns end-
        ing in, 7
Letters, dates on, 140
liegen, 258–59
los-, as separable prefix,
        160

Mädchen, das, personal
        pronoun and, 52
Main clause, position of
        verb in, 271–74
Mal, ordinal numbers with,
        134
-mal, cardinal numbers
        and, 131
man
    avoiding passive voice
        with, 204
    as pronoun, 58–59
Manch ein, 23
Manner, adverbs of, 277,
        278
Masculine gender groups,
        6–7
Masculine nouns, 6–7
nicht, negation of a spe-
        cific sentence unit
        with, 281
Meals, definite article with,
        16

Measurement, expressions
        of
    accusative with, 31–32
mehr, plus base form of
        adjective or adverb,
        122
miβ-, as inseparable prefix,
        158, 159
mit
    agent in passive sentence
        introduced by,
        198
    use of, 82–83
mit-, as separable prefix,
        160
Mixed adjective endings,
        105
Mixed verbs
    past participles of, 177
    present tense subjunctive
        for, 215–16
    in simple past tense, 171
Modal verbs, 163–67. See
        also specific verbs
    avoiding passive voice
        with, 205
    dürfen, 163–65
    in future tense, 186
    in indirect discourse,
        237
    können, 164
    meanings of, 163
    mögen, 164–65
    müssen, 165
    in passive voice, 194–97
    past subjective of,
        224–25
    past tense of special sub-
        junctive and, 234
    in present perfect tense,
        181–84
    present tense, 163
    present tense subjunctive
        for, 216, 217–18
    to express politeness,
        222
    in simple past tense,
        172–73, 183–84
    sollen, 165
    subjective use of,
        260–65
    meanings of, 262–65

past tense, 261–62
    present tense, 261
    subjunctive, 262
    without an infinitive,
        167
    wollen, 165
Modifiers. See also specific
        topics
    extended, 124
mögen, 164–65
    present tense subjunctive
        of, 216
    simple past tense of,
        172, 173
    subjective use of, 263
Months, 137
    gender of, 6–7
müssen, 165
    present tense subjunctive
        of, 216
    simple past tense of,
        172, 173
    subjective use of, 263

nach, use of, 83–84
nach-, as separable prefix,
        160
nachdem, 294
nachdem, nach, nachher,
        295
Names of people, genitive
        with, 41
neben, use of, 89
nehmen, present tense of,
        151
-nen, plural formed with,
        11–12
Neuter gender groups, 7–8
Neuter nouns, 7–8
Neuter ordinals, was used
        to refer to, 71
News value, word order
        and, 282–83
nicht, kein vs., 22
nicht ein, 23
Nominative case, 28–30
    in English, 27
    forms of, 28–29
    relative pronouns in, 64
    use of, 29
Normal word order,
        inverted word

order, difference
between, 272–73
Nouns
adjectival, 110–12
past participles as,
113–14
present participles as,
113–14
superlative, **was** used
to refer to, 71
capitalization of, 3–5
compound, 14–15
gender of, 5–9
feminine, 8
for human beings, 5–6
masculine, 6–7
neuter, 7–8
prediction of, 6–9
two genders, 9
in genitive case, 39
infinitives used as, gen-
der of, 7
plural, 9–14
always plural nouns,
13
in English, nouns that
are singular in
German and, 12–13
with **-e** + umlaut
sometimes, 10
with **-e** + umlaut
where possible,
10–11
general patterns in for-
mation of, 12
with **-(e)n,** 11
with **-nen,** 11–12
with nominative end-
ing + umlaut some-
times, 9–10
problem areas in for-
mation of, 12
predicate, nominative as,
29
weak, case and, 42–44
Numbers, 128–35
cardinal, 128–31
ordinal, 131–35
nur, in wishes, 220

ob, use of, 291
Objective case, 27–28

oder, use of, 287
ohne
infinitive phrases with,
250–51
use of, 79
Ordinal numbers, 131–35
-ens and, 134
fractions and, 133–34
with **Mal,** 134

Passive infinitives, 196
Passive voice, 192–210
active vs., 192–93
agent in passive sen-
tences, 197–98
avoiding, 204–6
dative objects used with,
200–201
dative verbs used with,
201
formation of, 193–95
impersonal verbs used
with, 199
modal verbs in, 194–97
tenses of, 194, 196
true vs. false, 202–4
Past participles, 175–84
as adjectival nouns,
113–14
as adjectives, 113
inseparable prefixes and,
178
of mixed verbs, 177
separable prefixes and,
178
of strong verbs, 176–77
of weak verbs, 176
Past perfect tense, 184–85
formation of, 184
passive voice in, 194
reflexive verbs in, 257
use of, 184
Past tense, simple, 167–75
mixed verbs in, 171
modal verbs in, 172–73
passive voice in, 194
present perfect tense vs.,
183
strong verbs in, 169–70
weak verbs in, 167–69
Percentages, 131
Permission, **lassen** used to

express, 247
Personal pronouns, 49–54
du, ihr, Sie, 50
forms of, 49–50
gender agreement of,
51–52
prepositions and, 99, 100
word order of, 53
Person's name, genitive
with, 41
Place, adverbs of, 277, 278
Plural, 9–14
always plural nouns, 13
in English, nouns that
are singular in
German and, 12–13
with **-e** + umlaut sometimes, 10
with **-e** + umlaut where
possible, 10–11
general patterns in for-
mation of, 12
with **-(e)n,** 11
with **-nen,** 11–12
with nominative ending
and umlaut some-
times, 9–10
problem areas in forma-
tion of, 12
two different plural
forms, nouns with,
12
Polite requests, subjunctive
in
English, 212, 213
German
present tense, 222–23
Possession, genitive for,
39–40
Possessive adjectives,
20–22
inanimate objects and,
20–21
Possessive case, 28
Predicate adjectives, 104
comparative and superla-
tive, 119–20
definition of, 105
Predicate noun, nominative
as, 29
Prepositional phrases
idiomatic

Prepositional phrases (*cont.*)
definite article with,
17
Prepositions, 77–103. *See
also specific prepo-
sitions*
accusative. *See*
Accusative preposi-
tions
accusative after, 32
conjunctions opposed to,
295
contractions with, 94–95
with **da-**compounds,
98–100
dative after, 38
either-or. *See* Either-or
(accusative-dative)
prepositions
genitive
anstatt, statt, 95
trotz, 95
während, 95
wegen, 96
genitive after, 42
interrogative pronouns
and, 100
personal pronouns and,
99, 100
reflexive verbs with,
256
in relative clauses, 69
relative pronouns with,
67–68
with **wo-**compounds,
100–101
Present participles
as adjectival nouns,
113–14
as adjectives, 113
Present perfect tense,
175–84
auxiliary verbs and,
178–79
formation of, 175
of modal verbs, 181–84
passive voice in, 194
past participles and,
175–84
reflexive verbs in, 257
simple past tense vs.,
183

Present tense, 147–55
endings, 148–50
passive voice in, 194
subjunctive. *See*
Subjunctive
use of, 154–55
vowel changes in the
verb stem, 150–52
Prices, 130
Pronouns, 49–76
demonstrative, 59–61
forms of, 59–60
der-words as, 61
ein-words as, 62–63
indefinite, 58
interrogative, 57–58
prepositions and, 100
as relative pronouns,
70–73
personal, 49–54
du, ihr, Sie, 50
forms of, 49–50
gender agreement of,
51–52
prepositions and, 99,
100
word order of, 53
reflexive, 54–57, 255
with body parts, 55
case of, 55
with clothing, 55
definition of, 54
to express reciprocity,
55–56
forms of, 54–55
reflexive verbs and,
56
selbst and **selber** and,
56
word order of,
accusative and
dative, 53
Proper names, capitaliza-
tion of, 4–5

Questions
indirect discourse in, 239
position of verb in,
274–76
Question words, to intro-
duce a subordinate
clause, 252

Quote
direct, 232–33
indirect. *See* Indirect discourse

raten, present tense of,
152
Reciprocity, reflexive pronouns used to
express, 55–56
Reflexive, avoiding passive
voice with the, 206
Reflexive pronouns, 54–57,
255
with body parts, 55
case of, 55
with clothing, 55
definition of, 54
to express reciprocity,
55–56
forms of, 54–55
reflexive verbs and, 56
selbst and **selber** and,
56
Reflexive verbs, 56,
254–55
accusative vs. dative,
256
in commands, 257
list of common, 255–56
in perfect tenses, 257
with prepositions, 256
Relative clauses, 63
prepositions in, 69
referring back to entire
clauses, 71
word order in, 66
Relative pronouns, 63–73
accusative, 65
dative, 65
definition of, 63–64
forms of, 64
genitive, 65–66
interrogative pronouns
as, 70–73
nominative, 64
ommited after, in
English, 70
with prepositions, 67–68

sagen, subordinate clause
following, 252

Saying, subordinate clause
following verbs of,
252
-schaft, gender of nouns
ending in, 8
Seasons, 137
definite article with, 16
months, 6–7
Second person, possessive
adjectives for, 21
sehen, 245, 246
sein
avoiding passive voice
with, 205
false passive formed
with, 203
future perfect tense
formed with, 187
imperative forms of,
156–57
indefinite article
ommited after, 17
nominative as predicate
noun after, 29
past perfect tense formed
with, 184
past tense of special subjunctive formed
with, 234, 237–38
in present perfect tense,
180
present perfect tense
formed with, 175,
178–79
present tense of, 153
present tense subjunctive
for, 215, 217–18
to express politeness,
222
in simple past tense, 171,
183
seit, use of, 84
seitdem/seit, 292
selber, 56
selbst, 56
Sentence fragments, case
in, 44–45
Sentence structure, basic,
281–82. *See also*
Word order
Separable prefixes, 159–62
avoiding passive voice

with, 205
past participles and,
178
pronunciation and, 161
in simple past tense,
168
Separable prefix verbs, in
infinitive phrases,
249
setzen, 258
sich lassen, avoiding passive voice with, 205
Sie, 50
Simple past tense, 167–75
mixed verbs in, 171
modal verbs in, 172–73
passive voice in, 194
present perfect tense vs.,
183
strong verbs in, 169–70
weak verbs in, 167–69
sitzen, 258–59
so, conclusion of conditional sentence
introduced by, 218,
219
solch ein (so ein), 23
sollen, 165
direct commands
reported indirectly
with, 240
present tense subjunctive
of, 216
simple past tense of,
172, 173
subjective use of, 263
sondern, use of, 286–87
so...wie, 121
Special subjunctive,
232–44. *See also*
Indirect discourse
future tense, 234
general subjunctive vs.,
236–40
past tense, 234
present tense, 233–34
States, gender of, 7–8
statt, use of, 95
stehen, 258–59
stellen, 258
stoßen, present tense of,
152

Strong adjective endings,
105
Strong verbs, 150
past participles of,
176–77
present tense subjunctive
for, 214–15
in simple past tense,
169–70
Subject, nominative as, 29
Subjunctive (special sub-
junctive). *See*
Special subjunctive
Subjunctive (general sub-
junctive), 211–31.
with **als ob, als wenn,** or
als, 223
in English, 211–14
in hypothetical situations
English, 212, 213
German, 221–22, 227
in indirect discourse,
242
indirect discourse and,
236–40
past tense, 224–27
in hypothetical situa-
tions, 227
modal verbs, 224–25
in unreal conditions,
225–26
in wishes, 226
in polite requests
English, 212, 213
German, 222–23
present tense, 214–24
conclusion clause
first, 219
for **haben,** 215,
217–18
to express politeness,
222
in hypothetical situa-
tions, 221–22
for mixed verbs,
215–16
of modal verbs, 216,
217–18
to express politeness,
222
one-word form,
214–16

Subjunctive (general sub-
    junctive) (*cont.*)
    one-word form vs.,
        217
    in polite requests,
        222–23
    for **sein,** 215, 217–18
        to express politeness,
            222
    for strong verbs,
        214–15
    in unreal conditions,
        218–20
    use of, 218–24
    for weak verbs, 214
    wenn clause in, 219
    wenn-clause in,
        217–22
    for **werden,** 215,
        217–18
        to express politeness,
            222
    in wishes, 220–21
    word order in, 218
    würde paraphrase
        and, 216–18, 222
    one-word form vs.,
        217
    in unreal conditions
        English, 211–12
        German, 218–20,
            225–26
    in wishes
        English, 212, 213
        German, 220, 226
Subordinate clauses
    English infinitive
        phrases vs., 252–53
    following anticipatory
        da-compounds,
            253–54
Subordinating conjunc-
    tions, 288–97. *See
    also specific subor-
    dinating conjunc-
    tions*
    meanings of, 289–90
    word order and, 289
Superlative, 116–23
    formation of, 117
    irregular, 118
    use of, 118–21

Superlative adjectives as
    nouns, **was** used to
    refer to, 71

-tät, gender of nouns end-
    ing in, 8
Time expressions
    case with, 138–40
        accusative, 31, 41
        dative, 37–38, 41
        genitive, 41
    dates, 140–41
    days of the week and
        parts of day,
            135–36
    indefinite, genitive with,
        41
    -lang with, 138
    -lich with, 138
    months and seasons,
        137–38
    other units of time,
        138
    telling time
        colloquial time,
            141–42
        official time, 142
Towns, gender of, 7–8
Transitive verbs, 258
treten, present tense of,
    151
trotz, use of, 95
Two-way prepositions.
    See Either-or
    (accusative-dative)
    prepositions

über, use of, 89–90
    special meanings, 93
um
    infinitive phrases with,
        250–51
    use of, 79–80
Umlaut, in plural, 9–10
und, use of, 287
-ung, gender of nouns
    ending in, 8
Unpreceded adjectives,
    108–9
Unreal conditions, subjunc-
    tive in
    English, 211–12

German
    past tense, 225–26
    present tense, 218–20
unter, use of, 90
-ur, gender of nouns end-
    ing in, 8
ver-, as inseparable prefix,
    158
Verb prefixes
    inseparable, 158–59
    separable, 159–62
    in simple past tense,
        168
Verbs. *See also specific
    verbs*
    dative, 34–36
        passive constructions
            with, 201
        reflexive, 256
    of expecting, subordinate
        clause following,
            252
    impersonal, passive con-
        structions with, 199
    infinitive of, 147
    intransitive, 258
    mixed
        past participles of, 177
        present tense subjunc-
            tive for, 215–16
        in simple past tense,
            171
    modal. *See* Modal verbs
    reflexive, 56, 254–55
        accusative vs. dative,
            256
        in commands, 257
        list of common,
            255–56
        in perfect tenses, 257
        with prepositions, 256
    of saying, subordinate
        clause following,
            252
    as separable prefixes,
        161
    strong, 150
        past participles of,
            176–77
        present tense subjunc-
            tive for, 214–15
        in simple past tense,

169–70
transitive verbs, 258
of wanting, subordinate
clause following,
252
weak
irregular (mixed), 171
past participles of, 176
present tense subjunc-
tive for, 214
in simple past tense,
167–69
word order and
coordinating conjunc-
tions as first ele-
ment of a clause
and, 273
in direct and indirect
questions, 274–76
interjections as first
element of a clause
and, 273
in a statement, 271–74
Verb stem, 148
vowel changes in,
150–52
Verb tenses, 147–91
future, 185–87
formation of, 185–86
modal verbs in, 186
passive voice in, 194
use of, 186
future perfect
formation of, 187
passive voice in, 194
use of, 187
imperatives, 155–58. *See
also* Commands
bitte and, 155
familiar plural, 156
familiar singular,
155–56
formal, 156
infinitives as, 157–58
of **sein** and **werden,**
156–57
wir imperative, 157
past perfect, 184–85
formation of, 184
passive voice in, 194
reflexive verbs in, 257
use of, 184

present perfect, 175–84
auxiliary verbs and,
178–79
formation of, 175
of modal verbs,
181–84
passive voice in, 194
past participles and,
175–84
reflexive verbs in,
257
simple past tense vs.,
183
present tense, 147–55
endings, 148–50
passive voice in, 194
subjunctive. *See*
Subjunctive
use of, 154–55
vowel changes in the
verb stem, 150–52
simple past tense,
167–75
mixed verbs in, 171
modal verbs in,
172–73
passive voice in, 194
present perfect tense
vs., 183
strong verbs in,
169–70
weak verbs in, 167–69
subjunctive. *See* Special
subjunctive; Sub-
junctive
von
agent in passive sentence
introduced by,
197–98
use of, 84–85
vor, use of, 90
special meaning, 93
vor-, as separable prefix,
160

während, use of, 95
wann, use of, 290
Wanting, subordinate
clause following
verbs of, 252
was, 57
as relative pronoun,

70–71
was für (ein), 23–24
Weak adjective endings,
105
Weak nouns
case and, 42–44
entire sentence negated,
279–80
identification of, 43–44
Weak verbs
irregular (mixed), 171
past participles of, 176
present tense subjunctive
for, 214
in simple past tense,
167–69
weg-, as separable prefix,
160
wegen, use of, 96
weil, use of, 292
Welch ein, 23
wenn, use of, 290, 291
wenn clause
to express wishes, 220
omission of, 219, 220
in present tense subjunc-
tive, 217–22
wer
declination of, 57
as relative pronoun, 71
werden
future perfect tense
formed with, 187
future tense formed with,
185, 206–7
future tense of special
subjunctive formed
with, 234
imperative forms of,
156–57
indefinite article
ommited after,
17
as main verb, 206
nominative as predicate
noun after, 29
passive voice formed
with, 193–94,
194–95, 207
in present perfect tense,
180
present tense of, 153

werden (*cont.*)

    present tense subjunctive for, 215, 217–18

    to express politeness, 222

    in simple past tense, 171

Wishes, subjunctive in

    English, 212, 213

    German

        past tense, 226

        present tense, 220–21

wissen, 153–54

    present tense of, 153

wo, as relative pronoun, 72

wo-compounds, 100–101

    as relative pronoun, 73

wollen, 165

    present tense subjunctive of, 216

    simple past tense of, 172, 173

    subjective use of, 263–64

    wishes introduced with, 221

wor, in conditional sentences, 218

Word order, 271–84

    coordinating conjunctions and, 285–86

    position of verb, 273

    direct and indirect objects and, 276–77

    English, 28

    in independent clauses with double infinitives, 225

    inverted, 272–73

    nicht and

        entire sentence negated, 279–80

        specific sentence unit negated, 281

    news value and, 282–83

    normal, 272–73

    of accusative and dative pronouns, 53

    in relative clauses, 66

    with subordinating conjunctions, 289

    variations in, 281–82

    verbs and

        coordinating conjunctions as first element of a clause and, 273

        in direct and indirect questions, 274–76

        interjections as first element of a clause and, 273

        in a statement, 271–74

wünschen, wishes introduced with, 221

würde paraphrase, 216–18, 222

    wenn-clause and, 217

Year, expressing a, 140–41

You, forms of, 21, 50. *See also specific forms*

Your, forms of, 21. *See also specific forms*

zer-, as inseparable prefix, 158

zu

    avoiding passive voice with, 205

    use of, 85

zu-, as separable prefix, 160

zurück-, as separable prefix, 160

zusammen-, as separable prefix, 160

zwischen, use of, 90–91